Eritrea

ERITREA

MAKING OF A NATION

Redie Bereketeab

THE RED SEA PRESS
TRENTON | LONDON | NEW DELHI | CAPE TOWN | NAIROBI | ADDIS ABABA | ASMARA | IBADAN

THE RED SEA PRESS
541 West Ingham Avenue | Suite B
Trenton, New Jersey 08638

First Printing 2007

Book and cover design: Saverance Publishing Services

Library of Congress Cataloging-in-Publication Data

Bereketeab, Redie.
Eritrea : the making of a nation, 1890-1991 / Redie Bereketeab.
p. cm.
Originally published: [Uppsala, Sweden] : Uppsala University, c2000.
Includes bibliographical references and index.
ISBN 1-56902-251-8 (hardcover) -- ISBN 1-56902-252-6 (pbk.)
1. Eritrea--History. I. Title.
DT394.B47 2004
963.5--dc22

2005033725

Table of Contents

List of Maps, Tables and Figures

MAPS

TABLES

FIGURES

Abbreviations

AESNA	Association of Eritrean Students in North America
AEWNA	Association of Eritrean Women in North America
BMA	British Military Administration
BOAC	British Overseas Airways Corporation
EDF	Eritrean Democratic Front
EDM	Eritrean Democratic Movement
ELF	Eritrean Liberation Front
ELF-CC	Eritrean Liberation Front - Central Committee
ELF-PLF	Eritrean Liberation Front - Popular Liberation Forces
ELF-RC	Eritrean Liberation Front - Revolutionary Council
ELM	Eritrean Liberation Movement
EPLF	Eritrean People's Liberation Forces
	Eritrean People's Liberation Front
EWN	Eritrean Weekly News
FO	Foreign Office
FPCI	Four Power Commission of Investigation
IB	Independence Bloc
LPP	Liberal Progressive Party
ML	Moslem League
NLM	National Liberation Movement
OAU	Organisation of African Unity
PFDJ	People's Front for Democracy and Justice
PLF	Popular Liberation Forces
RC	Revolutionary Command
RDC	Research and Documentation Centre
RICE	Research and Information Centre on Eritrea
SC	Supreme Council
SCAO	Senior Civil Affairs Officer
SLCE	Society for the Love of the Country of Eritrea

SUEE	Society for the Unification of Eritrea with Ethiopia
UNO	United Nations Organisation
UP	Unionist Party
WO	War Office
ZC	Zone Command

Map 1: Administrative Map of Eritrea

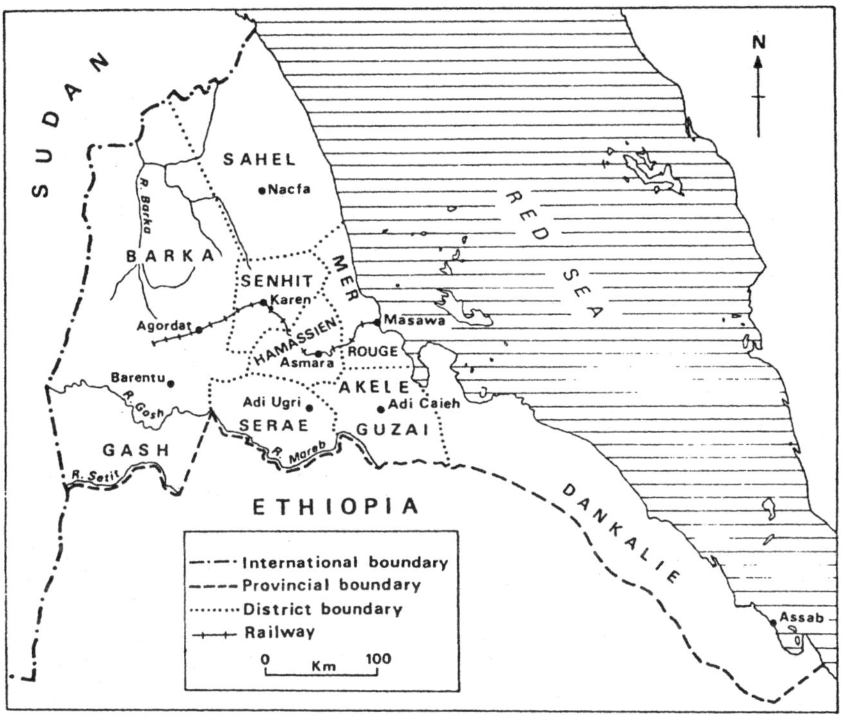

Source: Pool D; Eritrea Africa longest war (London, 1979), p. 6.

Preface

Eritrea had fought Africa's longest war of liberation when it won its independence in 1991. Unlike many other conflicts, however, this protracted war attracted little attention from the international community. The major powers, the UN and the OAU, remained until its conclusion at the outermost fringes of the conflict. Several reasons can be offered to explain this marginalisation. The prime reason is that it was seen as an internal problem of the Ethiopian State. The physical size and the international diplomatic privilege that Ethiopia enjoyed also prevented the problem from being taken up in the international arena. The major actors of global power politics patiently waited for Ethiopia to find a solution to the nuisance the Eritrean nationalists were causing for its internal stability. Many observers were convinced that the Eritrean struggle would eventually be defeated, and it was written off more than once. In fact, virtually every time Ethiopia scored a major military victory against the liberation fronts, the end of the Eritrean struggle was predicted (Connel 1980: 54). One such occasion was the highly advertised, Soviet backed campaign of the Dergue in 1978. The Ethiopian regime, as well as international observers, declared that the Eritrean problem was once and for all resolved: "Practically, the Eritreans' chance for achieving self-determination was gone" (Erlich 1983: 15).

To the likely surprise of many, the Eritrean struggle endured despite the effort by successive Ethiopian regimes to defeat it. First, the Haile Selassie regime with the support of USA, and later, the Dergue regime with the massive support of the Soviet Union, failed to resolve the confrontation to the benefit of Ethiopia. Finally, Eritrea emerged triumphantly as an independent state to earn its place as the first secessionist movement to become free from an African state (cf. Pool 1997: 5). The designation of 'successful secessionist movement' originated from the fact that several secessionist movements' attempting to form their own state ended in failure. The question posed by many is how the Eritrean revolution survived and triumphed. How could a tiny Eritrea fight against a giant Ethiopia and win? Some observers tried to compare it with the Biafra rebellion in Nigeria, the Katanga in Congo and the South Sudan question (see Young 1983) and wondered how the Eritreans succeeded where the others failed. These analogies, however, appear to be misapplied. The Eritrean case can only be appropriately compared with the Namibian and Western Saharan case, which are like Eritrea — but unlike Biafra, Katanga and South Sudan — the creation of European colonialism.

The Eritrean question, in addition to being the most forgotten and ignored, was perhaps also the most misunderstood. It was quite often depicted as an ethnic, secessionist and religious movement. Reality, however, suggests otherwise. Eritrea is home to nine ethno-linguistic groups with different religions. Thus, the struggle cannot be ethnic or religious. As for the connotation of secessionism, in the eyes of the Eritreans and their supporters, Eritrea was created by Italian colonialism, as were many African states, entitling it to the right to decolonisation and self-determination. Therefore, Eritrean nationalists were convinced that the liberation struggle was not a secessionist effort, but rather the continuation of an aborted decolonisation process. This conviction was the underlying factor behind their resilience and eventual victory. Misunderstanding of these elements complicated efforts to find a solution to the problem. Because many did not recognise it as a national question involving a legitimate right to self-determination, finding a diplomatic settlement became difficult.

When Italy lost the war in 1941, Eritrea fell into the hands of the British. They were to administer it on the basis of the principles of the Hague Convention of 1907, which rest on "care and maintenance" (Becker 1952: 30) of the Trust Territories. Since its inception, the British Military Administration (BMA), probably deriving from the Mazzinian threshold theory and guided by the non-viability principle (cf. Heater 1998), advocated for the partition of Eritrea. At the root of the British policy was the belief that the territory could not constitute a viable, independent state. As a result, the British position toward all attempts to find a settlement for the Eritrean problem was guided by this non-viability principle. The partition project came close to realisation with the rise of the Bevin-Sforza proposition, worked out by the British and Italian Foreign Ministers, but which was voted down by the UN General Assembly. When the case of the former Italian colonies was brought to the UN General Assembly in 1949, it was the most challenging issue that the UN had encountered since its formation. The UN had recently endorsed the Declaration Regarding Non-Self-Governing Territories, in which the inhabitants of these colonies were guaranteed the right to self-government (Becker 1952: 233). This declaration formed the foundation for the principle of decolonisation through which colonised societies were to be afforded their independence. It was envisioned that people who did not already have their own government would be allowed to form one. The implementation of this principle, for example, ensured the independence of Libya and Italian Somaliland. Eritrea, far from benefiting from the principle, was bound to Ethiopia through the eventually aborted Federation. What was the reason behind denying Eritrea the opportunity to exercise its rights according to the principle of decolonisation that was followed with respect to the other former Italian colonies? Was it because the big powers were concerned about its viability as an independent state? Was it a consideration of the legitimate rights of Ethiopia to have outlet to the sea? Was it global Cold War politics? Was it the consideration of the wishes of the Eritrean people? It is not my intention here to indulge in giving elaborate answers to these questions. However, a few brief comments seem appropriate. Certainly, it was not for lack of a majority in Eritrean society craving independence. Recently released documentation of diplomatic exchanges that took place between Britain and the USA at the time proves that a clear majority among the Eritrean people supported independence (Habte Selassie 1989, Yohannes 1991). The Four Power Commission Report also presented in its finding that by 1947, more than seventy percent of the population was opposed to union with Ethiopia (cf. Ellingson 1977: 270). As a matter of fact, even the poll that was used as a basis for the UN resolution pointed to the existence of a majority supporting independence.

The preamble of the UN Resolution of the Federation stated that the endorsement of the Resolution was based on: a) consideration of the welfare of the Eritrean people; b) the legitimate right of Ethiopia to have an outlet to the sea; and c) a desire for world peace and security. However, as US Secretary of State John Foster Dulles later revealed, the UN was guided by principles that did not appear in the preamble of the Resolution. It was the strategic interest of the United States that made it necessary to connect Eritrea with Ethiopia (Medhanie 1986: 19). Ethiopia was provided with an outlet to the sea and American strategic interests were also protected. However, far from assuring the welfare of the Eritrean people or safeguarding peace and security, the decision of Federation, as Ellingson (1977: 281) put it, "planted the seeds for future conflict. The issue was determined in an international political arena in which the participation of the members of Eritrean society was entirely absent. One might wonder how a deliberation on supposedly democratic principles which intentionally excluded the subjects of the matter from involvement in the decision intended to determine their destiny, could, at the same time, take into consideration their welfare. Not unexpectedly, the resolution of federation satisfied no one (Ellingson 1977: 281).

The issue of the settlement of the former Italian colonies appeared on the agenda of the UN General Assembly after the failure of the Big Four Powers, and when the Cold War was in full swing. The UN was embroiled in power politics and ideological frictions. So when the debate on Eritrea began, the Assembly was divided based on ideological blocs. The Socialist Bloc and third world countries were reported to have supported the independence of Eritrea while the Western bloc supported federation. Through its Resolution 390A (V) of 1950, the UN tied Eritrea with Ethiopia. The Federation Resolution entitled Eritrea to a far-reaching autonomy. If there had been an environment conducive to its development, and if there had been control mechanisms for its proper implementation, the federal arrangement might have worked. But, as the Tigrinya proverb goes "the devil makes a beautiful dish but leaves it without a lid". The UN, in its resolution, stipulated a wide-ranging federal system without providing adequate mechanisms for implementation, control and supervision. The absence of such mechanisms became one of the main sources of its failure.

For the Eritreans, the fundamental cause of the Eritro-Ethiopian conflict was the disruption of the decolonisation process and the abrogation of the Federation. The abrogation of the Federation compelled the Eritreans to appeal to the UN General Assembly to take necessary measures to protect the federal arrangement, but their plea was not heeded. As a result, they became convinced that there was no alternative other than the use of violence for the realisation of their national aspirations. Hoping that the world would pay attention to their plight, they launched an armed struggle for the liberation of Eritrea. To their dismay, the world response never came. Several different reasons can be suggested to explain this lack of interest. At the geopolitical and geo-strategic level, the need to control the Red Sea had been a factor (Chaliand 1980: 53). The Arab-Israeli conflict, too, was a factor that complicated the Eritro-Ethiopian conflict. The fear of the conversion of the Red Sea into an Arab sea attracted the active involvement of the state of Israel in the undermining of the liberation struggle of Eritrea (Erlich 1983), while Arab support for Eritrea was irregular. In the UN debate on the disposition of Eritrea, the Arabs supported the independence of Eritrea, but when the actual vote on the federation resolution came, Egypt voted for it. Throughout the armed struggle, Arab support was characterised by vacillation. There seems little doubt that it was governed by regional and global circumstances. For instance, when a shift of regime occurred in Ethiopia, states like Libya, PDRY (People's Democratic Republic of Yemen), and Syria forged a close relationship with the Dergue.

For the emerging OAU, the issue of territorial integrity of the African states on the basis of the recognition of the colonially created international boundaries was more important than the question of Eritrea. Through a shrewd diplomatic manoeuvre, Ethiopia had succeeded in convincing the founders of the OAU that the principle of colonial boundaries did not apply to Eritrea (Babu 1986). The paranoia of Balkanisation coupled with the Arabs' evil intention of undermining the African Christian state advocated by Ethiopia (cf. Pool 1997: 11) deterred the OAU member states from involving themselves in the plight of the Eritrean people. For the sake of a higher goal, the sanctity of the "master principle" (Young 1983:199) of territorial integrity, the Eritrean cause had to be compromised. The UN, the author of the aborted Federation, shied away from intervening in spite of the legal responsibility the Organisation bore. The logic of power politics and international relations, marked by a Cold War, paralysed the UN and diminished its capability for upholding the legitimate rights of peoples, one of the cardinal provisions of the Organisation. It became a pawn of superpower politics and ideological rivalry. Therefore, Eritrea fell victim to these global power politics (Yohannes 1991).

Eritrean disappointment in the UN's silence grew as the war dragged on. They felt betrayed and grew increasingly vocal in their condemnation. The criticisms levelled against the UN by the Eritreans included: 1) the failure to afford

Eritrea its independence rather than that binding it with Ethiopia through its Resolution 390A(V) of 1950; 2) the failure to intervene when the Federation was abrogated by Ethiopia in 1962; and 3) the lack of interest in actively seeking a peaceful resolution to the armed conflict between Eritrea and Ethiopia – one that raged for thirty years.

The Eritreans and the Ethiopians entertained opposite views regarding the root cause of the problem and its proper solution. For the Eritreans, the root cause of the Eritro-Ethiopian conflict was the aborted decolonisation process, which led to the UN-sponsored Federation. Eritrean nationalists were convinced that Eritrea was a creation of Italian colonialism. Eritrea, therefore, should have been treated according to the principles of decolonisation and the right to self-determination accorded to all other former colonies in Africa. The UN Resolution on the problem thus misrepresented the facts in its claim to be upholding the principle and the right to self-determination (ELF 1971, 1977; EPLF 1977, 1987). In Ethiopia's view, the cause of the problem was the rise of a small group of secessionist bandits manipulated by Arab petrodollars (see Erlich 1983: 68). Ethiopia's argument was that Eritrea constituted the cradle of the three thousand years old history of Ethiopia, except for the short-lived aberration represented by the period of Italian rule. Ethiopia argued that Italy forcibly separated Eritrea from Ethiopia for a half a century. According to Ethiopia, Eritreans are Ethiopians, and they expressed their wish to join their "motherland" when Italy was defeated as a confirmation of their Ethiopia-ness. These different interpretations of history and identity and their competing claims formed the basis for the war. Both sides were locked into intractable positions in which negotiated settlement was nowhere to be found. Thus, the war dragged on for thirty years.

There were a number of questions which intrigued many Eritreans. Why was it that the Eritrean National Liberation Movement and the Eritrean struggle for independence the most misunderstood liberation struggle? Why was there less international attention to the plight of the Eritrean people? These and other questions became the impetus for my interest in undertaking this study. And I came to the realisation that there are at least three reasons for this misinterpretation and the lack of attention. This study seeks to address them.

(1) Generally, the Eritrean struggle was seen as an internal Ethiopian problem. This understanding was grounded in the view that Eritrea has been an integral part of Ethiopia. Since the collapse of Italian colonial rule in Eritrea, Ethiopia has been trying to convince the world, with considerable success, that Italy had forcibly snatched Eritrea from Ethiopia. Ethiopia retrieved it back, wishing for it to remain as its integral part. This view was, therefore, the primary reason why the international community did not intervene to find a just settlement for the conflict. For Eritrean nationalists, however, Eritrea, like any African state, is the creation of European colonialism, entitling it to the right of decolonisation and self-determination. The only durable, equitable solution would be to grant the Eritreans their rights. The international community's silence was,

thus, incomprehensible to them. How could these diametrically opposite views be explained?

(2) Internal conflicts in post-colonial Africa in which one of the contestants is aiming at establishing a sovereign state are described as secessionist, meaning that some disaffected groups are trying to destabilise and break an already established state. The Eritrean struggle was seen instead of a genuine nationalist movement, as an externally instigated sectarian movement that aimed to destroy the Ethiopian State. This view contributed to the neglect of the Eritrean question by the international community. Many of the so-called secessionist movements like the Biafra, Katanga were not successful, making Eritrea the first to break away from an African state. What are the reasons that enabled Eritrea to succeed in achieving its goals?

(3) An aspect of a theoretical nature that probably contributed to the misunderstanding of the Eritrean case is the theoretical debate regarding the formation of new states. Current theories dealing with nationalist movement trying to break away from established, "old" multiethnic nation-states are confined to ethnic homogenous groups. Regardless of their diversity, they are studied under the label of ethnic movements. In other words, there is a theoretical bias that tends to treat nationalist movements as ethnic secessionist movements. This has led to the designation of ethno-nationalism for these movements. These movements are often seen negatively, as narrow chauvinistic struggles. In addition, whenever a movement displays diversity there exists a theoretical and definitional chaos. This could have contributed to the misunderstanding of the Eritrean case, which many, in fact, categorised as an ethnic movement. Yet, perhaps because the Eritreans did not define their struggle as an ethnic movement, they remained unsuccessful in enlisting international support of their right to self-determination. Calhoun (1997: 65) makes the same point, noting that "the Americans and many others found it hard to comprehend self-determination for people who did not define themselves as mono-ethnic nation". Eritrea is multiethnic nation, which defies the assumptions of the current theoretical orthodoxy. This phenomenon of a multiethnic entity breaking away from a multiethnic state presents a theoretical challenge to current mainstream theory of nation formation. The question is, can a theoretical explanation be found for how an Eritrea comprised of various ethno-linguistic groups was able to form its own state?

Chapter 1

INTRODUCTION

INTRODUCTION

This chapter elaborates (i) the research problem; (ii) sources and method; and (iii) theoretical and conceptual elements. The objective of the chapter is to delimit and specify the research problem, outline sources and method, and to provide a succinct review of selected literature that deals with the concepts of nation and the theories of the process of nation formation. The subject of nation formation is one of the difficult areas of social science in general, and political sociology in particular. The difficulty in characterising the subject arises primarily from the plethora of theories, definitions and methodological approaches. This multiplicity is partly to be explained by the existence of varieties of societies reflecting a plurality of distinctive characteristics in the context of social, economic, cultural and historical backgrounds. These are conditions that make it impossible to parcel them into a single, grand theoretical model. The various processes and paths that these societies follow in their actual development further add to the lack of clarity surrounding the subject. Consequently, efforts to create a general theoretical model to explain and analyse the processes of nation formation seem not to have born fruit. Rather, today we have different models and theories claiming to represent and explain the various historical experiences. Moreover, we encounter contradicting claims and counterclaims regarding the validity and applicability of those models and theories to different cultural contexts. A variety of authors have expounded one or another explanatory theoretical model without advancing the objective of understanding the subject. This not only makes it impossible, but probably also undesirable to have a single grand theory with the capacity to explain everything. Saying this, however, it is important to bear in mind that it is quite possible to have a general theory that explains some universal trends that are of relevance to all of the cultural settings.

THE RESEARCH PROBLEM

This work is a study of social transformation induced by (a) colonial capitalist penetration, and (b) nationalist movements. More precisely, the focus is on (1) the impact of Italian colonialism on the socio-economic structure of the Eritrean society; (2) the influence of the nationalist political movement during both the British Administration and the Federation, on Eritrean national consciousness; (3) the impact of Ethiopian involvement in Eritrea and the resistance to it by Eritreans in the creation of Eritrean identity; and (4) the role played by the National Liberation Movement in the process of the formation of the Eritrean nation. Related to this, we can identify three historical periods in the process of formation of the Eritrean nation, notably (a) the Italian colonial period, during which capitalist political economy is assumed to have induced socio-economic changes; (b) the British Administration and the Federation, during which, as a result of the political activities of the period, it is widely believed that national political consciousness was promoted; and (c) the National Liberation Movement (NLM), which, as an intentional agent in the struggle against Ethiopian occupation, enhanced the process of nation formation. This focus and periodisation enables us to formulate the following questions, which constitute the basis of the study: Did Italian colonialism affect the socio-economic structure of the Eritrean society? What were the indications of the changes that took place as a result of Italian colonialism? What were the implications of political liberalisation for Eritrean society during the British period of occupation? What role did the Federation play in the development of the national consciousness of Eritreans? What was the role played by the nationalist movements in the process of nation formation? How successful was the NLM in its effort to build a cohesive modern civic nation? What was the impact of Ethiopian occupation on the creation of Eritrean identity?

This study seeks to provide a sociological interpretation of the process of formation of the Eritrean nation by examining the chronological events through which this formation process advanced. Based on the existing general paradigm of theories of nation formation, six analytical dimensions have been selected. These include (1) territorial integration; (2) socio-economic integration; (3) politico-legal integration; (4) common history; (5) common culture; and (6) the will to live together. In the inquiry into the process of the formation of the Eritrean nation, a thorough investigation is undertaken to determine the impact of the Italian colonial political economy on the socio-economic structure of Eritrean society. This investigation is intended to enable us to make an assessment of the social transformation that resulted from Italian colonial rule. The investigation of the British Administration and the Federation assesses the impact of political liberalisation and the accompanying emergence of political parties on the political consciousness of Eritrean society. The political activity, which began under the British Administration, extended to the first half of the Federation period, and that is why both the British Administration and the Federation are treated together.

The study also investigates how the National Liberation Movement (NLM) functioned as a purposive agent of nation building by operating at two levels; one political, the other social. Moreover, I argue that at the political level, the principal objective of the NLM was the achievement of the political sovereignty of Eritrea. At the social level, the aim was the transformation of the society into a cohesive modern one. The achievement of political sovereignty was to be accomplished through combating Ethiopian occupation. In the implementation of the project of social transformation, the *Field* served as a significant experimental space for pursuing the social vision of the NLM, in which extensive social, economic political and cultural projects were undertaken. Adopting the strategy of social engineering, the agents of the NLM, particularly since the 1970s, acted to implement social mobilisation, they undertook the all-encompassing task of engaging, organising and mobilising the masses in the liberation struggle and in the process of nation building.

The focus of this investigation is the century-long (1890-1991) process that eventually culminated in the formation of the Eritrean nation, its liberation from foreign rule and the emergence of The State of Eritrea as an independent nation-state. It begins with the initiation of the territorial integration of the various ethno-linguistic groups in 1890, and concludes with their emergence as integral components of the sovereign nation state of Eritrea in 1991. My thesis is that the making of Eritrea was fundamentally the result of the actions of two groups of collective actors, the colonial powers (Italy, Britain and Ethiopia) on the one hand, and nationalist movements (the various groups, parties and organisations opposing colonial rule) on the other. More specifically, my thesis can be summarised in five points (see figures 1.1 and 1.2)[1]:

1. The pre-colonial societies (the Afar, the Highlanders and the Lowlanders) with no common history, culture or state-like organisation, were initially integrated under Italian colonialism in what came to be known as the Colony of Eritrea (1890-1941). Although territorial integration was completed under Italian rule, the process of socio-economic and politico-legal integration continued during the British Administration (1941-1952) and even afterwards, under Ethiopian domination (1952-1991).

2. A commonly experienced history and shared culture began to develop among the peoples originally living in the territory. This resulted from this integration by force, and also out of the struggle against colonial rule by a variety of groups, parties and particularly, by the National Liberation Movement (NLM, 1961-1991). As shared history and distinctive patterns of culture emerged, the people of Eritrea began to develop a will to live together, experiencing themselves as a "nation".

3. Territorial, socio-economic and politico-legal integration, on the one hand, and common history, common culture and will to live together, on

Figure 1.1: The Making of Colonial Eritrea

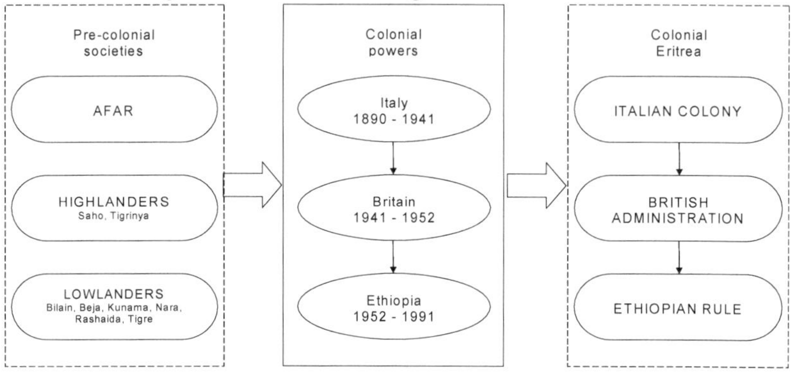

Pre-colonial societies
AFAR
HIGHLANDERS
Saho, Tigrinya
LOWLANDERS
Bilain, Beja, Kunama, Nara, Rashaida, Tigre

Colonial powers
Italy
1890 - 1941
Britain
1941 - 1952
Ethiopia
1952 - 1991

Colonial Eritrea
ITALIAN COLONY
BRITISH ADMINISTRATION
ETHIOPIAN RULE

the other, characterise the emergent dimensions of nation formation in the case of Eritrea.

4. A duality of identity characterises the Eritrean path to nation formation - sub-national identity (i.e., primordial, ethnic identity) and national identity (civic, common identity). Ethno-linguistic integration (at times suggested as a necessary condition for becoming a nation, e.g. Smith 1986) cannot be said to have had any bearing in the making of Eritrea. Eritrea emerged as a polyethnic nation composed of nine ethno-linguistic groups.

5. The State of Eritrea (1991-) emerged out of the struggles between the Ethiopian rulers and the NLM, shaping and reshaping the web of relationships between the aforementioned six emergent dimensions of nation characterising Eritrea.

The remainder of this chapter provides a historical overview, sources and method, concepts of nation, paths of nation formation, theories of nation formation and analytical dimensions. Two paths of nation formation, notably the European path and the African path are discussed. The legacy of colonialism is also elucidated. Here, the focus is mainly on the British and French colonial legacy in Africa and the implications of their political philosophy for the nation formation process. The reason for the limitation to the British and French legacies is both the availability of literature and also the fact that they are representative. The Italian type was closer to the French approach, except that the Italians were much less interested in the cultural promotion of the society. The theories of nation formation are analysed in order to provide the theoretical framework of the study. The last section of the chapter, Analytical Dimensions, deals with six dimensions whose value to the analysis of the process of formation of the Eritrean nation is thought to be justifiable on the basis of elucidating important elements.

Figure 1.2: The Making of the Eritrean Nation

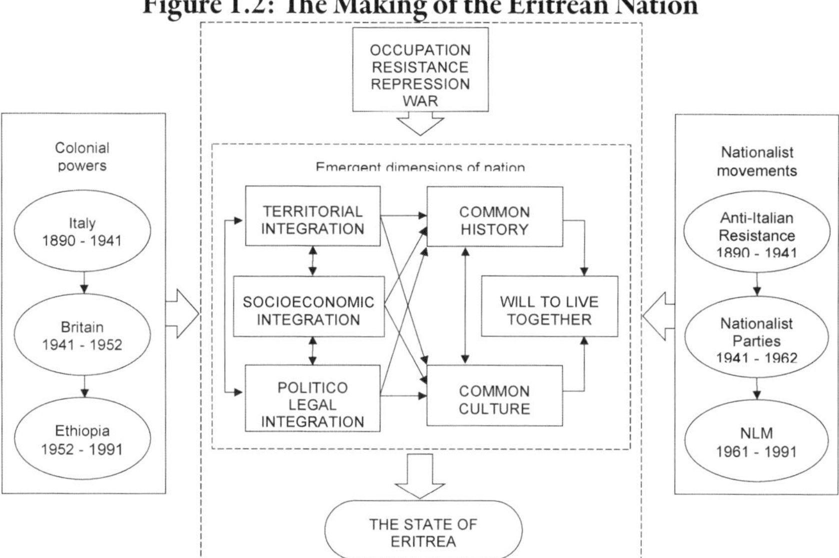

Chapters 2-6 deal with the empirical materials, while Chapters 7-8 represent an effort to theorise based on the social-historical development of Eritrea. The final chapter briefly summarises the entire work. Chapter 2, *A Synopsis of Pre-colonial History*, discusses the people and economic and socio-political organisation. As the heading indicates, the chapter gives account of the conditions immediately prior to Italian colonisation, before the territorial integration of the various ethno-linguistic groups. This is intended to serve as the backdrop of the study. Chapter 3, *Territorial Integration: The Birth of Eritrea,* studies how Eritrea evolved into a unified, geo-political entity. The aspects studied in this chapter include the demarcation and consolidation of international boundaries, the establishment of administrative divisions and provinces, which gave Eritrea its modern political structure, and the consolidation of legal and administrative unification of the territory.

After investigating how the Colony of Eritrea came into being as the outcome of Italian rule, the study proceeds to examine the effects of European colonialism. Chapter 4, *Socio-Economic Integration: Capitalist Penetration Under European Rule,* makes an attempt to establish the significant changes that took place. This chapter provides an account of socio-economic transformation. Italian colonial rule and later British Administration introduced a centralised politico-legal system of rule of the Western model. The politico-legal dimension is discussed in Chapter 5, under *Politico-legal Integration: The Emergence of Politico-Legal Institutions.* The chapter focuses primarily on the British occupation and the Federation period. This is because of the emergence of political parties, Eritrean constitution and the autonomous Eritrean State during the period. Chapter 6 deals with *the National Liberation Movement (NLM) As An*

Agent Of Nation-Building, in which mobilisation, recruitment and participation in national politics became the chief priority.

The final two chapters are an attempt to construct the emergence of common Eritrean political culture and nationalism on the basis of the material presented in Chapters 2 to 6, which constitute the common historical experience. Chapter 7, *Common Historical Experience and Growth of Common Culture*, examines the development of common culture which is a result of common historical experience. Chapter 8, *The Will to Live Together: Nationalism,* discusses the development of Eritrean nationalism and the crystallisation of the will to live together. Finally, Chapter 9 provides a summary of the research and suggests possible future developments.

AN HISTORICAL OVERVIEW

The exposure of the region to foreign powers began with the arrival of the Ottoman Empire in the 15th century. Beginning with this development, we can categorise the colonial history of the region into three periods, the pre-European colonial era (1557-1885), the European colonial era (1882-1952), and the Ethiopian occupation (1962-1991). The pre-European colonial era pertains mainly to the Ottoman domination. The Ottoman presence in the Red Sea started in 1557 and lasted for about three centuries, up to 1865, when the Egyptians succeeded them (Habte Selassie 1980: 34). Despite several attempts to occupy the interior part of the region, the Ottomans never succeeded in controlling the highland region for any enduring period, largely confining the three-century Ottoman presence to the coastal areas. When the Ottoman Empire began to crumble, the Egyptians emerged as the dominant force in the region. Egyptian hegemony began with their gaining control of Massawa in 1865 (AESNA 1978: 37). From Massawa, they were able to extend their influence over most part of the coastal area on the African side of the Red Sea. As successors to the collapsing Ottoman Empire, they were also put in charge of the Sudan. This allowed them to occupy the western part of present-day Eritrea that was subject to the rule of the Fung Dynasty of the Sinar in the Sudan. For a brief period, the Egyptians were able to control three-quarters of Eritrea. The Egyptian effort to expand their control to the highland of Eritrea placed them on a direct collision course with Abyssinia. This led to two confrontations between Egypt and Abyssinia, in 1875 and 1876 (Erlich 1982: 10-11). Emperor Yohannes succeeded in bringing the three highland provinces under his effective control beginning in 1879, until the Italians colonised Eritrea in1889.

The first time Italy set foot on the coast of the Red Sea was in 1869, when it bought a piece of land in Assab through a shipping company. But it was not until July 1882, that Assab was formally declared an Italian colony (Negash 1987). From Assab, the Italians extended their colonial grip and replaced the Egyptians, taking Massawa in 1885 with the consent of the British. Since the aim of the Italians was to join in the scramble for Africa, their main target was the mainland. Using Massawa as their base, they penetrated inland, occupying

Asmara in 1889. In 1889, the Wichale Treaty was signed between Italy and Emperor Menelik II. Abyssinia recognised Italy's right to the Eritrean colony, while Italy recognised Menelik as the successor to the Abyssinian Crown in return. Finally, on January 1, 1890, Italy declared the birth of its first colony, naming it Eritrea after the Greek name of the Red Sea. Eritrea, in its present day form, came into existence as a product of Italian colonial rule. Before that, Eritrea had never experienced the rule of any single political system or political power as a unified entity. After nearly six decades, Italian colonial rule came to an end in conjunction with their defeat in 1941, and the British replaced them as the new masters of Eritrea. British rule was not, in a technical sense, colonial rule. As a victorious power, Britain assumed responsibility for administering the territory of the former Italian colony until the destiny of that colony could be decided. Accordingly, Britain administered Eritrea from 1941 up to the enforcement of the UN-sponsored Federal Pact in 1952.

The victorious Big Four Powers (USA, USSR, Britain and France) were entrusted with the responsibility of the settlement of the territories of the former Italian colonies. It was in the summer of 1945, at the Potsdam conference, that the issue of the former Italian territories was placed on the agenda of the three Big Powers (USA, USSR and Britain). After an exchange of ideas, it was decided that the issue should be discussed fully in the September 1945, London Meeting of the Council of Foreign Ministers (CFM) (Becker 1952: 77-8). However, the intractability of the issue was soon to become clear. After the London Meeting of the CFM failed to produce a settlement, it was postponed to the Paris Meeting. When even the Paris Meeting was unsuccessful in producing a settlement, it was decide to establish a commission, the Four Power Commission of Investigation (FPCI), with the aim of ascertaining the wishes of the people of the colonies. The FPCI failed to present a unified report; and thus also failed to lead to the settlement of the matter. Subsequently, the case of the former colonies was formally submitted to the United Nations in 1949. The UN General Assembly began by dispatching a five-nation-member commission to Eritrea to investigate the wishes of the people. The Commission arrived in Eritrea on February 8, remaining until April 6, 1950 (Becker 1952: 221-3). The Commission presented three proposals to the UN General Assembly, contained in two reports. These recommended three separate alternatives: a) that Eritrea be constituted a self-governing unit of a federation with Ethiopia under the sovereignty of the Ethiopian Crown; b) a reunion of the whole territory with Ethiopia; and c) Eritrea be placed under direct United Nations trusteeship for a maximum period of ten years, at the end of which it should become completely independent (Becker 1952: 225-6). After two years of wrangling and acrimonious debate, the UN General Assembly, in its session of December 2, 1950, passed Resolution 390A(v) to federate Eritrea with Ethiopia. The federation of Eritrea with Ethiopia was to be implemented within two years of its approval. During the interim period, an Eritrean Government would be organised and a constitution prepared. Once the Eritrean Assembly had been established, the Eritrean Constitution drafted, and the Constitution endorsed by the Eritrean Assembly and the Emperor of Ethiopia, the Federation was put in force on September 11, 1952.

The period between 1952 to 1962 is known as the Federation Period. During that time, Eritrea constituted an autonomous unit of the Eritro-Ethiopian Federation, with its rights and duties constitutionally defined. According to the federal act, Eritrea was to possess its own legislative, judiciary and executive state organs. However, during the process of drafting the Eritrean constitution, the UN Commissioner caved in to Ethiopian pressure. Therefore, contrary to the UN Resolution's stipulations, the Ethiopian Constitution and Government became the federal constitution and government of Eritrea (see ELF 1977: 43-7). This was not only in violation of the UN Resolution, it also provided the basis for the abrogation of the Federal Act. In the Eritrean Constitution, democratic provisions had been enshrined which were assumed to regulate the political activities of the Eritrean government. The Constitution guaranteed freedom of speech, freedom of association and demonstration. It also guaranteed the right to form trade unions and political parties. The second election of Parliament, which took place in 1956 after the parties for independence were silenced, ensured the absolute domination of the Unionist Party (UP). Predictably, the Federation did not work as it was stipulated. All the provisions of the Federation upholding the autonomous status of Eritrea were discarded. Finally, the Federation was formally abrogated on November 14, 1962.

A year before the formal abrogation of the Federation, the armed struggle for Eritrean independence was launched. Eritrean exiles, predominantly from the Moslem communities, met in Cairo in 1960 and formed the Eritrean Liberation Front (ELF). A year later, September 1, 1961, a dozen poorly-armed guerrilla fighters proclaimed the start of the armed struggle for independence. As the number of the Eritrean fighters began to grow, drawing from the experience of the Algerian liberation struggle, the leadership of the ELF divided the army into zone units. However, the experience of the *zemene kflitat* (period of the zones) was fraught with serious problems. The Rectification Movement was undertaken to unite the zones, resulting in the unity conference of Adobha in 1969. But the National Liberation Movement (NLM) was soon to experience a more serious split, leading to the formation of the Eritrean People's Liberation Forces (EPLF). This was followed by the first Civil War (1972-1974). Realising the depleting effects of the Civil War on the NLM, initiatives seeking unity were undertaken by the fighters and the population. The first measure taken was to stop the Civil War. As a next step, a unity process was set in motion, which led to the Khartoum Unity Agreement of 1975. By the middle of the 1970s, the liberation movement grew considerably in size, resulting in the liberation of many villages and towns. At the end of 1977, except for four towns, all of Eritrea was under the control of the NLM. However, with massive support from the Soviet Bloc, the Dergue was able to recapture most of the towns. In addition to the military setback in the confrontation with the Dergue, the NLM was beset

Figure 1.3: The Evolution of the Eritrean Nation, 1890-1991

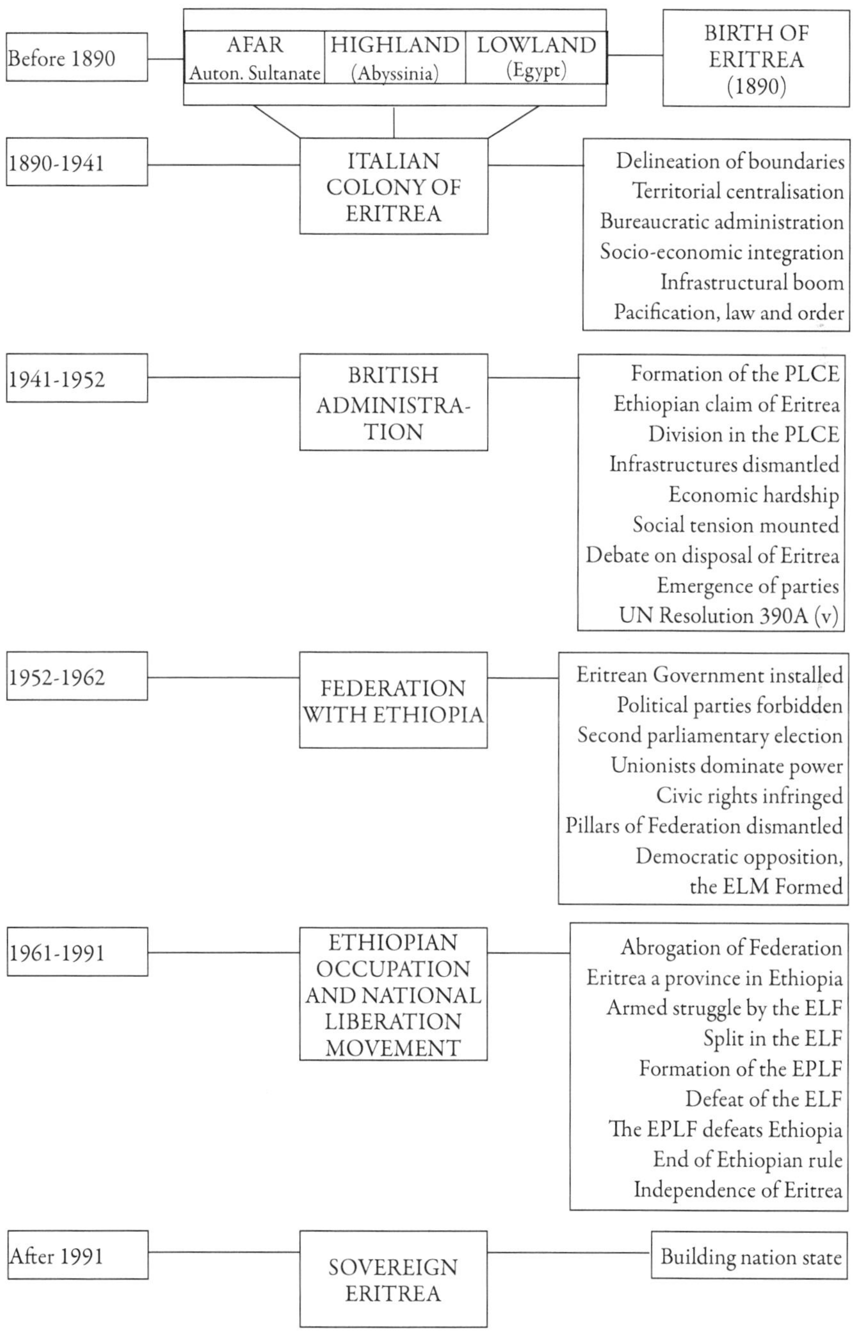

by another problem, a second Civil War. After raging for a full year (August 1980 to July 1981), the Civil War ended with the defeat of the ELF. For the next ten years, the EPLF confronted the Dergue with remarkable success as the sole dominant organisation. The armed struggle, after a bloody war of thirty years, came to an end with the military defeat of Ethiopian forces in May, 1991. This ensured the liberation of Eritrea, and after two years of preparation, a referendum was held, making Eritrea formally a sovereign state in May 1993.

Figure 1.3 provides a schematic presentation of the highlights of Eritrean social history from its birth in 1890 to its emergence as an independence state in 1991. It describes very briefly the process of formation of the Eritrean nation. It begins from the time the territorial integration of the three regions – the Afar, the Highland and the Lowland – took place, extending through the historical trajectory until Eritrean independence. The figure brings to the fore in a summary fashion the main body of the study.

Beginning with the Italian period, the developments that took place can be summarised as follows. The first step taken by the Italian colonialists that established the foundation for the formation of the Eritrean nation was the delineation of boundaries, followed by territorial centralisation. They also introduced bureaucratic administration, which promoted administrative centralisation. The socio-economic integration combined with the dramatic expansion of infrastructure further consolidated the integration of society. Overall, Italian colonialism is considered to have pacified the society, thereby promoting law and order, widely believed to be an indication of the emergence of a modern society.

After more than fifty years, 1890-1941, Italian rule was replaced by the British Military Administration (BMA). The British Administration, 1941-1952, is characterised by its most important contribution, the introduction of political liberalisation. The first Eritrean organisation to emerge during the British Administration was the *Mahber Fikri Hager*. When Ethiopian claims to Eritrea were followed up with its increasing intervention in Eritrean internal affairs, the *Mahber* was split. Urged by the need to find a settlement for the ex-Italian colony, the Administration allowed the formation of political parties, and several different parties were formed as a result. When the economic difficulties that hit the territory coincided with the onset of the debate of the disposition of the territory in the UN General Assembly, a high degree of social tension and disturbance arose in Eritrean society. This resulted in the political parties splitting into two blocs, an independence bloc and a unionist bloc. Amid this division, the UN passed Resolution 390A(v) by which Eritrea was to be federated with Ethiopia.

The Federation, 1952-1962, brought with it national institutions and symbols, and these further enhanced the unique identity of Eritrea. These institutions included a government, a parliament, political parties and a constitution. National symbols such as a flag, seal, and official languages were also introduced. The constitution further enshrined political and civic rights, freedom of the press, of demonstration, and of organisation and assembly. However, these institutions, symbols, and civic and political rights were not respected. Consequently, the pillars of the Federation were dismantled, sparking resistance from the Eritrean nationalists.

The peaceful protest against the infringement upon the Federation failed to produce any of the desired results. Instead, Ethiopia responded with violent repression and proceeded with the annexation of Eritrea, making it a simple province of that country. Therefore, an armed struggle was initiated to challenge the Ethiopian occupation of Eritrea, 1961-1991, a year before the formal annexation. The National Liberation Movement (NLM), as a purposive agent of liberation struggle and nation-building, took up this fight on two fronts. On the one hand, the effort to achieve sovereignty was undertaken through combating Ethiopian occupation. On the other, building a nation through embarking on socio-cultural activities aiming at transforming society was carried out. Over the course of its thirty-year struggle, the NLM experienced internal splits and civil wars. In the end, however, it succeeded in reaching its first target, the independence of Eritrea, in 1991, where this research ends. The post-liberation period, after 1991, is devoted to the task of building nation state.

In this study, I have sought to investigate the Eritrean case from within, that is, from the perspective of the internal development of the Eritrean nation. I have also attempted to approach it from an Eritrean viewpoint. In doing this I have undoubtedly emphasised certain aspects while glossing over others. One of those aspects that was given less emphasis is the Eritro-Ethiopian conflict. The reason for this is my understanding that the process of nation formation is, above all, an internal process. However, this should not be interpreted as implying that external factors are of no significance. I believe they are quite important, but would suggest that they play a secondary role. In a broad sense, this study can be distinguished from other studies of Eritrea on the basis of the following emphases:

1. It traces the social changes that took place over the hundred years of the social history of Eritrea - starting from the territorial integration of the various ethno-linguistic groups in 1890 to the independence of Eritrea. The dates 1890 and 1991 are chosen as starting point and ending point of this study respectively, because they represent specific events of great significance in the social history of Eritrea. The former represents the time when the various ethno-linguistic groups were integrated to form the territorial unit that was to become Eritrea. The latter represents the end of an epoch characterised by the domination of alien powers on the one hand, and the struggle of the Eritrean people for independence on the other, ending in the emergence of Eritrea as a sovereign nation state.

2. It investigates the internal development of the process of formation of the Eritrean nation. It examines the internal development process starting from its very beginnings in the isolated and sporadic resistance to the Abyssinians and Mahdists, to its zenith, the upper stage of the NLM, during which virtually the whole of Eritrean society was mobilised to fight as a unit to achieve its

independence. In contrast to many other studies, which attempt to examine the Eritrean question in conjunction with the Eritro-Ethiopian conflict, the aim of the present study is to analyse it from within. In this respect, it has paid less attention to the debate on the Eritro-Ethiopian conflict.

3. Since the study deals with the process of nation formation as such, it has to be analysed from within. Nation formation is directly connected with internal social transformation. A social transformation, which generates social institutions and arrangements conducive to the development of nations, is required as a necessary condition. It is the institutions, symbols, values, historical experiences, and memories that are the outcome of that social transformation, and which constitute a nation. These are essentially internal elements, and require investigation from the inside. Commenting on nation formation as an internal process, Calhoun (1997: 79) notes, "Nations are made by internal processes of struggle, communication, political participation, road building, history writing and economic development as well as by campaigns against external enemies".

In writing about the process of formation of the Eritrean nation beginning from the inception of its territoriality and culminating in its emergence as a sovereign nation state, I have followed a linear historical trajectory of development (of the sort that it starts in year one and ends in year one hundred). The specific aims of the study necessitated that I make certain choices. Thus, it has been necessary to emphasise certain patterns, issues, phenomena and periods that make sense in describing, analysing and explaining the social-historical development of the Eritrean nation.

SOURCES AND METHOD

A variety of different methodological approaches has been used to analyse and explain the processes of nation formation. The dominant ones are the dichotomous 'generality-specificity' variant. In this category, proponents of the generality/universalist approach seek to create theories, concepts and methodological approaches that have a general application. Advocates of the specificity/historicist approach tend to deal with the historically specific, unique events and phenomena (cf. Sheth 1973, Ragin 1987). The latter approach is more sensitive to historical and cultural contexts, while the former tends to emphasise the general and universal, that is, the historical and culturally neutral. In addition, we have the macro- and micro-sociological, the case-oriented and variable-oriented approaches (see Iggers 1968, Anttila 1993) which are of significant relevance to the study of nation formation. Time and space do not allow detailed discussion regarding the various methodological debates. However, what is most relevant here is that the approach in this study leans toward more or less specificity, a macro-sociological and case-oriented constellation. It deals with the specific history of Eritrea. It is macro-sociological because the study of Eritrea is undertaken at a societal level, that is, social historical processes. Finally, it is a case-oriented because it is a case study of Eritrea.

The material that forms the basis of the study has been gathered from a variety of different sources. It consists of both primary and secondary sources of archives, books, journals, newspapers, interviews and my own personal experience. The distinction between primary sources and secondary sources is given particular importance in historical studies. Primary sources refer to historical materials produced by individuals who were present when the historical events they account for took place (Marshall and Rossman 1995: 89). They are first-hand accounts. Most primary sources are written, these include personal correspondence, diaries, journals, memoirs, autobiographies and government documents. Secondary sources on the other hand refer to historical material produced by individuals who were not present when the events took place. They are second-hand accounts. The secondary sources constitute the chief source of material for this study.

Primary sources

Primary sources are important for developing an understanding of an event. They serve as evidence in developing an interpretation and in building an argument to support that interpretation. In studying political and social events in a historical perspective, archival records and content analysis are seen as vital (Rudestam & Newton 1992: 22). Moreover, it is stressed that content analysis entails systematic examination of documents (Marshall and Rossman 1995: 85). Archival records and content analysis form an important aspect of the research method in this study. The prime source material of the study is historical data. Hence historical archives are collected, analysed and serve to establish the mechanisms and processes leading to the formation of the Eritrean nation. The historical material is also used for the purpose of establishing the change that took place under colonial rule. The primary data consists of mainly of archival documents and interviews. The archival documents I used are collected mainly from the UK and Eritrea. In the summer of 1995, I spent three week in the Public Records Office in London. There, using the directory, I selected relevant information. Of course, to find relevant information I had to go through an enormous bulk of material, most of which was of no use to my study. In that sense, it was time and energy consuming. During the next summer, 1996, I travelled to the Netherlands and I spent two weeks at the African Study Centre in Leiden collecting data. The following year, 1997, I travelled to Eritrea, where I stayed for six months and ten days doing fieldwork.

In Eritrea, most of my data collecting was done in the Research and Documentation Centre (RDC). In addition to the RDC, I also visited the Pavoni Centre where most of the materials from the *Eritrean Weekly Newsletter*, 1941-1947, were collected. I also consulted the Research Library at Asmara University, where I was able to locate issues of the Unionists' newspaper *Ethiopia*. The RDC (previously owned by EPLF and now by the People's Front for Democracy and Justice) also have a large collection of documents. A substantial part of the data was gathered during the armed struggle in the Field through interviews, documentation of oral narratives, and collecting various documents from diverse sources that deal with Italian colonialism, British occupation, etc. The EPLF also tried to gather documents, books and other relevant materials from abroad, particularly through the Research and Information Centre of Eritrea (RICE). Documents and written materials of the various Eritrean political organisations are being collected and preserved in the RDC, for research purposes. Other important source of data for the collection of the RDC during the armed struggle were the various symposiums, conferences and seminars discussing different aspects of the Eritrean struggle held inside and outside Eritrea. These symposiums, conferences and seminars were largely concerned with the Eritro-Ethiopian conflict, thus attempting to establish the legitimacy of the Eritrean question. The research and documentation done in the Field are very important because they are primary and touch upon different aspects (ethnic, economic, cultural, political, demographic and historical) of Eritrean society. However, there are some obvious problems with many of these documents. They lack such important information as date of compilation, place of compilation and author. Nevertheless, the immense importance of their content compelled me to make use of them.

The actual procedure for obtaining material from the RDC is a long process. There is a directory in which materials are listed according to specific titles (culture, politics, economy, armed struggle, demography, ethnic, Italian rule, etc.). One has to go through the list, and after making the selection, order three documents of his/her choice at time through the serial numbers assigned to the documents. After receiving the documents, one can read them on the spot in the reading room, take notes or make copies. The number of copies one is allowed to make is limited to no more than five percent of each document. If the document is large, one is then compelled to sit in the reading room to read it and take notes, which takes a much longer time. Home borrowing is not allowed, and the reading must be done in the single available reading room.

In addition to collecting materials from the RDC, I also interviewed politicians and benefited both from formal and informal discussions. Concerning the interviews I conducted, a number of politicians were selected. Some were suggested to me by friends, while others were chosen because they are public figures. This type of interview is commonly known as the elite interview (Marshall and Rossman 1995). "Elite individuals are considered to be the influential, the prominent, and well-informed people in an organisation or community and are selected for interviews on the basis of their expertise in areas relevant to the research" (Marshall and Rossman 1995: 83). Out of the original number selected, I succeeded in interviewing nine. Two refused, and others could not be reached. Of those interviewed, three were leaders of the ELF, two leaders of the EPLF, two leaders of the ELF-PLF, two leaders of the ELM and one member of the LPP (several of them have, in the course of time, changed organisations). The choice to interview these particular politicians was justified by their political role in one or another Eritrean political organisation, either as founding member figures or in their place in the power hierarchy which enabled them to exercise a key role in shaping the national socio-political landscape during the armed liberation struggle. These are the category of people who, as agents of nation building, played a decisive role in the social history of Eritrea. Specific questions, which varied with respect to the role they played, were posed to all but one, covering practically the entire armed struggle. One of them was asked to read the chapter on the National Liberation Movement (NLM) and comment on it in detail from his organisation's point of view and his personal experience. Some of the questions posed to the respondents were formulated in a fashion that they would serve to check and confirm or, as the case may be, disconfirm the correctness of the answers given. The questions were intended to illustrate and highlight certain historico-political events and actors' views and understandings of the NLM as well as the nation building process. Moreover, these interviews had the intention of demonstrating the problems and successes of the Eritrean revolution. They intended to examine the nature of the internal contradictions, the way they were tackled. They also aimed at inquiring into the effects of these internal contradictions on the achievement of national sovereignty, national cohesion and integration, and ultimately on the process of nation formation. It was also the aim of the interviews to investigate the role of political actors, either as individuals or members of organised groups. The interviewees were asked to give the view of their respective organisation as well as their own.

Any research method has its particular problems and shortcomings. Here, I would like to highlight three general aspects of problems connected with methodological reliability. These are (i) problems embedded in interviews; (ii) problems which archival sources pose; and (iii) the researcher's own bias.

(i) The most common limitation of interviews is that respondents may be uncomfortable about sharing their experience – or simply unwilling to (Marshall and Rossman 1995: 81). The reasons given by the two who refused to be interviewed seem to suggest that they were uncomfortable sharing their experience. The elite type of interview also poses both advantages and disadvantages. "Valuable information can be gained from these participants because of the positions they hold in social, political, financial, or administrative realms. Elites can usually provide an overall view of an organization or its relationship to other organizations" (Marshall and Rossman 1995: 83). Elites are also in a position to give an account of an organisation's policies, past history and future plans. Several weaknesses can also be pointed out. For example, interviewees can be influenced by present conditions, which may consciously or unconsciously affect their descriptions of the past. They can also be influenced by their political convictions in the sense that they may be tempted to convey or promote their political outlook through the interview. This is particularly true when they comment on their opponents. The common view is the "we were right while the other side (other organisations) was wrong" type. When I encountered such situation, I tried to ignore the politically-laden information and concentrated on the information relevant to the study. Here I made use of my own experience to distinguish between politically or ideologically-motivated responses and factual responses.

(ii) The use of colonial archives poses its own shortcomings. In spite of the important information contained in the historical archives compiled by the former colonial powers, still they are accompanied by wide range of limitations. The colonial powers gathered their information largely for the purpose of facilitating their administrative operations. In addition, colonial powers were not adequately equipped to understand the culture of the colonised people, because of, for instance, language barriers. Therefore, their understanding and interpretation of the colonised population was quite often derived from their own cultural codes, perceptions and assumptions. The result is that the archives typically reflect colonial aims, values and interpretations. In other words, they do not reflect the feeling, views, aspirations and interpretations of the colonised people. This is to say that although the archives are of significant importance, they should be treated with caution. Thus, any research conducted solely on the basis of colonial archives cannot adequately represent reality and can be misleading. The interviews are intended to compensate in part for this shortcoming.

(iii) My own background and participation in the National Liberation Movement poses its own advantages and disadvantages. As a participant, one has the privilege of witnessing events as they are unfolding. This gives one an insight that the non-participant lacks. Of course, one also becomes socialised in the nationalist discourse and internalises the standard view of the nationalists. This may cause the participant to develop a difficulty in seeing things from other angles. Therefore, in a situation in which a participant is turning researcher, resocialisation in an academic milieu, in which the researcher is trained to use scientific tools, is quite important. These scientific tools serve the researcher to treat the information sources as objectively as possible. They also help to create distance between the researcher and his subject of study thereby reducing subjective attachment. I would not say that I have been free of bias. I have, for instance, approached the study with a sympathetic, Eritrean eye. Nevertheless, the problem of subjectivity is minimised by a number of factors. First, my direct participation pertains to a relatively small section of the research subject (the NLM). Second, the archival sources and the interviews serve as firsthand sources, which go beyond my subjective limitations, thereby diluting the problems of subjectivity. Third, the secondary sources which are widely used in this study represent the interpretations of other scholars which makes them transcendent, thus, providing a counter to my own subjectivity.

Secondary sources

Another major source of information used in the research is secondary material such as books, journals and newspapers. The secondary materials used can be divided into two groups, those dealing with the empirical work (Eritrea) and those dealing with the theories of nation formation. Much of the published materials dealing with Eritrea were written for different purposes than those of the present research. All research done during the liberation struggle focused mainly on trying to grapple with the question of whether the Eritrean question was legitimate and its people entitled to make claims for the right to self-determination. As such, it was oriented towards the Eritro-Ethiopian conflict. This study, on the other hand, is oriented toward the internal processes of development of the Eritrean nation. In this area, there is no major work from which this study can directly benefit. This dissertation attempts, therefore, to reconstruct the process of formation of the Eritrean nation by extracting information from the available work. Such work chronologically includes: Nadel 1946; Trevaskis 1960; Gebre-Medhin 1979, 1989; Sherman 1980; Houtart 1982; Leonard 1982; Erlich 1982, 1983; Killion 1985; Medhanie 1986, Negash 1987, 1997; Markakis 1987, 1988; Mesghenna 1988; Habte Sellasie 1989; Bondestam 1989; Gayim 1993; Iyob 1995. Published materials of the Eritrean organisations (ELF and EPLF) are also included.

An analysis of the process of formation of the Eritrean nation needs to be supported by the theories, concepts and models that can be found in the research on nation formation. This was done, in part, on the basis of available information in the literature concerning Eritrea. Therefore, a number of authors thought to be representative in the field have been selected and discussed. These include chronologically: Hodgkin 1956; Emerson 1960; Kemiläinen 1964; Bendix 1964; Rustow 1967; Rokkan 1973; Seton-Watson 1977; Mazrui 1983; Gellner 1983; Smith 1983a, 1983b, 1986, 1991, 1998; Hobsbawm 1990; Anderson 1991; Breuilly 1993; Hutchinson 1994; James 1995; McCrone 1998. These theoretical works help in the exposition of (a) the definition and historical genesis of the concept of nation; (b) the difference between the primordialist school of thought and the modernist school of thought; and (c) the colonial school of thought. Inasmuch as they are intended to help in the exposition of these three elements, they also provide the conceptual and theoretical framework of the study.

CONCEPTS OF NATION

This section will very briefly discuss the historical evolution of concepts of nation. The nation and its corollaries, such as nation-state, multinational state, nationalism, nationality, and nationhood are ambiguously and contradictorily described and defined concepts. This has certainly contributed to the confusion that characterises the subject. Thus, it seems appropriate to present some general ideas concerning the evolution and definition of the concept. The primary concern of this study is the process of nation formation. In this respect, the main focus of the definition will be the concept of nation. Other corollary concepts will be touched upon only briefly, since they are beyond the scope of the study.

In what follows, I grapple with the historical and etymological development of the concept of nation. Meanings have changed to fit into the specific historical, political, social and cultural circumstances in which it was operating. By presenting accounts of how the concept has developed, I demonstrate the amorphous and changing nature of the concept.

The Origin and Evolution of the Concept

The origin and historical evolution of the concept of nation represents a quite remarkable innovation. Three broad stages can be discerned in the etymological evolution of the concept, the ancient time, the Middle Ages and modern time. It originated from the Latin word "natio" (Kemiläinen 1964: 13, Greenfeld 1992: 4). In ancient Rome, the word "natio" had various meanings, including a foreign tribe or people, race, or a class (Kemiläinen 1964: 13). It had a pejorative connotation (Zernatto 1944: 352, Greenfeld 1992:4), referring to a backward barbarous group of people. The Church applied it to denote non-Christians or non-believers. It also bore the meaning that common origin or ethnicity was a characteristic hallmark of a group. The word "natio" is derived from the word "nascar" which means, "I am born" (Zernatto 1944: 351). Hence, "natio" in common parlance was perceived as a group of people who shared place of birth. The Romans, while considering "natio" as external and foreign – "exterae nationes" – they perceived themselves as "populus" or "civitas" (Kemiläinen 1964: 53).

Later, in the Middle Ages, while retaining the meaning it had in ancient Rome, nation picked up an additional meaning. Members of universities were divided into nations based on their nationality (birthplace) (Seton-Watson 1977: 8). Later; however, language was emphasised as a variable of category. Now these "nationes" of students represented a different meaning than that which was originally meant by the term "natio". Nation, at this point in time, evolved to mean "a community of origin, a union of purpose, and a community of opinion" (Zernatto 1944: 354, Greenfeld 1992: 4). Even in the Church, where the bishops were assembled in groups of nations to vote for their countries or geographical regions, a nation may constitute several countries (Kemiläinen 1964:22). Overall, two conceptions of the concept of nation came to dominate in the medieval period, notably 'council nation'[2] and 'university nation'. Yet, up to this point, the concept of nation was invariably associated with foreigners. This was soon to be changed. The new meaning that the word nation was to acquire originated primarily from the emerging political development that led to the rise of national states and national consciousness. Here "natio" was endowed with the meaning of a people living in a country. The medieval usage of "natio" in churches and universities was combined with home country. The word "populus" began to imply people of a state or city (Kemiläinen 1964: 24).

In more modern times, or the third stage, the term nation assumed yet another meaning. It began to take on the meaning of a number of people dwelling in specific territory under the same government (Kemiläinen 1964: 26). At another stage, for about two centuries before the French Revolution, the term "nation" denoted the whole people of a country. The designation "the people" referred to the lower class indicating the voters (Greenfeld 1992: 6), whereas the "nation" referred to the elite, the nobility (Seton-Watson 1977: 159). At this time, two distinct meanings could be identified. In France and England, "nation" indicated the whole people under the state, within the same country, the same laws and the same government. In Germany, "nation" represented linguistic community dispersed throughout the German Empire[3]. This included ethnic Germans living in different states. The characteristic markers of a nation in the German definition were common origin, language and custom (Hobsbawm 1990: 102-3, Kemiläinen 1964: 55). After the French Revolution "nation" began to take on a jurisdictional meaning. The Revolution declared that sovereignty lies in the nation. Prior to the Revolution, the nation had been viewed as state. The Revolution separated nation and state, and the nation came to be understood as the foundation of the state (Kemiläinen 1964: 31) and became a sacred entity. Now the nation came to mean a sovereign people, replacing that of an elite or nobility, and thereby referring to the whole population (Smith 1983b: 191).

Greenfeld (1992: 9) describes the transformation of the concept of nation as follows: (1) nation – a group of foreigners; (2) nation – a community of opinion; (3) nation – an elite; (4) nation – a sovereign people; (5) nation – a unique people. The first definition corresponds to the ancient Roman usage, while the second and third definitions correspond to the medieval age (universities and Church councils). The fourth and fifth correspond to the modern age. Within the modern age itself, the fourth definition pertains the first nations, particularly England and France. The fifth definition is associated with the formation of nation in the nineteenth century, which put great emphasis on language, ethnicity, and culture. Further, in discerning the distinction between a nation as a sovereign people and a nation as a unique people, Greenfeld discusses it in terms of particularistic and non-particularistic notions. The particularistic corresponds to the notion of a unique people while the non-particularistic corresponds to the notion of a sovereign people. A further parallel can be drawn, in that the non-particularistic matches the prototype nations, especially England, while the particularistic is matched with the nation in the second phase of the process of nation formation of the nineteenth century.

Greenfeld argues that the original idea of the modern nation, which implied sovereignty of the people, was based on the principle of individualism. Sovereignty of the people actually means sovereignty of individuals. In the category of a unique people, sovereignty derives from the distinctiveness of the people. The national principle is collectivism. She also describes two types of nationalism, the individualistic-libertarian and the collectivistic-authoritarian. The individualistic-libertarian vs. collectivistic-authoritarian perception leads to the membership criteria based on civic or ethnic status (Greenfeld 1992: 11). According to the former, nationality is voluntary and can be acquired, whereas according to the latter it is deterministic and inherited, arising from the fact of belonging to a unique ethnicity his or her nationality is predetermined.

In conclusion, as Kemiläinen suggests, one quality – group consciousness – stands as most important, irrespective of the number of different meanings the term nation might have possessed along its historical trajectory. While the concept of nation has changed a lot from its Latin roots denoting foreigners, it carries even today the connotation of foreigner expressed in the "we" and "they" exclusivity.

Finally, this section has attempted to describe the historical metamorphosis of the concept of nation. In this respect, roughly three stages have been distinguished, notably the ancient Roman period, the Middle Ages and modern times. We have also seen how the concept has possessed shifting meanings along its historical development, reflecting historical socio-economic changes.

PATHS OF NATION FORMATION

This section briefly reviews the historical paths through which the European and African nations evolved. First, the historical experience of Europe is examined, followed by a look at the African experience. Finally, in connection with the African path, the legacy of colonialism is examined briefly.

The rationale behind the juxtaposition of the European path and the African (colonial) path is grounded in the European spatio-temporal origin of the concepts and theories of nation and their diffusion to the rest of the world (see Tilly 1975). The diffusion to Africa was imported on the boat of colonialism. The colonial state, in a fashion similar to that of the absolute states in Western Europe, dictated certain conditions in the colonised societies. Even after independence, the post-colonial state inherited and perpetuated the legacy of the colonial state. These developments merit a comparative analysis of the European path and the African path (cf. Smith 1983a: 1-2, First 1983, Young 1994).

One underlying assumption of this study is that there exists a common pattern in the historical initiation of the process of nation formation in Western Europe and Africa. In both cases, the state played an indispensable historical role. The absolute state in Western Europe imposed certain standards, which led to the centralisation and homogenisation of a society, while at the same time detaching it from the surrounding societies. The colonial state compartmentalised societies in Africa in an effort to impose particular standards, which bear a remarkable resemblance to its own historical experience at home. Thus, a comparative analysis of the historical path of Europe and historical path of Africa is justified.

The European Path

There is a consensus among most social scientists in the Western world that modern nations and nation-states are the result of the socio-economic transformations that took place in Western Europe and North America. The advent of this transformation can be roughly traced back to the 16th century. Since then, it has diffused to the rest of the world. It was an evolutionary process that entailed economic, cultural, social, and political transformations based on scientific, technological, educational, and industrial revolutions. This, in turn, led to the rationalisation, secularisation, bureaucratisation, democratisation, centralisation, and standardisation of societies and the transformation of people from subject to citizenship. Emphasising the salience of citizenship, Hutchinson & Smith (1994: 132) suggest that it is the institutionalisation of citizenship that distinguishes post-eighteenth-century nations from earlier ethnic and territorial communities. Further, the principle of sovereignty – that is, the external recognition of the right of the state to establish internal order and defend itself from external aggression, and the internal view that sovereignty stems from the people or the nation – becomes universal. In a nutshell, nations are the consequence of what Smith (1986: 131) calls 'triple revolutions' notably, revolutions in the sphere of the division of labour, in the control of administration, and in cultural co-ordination.

It was within this general time frame, around the 16th century, that the French and English nations were consolidated (see Durkheim 1977). All the different revolutions that occurred are 'arbitrarily chosen dates' (Seton-Watson 1977: 8). Beyond this, it is difficult to designate a specific date (Balibar & Wallerstein 1988: 88) indicating when the formation of the nations exactly began. Seton-Watson distinguishes between two models of nation, notably 'old continuous nations' and new nations. The chief distinction between these two models is the types of developments that occurred. In the 'old continuous nations', the genesis of nations is believed to have begun in the Middle Ages and developed through an evolutionary process in which the integration of a greater section of society took place. This occurred as a result of state expansion, the development of communications, trade exchanges, and the emergence of vernacular literature. In the 'new nations', on the other hand, the rise of nations is believed to have taken place in the era of nationalism, "The new nations were formed in the era of nationalism and, as such, were the ideologized products of educated élites who moulded their populations according to the national model of the old nations" (Hutchinson & Smith 1994: 132). Moreover, according to Seton-Watson (1977: 17) the formation of the nation and the formation of the state in the 'old nations' advanced hand in hand. He maintains that the nation was shaped within the common framework of the state, and that those who were excluded from this common framework (boundary) were not considered members of the nation. In addition, the broad coincidence of the nation and language was perceived as a central pre-requisite (Emerson 1963: 113), that is, those who spoke English constituted England, and those who spoke French or Spanish constituted France or Spain. Of course, this assumption has its faults because there existed minorities, for instance, within the French nation who did not speak French or within the Spanish nation who did not speak Spanish.

The proponents of this idea acknowledge that there had been a transition period through which the prototype nations had to pass before the transformation of nations could take place. This transformation period was the formation of the absolute monarchy, which happened as a consequence of the configuration of the disintegrated feudal states of Princes. This transformation, with its inherent and characteristic consequences of monetary monopoly, administrative and fiscal centralisation and a relative degree of standardisation of the legal system and internal pacification, formed the threshold of the modern nation formation (Balibar 1988: 87, Seton-Watson 1977: 9). This sheds light on how bureaucratic state centralisation played a significant role in bringing the nation into existence.

In addition, in the elucidation of the process of nation formation, a distinction is made between two paths: (a) via culture and descent of a group, and (b) via state centralisation and territorial homogenisation of ethnically heterogeneous groups (Smith 1983b: xiii). This, in turn, was the outcome of the transformation of the two main types of *ethnie,* lateral and vertical[4] (Smith 1994: 147f). In elaborating the mechanisms of transformation, Smith suggests that in the lateral paths the upper class created the nation by incorporating the lower class and the periphery into a centralised bureaucratic state. Here a dominant ethnic group like the Franks (France), Normans (England) and Castillian (Spain) played a decisive role in the formation of nation by a bureaucratic incorporation of other minorities. In the case of the vertical path, a secularised intelligentsia mobilises the ethnic community around shared language, culture and ethnic descent to create a compact nation. This type of vertical *ethnie* transformation takes place in the era of nationalism and emergence of nations. This transformation entails the fulfilment of a range of conditions. These include a shift from a passive minority into an active political community, with the sole aim of establishing an internationally recognised homeland (territory). Such a shift is facilitated by the economic integration that takes place with members becoming masters of their own resources, changing the ethnic community into a political community and exercising all civic rights and duties, and finally, putting the people in the political and moral centre endowed with their national myths, symbols and memory (Smith 1994: 153-4). The creation of nations in Eastern Europe was on the basis of ethnic identity, whereas in Western Europe it was based on territory. These two historical routes, in turn, have produced two models of integration, civic and ethnic (Smith 1986: 146). The two historical experiences led to a conceptualisation of nations which Smith (1986, 1991: 9-11) refers to as the territorial (civic) conception and the cultural (ethnic) conception. While in the former, nationhood is based on citizenship, in the latter nationhood is based on culture. This discussion shows the existence of two main historical paths of nation formation, corresponding with two main models of societal unification. The diagram can illustrate this development.

Figure 1.4: Two paths of nation formation

Lateral *Ethnie* –––> Territorial centralisation –––> Civic nation
a) From lateral *ethnic* to civic nation

Vertical Ethnie –––> Ethnic centralisation –––> Ethnic nation
b) From vertical *ethnie* to ethnic (genealogical) nation

The diagram illustrates the two paths through which the transformation of nations took place. Ethnic politicisation and territorial integration are the extensions of the cultural community and the political community respectively (Smith 1983b: xii-xiii). The former is "based on belief in common descent, and a sense of identity and solidarity". The latter, "on shared administrative and military institutions, and common boundaries for protection and mobility of labour and goods within a common territory" (Smith 1983b: xii-xiii). It is widely believed that the formation of the nation and nation-state have passed through different stages (see Hague & Harrop 1982: 19ff, Habermas 1981: 358-61, Giddens 1985). It appears that at each stage, the state played a different role and had different functions. Behind this notion lies an evolutionary developmental theory.

This cumulative historical evolutionary perspective rests on the perception that the nation and nation-state have developed steadily and progressively from lower and less complex, to higher and more complex organisms, equipped with sophisticated modern institutions. This is a change from a primitive, mechanical differentiation to a modern, organic differentiation. Tilly (1975) presents a comprehensive overview of the development of the national state in Western Europe and its subsequent diffusion to the rest of the world. Tilly's emphasis is on the national state. It seems that Tilly does not make any distinction between state and nation. Seton-Watson persuasively discusses how the nation and the state developed simultaneously, particularly in the prototype nation-states thereafter to be inextricably cemented together thereby making a distinction between them meaningless or rather difficult. Amin (1980) has likewise noted that in the centre nation and state are inextricably entangled. The nation-state is of course neither a nation nor a state, but rather a blend of both nation and state, in other words a nation having its own state. Yet, an analytical distinction is made between the state and the nation. The following diagram illustrates the historical evolution of the nation and the state.

Figure 1.5: Nationalism as the mechanism of nation and state formation

State –––> Nationalism –––> Nation
Nation –––> Nationalism –––> State

Now it is clear that there have been two principal historical processes. The first process refers to the extension of power and administration from centre to periphery – the creation of territorial integration by different forms through state design. Many scholars of nation formation view this process and its concomitant upshot as the precursor to the emergence of nations. It is in this vein that Smith's (1986) model of state-to-nation historical process of the formation of the first nations of Western Europe should be seen. The second process includes the more or less deliberate creation of new states, orchestrated by the intellectuals. Yugoslavia and Czechoslovakia are taken as good examples, and the final consolidation of Germany and Italy also belonged to this category (Seton-Watson 1977). The early process of the formation of modern state – widely assumed to follow an era of absolute monarchy, and undertaken under intense internal warfare of expansion – established the framework for the formation of nations. In addition, in the first process, the widely-held conviction is that the emergence of nations was the result of unwitting societal developmental processes. It came as a consequence of transformations in various fields, which geared societies to more homogenous exclusivities. While in the second process, nations came into existence as intentional conscious acts of political actors. Whichever form the process took, the formation or growth of nations occurred, "in the sense of culturally homogeneous, territorially compact and economically unified political communities of destiny" (Smith 1983a: 14).

Smith, in his 'two routes model', discerns two paths of the formation of nations identical to those of Tilly. The two paths are the 'state-to-nation' route and the 'nation-to-state' route illustrated in figure 1.5. According to Smith the 'state-to-nation' path presupposes, "implicitly shared meanings and values, with common myths and symbols" (Smith 1986: 136). In the absence of these meanings, myths and symbols, it becomes imperative to construct them. Conversely, in the 'nation-to-state' path, nations are formed in a protracted transformation processes from the 'pre-existing *ethnie* and ethnic ties'. A transformation of ethnic to nation through 'mobilization', 'territorialization' and 'politicization' (Smith 1986: 137) takes place. This implies, in other words, the transformation of qualities already there in the form of primitive, primordial existence to modern, active, conscious and national ones. Generally, these two paths lead to the conceptions of what Smith designates as 'territorial nations' and 'ethnic nations'. These two models of nation formation have, thus, given rise to two different conceptions, one based on territory and another based on *ethnie*. Yet, both conceptions concede that in the end, the result of the two processes will culminate in the creation of culturally homogenous nations (in terms of civic culture). In the territorial conception of nation, for instance, this function (cultural homogeneity) is accomplished through the socialisation of community members into a, "uniform and shared way of life and belief-system" (Smith 1986: 136).

In this process of formation of the nation, the transition from feudal kingdom to an absolute monarchy represented a vital threshold in the rise of nations in Western Europe. Territorial centralisation, economic integration, cultural homogenisation, and above all, the emergence of vernacular languages under absolute monarchies paved the way for the formation of nations. The break from the Greco-Latin language and concomitantly, the development of vernacular language and the growth of national script (Rokkan 1975) played a determining role in the process of nation formation. Rokkan states that the emergence of vernacular languages had two consequences, one to reach all the segments or strata within the specific territory, and the second to limit the communication within the boundaries of the particular vernacular community, thereby producing linguistic homogenisation. The importance of the written language in the process of nation formation is also strongly emphasised by Gellner (1983), Anderson (1991) and Hroch (1994).

The prevalence of what Gellner describes as a 'pervasive high culture', which means, "standardized, literacy, and education-based systems of communication" (Gellner 1983: 54) was also a decisive factor in the formation of the nation. This leads to the creation of a standardised, homogenised, and centralised high culture, which is not only confined to the elite level, but penetrates the entire society, thereby encompassing all members of the society. This development is seen as a prerequisite for the rise of nationhood. Gellner's strong emphasis on language faces scathing criticism. Criticising Gellner's exaggerated stress on language Smith (1983b) asserts that Gellner equates language with culture and his perception (Smith's) is that culture is more than sheer language.

Smith (1991: 59) states that early nation formation in England, France, Spain, Holland and Sweden was associated with the revolutions in the fields of administration, economy, and culture, the 'triple revolution' (Smith 1986). In this context, it is argued that in actuality, the state created the nation (state-to-nation model), "activities of taxation, conscription and administration endowed the population within its jurisdiction a sense of their corporate identity and civic loyalty" (Smith 1991: 59). So the state was the prime driving force in creating the necessary conditions for the consolidation of national loyalty. In addition to the expansion of citizenship rights and obligations, the development of infrastructure connected remote parts of the country. Through expanded communications networks, more people from different areas and classes were drawn into the national political sphere, thereby creating the image of the national communities of "England, France, Spain, that evoke such powerful feelings of commitment and belonging to this day" (Smith 1991: 60). Elaborating on the processes through which nations came into existence in Western Europe, Smith writes:

> Here 'ethnic states' were gradually transformed, through the impact of the triple revolutions, into genuinely 'national states' through the unification of the economy, territorial centralization, the provision of equal legal rights formore and more strata, and the growth of public, mass education systems (Smith 1986: 138).

In this developmental path, two revolutions, one economic and the other cultural, appear to have been critical. The emergence of a market economy, which was first confined to several core, late-medieval Western states, was gradually to expand throughout the globe. The cultural and educational revolution in its turn, engendered "the development of secular studies, notably classical humanism and science, of university learning and ultimately of popular modes of communication – novels, plays and journal" (Smith 1986: 138). Thus, it was through the administrative, economic and cultural revolutions, that peripheral regions and ethnic groups and middle and lower classes were incorporated into the dominant ethnic culture through the agency of the bureaucratic state. "The creation of a secular, mass nation was ultimately the outcome of various programmes of political socialization through a public, mass education system" (Smith 1991: 61).

Rokkan has also developed a 'four dimensional models' scheme, which more sharply elucidates the integration process. These are:

> 1) the distinctiveness, the consolidation and the economic, political, and cultural strength of the territorial centre; 2) the cultural distance of peripheries from the centre and their economic and political resources for resistance against integration and standardisation; 3) the internal strength and the external resource links of cross-locally organized substructures such as churches, sects, casts; 4) the internal strength and the external resource links of cross-locally organized economic units, such as merchants leagues, credit networks, international cooperations (Rokkan 1973: 18).

As can be clearly seen from the quotation, Rokkan's argument is based on the dichotomy of centre-periphery. His argument is that the formation of a nation is determined by the success of the centre in bringing the periphery under its effective control, and the consent of the periphery to the legitimate dominance of the centre. This dominance and extension of the centre into its periphery promotes a homogenisation and standardisation of culture, the economic system, territorial integrity and uniformity of citizen allegiance, etc. These are vital prerequisites for the consolidation of a nation. The existence of competing centres, their ability to defend their cultural uniqueness and their capacity to furnish a fertile milieu for the autonomous survival and perpetuation of their periphery seriously inhibits the successful formation of a nation. The case of Spain is a good example (see Linz 1973). The competitive capability of Catalonia and the Basque country in terms of economy and culture has contributed to weak nation formation in Spain.

In conclusion, in this historical account we have discussed the two paths (vertical and lateral) within the European historical experience that led to the two conceptions of nation (ethnic and civic). We have also seen the role played by the state in the formation of the 'old nations'. The formation of nations was the result of transformation in the different spheres, which began in the 16th century. The 'new nations' – those of post-1789 – led by their secularised intelligentsia, had to struggle against the 'old nations', in their attempt to create their own states, while, at the same time, emulating the model of formation of the old nations. This discussion permits us now to shift our attention to the situation of Africa.

The African Path

The above presentation is intended to provide insight into the historical frame of reference against which the socio-historical evolution of African nations is compared. One might wonder why we should adopt the European model of nation formation as a frame of reference for studying nation formation in Africa. While acknowledging the legitimacy of the question, it is possible to point to the presence of several compelling reasons for doing so. There is widespread understanding that European experience was diffused to the colonial societies through colonialism (Tilly 1975, Smith 1983a, Mazrui 1983, Diamond et. al., 1988, First 1983, Young 1994). Among other things, an *ipso facto* attempt was made to implement the European historical experience in Africa through colonialism. The Berlin Conference of 1884-85 on the partition of Africa marked the formal beginning of the imposition of the European territorial model on the continent. Upon its establishment, the colonial state made efforts to implement the central aspects of the European experience in the colonial societies. In addition, an indigenous intellectual corps developed, trained in European educational institutions, which was to take-over state power (First 1983: 207). Many scholars have thus maintained that the impact of colonialism in the African continent was of considerable magnitude. This, in turn, has led them to argue for the validity of the European model – particularly the one invariably represented as 'territorial nation', 'civic nation', 'state-to-nation', 'state-sponsored'. A development that enhanced this view was that the inheritors of the colonial state pursued the same path, the European model of nation building. The fact that the intellectuals were the products of the philosophical and academic socialisation of metropolitan nations played a decisive role in their vision of nation formation (cf. Neuberger 1994/1977, Smith 1983a, Dzongola-Ntalaja 1988). These factors make it necessary to pay due attention to the European historical experience. It is a basic assumption of this study that there is a fundamental similarity between the path of the 'old nations' in Western Europe and the path in Africa, the state-to-nation path.

In arguing for the applicability of the European path to Africa, Smith (1983a: 1f) elucidates two main approaches. The first refers to the omnipresent transition from the feudal socio-economic order to the capitalist socio-economic order in the West. This is paralleled by a similar development in the non-western cultures from a non-capitalist order to either a capitalist or a dependent or a peripheral capitalist societal structure and economic mode of production. The other approach refers to the ubiquitous development from a traditional pattern of society to one that is modern, and concerns the process of modernisation by which this transition is effected. It is argued that the process displays an underlying pattern common to all cases, notwithstanding the individual circumstances that distinguish the pace, timing and intensity. This kind of debate is undertaken with the aim of making a persuasive argument that there are some basic elements that bind the development of general social history. By establishing that logic, it is possible to draw conclusions regarding the relevance of the European model to the African social history.

Besides the historical and materialist (in the economic sense) perspectives entailed in this approach – i.e., the perception of the transformation of societies from a relatively lower stage of development to a higher level – the role of the post-colonial state and the indigenous intelligentsia is accorded significant importance. These tendencies are considered to be generic and broadly common to all societies, however variable the particular historical route may be. There are certain obvious similarities between the roles played by the absolute state in Europe at the end of the Middle Ages and the colonial state in Africa. These similarities can be abstracted as the building of the bureaucratic centralised administrative order, the integration of the economy, establishing the basis for a standardised taxation system and the introduction of conscription. As the absolute state is credited for having laid the groundwork for the rise of the nation in Europe, the colonial state is in a similar fashion credited for having established the conditions necessary for the formation of the nation in Africa.

Many European scholars of nation formation contest the existence of nations in Africa prior to colonialism. Some social scientists in the West argue in earnest that nations never existed in pre-colonial Africa. Nations, which emerged as the consequence of the process of decolonisation, are also perceived to be in their rudimentary phase (see Hague & Harrop 1987, Hughes 1981, Käufeler 1988). Moreover, the viability of these post-colonial political units, as nations as well as states is highly questioned (Strayer 1963: 26). Conversely, others acknowledge that the only fair comparison that can be made is that the embryonic African nations are at a stage comparable to that of European nations at the start of 19th century. This is the view proffered by the modernist school of thought (cf. Smith 1986). As a faithful adherent of the modernist school of thought, Arnold Hughes (1981: 122) maintains that the reference to the recently-emerged countries of Africa as nation-states and their peoples as nations is dubious.

Scholars from Africa have argued to the contrary – that nations had existed in Africa long before the advent of colonialism. Indeed, these scholars point out that colonial powers destroyed many African political nations (Tokolor, Mandinka, Fulani, Zulu, etc.) for the purpose of establishing their own political order (Mazrui & Tidy 1984: 186). Nzongola-Ntalaja (1988: 27), vigorously rejects the view that says that nations did not exist in pre-colonial Africa, arguing that nations did, in fact, exist. As an illustration, he mentions the kingdoms of Kongo, Kuba, Luba and Lunda, which clearly exhibited nationhood. Yet, he acknowledges that most present-day African nations are the creation of colonialism (Nzongola-Ntalaja 1988: 38).

Other researchers of nation formation also agree that most of the nations in contemporary Africa are the construction of colonial rule. The colonial powers amalgamated a variety of geographical regions and ethnic groups into artificially constructed territorial nations. In doing this, Europe transferred its own state system to Africa, without prior study, in order to assure that statehood coincided with nationhood. But the state system which Europe transplanted in Africa differed in one fundamental respect, that of the divergence between politics and culture. As Lewis puts it, "It is a remarkable irony that the European powers who partitioned Africa in the late 19th century when the idea of the nation-state was paramount, should have created in Africa a whole series of Habsburg-style states, comprising a medley of peoples and ethnic groups lumped together within frontiers which paid no respect to traditional cultural contours" (Lewis 1983: 73). Little effort was made to ensure congruence between the political unit (state) and the cultural unit (nation), not even for the cultural similarities among the different units being ruled by the same colonial government (Diamond et al 1988). Nzongola-Ntalaja (1988) stresses that existing social, political, cultural and institutional structures were dismantled to pave the way for the alien imperialistic ones. Mazrui & Tidy (1984: 185) also argue that even today after decolonisation, the geopolitical boundaries that were devised in the scramble for Africa are intact. It is emphasised that the state forms that Africans tried to build following decolonisation were modelled after those of the West European models (Mazrui & Tidy 1984). As a matter of fact, even the constitutional structures that were installed in the aftermath of decolonisation were designed in the constitutional tradition of the particular ex-colonial power.

I will now set out some tentative, specific propositions concerning the particular types of development that took place during colonial rule. This development shaped African societies and has had a great impact in the nation formation processes of the continent. The focus will be on five spheres of development: a) the territorial sphere, b) the political sphere, c) the cultural sphere, d) the economic sphere and e) the communications spheres.

a) Territorial sphere: Much of the literature on colonialism underscores the fact that the territorial centralisation and integration engendered by the colonial state established the foundation for the development of nations (Hodgkin 1956, Goody 1973, Smith 1983a, Clapham 1985). This integration is effected by the boundary delimitation, which involves the act of exclusivity and inclusivity leading to the evolution of a nation. It is a process of exclusivity because those physically separated are considered to be different, constituting the "they" category. It is, at the same time, a process of inclusivity in that those who are included within the delimited space, through abstract imagining, form the "we" category. Thus, the arbitrary delimitation of geo-political boundaries constituted the first step in the long process of nation formation in Africa. In that sense, the first and primary task of the colonial state, akin to its predecessor (the absolute state), was to delineate and integrate the territories which were to be recognised as sovereign political units. However, in a marked departure from the patterns and practices of the absolute state, these boundaries were rarely based on the pre-colonial units. Most of the time, they were founded on expanded territories, and with no prior consideration given to the cultural and ethnic composition of the populations (Goody 1973: 354, Clapham 1985: 18). What mattered most was that this mapping should satisfy the intention of the scramble. As a result many ethnic groups were unjustifiably divided and dispersed into different territorial units generating multiethnic societies. The perpetrators thought that these territories would develop into compact nation-states along the Western model. The salience of this territorial integration with regard to the process of nation formation can be seen in its similarity to the role played by the centralising bureaucratic state in Europe in creating a compact administrative unit (discussed earlier). This is often perceived as a precursor to the emergence of the nation.

b) Political sphere: The establishment of a system of political rule presupposes territorial integration. Following the establishment of territorial integration, the colonial state set out to forge a territorially-centralised political system based on bureaucratic, administrative rule. In contrast to the West European type, which was founded upon a relatively homogenous cultural political entity (where there existed at least one dominant ethnic group playing a determining role, e.g. the Franks, the Normans), the political system in Africa was founded on forcibly-integrated territorial political units made up of polyethnic entities. This peculiarly African historical experience, in marked variance with the experience of the European nation-state formation processes, is culminated in the formation of what Smith (1983b) and Gellar (1973: 392) identify as the 'state-nation' political system. The argument here is that, while in most European nations the state was coterminous with the nation, in Africa, this condition was starkly lacking. In Africa, many scholars seem to agree the state preceded the nation. Of course, the story is not fully told here, because this is not entirely peculiar to Africa. Initially, in Western Europe, too, the state preceded the nation. But in any case, colonialism resulted in the establishment of the bureaucratic state system, resulting in the state shouldering the responsibility for building a nation.

c) Cultural sphere: Theories of nation formation inform us that the nation system in Europe is characterised by the homogeneity of culture. Further, we are also informed that language, as a medium of communication, plays a salient role in the unification of a community. The emergence of vernacular script in Europe is perceived as a revolutionary development in the creation of a homogenous identity (see Gellner 1983, Smith 1983b, Anderson 1991). In most colonial and post-colonial African countries, the ex-colonial metropolitan language, such as French, English or Portuguese, has become the dominant national language. This reality, in a multilingual and multiethnic community, serves a vital purpose as a medium of communication across ethnic and linguistic communities. This has engendered relative unity and integration, particularly within the well-educated social stratum. In other words, these alien languages spreading across ethnic and linguistic communities create a sort of sense of commonality. In addition, these languages serve as a vehicle of cultural socialisation in their role as the medium of education. Education mediated through a common language to all sections of society, across polyethnic and polyglot (multilingual) communities, engenders a certain level of shared sentiment, ideas, aspirations, symbols and myths which are expressed in an overarching common general civic culture. Ostensibly, in several of these colonial societies, the colonial language has contributed towards the formation of a transcending, common national culture.

d) Economic sphere: As Smith (1983a) observes, colonial capitalist economic penetration introduced the capitalist economic system into colonial societies, thereby affecting their socio-economic structure. The establishment of a centralised economic system linked to the metropolitan economic system created a centre-periphery relationship. The development of roles took place, in which the colonial territory was assigned with supplying raw materials, while the imperial power supplied industrial products. Within the colonial territory itself, a geographical division of labour between rural and urban areas and class stratification developed. Central market places in urban sites flourished (see Hodgkin 1956). This in turn opened up the possibility of exchanges of products both modern and traditional, promoting the intermingling of the various linguistic and ethnic groups. The colonial economic system, to a certain degree, created a centralised economic structure through which the various sections of the territory were interconnected. These eventually produced a hierarchically structured economic system. This, in turn, played an important role in metamorphosing the communities, thereby fuelling the processes of nation formation. Hence, the economic integration effected by colonialism laid the basic foundations for the rise of territorially-based civic nations.

e) Communications sphere: Colonialism brought with it modern communications and transportation technology. Infrastructure, in the form of roads, railways, towns, hospitals, schools, sea and airports was constructed. Telecommunications, in the form of postal systems, telephone and telegraph communications were established (Hodgkin 1956: 29). Radio, newspaper and other media infrastructure were also introduced. These developments facilitated physical communication between different geographical and ethno-cultural regions. They also led to exchanges in the material and cultural dimensions between the different groups and the gradual learning of each other's mosaic cultural features. These exchanges of cultural and material values, norms and symbols made a socialisation process possible, which finally culminated in the creation of certain common national symbols and values. Overall, this helped in generating a sense of 'imagined community'.

These are the five predominate spheres in which centralisation and integration have taken place. Critics, however, maintain that integration and centralisation is weak, pointing to the polyethnic composition of the embryonic African 'state-nations'. This development undoubtedly shows certain similarities with the European path, though in Africa the configuration of various ethnolinguistic groups into territorial political units led to what some scholars have characterised as 'empire-building' (cf. Gellar 1973). In expounding upon the process of nation building in Africa, Mazrui summarises five dimensions of this integration:

> Firstly, some degree of cultural and normative fusion; secondly, the promotion of economic interpenetration between different strata and sectors of society; thirdly, the process of social integration; fourthly, the process of building institutions for effective conflict resolution; and fifthly, the psychological accumulation of a shared national experience (Mazrui 1973: 469).

To conclude, the overall assumption is that taken collectively, these developments are responsible for the emergence of the dialectics of unity within diversity and diversity within unity. This means that the various ethno-linguistic groups form unity while at the same time maintaining diversity. The particularistic coexists with the universalistic. In other words, there will exist a duality of loyalty and identity. The different ethnic groups will pay allegiance to their *ethnie* – and to the transcending civic nation.

The Legacy of Colonialism

This section briefly discusses the implications of the imperial colonial policies and philosophies for the process of nation formation. The focus is primarily on British and French policies. This is due to their representativity and the availability of literature. Several scholars (e.g. Hodgkin 1956, Rivkin 1969, Seton-Watson 1977, Mazrui 1983, Smith 1983a, Clapham 1985) have surveyed the policies of the imperial powers. Mazrui (1983) argues that the Francophone colonies were more of becoming nations than the Anglophone colonies. On the other hand, the Francophones were weaker than their Anglophone counterparts with respect to state formation.

This contrast is explained as having originated from the different policies of the two imperial powers toward their colonies. The policies are believed to have been based on the history and political culture of respective nations. In a broad sense, the distinction is made along the policies of 'direct rule' and 'indirect rule'. The British policy was known to emphasise the policy of indirect rule[5], which was intended to engage the indigenous population in local administrative affairs and utilise native institutions. The French policy, on the other hand, emphasised assimilation and integration of the native people into the French culture, thus direct rule (Mazrui 1983: 27-8, Clapham 1985: 21f, Diamond et al 1988: 6f). These scholars believe that these policies had significant consequences in terms of nation and state formation in Africa.

The British doctrine was based upon the belief that people are more easily ruled through local authority and institutions. They believed that it becomes easier for them to accept authority based on institutions they could understand and conventions they could identify with. On the basis of this understanding, the British sometimes even initiated local authorities and institutions where they did not already exist, and incorporated them in the colonial structure. They found this an economical strategy, not only financially, but also culturally. It was financially economical because it employed local manpower. It was also culturally economical because it spared the colonial power many of the conflicts and tensions that arise due to cultural disruption in the process of cultural change. Thus, the adaptability of the local population to colonial culture was expected to be gradual and peaceful. This colonial philosophy of indirect rule is believed to have been a carry-over from British political culture, which disapproves of radical fundamental change – a conservative political philosophy that favours the preservation of old institutions and norms while abhorring the sudden change of customs, traditions, values and institutions. This philosophy saved the power of the emirates of Northern Nigeria and the Kabakaship of Buganda (Uganda) until it was removed by military force after the independence (Mazrui 1983, Diamond et al 1988:9). The negative effect of the doctrine was that it preserved some archaic divisive institutions, hampering the integration of those societies and delaying the process of nation formation.

The contribution of the Francophone legacy is in the formation of nationhood. A variety of practices is suggested as the underlying cause. A first factor is the French policy of centralisation and assimilation. For the purpose of assimilation, a highly centralised educational policy throughout the Francophone colonies was introduced. In the Anglophone colonies, indigenous languages were used as a medium of instruction, though at lower levels. In Francophone colonies, a rigorous 'Frenchisation' policy was undertaken from the very outset of educational life, without any concession to indigenous traditions. The educational system was viewed as the main instrument in producing Frenchmen and Frenchwomen within the colonial population (Mazrui 1983: 30). A second factor in Mazrui's scheme is the federal system of government. The French ruled West Africa and Equatorial Africa as two Federations. This might had the effect of producing national consciousness among the competing constituent units of the federation. Hence, the peaceful competition among the French colonies fostered a regional awareness, thereby intensifying national consciousness. Mazrui discusses other factors that are implicitly related to French policy, and which may not be peculiar to French colonies, including the comparatively small size of the colonies and the relative ethnic homogeneity. What we can understand from Mazrui's exposition is that the French colonial legacy tended to expedite the rise of nationhood while at the same time repressing the formation of statehood. The French policy of assimilation and integration coupled with its centralised political culture contributed to the weak statehood in its colonies. The British doctrine of indirect rule, conversely, contributed to relatively strong prospects for statehood.

The variation of policies of the two colonial powers is, further, assumed to be based on the distinction between the Teutonic culture (Germanic) and the Latin culture (Romanic). Generally, the British were more racially arrogant than the French (Seton-Watson 1977: 330), while the French were more culturally arrogant than the British. The British attitude of racial arrogance resulted in physical segregation of races in the colonies in the form of having separate clubs, restaurants, hotels, schools, lavatories etc., for indigenous people and whites. Conversely, the French practised a segregation that rested on culture. The French actively and consciously tried to disseminate the French culture, in the hope of creating Frenchmen from Africans (Seton-Watson 1977: 329). An indigenous person assumed to be cultured had a better chance of being accepted in French socio-cultural circles than in British socio-cultural circles. Indeed in some French colonies, a competent knowledge of the French language and culture was a ticket to French citizenship (Mazrui 1983: 35f). Mazrui asserts that the French cultural arrogance, by striving to create a homogenous culture, brought about a normative integration in its colonies, thereby laying the foundations for nationhood. The British, on the other hand, by being culturally less bigoted entertained cultural relativism. The policy of indirect rule was to some extent a consequence of this cultural relativism. This indirect rule facilitated state formation, but hampered nation formation. Mazrui concludes that nationhood, as a level of identity was forged by French rule, while statehood as a level of authority, was consolidated by British rule.

To conclude, a range of postcolonial theorists have shed light on the negative effects of colonialism on the colonised societies. This is particularly true with regard to the European-imposed state model, which conflicts with the socio-economic and historico-cultural bases of these societies. We are informed that grave damage was inflicted upon the social structure of African societies. While it started as the "white man's burden", it ended as the "black man's burden", to use Davidson's (1992) thesis.

THEORIES OF NATION FORMATION

This section briefly discusses theories of nation formation. The aim is to frame a theoretical platform that can serve as a tool for understanding and interpreting the empirical case, the formation of the Eritrean nation. The study of nations and nationalism is rife with controversy, which revolves around the theories and paradigms dealing with the subject. It is widely agreed that classical social theory, and classical sociology in particular, did not generate a systematic theory of nation formation. This failure is attributed to the fact that the central agenda of the discipline as it developed was to explain the Great Transition from pre-industrial, pre-modern to industrial, modern society, and in doing so, to develop a more general theory of society. Though they wrote on the subject of nation, the founding fathers of sociology, Marx, Durkheim and Weber, never took it up as a central subject of their work. Thus, they never developed elaborated theory (James 1996, Guibernau 1996, Smith 1998, McCrone 1998). It is obvious that classical social theory and classical sociology dedicated considerable time to elaborate theories of development. The theory of developmentalism,[6] in its more generic forms is the pre-dominant theoretical edifice for the analysis of social transformation. Its multiple variants include modernisation theory (cf. Rustow 1967, Käufeler 1988), social mobility theory (cf. Huntington 1968, Kothari 1973), diffusion theory, evolution theory, assimilation theory (cf. Tilly

1975, Hobsbawm 1990) and progress theory (cf. Nisbet 1980, 1986; Sztompka 1993).

These theoretical variations attempt to explain how human societies have evolved gradually, but steadily into compact, modern associations called nations. They discuss how communities within confined territorial boundaries metamorphose into homogenous human units in terms of a political and legal system, territorial integration, cultural and social cohesion, economic centralisation, bounded by common history and the will to live together. A common denominator for all these theories of developmentalism is the implicit assumption of a linear evolutionary development process (Cf. Sztompka 1993). At the root of the theories of nation formation lies the theory of social transformation, which rests on the Great Division of traditional-modern of classical social theory of the Durkheimian-Weberian tradition (James 1996). This theme is adopted by contemporary scholars of nation formation like Gellner, Giddens, Hobsbawm and Anderson, who belong to the modernist school of thought. Following this tradition, scholars of nation contend that nation formation becomes a reality when social integration based on embodied concrete face-to-face relationships gives way to social integration governed by disembodied, abstract relationships. The mediation of these disembodied, abstract relationships, it is suggested, takes place through the extended agency that works through institutions such as print-capitalism and the state (Anderson 1991, James 1996).

The validity of developmentalism as the underlying theoretical perspective in the debate about the genesis of nations is justified on the basis of the contribution of classical sociology. Tilly (1975), for instance, asserts that Durkheim, Comte, Marx, and Weber were all developmental theorists. These classical fathers of sociology devoted most of their life to the study of societal development. Durkheim's monumental work, his theory of the division of labour as a causal factor in the development of society from mechanical solidarity to organic solidarity; Marx' theory of historical materialism and the five stages of socio-economic development processes which characterise social transformation; Comte's law of three stages (Nisbet 1986: 33); or Weber's theory of the persistent rationalisation of society, are some of the perspectives debated by classical sociologists in the theory of developmentism. Arguing along the lines of diffusion theory, Tilly (1975) describes how national states, which first emerged in England and France, spread throughout Europe and eventually across the globe. These social theoretical constructs are fundamentally based upon the classical sociological belief of the persistent "transformation from small, face-to-face communities or *Gemeinschaften,* to large, complex and impersonal societies, or *Gesellschaften*" (Smith 1986: 153).

Tilly discusses three explanatory theoretical approaches that are employed in analysing nation formation, notably developmental, functional and historical. Of these three theoretical approaches, the developmental theory has more power and depth in explaining nation formation because it deals with the processes typical of socio-political transformations (Tilly 1975: 602-3). A theory in current, widespread use in connection with the process of formation of nations is modernisation theory. More than any other theory, the theory of modernisation rests upon the dichotomous assumption of tradition and modernity in which a nation is assumed to evolve in the period of modernity (Gellner 1983, 1993; Hobsbawm 1990, Anderson 1991). Modernisation entails the secularisation and individuation of society, whose potent result leads to the emergence of social relationships based on rational individual calculation. Based on this expectation, social transformation would indicate a transition from community to society. The process of nation formation is intimately linked with the process of social transformation leading to modernisation, secularisation and individuation. Underscoring this, James (1996: 45) argues: "Nation formation only becomes possible within a social formation constituted in the emerging dominance of relations of disembodied integration". Further, this transformation also gives way to the rise of civic institutions, which are in turn seen as a necessary prerequisite for the emergence of civic nations. Such civic institutions would include the legal (law, courts, judges, jury), political (parties, parliament, enfranchisement, election), economic (market, bank, credit institutions, money and finance institutions), and cultural (values, norms, symbols, music, theatre, cinemas, national holidays) which bound together the French, the Spanish, the English and the Americans as nations (Seton-Watson 1977, Smith 1986). Thus, nations are described as abstract communities of strangers (James 1996), imagined communities (Anderson 1991). This abstraction and imagining is facilitated by the emergence of print capitalism and communications technology (Anderson 1991, Gellner 1983, Deutsch 1966), whose genesis in Europe and America is connected with the emergence of industrial societies. In Africa, these developments occurred with the advent of colonialism.

In this theoretical debate, the primordialist school of thought provides the counterpoint to the modernist school. Unlike the modernist school of thought, the primordialist school contends that nations prevailed before modernity (cf. Geertz 1963, Van den Berghe 1978, Smith 1986). The adherents of the primordialist school, which ground their perception upon primordial bonds such as race, ethnicity, religion, language, homeland, etc., contend that nations are the natural units of human beings (cf. Heater 1998). Moreover, in conformity with this belief, they argue that nations have existed as long as human history. This historicist political perspective was heavily influenced by the German romanticism elaborated by German writers like Herder and Fichte (see Breuilly 1993: 56, Heater 1998). A sociological variant of the primordialist perspective advocates that religion, language, race, ethnicity and territory have been the cardinal precepts of organising societies throughout history. Therefore, nations are considered primordial in that they precede polities that are more complex. The advocates of this view further argue that primordial bonds have always divided human kinds, as have sex or geography. In that sense, adherents of this view assert that there is nothing modern about nations and nationalism (see Smith 1986: 12f). They postulate that human beings have an inherent need for kinship and group belonging (Allahar 1996) entailing a requirement for cultural symbolism that facilitates communication and meaning shared between members. These elements have always been present. In contrast, the champions of the modernist school maintain that there is a radical break between the pre-modern units and sentiments and modern nations and nationalism. Theorists of the primordialist school (its perennialist version) respond by insisting on an uninterrupted continuity between traditionalism and modernity, argue that nations and nationalism "are simply larger, updated version of pre-modern ties and sentiments" (Smith 1986: 13).

In emphasising the modernity of nations, modernist theorists argue that the primordial premises are merely relevant for small, simple primitive communities. The features embedded in the primordial characteristics are inadequate to explain and analyse the development of modern nations. They suggest that what is needed is to introduce premises and mechanisms that stretch beyond primordial characteristics. Amid the seemingly endless debate between the modernists and primordialists, a genuine attempt is made to close the lacuna between them. Anthony D. Smith makes one such attempt. Criticising both the primordialist and the modernist schools, Smith asserts that there is a connection between the traditional and the modern. According to Smith's synthetic approach, modern nations trace their root from the *ethnie* (pre-modern community). His argument is first, that nations are not something suddenly handed down from nowhere, and second, that there are some features of the primordial ties and sentiments which still persist in modern nations. By maintaining that it is only when a cultural community (*ethnie*) is transformed into a political community that it constitutes a nation, Smith proposes continuity projecting from the traditional to the modern, thereby bridging the gap between the primordialist and the modernist notions.

Yet, in spite of this effort, it seems that the modernist orthodoxy is predominant. There are obvious variations of the modernist explanations of how nations emerged. Hobsbawm (1990), for instance, elucidates two theories[7] directly connected with the theory of development or progress. The first is the assimilation theory, which is used to explain that a certain size is required for a nation to arise. This viability criterion, i. e., cultural and economic viability, is taken as a base for the rise of nationhood (Hobsbawm 1990: 32). The understanding here is that small communities are not able to constitute nations. Therefore, a successful assimilation of small communities into larger ones is perceived as a precondition for the emergence of nations. In other words, contrary to the primordialist belief, nations came into existence when small communities transcended the primordial barriers that existed between them and built a larger, expansive and complex society. These communities were presumably welded together by a process of expansion, trade, and other means of communication and exchange of culture. This assumption is closely related to Smith's (1986, 1991) view of the territorial perception of nation where territorial integration is seen as the foundation of the formation of nations. That is, as an outcome of the different revolutions, societies residing within compact, demarcated, boundaries develop civic norms and values which wrap them together so as to form nations. In the case of the colonial societies, the process was undertaken through the colonial territorial integration and the ensuing socio-economic transformations.

The second is the evolution theory, which explains that the formation of nations is the inexorable outcome of human expansion. In the evolutionary process, the scale of human social units enlarges from family and tribe to country, from local to regional, from national to global (Hobsbawm 1990: 33). This fits well into Durkheim's (1984) principle of density and volume. In this respect, nations are perceived as the natural outgrowth of historical developmental processes. For the liberal thinkers of the 19th century, the development of nations was an inevitable phase in human advancement from the small group to the larger. It evolved from family, to tribe, to region, to nation and to the united world of the future (Hobsbawm 1990: 38). This idea is based on the classical theory of progress (cf. Nisbet 1980, Sztompka 1993), which envisions human advancement as a unilinear, gradual, continuous trajectory moving from low to high, from small to large, from simple to complex, from worse to better, from ignorance to knowledge, from barbarism to civilisation. Accordingly, nations arise at a certain level in the hierarchical stage of the logically connected organisational continuum of societal ascendancy.

The chief tenet of modernisation theory rests on the belief that changes in the economic realm will generate unanticipated innovation in the social, cultural, and personal realms (Harrison 1988: 9). Modernist theorists argue that the accumulation and mobilisation of capital, the introduction of technology, modern skills and rationality will change the traditional socio-economic structure leading to the rise of nations. Another variant of modernisation theory is the convergence theory. Sztompka (1993: 13) writes, "various societies, of utterly diverse traditions, eventually reach similar civilizational or technological achievements, be it in machine production, democratic rule, automobile transportation, telecommunications etc.". The modern society is, thus, perceived as equally capable of disseminating and absorbing cultural influences (Rustow 1967: 10-11). The explicit conclusion of all these theories is that societies will resemble each other as they fully industrialise (Bendix, 1964: 8) giving way to the world of nations. The nation system becomes universal.

A distinction relevant to the conditions of the developed societies and developing societies is made between modernisation as a process of socio-cultural evolution and modernisation as a policy of socio-cultural adjustment (Käufeler 1988: 16-7). As a process, it refers to the original European evolutionary process. As a socio-cultural adjustment, it refers to the efforts made by developing societies to modernise themselves. Moreover, in the former case, modernisation was spontaneous, the result of unintentional and unconscious actions. Everything took its own natural course. In the latter case, everything is consciously planned. This planned process of nation building is made plausible thanks to the already existing models and forms of nations embodied in the modern societies, which serve as templates for the late-comers. The difference between planned and unplanned is expressed by the concepts formulated by Deutsch (1963: 3) as 'national growth' and 'nation-building'. The first one refers to the unplanned, spontaneous development of nations. The second refers to the intentionally designed efforts of agents to construct nations. 'Nation-building' carries an architectural connotation implying intentional human action, social engineering. 'National growth', in contrast, carries an organic connotation, evincing natural growth.

In the late nineteenth century and early twentieth century, social science witnessed a paradigm shift in the perception of the concept of nation. As a result of the profound influence from romantic political thought, ethnographic and philological theories started to become dominant. Subsequently the 'threshold principle'[8] hailed by writers like Mazzini and Mill was abandoned, giving way to the Wilsonian Doctrine (see Hobsbawm 1990: 32, 102). As a consequence, ethnicity and language came to occupy a central position in the theory of nation formation. In other words, the congruity of the cultural community and the state, the nation-state (monoethnic state), was placed high on the agenda (see Gellner 1983). The contradiction between cultural theories and political theories concerning the debate of the process of nation formation form the fundamental basis of the cleavage surrounding the subject. The theory of culture, which is more or less grounded upon primordial premises – the unique, the historicist and the idiographic hallmarks of small, disjointed communities – ends up in the narrow particularistic ethnic genealogy in its effort to analyse and define the nation. The theory of politics, on the other hand, is grounded upon the principle of a civic polity (Hutchinson 1994:122), which, by transcending the primordial premises, emphasises citizenry, common law, mores, etc. as constitutive elements of the nation. It is this principle of civic polity which is valid for the present study.

Recently, however, the notion that all societies will eventually resemble one another has come under severe criticism. The most criticised aspects are its underlying evolutionary theory and its linear methodological approach, its two basic supporting pillars. The failure of the development predicted by the modernisation theory led to the upsurge of contending theories such as the underdevelopment theory, dependency theory and world system theory (Kiely 1995).

In conclusion, the theory of developmentalism helps to explain the process of development through which nations evolve. It explains the historical, social, political, economic and structural changes. The relevance of the theories discussed here to the empirical study is that they serve as a tool to understand and explain the social transformation, which started with the territorial integration of Eritrea. In general, they serve to explain the developmental process that led to the integration of the various ethno-linguistic groups and regions and the formation of the Eritrean nation.

ANALYTICAL DIMENSIONS

The most important concepts employed to analyse the process of nation formation are considered to be the centralisation and integration of a specific territory, followed by politico-legal and socio-economic integration. It is further suggested that as a result of accumulated historical experience, a common culture develops within that demarcated territory that binds the people who inhabit the territory. In the process, common values and norms, common identity and experience generating the will to live together are nurtured. The civic conception of nation focuses on the emergence of modern institutions in terms of legal, economic, cultural, social, territorial, technological, scientific and ideological. The focus in this section, therefore, will be on that dimension of nation formation which deals with the civic aspect.

The aim of this section is to review a number of dimensions of the processes of nation formation. Six dimensions are selected on the basis of the central role they play in explaining the process of nation formation. The construction of these dimensions is inferred from my reading of the literature on nation formation. Hence, they may not be found in their present form in the works of the various authors referred to here. Moreover, it seems appropriate to point out from the very outset that the dimensions dealt with here are by no means exhaustive, they should rather be viewed as suggestive and tentative. These dimensions will be presented in the sequence in which they are thought to appear in the process of the formation of a nation. Therefore, according to the scheme introduced in this research, the first prerequisite will be territorial integration. Within this integrated territoriality, a centralised politico-legal system is established. When these two dimensions are set in place, the process of socio-economic integration begins. In general, common historical experience represents a subsummation of the other three dimensions. Common culture results from the accumulation of common historical experience. And finally, because of those common historical experiences and the development of a common culture, the will to live together may flourish. In a nutshell, the assumption is that a nation emerges when a group of people are brought together by territorial, socio-economic and politico-legal integration, which leads to common history and common culture, and ultimately the development of the will to live together.

1 Territorial Integration: The notion of territoriality occupies a centre-stage position in the discourses of nation formation (see Tilly 1975; Seton-Watson 1977; Rokkan & Urwin 1982; Smith 1983a, 1986). Territorial integration pertains to the process of compartmentalisation wherein a clearly defined territoriality evolves. To retain legitimacy, nations need to be identified with a certain territorial jurisdiction. In a broad sense, territorial integration and centralisation is the first stepping-stone in the process of nation formation. This occurred in Europe when the absolute monarchies created unified political and jurisdictional territorialities.

> The origins of the transition to nationhood are shrouded in obscurity. In principle, they can be traced back to the gradual unification

> by Saxon and Frankish kings of the territories which later became known as 'England' and 'France' in the early Middle Ages (Smith 1986: 130).

The process of territorialisation in Europe began with the collapse of the Roman Empire (Seton-Watson 1977: 15) and the emergence of the absolute state. The absolute state imposed a single national identity, which led to the emergence of compact territories with more culturally and linguistically homogenous communities. The competition between monarchies for trade dominance, tax collection and expansion of territories necessitated the creation of a standing army. This, coupled with bureaucratic administration, made the centralisation and integration of the territories feasible. The centralising state ensured that all people residing in its territory were considered subjects or citizens having duties and rights, thereby fostering an intimate bond between the people and the territory. The territory bore a great affective and psychological meaning, because it provided both the habitat and the means for living (Väyrynen 1993: 164).

The decision regarding territorialisation in Africa was made in Europe at the Berlin Conference of 1884-85. The scramble for Africa necessitated the compartmentalisation of territories so that the European powers could avoid conflict. Once the colonial state was in place, it attempted to take measures comparable to those taken by the absolute state in Europe. After the creation of the territories, developments were to follow which would have the effect of building nations.

Territorial centralisation and integration aims mainly at the territorial homogenisation of ethnically heterogeneous societies (Smith 1983b: xiii). The common domain is the centralisation and standardisation of the community on the basis of common territory. Recognition of and loyalty to the unified territory by its members creates the foundation for the sense of common identity, purpose and destiny. In that sense, a building block is set in place in the process of nation building.

2 Socio-economic Integration: Our second dimension refers to the development of an integrated socio-economic order. It is argued that this order creates socially and economically compact and cohesive societies. Smith (1986) depicts the triple revolution – 'socio-economic', 'military-administrative' and 'cultural-educational' – as the underlying factor in the rise of nations in Europe. Here the 'socio-economic' pertains to the revolution which led to the dramatic expansion of capitalism. In Africa, the penetration of colonial capital brought a socio-economic integration, which constituted the foundation of nation formation.

In the capitalist socio-economic enterprise, three component variables are accorded particular importance: modernisation, urbanisation and industrialisation. Modernisation involves on one hand, material (economic), scientific and technological innovations. On the other, it involves cognitive innovations in terms of belief systems, values, norms and modes of thinking. Bendix (1964: 5) emphasises the claim that modernisation pertains to the economic and political transformation. Modernisation theory explains that in social history, socio-economic changes advance through roughly three stages, the traditional, transitional and modern. In such a trajectory, the socio-economic revolution that takes place in agrarian societies, transforming them into industrial or semi-industrial societies with all its novelty of norms, values, ideas, and ways of doing things, is thought to provide the necessary condition for the appearance of nations (see Gellner 1983, Hobsbawm 1990, Anderson 1991).

The basic tenets of the theory of urbanisation entail the uprooting of people from their primordial villages and age-old habitat and mode of life, subsequently placing them in a sort of melting-pot in which people from different places and traditions blend and adopt a new identity (Huntington 1968: 33-4, Pye 1962: 50). In this sense, the continual processes of transformation which transcend parochial associations like kinship and region bring about the organisation of society at a national level, providing the basis for the growth of the nation. Here a process of differentiation, complexity and geographical division of labour between urban and rural arises. This necessitates functional interdependency between the regions. These dynamic changes alter societies radically and dramatically in such a manner that a new form of societal organisation emerges. It is argued that following urbanisation, socio-culturally and politico-legally altered societies develop, embodying the new socio-economic reality.

In conclusion, modernisation, urbanisation and industrialisation reinforce each other, consolidating the nation formation processes. They extract the individual from the age-old traditional communal bonds of face-to-face relationships, leaving him to stand as a free person who is enmeshed in a network of anonymous interrelationships in the imagined community. Hence, the social and economic integration embedded in the new socio-economic order constitutes a basic dimension in the rise of a nation.

3 Politico-legal Integration: Territorial integration brought with it the centralisation and standardisation of polity and jurisprudence. The establishment of a standardised and centralised politico-legal system encapsulating the whole society across geographic, linguistic, ethnic, religious, class and gender boundaries is perceived to be a necessary condition for the development of a civic nation. The politico-legal dimension refers to the development of political and legal institutions, which unite a society in such a way that it constitutes a uniform identity. Accordingly, nations are viewed as "group of people inhabiting a given territory and obeying the same laws and government" (Smith 1986: 135). In the 'territorial nation' model, political and legal values, civic rights and legal codes are the basic features of identification, although the ethnic cultural dimension may remain in the background.

A collectivity governed under a unified political and legal system constitutes a nation. The definition of the 'old nations' (England, France, Spain, Holland and Sweden) was based on this dimension (Smith 1991: 59). Similarly, this definition is also applicable to the colonised African peoples, where the colonial state imposed a political and legal rule system in similar ways. A nation comes into existence when its members acquiesce to the legitimacy of its politico-legal system, notwithstanding the discrepancies of language, religion, and ethnicity. The ideal case is Switzerland (Renan 1991). In this respect, the nation is formed only when an orderly, nation-wide exercise of public authority is achieved (Bendix 1964: 18). The codification of the rights and duties of all adults upon whom the title of citizenship is conferred is also an important prerequisite of nation building. Smith (1986: 137) also supports the claim that in the territorial nations, legal codes and institutions provide the cement in fashioning nations. In other words, legal codes and institutions furnish the ideological bonds of nationhood. The notion of patria – "a community of laws and institutions with a single political will" – refers to common regulating institutions and structures which generate the feeling of common political sentiments and purposes (Smith 1991: 10). A nation presupposes a measure of common political and legal culture and a civic ideology, as well as a certain set of common understandings and aspirations, sentiments and ideals that cement the unity of the community (Smith 1991: 11).

In short, the essential theme of this dimension is that the establishment, consolidation and maintenance of a centralised political and legal order, penetrating and encompassing the entire society from centre to periphery, creates the necessary milieu for the evolution of a nation. Common values and norms, founded upon the legitimate legal and political institutions and structures accepted and revered by all members, furnish the needed requirement for the development of the nation. When the rule of law and legal bureaucratic domination in the administration of societies triumphs, then, and only then, is the formation of nations plausible.

4 Common Historical Experience: If the three dimensions discussed in the preceding paragraphs are to function as constitutive dimensions of the processes of nation formation, they need to be wrapped and stored into a common repertoire of historic memory. The belief in inheriting and the experience of a common heritage – and the will to pass it to future generations – create a collective identity. Shared history is to be understood as an accumulated depository of past deeds that lead to the creation of collective social memory. The consciousness about a common history, whether actual or imagined, is indispensable to the construction of national identity. In a historiographic context, a nation entails a sense of common historical heritage of the past and the awareness of a common destiny for the future (Rustow 1967: 42, Emerson 1960: 95, Renan 1991:11). Communities which shared common habitat and have accomplished actual or imagined great deeds, or who were made to believe that their great-great-grandparents had made history, develop a strong sense of nationhood. They are prepared to make great sacrifices in the service of a noble mission.

History, for nationalists, serves as a toolbox from which they wittingly select past themes that fit with their present purpose. In light of this, it should come as no surprise that nationalists frequently alter their point of reference in accordance with the purpose at hand. Historical presentations should mediate the best part of past memories, present realities and visions of the future. There is always the need to portray and inculcate the feeling of continuity between the past and present (Rustow 1967: 42). Those sacred symbols and events are to be praised, while the profane are to be repudiated. In times of uncertainty and rapid change, a new historical consciousness has to be fostered. This can be more clearly elucidated by the famous Renanean proposition, "Forgetting, I would even go so far to say historical error, is a crucial factor in the creation of a nation" (Renan 1991: 11).

History is also intimately connected with the land. Expressions like the 'historic' land and the 'homeland' possess a great appeal for the common person. "A 'historic land' is one where terrain and people have exerted mutual and beneficial influence over several generations. The homeland becomes a repository of historic memories and associations, the place where 'our' sages, saints and heroes lived, worked, prayed and fought" (Smith 1991: 9). Such beliefs, based on real or legendary sagas, shape the consciousness of common history and destination. Historical narratives serve, externally, to distinguish a group from both allies and enemies, and internally, to instil solid awareness of common history. A distinction is also made between 'old histories' and 'young histories'. The latter refers to African peoples where the common history is the result of colonialism. Imperial exploitation and oppression and the resistance to it form African common historical experience.

Historiographic mythologies are reinforced by oral or written narratives that depict glorious wars and historical achievements. Those inherited are to be preserved and passed to future generations. This collective consciousness of common history constitutes a nation.

5 Common Culture: In our scheme territorial integration, politico-legal integration, socio-economic integration and common historical experience generate common culture. Common culture is used here in a broad sense. It is used in a different way from that used by anthropologists - in reference to a particular dance or marriage ceremony, a particular kind of axe, spear, food, clothing, etc. (cf. Deutsch 1966: 88). It should be understood as an expression of the accumulated experience of a society, which gives the society its common values, norms and meanings through which communication takes place, and through which the society is also bound together.

In the axiom of 'High Culture', advocated particularly by Ernest Gellner (1983, 1993), a nation evolves as a result of the development of a pervasive culture mediated through a standardised educational system and embracing the whole society. Gellner (1993: 21) notes, "the satisfaction of the nationalist principle is that the political unit and the cultural unit should be congruent, that the state should be an expression of culture". This restricted understanding of culture is not helpful in understanding the African situation, where territorial delineation failed to pay attention to cultural units. In the African case, it is rather the civic (political) culture, as advocated by Smith, which is appropriate. Common culture is also approached from the notion of communications. Deutsch (1966: 88) elucidates common culture as "a common set of stable, habitual preferences and priorities in men's attention, and behaviour, as well as in their thoughts and feelings". He also notes that "many of these preferences may involve communication", and this leads him to conclude that by facilitating communication, common culture "forms a community". Culture is simultaneously inclusive and exclusive. It is inclusive in that members are interconnected by a common communicative system. It is exclusive in that non-members are unable to communicate due to unfamiliarity with the code of conduct, and are thus excluded from the community. Depicting this, Smith notes, "the solidarity of citizenship required a common 'civil religion' formed out of shared myths and memories and symbols, and communicated in a standard language through educational institutions" (Smith 1986: 136). Shared myths, memories and symbols, while unifying communities internally, distinguish them externally by delineating the boundaries.

The development of vernacular languages and the development of national scripts played a prominent role in the consolidation of common culture in Europe (Rokkan 1973). Similarly, the emergence of the *lingua franca* played a prominent role in the development of common culture in Africa (cf. Anderson 1991). The collective colonial experience has created a political culture that cannot be identified with a specific group within the African State. This type of culture springs from citizenship rights, a common code of law, and a common secular political system based on a compact specific territory. It is suggested that the rise of a homogenous political culture leads to the emergence of a civic nation. The polity is here understood as culture.

6 Will to Live Together: This leads us to our final dimension. This final dimension is the product of all the other dimensions. The society is expected to develop a sense of commonality and the feeling of uniqueness. The combination of all the dimensions generates common values, which evoke in the hearts and minds of individual members the feeling, need and aspiration to constitute nationhood. Renan (1991) strongly advocates that it is the subjective will of a community to be united and have a life together that determines its nationhood. The nation exists as long as the members agree to live together. What constitutes a nation is thus, "To have common glories in the past and to have a common will in the present; to have performed great deeds together, to wish to perform still more" (Renan 1991: 19). Accordingly, all other criteria such as geography, religion, ethnicity, language are given less significance in determining the formation of a nation (see Renan 1991: 19).

In short, a nation exists when a considerable number of the people in a society perceive themselves as constituting a nation, or behave as if they constituted one (Seton-Watson 1977: 5). This voluntaristic approach identifies the determining factor for the formation of a nation in the will of the members of the specific nation. The inherent connection between nationhood and consensus is also emphasised. "Nationhood is an idea which causes people who believe in it to come together, work together, and fight together" (Slowe 1990: 88). Nationhood, thus, involves a sense of belonging; it heralds a certain degree of mutual understanding and consensus. Yet in a broader sense the will to live together – or the subjective consciousness – stems from some basic objective criteria. These objective criteria are the five dimension discussed. They create common values, norms, and belief-systems, which ultimately inculcate a strong sense of common destiny, belonging, hope, solidarity and aspirations. All these in turn produce the will to live together.

In the final analysis, the volition of the people determines the rise of nations. Most of the authors referred to here seem to agree, although to varying degrees, that in the long run, without the acceptance and acknowledgement of the individual members, the nation can not exist. More than anyone, Renan strongly advocates that the foundation of the emergence and perpetuation of the nation rests on the soul and spirit of its members.

SUMMARY AND CONCLUSIONS

In this chapter, we have discussed paths, theories and concepts of nation. Two paths of nation formation were identified, one European, and the other African. As historical trajectories, these paths may be qualified in principle by the uniqueness of the specific historical patterns they represent. The question that follows, of course, is what connects the two paths at hand. The brief account presented in this chapter shows that the European and African historical paths of nation formation differ in fundamental dimensions, while simultaneously containing important common denominators. The differences in historical experience have created different types of nations, but the common causal factors are also powerful. A number of these elements have been pointed out. The colonial state in Africa has a number of characteristics in common with the absolute state in Europe: it a) created centralised territories; b) adopted the European model of bureaucratic administration; c) effected the socialisation of the intellectual and political elites in the European political and philosophical thought; and d) provided the structural and experiential bases that have compelled the post-independence African states to pursue the European model. All these, thus, reinforce the validity of such comparisons.

In spite of their differences, the African path and the historical West European path also share common elements. As in today's Africa, the historical path followed by the 'old nations' of Western Europe was from state to nation, known as the 'territorial model'. As Neuberger notes, the African situation of states without nations has its parallels and analogies in European history. Neuberger draws parallels between what he calls the *kulturnation* of Central and Eastern Europe and the separatist nationalism in Africa, on one hand, and between the *staatsnation* of Western Europe and state-nations of Africa which are the heritage of colonialism, on the other. Many have come to the conclusion that there is no unique African historical process or unique European historical process. Saying this, they insist on the existence of general laws and trends guiding the formation of nations, states, and nation-states.

Introduction

The most basic problem with the debate on nation formation seems to rest with the concept of nation itself. The history, usage and conceptualisation of the term nation abounds in concepts denies us clear definitions and meanings. Historically, the evolution of the concepts of nation has passed through three stages. In each of these stages and time periods – the ancient times represented by the Roman period, the Middle Ages, and finally, modern times – it bears different meanings. The meanings and usage of the concept have continuously changed in the course of this time, which perhaps is one of the reasons it is intractable. This multiplicity of meanings, coupled with the profusion of theories and methodology, appear to be what make the concept difficult to manage. In addition, most of the contemporary theories of nation formation fail in giving due attention to situations in Africa. However, the theory of developmentalism, in spite of its spatio-temporal parochiality, has been shown to have explanatory value and broader utility with respect to nation building in Africa.

Notes

1. Symbols in figures:
   block arrows = input/output relations,
   one-headed arrows = causal relations,
   two-headed arrows = interrelations,
   boldface one-headed arrows = time flow;
   ellipses = collective actors,
   ovals = societies;
   solid rectangles = subprocesses,
   dashed rectangles = blocks of subprocesses,
   solid boldface rectangles = sets of collective actors.
2. A council, to grapple with the Great Schism which befell the Church, was summoned in the town of Constance in 1414. The crises of the Christian Church emanated from the split which it encountered and which led to the establishment of two rival leaderships sites, one centred at Avigon and the other in Rome. Representatives from various places, ranks, and sections of the Christian Church as well as secular groups were present. These various groups were designated as nationes (Zernatto 1944: 356-7).
3. While in both England and France the criteria used to define a nation were political, in Germany it was ethno-linguistic. This discrepancy is suggested to have derived from the historical differences which characterised the nations. In England and France, a unified nation-state was achieved, whereas Germany lacked a unified nation-state. Ethnic Germans were dispersed throughout central and eastern Europe, thus in order to encompass all ethnic Germans philologists and philosophers designed ethno-linguistic or cultural criteria for the existence of a nation (Hobsbawm 1990: 99, Kemiläinen 1964). The case of Italy is also similar to that of Germany. Italy was not unified till the late 19th century. Thus Italian thinkers and politicians emphasised the Italian language and culture to unify the dispersed Italians.

4. The concept *ethnie* is constructed by Smith intended to depict the pre-modern ethnic communities. He distinguishes two types of *ethnie* (Smith 1994), which he designates as the lateral and the vertical type. The lateral, aristocratic type is identified as territorially extensive, however socially it is characterised by the paucity of penetrating deep in society. The vertical, demotic type, on the other hand, is more compact and often tied to religious identities. Both types are presumed to pursue two distinctive roads in their respective journeys toward the formation of a nation. Whereas, in the case of the lateral type the formation of nation was the work of the bureaucratic state through its incorporation of the lower classes, in the vertical type national autonomy it is achieved by the effort of the intelligentsia who strive against a hostile state and simultaneously against internal "religious custodians of ethnic tradition".
5. The doctrine of 'indirect rule' is often attributed to British policy. But Rivkin (1969: 221) suggests that the experiment was also tested in French Morocco. The doctrine known as the 'Lyautey Doctrine' preserved some selected customary and traditional institutions for the purpose of exercising colonial authority with a minimum of manpower. The doctrine, as used by both colonial powers is better known for its instrumentalist intention; it was designed to facilitate the colonial rule. Both colonial powers realised that it was easier and cheaper for the daily bureaucratic function to run smoothly if a certain level of self-administration of the indigenous population was permitted.
6. For a more elaborate discussion on the concept see Robert Nisbet (1986: 33ff). Nisbet traces the origin of the notion of developmentalism as a method of analysis of social progress which refers to the gradual, steady, accumulative advancement, back to Greek philosophical tradition. Nisbet does not make a distinction between the terms development, evolution and progress. Further, he, while admitting that the classic notion of developmentalism is nowadays discredited, nevertheless acknowledges the viability of the revised version of tenets of developmentalism.
7. These theories are not to be viewed as two exclusively different, but rather as the author expressed it 'two faces of one coin' (Hobsbawm 1990: 41). They are two variants of developmental or progress theory perhaps emphasising different aspects of the same object.
8. The concept was used to demonstrate boundaries between big nations and small nationalities. It was regarded that viability to sustain economic and cultural development was a condition for the emergence of a nation. Small-sized communities were considered unable to form nations. Thus according to this principle, and according to many nineteenth century thinkers, the small nationalities were thought to benefit by joining big nations. Thinkers like Mazzini, John S. Mill upheld such notions (Hobsbawm 1990).

Chapter 2

A SYNOPSIS OF PRE-COLONIAL HISTORY

INTRODUCTION

This chapter discusses in general terms, the origins of the people of Eritrea, the mode of life they pursued, their forms of social organisation and their political status immediately before the beginning of Italian colonialism. The aim is to give a brief account of the roots and origins of the people and to illustrate the social, economic and political relations and structures of the period. The account presented in this chapter is intended to serve as a point of reference for the socio-economic transformation that took place under colonial rule. The study therefore, does not delve into historical investigations that stretch back into earlier history.

There is a variety of different views concerning the impact of the Italian colonial rule on Eritrean social structure. There are many, for example, who argue that fundamental structural changes took place, including Gebre-Medhin (1979, 1989), Pool (1979), Sherman (1980), Leonard (1982), Houtart (1982), Killion (1985), Pedersen (1987), and Bondestam (1989). Others argue that no substantial change took place. These include Haliday (1971), Erlich (1982), and Negash (1987). In light of these contending views, a succinct account of the structural circumstances that existed prior to the establishment of colonial rule will be helpful in shedding light on our assessment of the changes that took place under colonialism. Through comparing circumstances in Eritrea both before and after colonialism began, we can make some reasonable judgements as to whether or not socio-economic transformation had, in fact, taken place. The overview provided in this chapter is intended to serve as background for the discussion in the chapters that follow. It will also serve as a starting point for the examination of the process of formation of the Eritrean nation. Consequently, I do not intend to provide a detailed account of the history of Eritrea before the genesis of Italian colonialism in 1890. The socio-economic transformation that

I finally conclude took place under European rule will be discussed in Chapter Four.

The chapter consists of four substantive sections. Section two briefly discusses the origins and composition of the people of Eritrea, while section three analyses economic organisation. Here the two dominant modes of life, notably nomadic and sedentary, are discussed. In section four, socio-political organisation is discussed. The traditional communities of the highland and of the lowland, respectively, are discussed separately. Finally, section five offers an account of the status of Eritrea on the eve of incipient Italian colonialism. Sections one and six represent the introduction and conclusion of this chapter, respectively.

THE PEOPLE

The Eritrean[1] society is composed of several ethno-linguistic groups. From a philological point of view, we can discern three basic linguistic families. The Semitic (Ge'ez - derived linguistic group) is composed of the Tigrinya-speaking and Tigre-speaking groups. The Hamitic (Cushitic) linguistic family is composed of four groups, the Beja, the Saho, the Bilain, and the Afar. The Beni Amer, part of the Beja, later adopted the Tigre language (Nadel 1945, Bondestam 1989: 25). The third basic linguistic family is the Nilotic. This last family consists of two groups, the Nara and Kunama (cf. Trevaskis 1960: 4, Bondestam 1989: 24). As derivatives of these philological families, we have then eight basic ethno-linguistic groups, plus a small Arabic-speaking group called Rashaida. This brings the total to nine ethno-linguistic groups, or nationalities[2].

Fig. 2.1 Linguistic Configurations

SEMITIC			HAMITIC				NILOTIC	
Tigrinya	Tigre	Arabic	Saho	Afar	Bilain	Beja	Kunama	Nara

Historical studies indicate that these ethno-linguistic groups came to settle in Eritrea in different historical periods, bringing with them different cultures and civilisations, values and norms, and ways of life. It is widely believed that the earliest inhabitants of the region were the Nilotic group, the Nara and Kunama, which are believed to have had moved from south-eastern Sudan into the Gash-Setit area of present day Eritrea (Pollera 1935, Trevaskis 1960: 4, Sherman 1980: 4). The next groups to follow into the region were pastoral Hamitic tribes who migrated from Northern Sudan. They subsequently occupied the Barka Lowlands and Northern Highland by either subjugating or expelling the previous Nilotic inhabitants (Trevaskis 1960: 4). Gradually this group spread along the coastal regions to the Dankalia area.

A third group, which were to have a substantial social, economic, and cultural impact, were the 'Sabaeans', Semites who crossed the Red Sea and finally settled in the highland, which they found climatically suitable (Trimingham

Map 2: Language Map of Eritrea

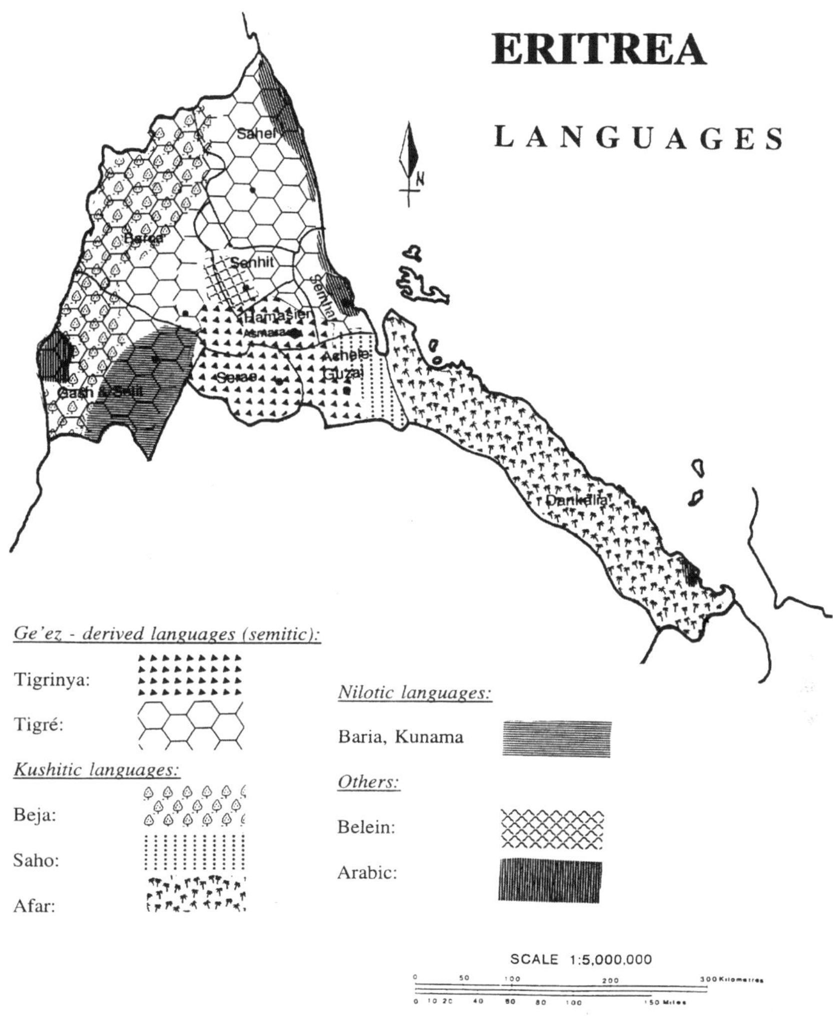

Source: Tore Sivertsen; National Atlas of Ethiopia (AA. 1988)

1952: 32-33, Machida 1987: 5). This group was more highly developed than the previous two groups, and presumably brought with them their social institutions and knowledge of political organisation, agricultural techniques, and commercial experience (Trimingham 1952: 7, Trevaskis 1960: 4). In addition, it is believed that they brought with them the camel, the horse, sheep, new plants and cultivation techniques, also introducing them to the communities already inhabiting the region. Further, they brought with them the art of writing, more tools of war, the embryo of a ruling elite, and the tradition of group life (Trimingham 1952: 33, Sherman 1980: 5). This means that they were already practising a sedentary mode of life and brought this habit or tradition of life with them to the region. Archaeological discoveries today indicate that this group had a highly civilised way of life – one which was to radically alter the social, cultural and political landscape of the region. This group later came to be known as the Abyssinians. Interestingly, there are two theories regarding the origin of the term Abyssinians. One theory contends that the term Abyssinian was derived from the Arabic term "Habasha" or "Habash" meaning mixture. In this conceptualisation of the term and the people it denotes, it is believed that when the Sabeans crossed the Red Sea from the Arabian Peninsula, they mixed with the Beja people, who were already living there. As a result, a mixture or "Habash" community emerged. The second theory speculates that the term originated from a tribal group in Yemen, from which these immigrants were supposed to originate. That tribe was called "Habashat". So the Abyssinians assumed their name from the tribe[3], from which they were descendants (Cf. Longrigg 1945:11, Trimingham 1952: 5, Gayim 1993: 267).

These various ethno-linguistic groups occupied, and still occupy, specific identifiable regions. It was by integrating these various regions and ethno-linguistic groups that Italy created Eritrea. On the eve of the founding of Italian colonial rule, three distinct regions existed. These were the plateau (Medri Bahri), the western and northeastern lowlands and northeastern highland, the northern highland, and the Afar (Dankalia). The Medri Bahri was under Abyssinian control, the western and northeastern lowland and northern highland under Egyptian control and the Dankalia region was ruled by autonomous local leaders. A central contention of this study is that the process of formation of the Eritrean nation commenced with the territorial integration of the various ethno-linguistic groups, which resulted from the centralisation and boundary-delineating measures of Italian colonialism.

ECONOMIC ORGANISATION

From the economic point of view, traditional Eritrean society was composed primarily of two 'economic communities'. These were a settled agriculturist (sedentary) type and a pastoral nomadic or semi-nomadic[4] one. In addition, these distinctions followed a geographical pattern of division, based on a division of plateaux and lowlands[5]. Accordingly, a settled, agricultural mode of life was to be found in the highland (*Kebessa*) region, while nomadism prevailed in the lowland (*Metahit*) region (Houtart, 1980: 84).

The distinction between the sedentary and the nomadic modes of life portrays two basic modes of economic production and means of subsistence. It also indicates, and determines, a people's relationship to the land. In traditional agrarian communities, the relationship of people to land determines the basic, existential being of humankind. The sedentary pattern of life necessarily requires an intimate relationship between people and land. Conversely, the nomadic pattern of life entails an inherently loose relationship between people and land. The nomadic pattern of life, unlike the sedentary pattern, displays a cohesive connection between a people and pastoralism, or the rearing of livestock. Here, livestock is the basic means of subsistence. In the sedentary mode of life, there is always a deeply ingrained sense of localism – an attachment to a specific piece of land – which is characteristically absent in the nomadic mode of life. The peasants are emotionally attached to the land from which they extract their subsistence. They also have clear, absolute property rights to specific land. In the case of the nomadic peoples, emotional attachment to the land is relatively weak, unlike their strong emotional attachment to their livestock.

The distinction between sedentarism and nomadism also has an influence on the socio-political organisation of a community. Sedentarism permits a cohesive social and political organisation, while nomadism discourages such cohesive organisation. The following two subsections briefly discuss the economic organisations of sedentarism and nomadism, respectively. The following section deals with the socio-political organisations.

The Sedentary Mode of Life

All historical indications suggest that when the Semitic ethno-linguistic group immigrated to the Horn of Africa, they brought with them agricultural techniques. In the Eritrean part of the Horn of Africa, this group settled in the *Kebessa* region, perhaps later expanding to various other regions. The favourable climatic conditions that they encountered in the region enabled them to pursue their old profession of practising agriculture. Farming requires a more settled way of life, in terms of both space and time. A group must be located in a given area for a relatively longer duration in order to cultivate and harvest the produce, and is compelled to follow the seasonal rhythms of the year. This, in turn, demands specific patterns of social organisation, compatible with the modes of economic production. Predominantly peasants, the people living in the highland area of Eritrea earned their subsistence primarily from agricultural products, their whole lives pivoting around farming activities. Hence, the relationship of people to land in the highland had a special importance. In the following paragraphs, an effort will be made to describe the structure and form of the land tenure system in the *Kebessa* region of Eritrea. During the early 1940's, elements of the British Military Administration (BMA) had undertaken comprehensive anthropological studies about the socio-economic realities of Eritrea (e.g. Nadel 1945, 1946; Longringg 1945; Trevaskis 1960). These works have since become so influential regarding the social history of Eritrea that they are treated almost as classics. As a result, these works are used as important references for this, as well as the following sections.

The highlanders, as settled agriculturists, were organised in village communities of extended families. Members of villages were often divided into two groups. The majority of them, who were the original inhabitants, were known as *restegnatat*[6]. The term *restegnatat* is derived from the word *resti*, which is a form of land ownership, and means "inheritance". Those who immigrated to the village at a later stage, were known as *makalai ailet* (see e.g. Bondestam 1989:58, Houtart 1980: 84, Trevaskis 1960: 11, Nadel 1946: 6). These types of status determine one's relationship and position to the land, to social matters and to politics. The *restegnatat* were entitled to political power and land rights prerogatives. The *makalai ailet*, on the other hand, were not entitled to participate in political affairs of the village, or did not have rights to ownership of land except in the *diesa* land tenure system. In the *diesa* land tenure system, land was collectively owned and every member of the village was entitled to the use of the land (Joireman 1996: 271) but not of private ownership. In principle, the *makalai ailet*, after residing in the village for a specific time, were given a full right of 'citizenship'. This awarded to them all the benefits that a citizen was entitled to, for instance the right to formally own the land. Generally, there were three types of land ownership, notably *diesa* (*shahina* in Akele Guzai - collective ownership), *meriet risti* (inherited land), and *meriet worki* (land bought). These corresponded to village ownership, family ownership, and individual ownership respectively (cf. Nadel 1946: 6).

The predominant type of land ownership in the highland was the *diesa* type (Houtart 1982: 211) in which the land was owned by the village and distributed among its members at regular time intervals. Usually, in principle, land distribution in the *diesa* system takes place every seventh year, whereas in the *meriet risti* form the land is under family private ownership. The *risti* form of ownership displayed multiple types of land titles (Nadel 1946). Nadel argues that they had three basic common features: "their relative absoluteness; their hereditary nature; and their derivation from the historical right of a first possession by some remote ancestor" (Nadel 1946: 7). A third type of ownership, which was rarely prevalent, is the *meriet work*i. Here the land was privately owned (Houtart 1980: 84) – an individual person becomes a private owner by buying a piece of land. Perhaps one can also categorise as a fourth form, the *gulti*[7], which was a land rented to those who did not have the right to own land. It was particularly found in the Akkele Guzai and Serae regions (Bondestam 1989: 59). What is important here are the jurisdictional rights associated with every form of ownership, and the social status they conferred on the individual owner. In the *diesa* property rights system, land could not be bought or sold. In the *meriet risti,* the consent of all members of the extended family was required if the selling of the land could be contemplated at all, which happened very rarely. The *meriet worki* was an individual private property; thus, all rights conferred on private ownership were exercised.

In addition to farming activities, the traditional community of the highland was also involved in livestock, cattle, goat, sheep, donkey, and horse rearing. Animal husbandry was a vital supplementary in the subsistence production. The use of animals provided a source of power for farming implements, means of transportation and sources of food. The peasants utterly depended on their own human labour and the domestic animals as supplementary source of power to plough and harvest their fields for their basic subsistence.

The Nomadic Mode of Life

These two modes of life, the sedentary and the nomadic were roughly separated along the same lines as the geographical divisions. As we have already seen, the people in the highland of Eritrea lived a sedentary way of life. The rest of the society lived a nomadic or semi-nomadic life. Those engaged in this nomadic and semi-nomadic socio-economic system included the various ethno-linguistic groups of the lowland (cf. Houtart 1980, Sherman 1980: 4). The nomadic mode of life was based on pastoralism, or livestock rearing. In this socio-economic system, people's relation to the land was very loose. Usually, the jurisdictional right to a plot of land was not clearly specified. On the other hand, the relation between man and livestock was quite strong. But this does not mean that the claim for land was absent; in fact, a large area for grazing was always needed, leading to incessant intra-ethnic feuds and inter-ethnic raids and skirmishes.

The traditional communities of the western lowland and northern highland, that is, the two Bejas, the Hadendowa and Beni Amer, and the Semitic Tigre-speakers, were predominantly pastoralists. They were in perpetual movement with their livestock, in search of grazing land and water. The mode of life they pursued did not allow them to settle in a specific place. This continuous mobility in turn precluded farming activities. Therefore, they depended solely on their livestock for their subsistence. In contrast to the community in the highland region (*Kebessa*), the relationship of these communities with the land was very diffuse.

One of the hallmarks of the nomadic mode of life is that a gathering of small groups of people at one time and place constitutes collective life. By its very nature, it is more amenable to a mode of life based on mobile small groups of individuals. Livestock, because they move and need large grazing area, occupy a vast space, thereby making it almost imperative to live in small groups and adopt a life-style that is not compatible with large settlements. The nomadic people of the lowland of Eritrea lived scattered. Sometimes not more than one or two families were living at the same place and time. The life of the nomads was contingent on the seasonal climatic conditions, and their movement shifted with the seasons. Instead of people steering nature, conversely, nature steered people. The adverse climatic conditions – shortages of rain (water) and scarcity of grass compelled them to wander according to the rhythms of nature in search of water and grass for their livestock. But this kind of life was to change soon – at least for some. The penetration of colonial administration was to produce a differentiation in the life style of the nomads. The emergence of urban centres such as Keren, Nacfa, Agordat, Barentu, Tessenai, etc. (Longrigg 1945: 138), conscription in the colonial army, and employment in the construction and agricultural projects permanently shifted the mode of life of many nomads. New social groups emerged as settled urban and semi-urban dwellers. This social and geographical mobility led to the gradual separation between those who became urbanised (urban middle class) and settled and those who persisted with their nomadic way of life. It was in this way the socio-economic transformation began (to be discussed later).

Other groups that shared their habitat with the Bejas included the two Nilotic groups, the Kunama and Nara. These ethno-linguistic groups were agro-pastoralists, i. e., they practised both cattle rearing and farming. Therefore they were less mobile, and it seems that they had a more stable life than did their Beja neighbours. Nadel (1945: 53) described these groups as sedentarians. Towards the southeastern lowland the Afars, who were predominantly pastoralists, were located. Like the other nomadic groups, they spent most part of the year wandering with their livestock in search for better grazing ground and water. The Saho who were also pastoralists occupied southeastern of the *Kebessa* region adjacent to the eastern lowland. In the centre of Eritrea, the Keren region, were to be found the Belain. This area was characterised by the widespread practice of agricultural activities (Longrigg 1945: 156, Trevaskis 1960: 16, Sherman 1980: 4). The Keren region is geographically situated between the highland and lowland regions. Topographically, it is classified as intermediary between the two main regions. Even in a cultural context, the people of this region are known for their mixed features. The economic mode of life was predominantly sedentary. After examining the economic mode briefly, the social and political organisation of the communities will be examined.

SOCIO-POLITICAL ORGANISATION

Now, we will examine the socio-political organisation of these communities, as social and political organisation is directly connected with the economic organisation. The scanty studies available indicate that the social and political organisation of the Eritrean communities immediately prior to Italian colonial rule was feudal and semi-feudal (cf. Nadel 1945, Houtart 1982, Leonard 1982). Houtart (1982), among others, attributes this feudal and semi-feudal organisation to the lowland Moslem communities, in which serfdom existed. The pastoral communities which exhibited feudal or semi-feudal structures were characterised by loose organisational structure and dispersed communal life. This weak organisational structure contributed to the absence of national identity. Thus, the disparate ethno-linguistic groups and geographical units did not constitute a unified geo-political territorial entity before the advent of Italian colonial period (cf. Trevaskis 1960: 4, Longrigg 1945: 132).

In socio-political and administrative terms, Eritrean society before the Italian colonial rule can thus be categorised into three units: the western and eastern regions, the Dankalia region and the Kebessa. The following two sections examine social and political organisation, how the precolonial communities were socially structured, and how political affairs were arranged, run and administered. Also examined are power relationships and allocations, the sources of social norms and status.

For the sake of simplicity and analytical manageability, I have separated Eritrean communities into traditional communities of the highland and traditional communities of the lowland. However, it should be pointed out that while this analytical approach is quite useful, it also conceals significant details, such as divergence within the individual blocks. For instance, if we more closely examine the traditional communities of the lowland, we can see that they encompass disparate ethno-linguistic communities with a variety of discrepancies within the socio-cultural context. Characteristics in a number of categories, such as ethnicity, language, religion, tradition separate them. Given an awareness of this problem, an effort is made to represent the component element as much as possible in the section that deals with this subject. Another point that requires clarification is the concept of traditional community – a concept that is frequently misused. Traditional community is here used as it is in Ferdinand Tönnies' Gemeinschaft-Gesellschaft concept, in which a distinction is made between traditional and modern. By traditional is meant simply the paucity of modern qualities –in terms of both the spiritual and material context. In this research, it denotes the socio-economic condition preceding the start of Italian colonialism, that is, before the penetration of European capitalism.

In general terms, it is possible to discern differences in political organisation between the sedentary social mode of life and the nomadic social mode of life. The political organisation of all sedentary groups is based on territoriality whereas that of the nomadic is based on tribalism or kinship. In the latter case geographic frontiers are rendered meaningless. Another fact worth mentioning is that almost all the aristocratic classes, or nobility, in the serf system of the various tribes were believed to have come from outside the masses of the serfs, and eventually had to adopt the language and religion of their serfs. The time frame that the study in this section covers stretches to the initial period of the Italian colonial era. The data and researches available circumscribe this time-space. To indicate the time limit all verbs are used in the past tense form.

The Traditional Community of the Highland

The people of the highland, the *Kebessa,* are predominantly composed of the Christian Tigrinya ethno-linguistic group, notwithstanding a small minority groups of Islamic faith, known as *Jiberti,* and the Saho on the southeastern escarpment. This section is concerned only with the Tigrinya ethno-linguistic group. The class composition of the Tigrinya-speaking group in the period under discussion was believed to consist of the peasantry, the higher echelons of the clergy and the ruling elite (Negash 1987: 4-5).

The available studies show that the traditional population of the highland were organised in village communities of extended families (see Longrigg 1945; Nadel 1946; Trevaskis 1960; Pool 1979; Sherman 1980; Gebre-Medhin 1979, 1989; Negash 1986, 1987; Bondestam 1989). The smallest social organisation of the village community was the *enda* (an extended family group). Village elders, elected by the village members, largely administered the local affairs. Heading the group of elders was the chiqa, or headman (Nadel 1946). Thousands of villages of peasant communities were scattered throughout the highland with a very limited link between them. The individual village community usually consisted of two groups, the *restenya* and the *makalai ailet*. As it was mentioned earlier, the former were the original settlers, while the latter were late-comer immigrants. These two groups enjoyed different rights and responsibilities. The *restenyatat* enjoyed the right to use and own the land, and the political management of the village. The *makalai ailet,* according to the *diesa* tenure system, were by contrast, required to wait for forty years for the right of land allocation and generally to be incorporated in all village socio-political life. Regarding internal political affairs, responsibility was conferred upon a committee composed of village elders elected from the *restenya* families (Houtart 1980: 84). "Governmental" tasks were executed by the *chiqa,* who was appointed from a *restenya* family (Nadel 1946: 4, Trevaskis 1960: 11, Negash 1986: 30). Generally, it appears that the political system was based on a democratic and egalitarian principles . Land was distributed equally, particularly in the *diesa* system, village elders were elected democratically to administer village affairs, and open discussion to settle problems was a common way of dealing with decisions and conflicts through the *baito* (assembly) system.

The basic unit of the traditional social organisation was the *enda.* This was an outgrowth of the individual family, often binding several families. The *enda* was based on genealogical foundations. The village, on the other hand, was a territorially-based political unit (Nadel 1946: 4). In other words, while the village was a result of political integration, the *enda* was a kinship association, based on descent from a common ancestor, real or mythical. The *enda* was known by the name of the common ancestor (Trimingham 1952: 12, Nadel 1946: 5). Nadel contends that historically, the political unit, that is the village, probably evolved from the *enda*. If that is the case, then the village can be comprised of either an enlarged single *enda,* or several *endas.* Nevertheless, as the social transformation advanced, the village gradually superseded the *enda* as a social organisation (Sherman 1980: 9). The village as a territorial unit constituted the smallest political unit. After the village, came the district in the territorial organisational hierarchy. A district chief governed the district, called *Meslenie* (Nadel 1946: 4). The district consisted of several villages. Contiguous villages were connected in a quite loosely-arranged relationship for the purpose of limited political and social functions, such as collecting tributes, and dealing with community problems that extended beyond local boundaries, such as safeguarding security of villages, etc. Beyond these relatively limited social and economic connections, the village was a virtually self-sufficient, autarkic unit. Above the district level there were different chiefs, whose rule expanded and contracted depending on their political power and strength, sometimes extending through the whole region. Some studies indicate that the whole highland region was divided at this time, for administrative purposes into five zones[8] (Negash 1986).

Figure 2.2: Socio-political Organisation in the Traditional Community of the highland

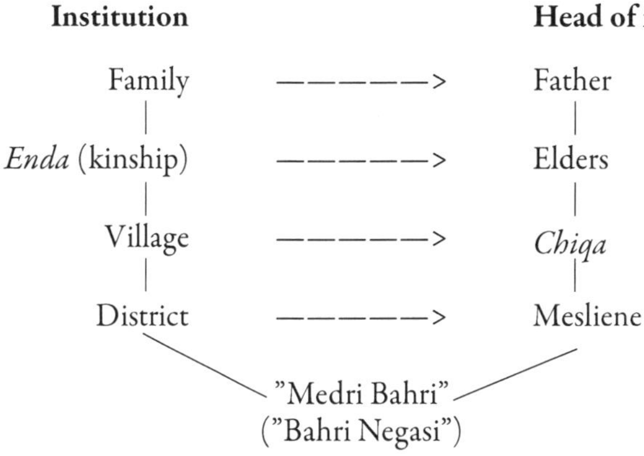

Figure 2.2 roughly illustrates how the traditional highland community was organised, beginning with the family and ending with the Medri Bahri – a name by which the Kebessa was known. When the entire Medri Bahri was under common rule, the ruler was known as Bahri Negasi. Yet, the *enda* was so dominant that it almost completely overshadowed the role of the individual family. In a political context, the village was informally autonomous, self-contained and self-sufficient. The relationships among the hundreds of villages were constrained, first, because autarky prevailed in the villages, which operated as self-sufficient administrative units. Second, an effective structural mechanism that could coherently combine the various village communities into a unified administrative unit was absent. From a functional and structural point of view, and particularly from the functional necessity of the villages, it also seems that there was little need for centralisation. The obvious result was a dispersed, decentralised independent village communal life.

What we appear to have here is what is commonly identified in social theory and the theory of nation formation, as *Gemeinschaft*. It is a territorial community, constituted from extended kinship and displaying a limited division of labour with little social differentiation, a pre-national association. Social theorists, in describing social integration in such communities, argue that integration is ensured by a value system which is based on a dominant religion and imposed by the clergy through oral tradition on an illiterate community (Richmond 1994: 290). The emergence of Italian colonial rule changed the administration structure by imposing bureaucratic administrative regimes which transcended village units. It centralised and integrated all the villages to constitute a unified rule system.

The Traditional Communities of the Lowland

A number of scholars have argued that it was among the lowland's ethno-linguistic groups that actual feudal socio-political structures existed. This view seems to derive from the fact that serfdom was widely practised, particularly among the Beni Amer, Tigre and Belain. The ruling classes of the Habab (Tigre) were called *Shumagelle* and their paramount *Kantebai.* As for the Beni Amer, some contend that they probably borrowed their feudal social structure from the Habab, Bet Asgede (the ruling class of the Habab), who were presumed to originate from the highland region (Paul 1950). The socio-political formation of these groups was embedded in a very complex economic and cultural structural setting. At a general level, it can be said that these groups were divided into aristocrats (ruling class) and serfs (subjects). Further, within this bifurcation there were additional hierarchical levels, particularly within the Beni Amer aristocratic class. In their social relations these groups were characterised by inherited status, obligations and rights founded on customary laws, and the prevalence of slavery (Negash 1987: 7). The Nara, Kunama and perhaps the Saho, on the other hand, lacked chiefs and ruling classes (Negash 1986: 39). The Beni Amer[9] were divided into two hierarchically structured classes, the aristocratic class (*Nabtab*) and the serf (*Tigre*[10]) class. Within the *Nabtab*, the nobility acknowledged the legitimate authority of a paramount leader known as *Diglal.*

Nadel (1945), in his *'Notes on Beni Amer Society'*, gives a detailed account of the Beni Amer's socio-economic anatomy. He believed that the *Nabtabs* and the *Tigre* had different genealogical origin. The *Nabtabs* invoked their origin from mythical ancestry called "Amer". The serfs who were subjected by the *Nabtabs* were called *Hedareb* (in Beja) and *Tigre* (in *Tigre*). *Hedareb* is also a vernacular language of the group known as *Beja,* of the ethno-linguistic group, *which* spoke it. Likewise, *Tigre* also represents both language and people. One supposition for why the serfs were called *Hedareb* and *Tigre,* is that when the *Ja'aliin* from the Sudan invaded and subjected the *Hedareb* and *Tigre* tribes into serfdom, they simply called them *Hedareb* and *Tigre* respectively (Nadel 1945: 57). The Beni Amer became, in their heyday, the strongest group between the Gash valley and the Red Sea – by either conquering or absorbing all small groups in the vicinity (Paul 1950: 226). Paul is of the view that the *Nabtab,* originally established by the Fung, showed loyalty to the Fung Kingdom, paid their tribute without any protest, and had a good relation with Sennar. Even later, when the Egyptians became the dominant power in the region, the Beni Amer accepted their rule and agreed to pay tribute. The era of the Mahdists, however, created significant turmoil for the Beni Amer confederation. As a result, the Italian occupation came as a relief for them (Paul 1950: 226).

The *Nabtab* were organised in a vertically structured political network. The serfs, on the other hand, were dispersed and divided among the different *Nabtabs*. A distinct cultural difference between the ruling class, the *Nabtab*, and the serfs, which was manifested in terms of cloths, shoes, style of hair cuts and ornaments representing social status, could be discerned. The offspring of both classes were exposed to their respective distinguishing features at an early stage as a mechanism of the socialisation process, so that when they had grown up, they assumed their proper social and cultural position. The serfs' relationships to one another were formed on a horizontal basis. More correctly described, they had no connection because they were divided among their masters. This fragmentation was a result of a deliberate act of the aristocracy – an effort to keep them weak and divided (Paul 1950: 228). The serfs were allowed to own livestock and grazing land, but they were dependent upon, and tied to, the aristocratic class by numerous feudal obligations (Houtart 1980: 85). For example, they were forced to pay various feudal tributes and gifts to their masters.

Such gifts included the giving of a goat when a noblewoman gave birth; the payment of wedding dowries when a nobleman was married; monetary payments to the master when a serf girl was married; providing transport animals to be used by the master; delivering meat to the master when an animal was slaughtered; and providing milk cow (FO 371-69363, Appendix 18, 1947). All these gifts were compulsory, they had different names, and they took place on different social occasions of happiness and sorrow representing symbols and myths of the tribes. A failure to provide the appropriate gifts usually carried with it serious consequences, it could cost either one's life or one's freedom (through transference to a slavery). In spite of these differences, the different classes of the Beni Amer were believed to be internally connected by "religion, language, common customs and habits, and the link of common descent" (Nadel 1945: 53). The overlap of these features, however, varied considerably. In terms of language, the Beni Amer as a whole were 'bilingual' (Nadel 1945: 54). Accordingly, they could be classified into three groups: those who spoke Hedareb, those who spoke Tigre and those who spoke both. Nadel argues also that although religion was a common denominator, the depth and clarity of conviction varied greatly. Religion as an institution was not well established, there were no known religious shrines, no permanent mosques, and no organised priests similar to that of the Coptic Church. Because of the absence of these vital religious institutions, it seemed that the institutional influence of Islamic religion on the day-to-day activities of the individual members was not as strong as was Christianity in the highland. Moreover, because of the economic mode of life, the groups as a whole lacked cohesiveness. Therefore, the only strong bond that connected them together seemed to be the bond of common descent (Nadel 1945: 55). All this contributed to the relatively weak integration of the ethno-linguistic group.

The relationship between the aristocratic class and the serfs was based on paternalistic principles. The aristocratic class protected its serf members while the serfs contributed to the economic power of the aristocratic class (see Trimingham 1952: 13). The economic obligations of the serfs generated surplus income for the ruling class, which strengthened their social and economic status. The serfs had an absolute right to ownership of livestock and grazing land (Gebre-Medhin 1979: 99), which guaranteed a measure of economic autonomy and also enabled them to fulfil their economic obligations to their masters. Social distance between the two classes was strictly observed. Intermarriage was absolutely prohibited. The aristocratic class was anxious to maintain its 'purity of blood' by allowing only endogamy (Bondestam 1989: 60). Yet, this did not hinder individual *Nabtab* members from having secret mistresses from among their serfs.

The Beni Amer was a confederation of a variety of clans and tribes united by a hierarchically structured organisation (Paul 1950). To be more precise, the federation consisted of 21 tribes and each tribe was divided into tribal sections (Gebre-Medhin 1979: 99). Presumably, the basis of the unity of the tribes was primarily political. However, Nadel (1945: 58) contends that political unity was, in part, an upshot of cultural and familial affinities and, in part, the effect of conquest and coercion. Here, it is assumed that political unity operated on two levels, the first level being that of the nobility, where political integration was the outcome of unity of descent. The second level was that of the serf-class, where the relationship was characterised by that of the rulers and ruled, and brought about by conquest or resting on voluntary submission of the weaker to the stronger. Moreover, cultural assimilation and coalescence of livelihood had contributed to political integration (Nadel 1945: 59). Here, it is emphasised that although cultural assimilation and the necessity based on common livelihood was an element of integration between the two classes, the relationship nevertheless rested essentially upon coercive domination.

The weakness of the Beni Amer confederation is emphasised by many observers. The main source of weakness was the negligible level of political centralisation (cf. Nadel 1945, Gebre-Medhin 1979). One of the reasons for this lack of centralisation was the nature of the nomadic mode of life itself. A nomadic mode of life presupposes constant movement, with dispersed communities living and moving in small groups. These conditions inhibited strong, centralised political administration. The confederate structure as a political instrument of governance, therefore, had only a formal and abstract meaning. Different *Sheikhs* and *Omdas,* as heads of various *Nabtab* clans with their respective serfs, paid due loyalty to the *Diglel* where the symbolic confederate power was embodied. It was a sort of traditional ritual recurrence. But this self-perpetuating norm and institution required neither conscious analysis or reflection, nor the adherence of its members. In the Weberian tradition, it can be denoted as traditional authority. The allegiance to the paramount chief was no more than mere tributary obligation (Nadel 1945: 59-60).

The social and political structure outlined below primarily concern the *Nabtab*. The power structure of the *Nabtabs* was arranged hierarchically: Diglel (paramount chief), Sheikh and Omda (cf. Gebre-Medhin 1979: 103, EPLF 1982).

Figure 2.3 The Tribal Structure of the *Nabtab*

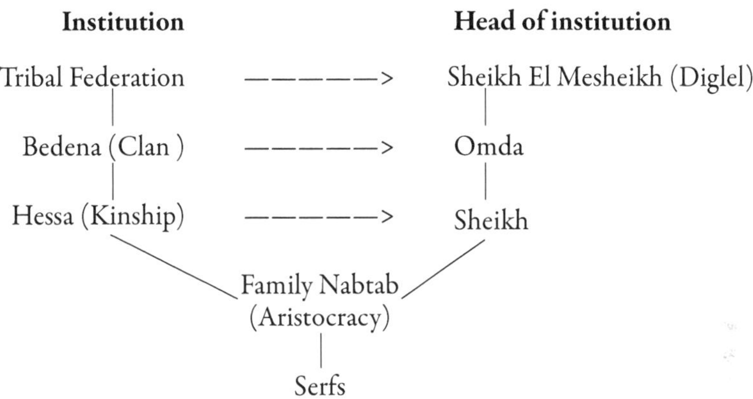

The succession to the office of *Omda* (clan-chief) was vested in only one of the kinship groups constituting the clan. When the head of the clan died, a meeting of all the *Nabtab* of the clan was held in *mahaber* (council). A larger council would elect a smaller committee of 3-4 members empowered to make a final decision. First, the sons of the late *Omda* were considered. If the sons of the late *Omda* were found unfit, the search would continue to another family in the same kinship group. Only as a last resort was the search of successor sought from a kinship group that traditionally did not supply the office holder. In the latter case, the new office holder was considered to have been adopted by the ruling house, and held the name of that kinship group. Afterwards, the *Diglel* would formally install the new chief in his office. The former had no power to refuse to install the *Omda* after the process had passed through all formal procedures (Nadel 1945: 61). The *Omda* had no judicial powers. Serious conflicts were solved by the clan-council, he "rules over men who are his equals in descent, status and economic resources, and his inferiors only by accord"(Nadel 1945: 62). He had only the function of intermediary between the *Nabtab* clan and the paramount chief (*Diglel*). The power of the *Omda* (clan-chief) may be strengthened at times of war, because then strict centralisation and loyalty was essential.

The principal chieftainship of the Beni Amer and its political organisation was believed to have appeared in the 16th century, introduced during the Fung rule. Then, the *Diglel* was a vassal chief of the Fung dynasty in the Sudan. However, the chieftainship survived the Ottoman and Egyptian rules. The Egyptians strengthened the *Diglel's* sovereignty, by incorporating into his rule non-Beni Amer groups. The advent of European colonial rule in both Eritrea and Sudan divided the Beni Amer tribes, and there emerged two principal chieftainships (Nadel 1945: 63). Like the clan-chief, the *Diglel's* power was limited, he had no judicial or executive power – clan feuds were resolved by the grand council of the *Nabtab*. The *Diglel* did not possess coercive state machinery such as an army or bodyguard (Nadel 1945: 65).

In addition to the Beni Amer, there were various ethno-linguistic groups in the lowland regions. In many respects, the social and political structure of some of these groups was similar to that of the Beni Amer. The Bet Asgede, composed of the Habab, Ad Tekles and Ad Temariam, were thought to descend from a common ancestor Asgede (Longrigg 1945: 156, Trevaskis 1960: 14, see esp. note 7). However, the three groups later existed independently from each other in a well-defined territorial exclusivity, constituting independent tribes under their own chiefs. Asgede, the mythical ancestor of the three groups, was believed to descend from the Tsenadegle, a kinship group in the Akkele-Guzai on the Plateau. The Asgedes lost their original language, Tigrinya, and adopted the language of their serfs, Tigre. The aristocracy was known by the name of *Shumagelle,* and the chiefs of the tribes had the title of *Shum,* except the Habab whose chief's title was *Kantebai* (BMA 1943: 19). The Bet Asgede were originally of the Coptic Christian faith, however were later converted to Islam, which was the religion of their subjects. The Habab and Ad Temariam pursued nomadic life, and their political organisation was tribal. The jurisdiction of the chiefs extended over their serf members wherever the latter migrated. The third group, the Ad Tekles, practised agriculture and led a sedentary life. This life brought with it a political orientation of chieftainship founded upon territorial jurisdiction rather than upon tribal jurisdiction which characterised the two other groups (BMA 1943: 19).

The Bilain, who were composed of two main groups, the Bet Tarke and Bet Tawke (Ghaber 1993: 6) were agriculturists. The aristocratic class was called *simager,* whereas the serfs were called *mikeru* (BMA-Eritrea 1943: 16-17, Trevaskis 1960: 15). The two sections of the Bilain were organised into numerous clan groups, each clan having its own *Sim* (chief) (Ghaber 1993: 27). Unlike the other tribes, they never succeeded in developing a common leader figure (Ghaber 1993: 28). The Maria, a Tigre-speaking group that was divided into two sub-groups, *Maria Tselam* and *Maria Keyah,* were believed to share common ancestry with the Tigre-speaking Mensa. The paramount chief of the Maria assumed the ancient hereditary title of *Shum,* and the "authentic" descendants of the ancestors provided the aristocratic class known as *Shumagalle* and the clans' chiefs and headmen. The serfs, the *Tigre,* on the other hand, were believed to be descendants of slaves and aboriginal inhabitants or weak clan factions, which ended up under the subordination of the Maria. Both the Maria and the Bilain were believed to have once been Coptic Christians (BMA 1943: 17, Ghaber 1993: 18-19). The Maria lived both a sedentary and a nomadic or semi-nomadic mode of life as cultivators and pastoralists.

The Mensa, whose sub-division formed Bet Abrehe and Bet Sha(h)kan, and who were situated in the vicinity bordering the Keren, Massawa and Hamasen regions, were believed to originate from a common ancestor called *Mensa'ai* (thus the name Mensa). The descendants of the legendary ancestor constituted the nobility, which ruled over the serfs, the *Tigre,* and the paramount chief was given the title of *Kantebai.* The Mensa were originally Orthodox Christians, and there still remain Orthodox Christians and converted Protestants of the Swedish Mission. In this group, Tigre and Tigrinya are spoken. Agricultural cultivation predominated as means of subsistence. Thus, they had a sedentary mode of life. The *Bet Juk* was another group believed to have descended from the Tigrinya-speakers of the plateau. Its serf system brought about the division between the nobility, the *Shumagelle*, on the one hand and the serfs, the *Sebmider*, on the other. The *Bet Juk* also practised an agriculturist sedentary life and their chief bore the title of *Kantebai* (BMA 1943: 18).

The Nara and Kunama, as sedentary and agricultural groups, were also believed to have had a political organisation based on territoriality rather than on kinship leadership. Unlike the Kunama, the Nara had a paramount chief called *Nazir* (Longrigg 1945: 159). Another distinguishing characteristic that differentiated the Kunama from the Nara was the practise of matriarchy – tracking familial descent from the maternal side (Longringg 1945: 38).

The Danakil, or Afar, was another mobile, predominantly nomadic group engaged in pastoralism, fishery, and trade. A small number of them supplemented their subsistence with agricultural activities, and they were socially organised into small clans or families (Sherman 1980: 4). The important political unit in the Afar community was the clan. Political institutions, such as leadership of the clan (*Kidhu Aba*), leadership of the sub-tribe and the sultans, played a vital role in the political life of the community (cf. Pedersen 1987: 15). These clans or families were subjected to loose control by the Sheikhs. These Sheikhs, at times assuming the title of Sultan, were able to exercise a territorial jurisdiction from their semi-permanent centres (Trevaskis 1960: 14). The clans traditionally paid loose allegiance to the Sultan, or Anfari, of Aussa (Trevaskis 1960: 14). The Afar community's members were well known for their independent minds, and several scholars have portrayed them as a fierce community that had preserved their independence from external dominance before European colonialism. As a group practising a system of serfdom, the Afar was divided into an aristocratic class, *Assaimara,* and a serf class, called *Adoimara* (BMA 1943: 23). The chiefs of the clans and headmen of the kinship families belong to the *Assaimara*.

The last group in our account is the Saho. Legend has it that the Saho-speaking Hazu and Asaworta groups have originated from Arabia (BMA 1943: 17). Geographically, the Saho share a common habitat with both the eastern lowlanders and the people of the plateau. This ethno-linguistic group consisted of five sub-groups: Assaworta, Hazu, Meniferi, Debrimaila and Sana'fay. It seems that, like the Kunama and the Bilain, they lacked a centralised common administrative structure. And while councils of elders carried out administrative affairs, they lacked chiefs (Trevaskis 1960: 15).

In conclusion, the serfs' loyalty to their masters, the *Nabtab, Shumaglle, Simager*, and *Assaimara,* was derived from the masters' obligation to protect them. This functional relationship was regulated by a mutual, although unequal, interest. The importance of this task of protection was given a significant weight in light of the continuous inter- and intra-ethnic conflicts. Although in principle, the aristocratic class gained its legitimacy by way of heredity (traditional legitimacy), in practice, legitimacy had to be earned through the capacity to protect the serfs. However, the involvement of a value-based rationale seems to have played a significant role in stabilising the system. Considering the ratio of serfs to aristocracy, and given the conspicuous absence of effective coercive means to subordinate the serfs, the most likely means by which the system could have been sustained was the symbolic value attached to it.

THE POLITICAL STATUS OF THE TERRITORY ON THE EVE OF ITALIAN COLONIALISM

The pre-Italian colonial history and status of Eritrea is marked by numerous controversies. These controversies are centred on the relationship between Eritrea and the successive Ethiopian empires. The Ethiopians have invariably claimed that Eritrea has been an integral part of their empire for thousands of years, whereas, the position of the Eritrean nationalists has always been that Eritrea has never been part of Ethiopia in the form we know it today (ELF 1971: 4ff, 1975: 7ff; EPLF 1978: 3f). The position of the Ethiopians, and of the scholars who support the view that Eritrea has invariably been an integral part of the Ethiopian empire, is founded upon an assumption of historical mythology which claims its validity in the assertion that there has been a continuation of unity and rule of the Ethiopian empire for the past three millennia (cf. Pool 1979: 13-20, 1980: 32-35; Tekle 1991).

Pool (1979, 1980) argues that the Ethiopian position arises from the belief that a centralised, compact state had existed during the mentioned period. However, before the end of the nineteenth century, no centralised and integrated state had previously existed in the modern sense of the concept. This study has no intention of indulging in repeating the claims and counterclaims that pertain to the pre-colonial history of Eritrea. Rather, the intention here is to briefly illustrate the status of Eritrea on the eve of the Italian colonialism. This is intended to help us to understand the role the Italians played in the creation of the present-day Eritrea by territorially integrating the various ethno-linguistic groups under unified bureaucratic administration which had never been unified before.

Immediately prior to Italian colonialisation, there were three distinctively discernible administrative regions in what was to become Eritrea: (i) the western and northern-eastern lowland and plateau regions, which were under Egyptian control; (ii) the Kebessa (highland) region, which was under the dominance of the Abyssinian Emperor Yohannes; and (iii) the Dankalia region, which was under the control of autonomous local aristocratic rulers (see Pool 1979: 15). The Medri Bahri or Merab Millash, as the *Kebessa* was called, comprised the three provinces of Akkele Guzai, Sarae and Hamasen. These regions were in continuous conflict with the rulers of Abyssinia, especially the Tigrean leaders. There were recurrent raids and attacks from the other side of the Mereb River by Abyssinian leaders. These were not only on the highland Tigrinya but also in the Bogos, the Habab/Mensa region, Saho and the Kunama regions (cf. Aren 1978,

Erlich 1982, Yohannes 1991). These raids and attacks usually evoked resistance, which in the long run were to constitute part of the accumulated history and political culture of resistance of Eritrean society. In that sense, perhaps they were the first building blocks in the creation of Eritrean history and culture. In this period, a number of resistance leaders emerged in the various regions. Those whose names are well known are Rasi Woldenkeal Solomon, Degeyat Bahta Hagos, Abubaker Nasser, Kafle Gofar, Ahmed El Idris (EPLF 1987: 31). The outstanding figures, however, were Rasi Woldenkeal and Degeyat Bahta Hagos. Rasi Woldenkeal, a hereditary chief from the Hamasen (Erlich 1982: 10), led a resistance effort from 1876 to 1879 in the Hamasen region against the forces of Emperor Yohannes. In the Akkele Guzai region, Bahta Hagos's uprising against the rule of Yohannes was reported to have endured until the complete colonisation of Eritrea by the Italians. However, he is much better known for his uprising against the Italians.

The Egyptians advanced upon Eritrea using two fronts. One front was from Sudan, where they first occupied the western lowland, which had earlier been under the influence of the Fung dynasty of Sinar in the Sudan. After some time they moved southward and occupied the Keren region. The second front stretched from the Red Sea. Using the port of Massawa as a spring-board, the Egyptians moved toward the hinterland and along the northern coast of the Red Sea (Sherman 1980: 10) under the leadership of a Swiss mercenary called Werner Munzinger (Dilebo 1974: 223). The Egyptian expansion was apparently facilitated by the obvious weakening and eventual collapse of the Ottoman Empire (Pool 1980: 41). At the same time, Menelik was busy co-ordinating his schemes with Munzinger and Ismail Pasha of Egypt to overthrow Yohannes and take over the imperial throne and title: Emperor of Ethiopia (Dilebo 1974: 223). The Egyptian campaign to occupy the Medri Bahri and Tigray, and their intention to depose Emperor Yohannes, was successfully challenged by the Emperor in 1875 and 1876 (Elrich 1982: 11-12). Though in the 1875 confrontation between Egypt and Abyssinia, Woldenkeal (a chief in the Hamesen region) supported Yohannes, this did not win him the needed trust from the Emperor. He therefore shifted his alliance and fought against the forces of Yohannes on the side of the Egyptians in the battle of Gura in 1876 (see Elrich 1982: 11, Perini [1905] 1997: 29). When the Egyptians were defeated in the Battle, Rasi Woldenkeal and his forces had to retreat to the Halhal region. Yohannes appointed Degeyat Haylu of Tze'azega as governor of Hamasen (Rubenson 1976: 333). When Rasi Woldenkeal heard about Degeyat Haylu's appointment he left his base in Halhal and went to confront him. In a battle at Wekidba in 1876 between the forces of Woldenkeal and Haylu, the latter was defeated and killed and his few followers who survived fled to Tigray (Kolmodin 1912, Rubenson 1976: 334, Elrich 1982: 13).

Outraged by the defeat and death of Degeyat Haylu Emperor Yohannes gathered his army and crossed over to Hamasen. Realising that he was not in a position to resist the force of Yohannes, Woldenkeal fled to Halhal. Yohannes, leaving Degeyat Tesema and Shaleka Alula, returned to Tigray. Followers of Rasi Woldenkeal arrived almost immediately at Hamasen, which forced Tesema and Alula to flee to Tigray, paving the way for Rasi Woldenkeal to resume the governorship of Hamasen (Kolmodin 1912: 232-6). Following this, in 1878, Yohannes sent a force of approximately 10,000 men, led by Rasi Bariau Gabra-Sadeg to dislodge Woldenkeal. The two hostile forces met in Asmara, where the battle concluded in success for Woldenkeal, and the forces of Bariau were destroyed and Bariau himself was killed (Perini [1905] 1997: 81-2, Kolmodin 1912: 237, Elrich 1982: 21). This battle was to leave a strong impact on the sentiments of the Eritrean nationalists, and songs and poems (discussed in Chapter Eight) were written praising Woldenkeal (EPLF 1987: 34-37). When this development reached Emperor Yohannes, who ordered his loyal Rasi Alula with 20 000 men (Rubenson 1976: 341) to cross over Hamasen and punish Woldenkeal, the latter was forced to again withdraw to Halhal. Finally, when Woldenkeal discovered the intentions of the Egyptians, who were engaged in negotiations with the Emperor and were conspiring to abandon him in the hope of mending their relation with Abyssinia, he decided to make peace with the Emperor. Accordingly, a reconciliation was reached and Woldenkeal was to be vice governor of Hamasen (Erlich 1982: 23). Shortly after, however, in 1879, he was arrested and deported to Tigray with his relatives and imprisoned for 10 years (Erlich 1982: 142). By the time he was free, Eritrea was under Italian rule. The Italians refused to allow him to return to Eritrea, and he spent the rest of his life in Tigray.

Alula ruled the provinces of Hamasen and Sarae for ten years, from 1879 until 1889, until the Italians colonised Eritrea (Sherman 1980: 10, Elrich 1982: 85). In the Akkele Guzai region, resistance against the Ethiopian presence by Bahta Hagos and his followers and the Saho continued until the end. The resistance of Bahta Hagos lasted more than 20 years (EPLF 1987). This resistance and the resistance from the lowland against the raids of Emperor Yohannes are considered by Eritrean nationalists to be the first phase of the Eritrean struggle against the Ethiopian occupation. Moreover, some scholars trace the genesis of Eritrean nationalism to these days (Yohannes 1991: 9).

The Egyptians, after their campaign to occupy the Kebessa and invade Ethiopia failed, were restricted to the lowland region of Eritrea. Consequently, two-thirds of the territory was subjected to their control, leading observers to believe that for the first time the larger part of Eritrea was centralised under unified governance (Machida 1987). Events unfolded rapidly during this tumultuous period. In Sudan, an Islamic movement known as the 'Mahdist Movement', which became a serious menace for the Egyptians, the British, and the Abyssinians, started to spread quickly. Threatened by its spread, the British convinced Emperor Yohannes of Abyssinia that if he helped in defeating the force of the Mahdists, he would get the port of Massawa and the Keren region of Eritrea. As the result of the June 3, 1884 accord between Britain, Egypt and Yohannes, the Anglo-Egyptian prisoners could be evacuated from the Mahdist camps in Eastern Sudan (Longrigg 1945: 114, Spencer 1984: 30). However, instead of sticking to their part of the deal, the British actively supported and encouraged Italy to occupy Massawa (Dilebo 1974: 226). In the meantime, Alula was undertaking raids on the lowland communities on almost a yearly basis to collect tributes or pacify the tribes. To safeguard their security, the tribes had to enter into various security pacts. These were sometimes with the Mahdists against the forces of Yohannes, and at other times, they had to ally with the forces of Yohannes against the Mahdists. When the threat of the Mahdists was finally minimised, they allied themselves with the Italians, who by 1885 became the masters of Massawa against the forces of Yohannes. Co-operation between the Bahta Hagos and the Saho, between Woldenkeal and the Mensa and the Belain against the forces of Yohannes were also common (cf. Elrich 1982). Beginning in the 1850s-1870s, the people of the Bogos, Mensa and the Catholics in Akkele Guzai had progressively been seeking protection from European missionaries and diplomats: "Here Eritrea was, in fact, conceived" (Rubenson 1976: 144). Aren Gustav (1978) about the Kunama and Nara also gives a similar description.

In depicting the status of the region, some observers have maintained that before the nineteenth century, the Tigrinya speakers of Eritrea and the Tigreans were politically independent from each other, with the Mareb River as their common front line (Dilebo 1974: 222). Dilebo further maintains that they were economically interdependent – the Tigreans for access to the sea through the Medri Bahri, while the Medri Bahrians had to procure their agricultural and dairy products from the Tigreans. This suggests that the Abyssinian state, or rather states, were decentralised feudal entities, often fighting against each other, at least from 1270 (Dilebo 1974: 222) until the time of Tewodros. After the death of Tewodros, the title of Emperor was conferred on Yohannes of Tigray. But Menelik of Shewa never accepted Yohannes's claim, and he subsequently sought to restore the throne to the Amhara dynasty. Menelik's dream was ultimately fulfilled by the sudden death of Yohannes. Thus, it was only under Menelik's rule that Abyssinia emerged as centralised modern state. Eritrea, rather the Kebessa region, could not evolve as part of the centralised empire of Menelik because Eritrea had already been carved out as an Italian colonial territory. The decentralised feudal tributary state structure could not support an all-embracing political unity. This political situation, it therefore seems, did not permit the Medri Bahri to have political unity beyond the Mareb River even with its neighbours and closest kin, the Tigreans, except for the short, 10-year rule of Alula. The Medri Bahrians had their autonomy (Dilebo 1974, Erlich 1982).

The rest of Eritrea was ruled under different alien and local rulers, as was mentioned earlier in this section. The Dankalia region was ruled by a local sultanate under Sultan Mohammed Hanfare of Afar, along with the rest of the Afar homeland (Dilebo 1974: 226). The Afar land was later partitioned both by Menelik's expansion and by the Italian and French colonial powers (Pool 1980: 7-8). The western and north-eastern lowland and the northern highland was ruled by Egypt as previously shown. Thus, Eritrea had never been politically united before the rise of Italian colonialism. To be sure, the different communities had economic relations with their immediate neighbours, stronger or weaker depending on the conditions of the particular point of time. On top of that, on many occasions they had been forced to pay tribute to one or another stronger power. The available information shows also that some communities share a common genealogical origin. These facts indicate that while no unified Eritrean political structure yet existed, it should not be denied that important relationships among the various ethno-linguistic groups did in fact, exist.

SUMMARY AND CONCLUSION

The account presented in this chapter shows that before the Italian colonialism, the various ethno-linguistic groups did not share a common history, cultural uniqueness and individuality, or territorial integration. Neither were they part of any unified state. Common history, cultural uniqueness and territorial integration are generally considered as necessary conditions for the successful advancement of the process of nation formation, as shown in the theoretical section of this dissertation. On the one hand, they help bind and integrate the society, and on the other, they help distinguish it from others, thereby engendering the "we-they" distinction. Hence, the logical inference that can be drawn in the conspicuous absence of these elements in the period prior to Italian colonialism is that the process of nation formation in Eritrea began with the initiation of the Italian colonial rule. This argument will become especially clear as the dimensions raised in the theoretical discussion in a later chapter highlight the dominant theoretical and conceptual discourse of nation formation.

The absence of the essential features of a nation makes it problematic to talk about an Eritrean collective identity before the advent of Italian colonial rule. In this respect, this pre-colonial period is intended to serve as a backdrop for the process of nation formation set in motion by Italian colonialism. The question of territorial integration (to be discussed in the next chapter) is assumed to be the basic prerequisite for the cohesion of a society, which may, in its turn, be seen as a yardstick for the emergence of a nation. The evidence presented in this chapter demonstrates unequivocally that the different ethno-linguistic groups of Eritrea rather had a separate existence prior to Italian colonialism. In terms of power structure, economic nexus, geographical and cultural communication and the socio-economic mode of life, they were separate. The paucity of these important ingredients almost certainly precludes the emergence of a common sentiment, feeling or identity based on mythical or actual historical memories and experiences. This absence was so evident that we can hardly expect a consolidated common sentiment and feeling within the different ethno-linguistic groups, let alone between them.

The sedentary mode of life in the highland of Eritrea was organised and revolved around traditional village community life. Traditional village life, as scholars like Smith (1983a, 1983b, 1986, 1991), Gellner (1983, 1993), Anderson (1991), Bendix (1964) describe it, is characterised by dispersed small cultures. Every village can be seen as an isolated island, bereft of cultural assimilation, political integration, territorial centralisation, social communication and interaction with the rest of the villages. For a national sentiment and consciousness to emerge, the erosion of the parochial and primordial village attachment is needed. It has to be replaced by a transcendent and more pervasive interaction and communication. Affinity and loyalty should rest on the nation. Exchange of goods and services need to be carried out at a national level. The submission to a higher politico-legal authority is also a prerequisite. In the village social formation of the highland of Eritrea, all these elements were absent. The absence of these elements was even more conspicuous in the lowland regions, because the nomadic social formations are, by their very nature, non-conducive, or even hostile to such interaction and integration. All these elements could only be initiated under Italian rule.

This reality makes a compelling case that the genesis of the process of nation formation in Eritrea coincided with the rise of Italian colonialism. This is so because the traditional social formation, which was quite limited at the clan and village levels of social organisation, could only accommodate parochial and primitive feelings and sentiments. Two particular fundamental conditions that precluded the possibility of emergent nationhood and nationalism can be mentioned. These were the socio-political organisational structure, which was limited to the *enda* and the village level in the *Kebessa*, and in the nomadic life-style in the *Metahit,* the absence of a centralised bureaucratic administration. Hence, beyond the primordial sentiments, no form of nationalism could develop.

In conclusion, this chapter has discussed the traditional social structures and socio-economic relations and formations of the Eritrean communities as they existed at the start of Italian colonial rule. It has also discussed the economic, socio-political organisation and status of the various ethno-linguistic groups. In addition, it has arrived at the conclusion that at this stage, before the initiation of Italian colonialism, fundamental characteristics of nation or nationalism could not have existed. In the next chapter, we will examine the changes that occurred as a consequence of European capitalist penetration, particularly the territorial and political centralisation. We will also study the transformation and evolution of Eritrea as a geo-political administrative entity which was the result of the various treaties and conventions.

Notes

1. Italy named its newly-created colony Eritrea in 1890. The name Eritrea originated from the Greek word *Sinus Erythraeus* a name given to the Red Sea by the Greeks. Later also the Romans called the Red Sea *Mare Erthraeum.* Prior to that the area was known from the fourteenth century onward as *Medri Bahri* (Land of the Sea), and the Ruler was called *Bahri Negassi* and approximately it embraced the provinces of Hamasen, Serae and Akkele Guzai (Machida 1987: 9; Haile 1988: 12).

2. The concepts tribe, ethnicity, nationality are confusing and the topic of a great deal of contention. This is due to the ideologically laden nature of the concepts. In the Eritrean nationalist movement, the concept of nationality(ies) was widely used to describe the various groups. However, it was recognised that only one ethno-linguistic group (the Tigrinya ethno-linguistic group) could really fit the designation of nationality. This understanding was reached on the basis of the politico-economic and socio-historical level of organisation of the various groups. Throughout this study, I employ a compound concept, which I believe to be neutral. In particular, I use ethno-linguistic groupings to distinguish the groups (to be discussed later).
3. The concept tribe is a much-abused, as well as much-contested concept. The use of the concept of tribe is becoming increasingly rare, and is being replaced by the concept of ethnicity. As noted above, I prefer to use the compound concept ethno-linguistic group to describe an ethnic collectivity. However, I have occasionally employed tribe when I refer to sub-groups within the ethno-linguistic group and in reference to their social organisation. I also use it in reference to groups who identify themselves as tribes. In the *Dictionary of Political Thought*, the concept of tribe is defined as: "A form of social organisation which is determined by kinship rather than by territory, but which nevertheless retains a distinct chain of command" (Scruton 1982: 470). The part of the definition "social organisation ... determined by kinship rather than by territory" is the sense to which I refer whenever I use the concept of tribe in reference to social organisation.
4. Some scholars discern three modes, notably agriculturalism, pastoralism, and agro-pastoralism (e.g. Bondestam 1989: 24). However, it should be noted that these distinctions had been blurred with the advance of time. For example, some ethno-linguistic groups had been transformed from an almost entirely nomadic mode of life to a wholly or partially sedentary mode of life.
5. The lowland and the highland are locally distinguished as *Metahit* and *Kebessa* (in Tigrinya) respectively. The *Kebessa* consisted of the three provinces of Hamasen, Serae and Akkele Guzai (cf. Nadel 1946, Longrigg 1945), while the *Metahit* generally consisted of the remaining part of Eritrea. The concepts are more than merely geographical connotations; they also denote culture, religion and economic life.
6. In addition to the advantages they enjoyed in the form of land ownership which entitled them to inheritance, the *restenya* also had a wide range of economic and social prerogatives which enhanced their social position. Such rights entailed, notwithstanding local variations, small, symbolic Easter-gifts, reed-crosses (*setti*) dipped in holy water; *lesane-manka* (tongue) was a privilege of the restenya elders who get all tongues of slaughtered cattles at weddings and funeral feasts. Further, it entailed more substantial matters such as political administrative affairs of the village, 'supervision and organisation of communal labour, care of the village church, the right to act as guardians of village fields and pastures, and the right to act as arbitrators in land disputes. Furthermore, the *restenya* were entitled to the most prestigious office of the village, which was properly known as *chikkenet* or *helkinet*. The above-described prerogatives even generated economic benefits. For instance the guardians of the fields got some share of the crops. Or when they acted as arbitrators in disputes got their share from the legal fee. They could also claim an extra plot of land for their services, etc. (Nadel 1946: 9-10). These were prerogatives exclusively conferred on the *restenya* families or *enda*.

7. The form of land tenure system known as *gulti* was, according to Nadel (1946) extraneous to the village land tenure system of the *Kebessa*. He maintains that it was introduced by the Ethiopian Imperial powers. Accordingly, land was expropriated from the villages and conferred upon chiefs and military leaders as compensation for services rendered.
8. According to Tekeste Negash (1986:23) the five zones were Hamasen, Akkele Guzai, Serae, Deki Tesfa and Deki Melega. However, the historically known division seems to be that involving the three provinces of Hamasen, Akkele Guzai, and Serae. The exact boundaries between them might have shifted around over time.
9. The name Beni Amer means descendants of Amer. According to S.F. Nadel (1945: 55-7) the legend behind this mystical ancestor is that he was the son of Ja'ali father (a tribe from the Sudan) and Bellou mother (inhabitants of present Eritrean side). The story goes as follows: a certain Ali Abu Gasim Jaaliin ventured into the Khor Baraka area and was married with the grand-daughter of the Bellou King, Idris Mohammed Adara - to whom he had, upon his arrival, explained that he had "sprung from the earth" (*nabata min al ard* - which later caused his descendants to be nicknamed Nabtab) (Paul 1950: 224). The Bellou killed Ali Abu Gasim, and after his death his son Amer was born. When Amer reached the age of manhood he went to the Nile Valley (his father's home area) and returned with an army to avenge his father's death. He conquered the Bellou and founded the Beni Amer tribe. Regarding the serfs, Nadel contends that the serfs were not the "sons of Amer" (Nadel 1945: 57). His assumption is that they were either descendants of the aboriginal Bellou or other tribes. Different narrations and interpretations countering Nadel's story about the pedigree of the Beni Amer federation of tribes are also available. For instance, we encounter historical narrations, which propose that the Beni Amer are a blending of the Beja and Semitic groups (EPLF, Beni Amer from past history 1928). Other views maintain that not all the Nabtab were the descendants of Amer. When Amer with the help of the Senar kingdom defeated the Ballou Kingdom, those who were defeated comprised the Nabtab aristocracy.
10. The term Tigre is confusing for a foreign reader because it has two meanings, or is used in two different ways. In one meaning it is a name given to the people who speak the Tigre language. It emanates from the language, Tigre, and the people are identified by the name of the language. The second meaning is the serfs who were also called Tigre. The aristocratic class, who invariably were alien to their subjects who were Tigre speakers, upon lack of alternative names used to call their serfs Tigre denoting their class identity, thus, endowing the term Tigre the meaning of serf. (I am indebted to Mohammed Nur Ahmed for this clarification.) This created problems for foreign scholars, although the second meaning has disappeared with the abolition of the serfdom system.

Chapter 3

TERRITORIAL INTEGRATION: THE BIRTH OF ERITREA

INTRODUCTION

The key point of departure of this chapter is that territorial integration leads not only to geographical integration, but also to societal, economic and political integration. Moreover, territorial integration is viewed as the fundamental landmark in the process of nation formation. Historical experiences seem to favour the view that territorial integration precedes other dimensions of nation formation. For example, it can be recalled that the absolute monarchies of Europe, by crushing the disintegrated feudal principalities and forcing them to submit to a centralised authority, created the necessary conditions for the emergence of modern nations (cf. Rokkan 1973, Seton-Watson 1977, Tilly 1990). Throughout social history, territorial organisation has been invariably given a prime position in the historical processes of the emergence of states and nations. Elucidating the importance of territorial integration in a historiographic context, Peter M. Slowe notes:

> It was part of that great change described by Homer and Aristotle, when several villages united into one community with some common interests to form the early city-state of ancient Greece and the river communities along the Nile and Indus and in Mesopotamia. Particularly in these latter cases, the need for territorial organisation was made more pressing by a drying climate and the need to control limited resources (Slowe 1990: 58).

Durkheim's *'Division of Labour in Society'* (1984) also deals with the formation of societies. His basic theme rests on the view that increasing population volume and density resulting from the integration of villages and communities leads to the transformation of societies and the integrating forces that hold them together. According to Durkheim, societies evolve from simple organisations based on the principle of likeness and bound together by "mechanical" solidarity, to highly differentiated societies based on the principle of interdependence and bound together by "organic" solidarity. This points out that when the dispersed and isolated village communities are integrated on the basis of territoriality a nation can be said to be emerging. Durkheim's work refers, of course, not to the formation of nations, but to the process of transformation from primitive village communities to modern societies. The theme of nation formation is also about the process of transformation of societies from a simple less cohesive to more compact, territorially integrated ones.

The general assumption in the theories of nation formation is that the prevalence of a 'homeland' or 'territory' is the necessary precondition for the emergence of a nation. It is only in the existence of an integrated territory that the 'practical business of nation-building' can be realised, and nationalists or elites are enabled to mobilise the masses to form a nation. This suggests an important reason for the great emphasis placed on the unification of Germany and Italy. In addition to the political and symbolic importance of a territory, economic aspects as a source of self-sufficiency are also much emphasised for the viability of a nation (cf. Smith 1986: 163). Moreover, it appears that territorial socialisation is an important aspect of the nation formation process. Territorial socialisation refers to the process through which members become rationally and emotionally attached to their territory, its way of life, its institutions and its culture. This territorial socialisation generates territorial consciousness, affinity and identification with a specific territory leading to the development of, to use Benedict Anderson's seminal concept, imagined community. Scholars of colonialism have repeatedly elucidated how colonial demarcation of territorial boundaries has created common territorial identities.

> Nevertheless, however artificial the colonial demarcation of territorial units may have been in relation to pre-colonial conditions, the administrative organizations of the colonial states created the basics for articulating new national units based on imaginary communities formed by these indigenous functionaries, communities which corresponded to the administrative domain of the highest administrative centre to which they could be assigned (Gledhill 1994: 79).

The important legacy of Italian colonialism in this context is that by centralising the territory of Eritrea in a colonial state, it has created in the people a sense of belonging to – and identification with – the territory. By severing the historical and cultural contact they had with their closest kin in the Sudan and Ethiopia respectively, the communities from the northern highland and western lowland, on the one hand, and the Tigrinya-speaking community in the highland, on the other, were progressively socialised to form a territorially integrated society.

The events and processes that contributed to the emergence, consolidation, and sustenance of territorial centralisation of Eritrea, will be also discussed in this chapter. The Eritrea of today came into existence as a consequence of the interplay between powerful local, regional and global actors. The treaties and conventions between regional actors (Ethiopia and Egypt), and regional actors and global actors (between Ethiopia and the various Western powers), and between global actors (Britain - Italy, Britain - France, Italy - France) shaped Eritrea (cf. Ghebre-Ab 1993). However, the treaties and conventions between Ethiopia and Italy had more impact than did others. In addition to Italy's campaign to delineate and consolidate the borders of Eritrea, the internal compartmentalisation of Eritrea into administrative provinces and the political and legal unification of the communities will briefly be analysed. In short, this chapter is devoted to the investigation of the process and mechanisms through which the present Eritrea was formed. This applies in the context of territorial demarcation, centralisation and provincialisation, as well as the unification in terms of the administration and judicial system.

Accordingly, the examination of these aspects is done in four sections. Section two discusses demarcation and consolidation of borderlines. Section three examines administrative compartmentalisation. In section four, the treaty of Wechale and its impact on Eritrean nationalism is scrutinised, whereas section five discusses legal and administrative unification. Sections one and six constitute the introduction and the summary respectively.

THE DEMARCATION AND CONSOLIDATION OF BOUNDARIES

The centralisation and integration process of Eritrea was actually set in motion by the Egyptians. As the rule of the Ottoman Empire declined in the 1860s, the Egyptians took over. Since the Sudan fell under Egyptian control, the western lowland of Eritrea, which was under the Fung rule of Sudan, was also incorporated under the expanded Egyptian rule. From the Red Sea side, first Massawa came under the Egyptian control, after which the Egyptians expanded their grip into the hinterland. The Egyptian attempt to occupy the whole of Eritrea, as well as their effort to colonise Abyssinia was frustrated on two occasions. They were badly defeated militarily and finally forced to withdraw from the highland of Eritrea, thereby limiting themselves to the lowland regions. At this time, the Egyptians succeeded in integrating two-thirds of the territory. This has led some observers to believe that it was under the Egyptian rule that Eritrea first came close to a unified existence (e.g. Machida 1987, Gayim 1993). However, the mission of creating an integrated territorial structure was left to the Italians, since they were the first to establish a formally united Eritrean territory.

The period between 1882 and 1907 is considered to be the time during which Italy consolidated its colonial grip on the region (Mesghenna 1988: 128-9, Gayim 1993: 57, Ghebre-Ab 1993). In other words, from a cartographic point of view, it was during this time frame that the mapping and documentation of the present day Eritrea was undertaken. The first stage of this mapping and documentation entailed the delineation of international boundaries and the signing of different treaties and conventions between the concerned powers. The process began when Italy declared Assab as its colony in 1882 (Gayim

1993: 57). After a while, the port of Massawa was occupied. The occupation of Massawa occurred with the acknowledgement–and encouragement, of Britain. In the game of international power politics, Britain preferred Italy, the less powerful and less potentially dangerous rival contender, to France. Assuming that the French would try to occupy the region, the British encouraged Italy to take the initiative. This does not mean, of course, that Italy had no plans to invade the entire region. As a matter of fact, Britain protested earlier against such an Italian attempt, favouring Egypt. After the successful conquest of Massawa, the hinterland became Italy's new target. But the campaign to conquer the highland of Eritrea initially proved to be quite costly for the Italians. In one battle, the Italians were almost wiped out by Emperor Yohannes's forces, with a total loss of 500 men. This represented a serious setback (Dilebo 1974, Sherman 1980, Trevaskis 1960).

Unlike the first attempt, the second campaign of expansion was successful. As a result, the Italians managed to penetrate the interior highland of Eritrea. Events were simultaneously unfolding on the Ethiopian side at an unprecedented pace. Emperor Yohannes lost his own life in the battle against the Mahdists, and Menelik was unexpectedly crowned as Emperor of Ethiopia. He began immediately to sign treaties with Italy. On May 2, 1889, a treaty of peace, friendship and commerce, known as 'Wechale Treaty' was signed between Menelik and Italy (Dilebo 1974: 226, Rubenson 1976: 385). The main theme of the treaty was an act of mutual recognition. Italy would recognise Menelik as the legitimate inheritor of the Abyssinian throne. In return, Menelik would recognise the sovereignty of Italy over Eritrea. In addition, this treaty clarified and defined the limits of the territorial boundaries of both states (Gayim 1993: 59). Of course, the area included in the Wechale Treaty embraced a smaller territory than what was later to become Eritrea, an expansion that required another agreement between the two states.

Following the signing of the Wechale Treaty, Italy further consolidated its grip on Eritrea. On June 2, 1889, Keren was occupied, followed by Asmara, whereby the whole of Eritrea fell under Italian colonial rule. This included area that had not been included in the Treaty. The appropriation of areas that had not been covered in the Wechale Treaty evoked little reaction from the Ethiopian side, including the Shewan Emperor. Instead, following this development, the treaty between Ethiopia and Italy was updated to reflect the new boundaries. Hence, on October 1, 1889, an additional convention was signed between the two countries, where Menelik reaffirmed his recognition of the sovereignty of Italy over Eritrea. Following this, on January 1, 1890 (Dilebo 1974: 221, Negash 1987: 2), Italy declared Eritrea as its colony, thereby creating the modern Eritrea (Longrigg 1945: 132). Various treaties and conventions between Italy and Abyssinia followed, for the purpose of further clarification and redrawing of the front lines between the colony of Italy and Abyssinia[1] (Gayim 1993: 59). This demonstrates how "Eritrea existed not only by Italian creation, but by Ethiopian renunciation" (Young 1983: 221).

The Italians attempted to further expand their territory with an effort to invade Abyssinia, which led to the battle of Adwa of 1896. The battle of Adwa resulted in a humiliating Italian defeat – and for Abyssinia, unprecedented victory. The treaty signed after the war reaffirmed the independence of Abyssinia and the sovereignty of Italy over Eritrea. Subsequently, many treaties were signed with the intention of redefinition and specification of the borderlines between Abyssinia and the colony of Italy (cf. Gayim 1993). Many scholars have argued that Abyssinia had the capacity to drive the Italians out of Eritrea after its victory at Adwa. The devastation incurred by Italy was thought to be so immense that Italy could by no means have resisted the force of Menelik (e.g. Dilebo 1974, Pool 1979, Sherman 1980, Bondestam 1989).

The international borders of Eritrea were delineated not only as the consequence of the conventions and agreements between Menelik's Abyssinia and Italy, but also as a result of agreements and treaties with other regional and European powers. The significant European actors besides Italy that participated in the territorial formation of Eritrea were Britain and France. Egypt played a role of a regional actor in participating in the demarcation and mapping of Eritrea. The border with Sudan was demarcated as a result of a series of accords with the Anglo-Egyptian Sudan, June 25, and July 7, 1895, December 7, 1898 and December 8, 1907 (Gayim 1993: 279). Meanwhile, the frontier facing Djibouti was established by treaties signed with France, January 24, 1900 and July 10, 1901 (Gayim 1993: 280). These series of agreements can be found documented in more detail in the British Foreign Office record (FO 371-69331). The Abyssinians, the Italians, the French and the British, as a consequence of their territorial positions, all participated in the shaping of the geo-political boundaries and structure of Eritrea. It was as a result of the agreements and treaties between these powers that today's Eritrea came into existence. Since then, Eritrean territorial integration and continuity has been preserved. It was at this time, in the objective sense, that the foundation of the Eritrean nation was established.

ADMINISTRATIVE COMPARTMENTALISATION

One of the effects of Italian colonial rule, particularly in the realms of politics, was the establishment of a centralised bureaucratic administration. The first stage of Italian rule took the form, as is discussed above, of defining and consolidating the international borders of their newly created colony. The next step, with a focus on internal needs, aimed at creating political institutions and mechanisms to facilitate the effective administration of the new colony. At this point, we will discuss only those dimensions of political institutions and administrative mechanisms that pertain to the creation of administrative structures, divisions and sub-divisions, provinces and districts, etc., aimed at creating a functional administration. Taken as a whole, the process can be described as one of both centralisation and decentralisation. On the one hand, the process established a centralised territorial administrative unit. On the other, decentralisation took place in the form of provincialisation for internal administrative purposes.

The concept of territorial centralisation rests on the perception of the prevalence of dominant centres. Centres can be characterised by monocephality, in which there is a single centre, or by polycephality, in which more than one centre exists. Further, it is based on the dichotomy of centre-periphery. The historical processes through which centres emerge vary greatly, as do the historical forces underlying the evolution of these centres. However, a common characterising feature is that the emergence of a dominant centre seems to be a necessary condition for the development of territorial centralisation and the resultant territorial identity. Generally, centres are defined as,

> privileged locations within a territory where key military/administrative, economic and cultural resource-holders most frequently meet; with established arenas for deliberations, negotiations and decision-making; where people convene for ritual ceremonies of affirmation of identity; with monuments that symbolize this identity; with the largest proportion of the economically active population engaged in the processing and communication of information and instructions over long distances. Centres, then, are both locations providing services and nodes in a communications network. ... measured in terms of the three conventional dimensions of differentiation: political control, economic dominance, cultural standardization (Rokkan and Urwin 1982: 5).

In the historical process of territorial and social organisation, there may arise two phenomena. Where there are various centres, it becomes imperative that one of the contending centres triumphs over the rest, thereby elevating itself into position as an unequivocal focal point around which the others pivot. Conversely, a single dominant centre may not emerge. Instead, various centres with equal distribution of the "resource-holders" and the three dimensions of differentiation (political, economic, and cultural) elucidated by Rokkan and Urwin coexist. In the latter case, the rise of cohesive integrated territory encounters substantial hurdles. The prevalence of monocephality or polycephality depends on several factors, which determine and characterise the details of social histories. In our case, it was the structure of colonialism. Seen from the conceptualisation of territorial centralisation, the significant Italian accomplishment in Eritrea was centralisation of the entire territory around the capital city, Asmara, triggering the rise of monocephality (one centre). The remainder was organised in such a way as to pivot around the capital city. This centre-periphery structure, brought about by Italian colonialism, was fashioned in two dimensions: a) urban-rural, b) capital city-provincial capitals and small towns acting as satellites of a single dominant centre. The connection between the centre (capital) and the rural area was very loose; yet, in terms of economic relationships, there arose interdependency. The provincial capitals were intended to function as administrative sites of the internally decentralised colonial territorial structure, which in turn was to be connected with the capital city in a hierarchical relation. The following figure illustrate the structure of the territorial organisation that the Italians created.

Figure 3.1: Territorial Organisation

CAPITAL CITY								
Provincial Capitals			Provincial Capitals			Provincial Capitals		
Province			Province			Province		
Village	Village	Village	Village	Village	Village	Village	Village	Village

Fig. 3.2 Administrative Divisions

DIVISION	HEADQUARTERS	DISTRICT*
I: Bassopiano Occidentale	Agordat	Barentu Tessenei Umm Hajar
II: Altopiano	Keren	Nagfa
III: Hamasien	Asmara	Decamere
IV: Accele Guzzai	Adi Caieh	Saganeiti Senafe Arafeli
V: Serae	Adi Ugri	Adi Quala
VI: Bassopiano Orientale	Massawa	Ghinda Nacra Thio
VII: Assab	Assab	

(*) Addition to H.Q.
Source: WO 230-106, 1942

The process of compartmentalisation – the division of Eritrea into administrative provinces – started around 1908 (Gayim 1993: 59). The country was divided into seven provinces (*Commissariati*). Each province was in turn, organised into districts (*vice-residenze*). These were to be administered by officials known as 'Commisari', 'Residenti', and 'Vice Residenti' respectively (FO 371- 69370). The seven provinces were the Hamasen Division, the Serae Division, the Eastern Division (*Bassopiano Orientale*), the Akale Guzai-Saho Division, the Western Division (*Bassopiano Occidentale*), the Keren Division, and Assab (WO 230-106 1942, Trevaskis 1960: 26, Sherman 1980: 13-4) as shown in figure 3.2. Under the British Military Administration (BMA) these seven administrative divisions were reduced to five. The administrative division of Assab was in 1944 included in the administrative division of Massawa, while the Commissariati of Keren and Agordat were amalgamated in 1947 into what was to be known afterwards as the 'Western Province' (FO 371-69370). The division into provinces, from the administrative point of view, indicates the introduction of modern administrative structures. In addition, one of the aims of the creation of administrative regions, from the political point of view, is often to accommodate and allocate central as well as regional political actors. It also helps to raise distinctive regions to a level political ground, through the mechanism of equalising the distribution of resources and creating political posts and powers. In other words, it can serve as a means of equalising the status of the different regions.

In this respect, three questions arise in connection with the creation of administrative provinces and corresponding administrative posts. What was the role of the indigenous population? What happened to the old power structures? Was there a distribution of resources and an allocation of power according to the principles of provincialisation? No pretension is made about having answers to these questions. But, generally, to understand the political behaviour of Italian colonial rule in Eritrea, it is useful to know the political philosophy of the Italians in handling the indigenous population. Italian colonial officials were known to have described their administrative system as a middle road between the French system of direct rule and the British system of indirect rule (Gray & Silberman 1948: 19). The underlying political philosophy behind the entire administrative arrangement was rooted in the Italian perception of direct rule. The Italians were against any thought of allowing the indigenous people to participate in administering themselves. Their philosophy was founded upon the belief that the whole ladder of power hierarchy should be placed under the control of the colonists in order to avoid the enlightenment and subsequent desire to seize power, of the indigenous population. Accordingly, the governance of the provinces was put in the hands of Italian administrative officials. In other words, no intermediary power structure was instituted that would accommodate the participation of indigenous people. Individuals from the traditional elites were given some posts, albeit at a lower level and in a manner which suited the colonial rule system.

Trevaskis (1960: 27) argues that the Italians did not institute a system of local government. The administrative design they pursued was based upon the assumption that the indigenous population should be separated from all political activities that might lead to national consciousness. While this is the widely accepted assumption, Gebre-Medhin (1989: 64) contends that Italian policy actually heralded a combination of direct and indirect rule. What Gebre-Medhin perceives as indirect rule is the fact that the Italians preserved some of the traditional structures and kept some chieftains in their positions because they found this to be expedient. David Pool shares this view. While noting the Italians' introduction of direct colonial rule system, Pool (1979: 17) contends that they encouraged the emergence of tribal and village leaders and facilitated the consolidation and legitimisation of their position in the community. This was a result of conferring upon them the power to resolve the disputes which could

Map 3: Showing the Establishment of Eritrea by Treaties

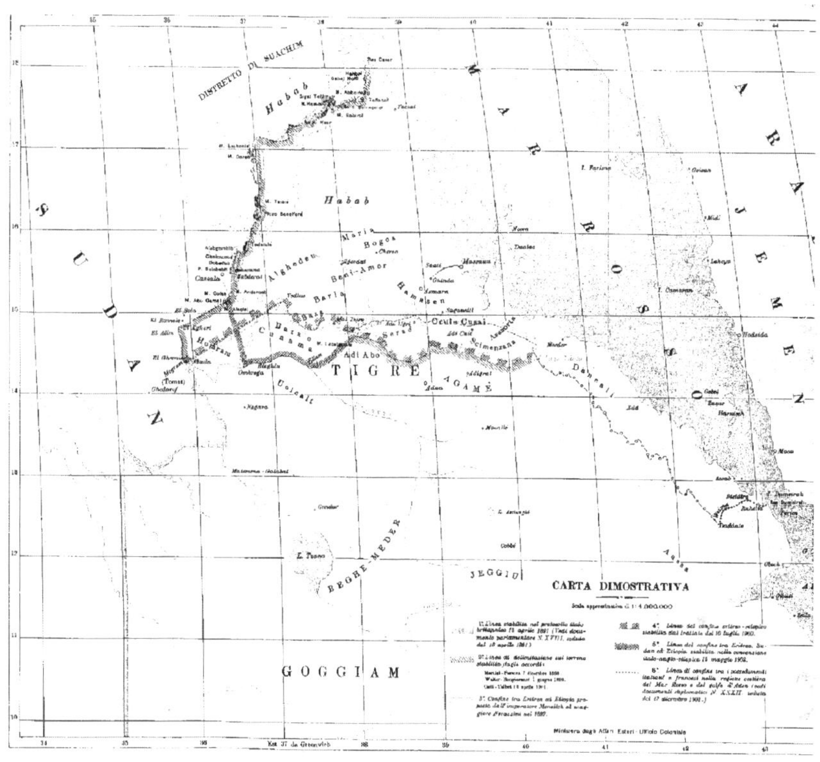

-·-·-·- Line of frontier between Dankalia and Ethiopia as laid down in the Convention between Italy and Ethiopia of the 16th May, 1908.

MAP

TO

ILLUSTRATE THE FRONTIER

BETWEEN

ERITREA AND THE SOUDAN,

AND

ERITREA AND ETHIOPIA.

See Protocol, Great Britain and Italy,
April 15th, 1891. No. 289, p. 949.
,, Local Agreements, Italy and Egypt,
December 7th, 1898. No. 340, p. 1110.
June 1st, 1899. No. 342, p. 1113.
April 16th, 1901. No. 343, p. 1115.
,, Treaty, Italy and Ethiopia,
July 10th, 1900. No. 125, p. 460.
,, Treaty, Great Britain, Italy, and Ethiopia,
May 15th, 1902. No. 100, p. 433.
,, Protocols, France and Italy,
January, 24th, 1900. No. 200, p. 663.
July 10th, 1901. No. 201, p. 664.

not be accommodated by either the Italian penal or civilian codes. Examples of these measures can be found well-documented in Nadel's (1945: 86) work on the Beni Amer community. For example, the Italians transformed the feudal office of the paramount chief, or the clan-chief, into a paid political office. The Italians also transformed the feudal obligation that the serfs had been required to pay into a state system of taxation. Here, it can be argued, in the Weberian tradition, that these acts amount to the conversion of these traditional offices and posts into bureaucratic offices and posts intended to serve and enable the new, modern administrative system. These changes do not appear to qualify as a status of indirect rule, because instead of setting up indigenous administrative structure, these were merely made to serve as tools of the colonial order of direct rule. In the face of such philosophy, they had to design politico-administrative mechanisms and systems that served their intention. Thus, the compartmentalisation of Eritrea into various administrative regions was no more than a tool for more effective rule of the territory.

In conclusion, the introduction of a provincial administrative structure was founded on the ideas of the liberal civic secular institutions of the Roman legal tradition. Italian colonialism transplanted these European administrative structures into the colonial society. Seen from the process of nation formation, therefore, the establishment of such administrative structures sets in place the basic foundation, in the objective sense, for the development of a nation.

The Treaty of Wechale and Its Impact

It is well known that while certain events and processes promote the creation of nations and states, others impede them. Conventions and treaties are some of these events and processes, and are not only juridical acts that bind signatories, but also have socio-economic implications and meanings. Many nations and states have been brought into existence as a consequence of conventions and treaties. Social history furnishes us with countless examples. The Westphalia Peace Treaty (1648) produced several dynastic territorial states (Smith 1986: 11). The congress of Vienna (Schulze 1998: 205) led to the creation of central European nation. The Versailles Treaty (1919), which paved the way for the principle of self-determination, facilitated the creation of the east European nations, and the Treaty of Berlin (1885) resulted in producing the present day African states (Duchacek 1987). The Versailles Treaty, not only explicitly endorsed the idea and philosophy of the creation of nations which was to result from the exercise of the right of self-determination, but also contributed to the actual formation, consolidation and perpetuation of nations. The fundamental tenet of this conceptualisation is that nations are amenable to construction and deconstruction. Hence, in history, conventions and treaties have often constructed or destroyed nations. As a political theory or philosophical belief, the doctrine which is commonly known as the 'Wilsonian Doctrine'–formulated after the end of World War I–established the theoretical and legal bases of the principle of self-determination in this century for the purpose of exercising the right to create a nation (cf. Wiberg 1983: 44). More closely related to our subject is the Berlin Conference of 1885. European powers sat in Berlin and divided the map of Africa into pieces. Latter they put their treaty into practice thereby creating artificial nations. By arguing along the lines of this perception, this section attempts to illustrate how the treaty of Wechale contributed to the emergence of present-day Eritrea not only physically, but also psychologically – in the minds of Eritrean nationalists.

As we have seen above, Eritrea was created as a result of the treaties and conventions signed between local, regional and global actors and powers. Some treaties, particularly those between Abyssinia and Italy, carried a special weight. The Wechale Treaty was the first official document which required Ethiopia to relinquish any claim it might have had on Eritrea. That treaty, in the Eritrean nationalists' eyes, proved two things. First, it was evidence that Eritrea was not an integral part of Ethiopia (EPLF p. 25, 1977; ELF 1971, 1975). Second, it indicated that Ethiopia itself was as much in the process of being formed as a unified modern state as Eritrea. Before Abyssinia succeeded in accomplishing its own process of formation, Italy effectively snatched Eritrea away. This is why Menelik entered freely into treaties with Italy, pursuing other priorities instead of trying to save Eritrea from the Italians in the Battle of Adwa and after. Both the south and Eritrea were territories outside the domain Menelik sought to conquer – he preferred to continue his expansion in the south, in part, because Eritrea was in the hand of the Italians. Eritrean nationalists argue that Menelik was not prepared to pay the necessary price for a territory that had never been under his control.

The Treaty of Wechale

The rapprochement between Italy and the Shewa rulers dates back to the 1870's and 1880's (Dilebo 1974: 221, Negash 1987: 1), when King Menelik signed a treaty in 1883 with Italy establishing a commercial connection between Shewa and Assab. In addition to commercial interests, Menelik's diplomatic manoeuvre was also driven by the need to procure weapons. The competition for power was becoming increasingly acute, particularly between the Amharas and Tigreans. This competition forced Menelik to do everything in his power to get diplomatic recognition and armaments. The power struggle between Shewa and Tigray, without any doubt, had contributed to the emergence, consolidation and persistence of the colony of Eritrea. According to Dilebo (1974), Menelik, in his effort to seize the imperial throne from the Tigrean rulers and in his intention to invade the South, started to play the game of, 'firearms politics'. Following that aim, he entered into trade accords, and subsequently had to trade off Eritrea as a material compensation for his firearms supply.

Sven Rubenson (1976), however, makes a more generous interpretation than that made by Dilebo. He claims that Menelik never sided with the enemies of Ethiopia. He adds, however, that Menelik's contribution to the defence of Ethiopia was marginal. It is clear from the accounts given by Rubenson that the power struggle between the Abyssinian leaders was the chief reason behind the genesis of the Treaty of Wechale and the subsequent loss of Eritrea.

> In the very last year of Yohannis's reign, however, Minilik came perilously close to allying himself with Ethiopia's potentially most dangerous enemy, Italy. In October 1887, he had promised neutrality, and neutrality only, on condition that the Italians dropped all territorial aspirations. This attitude he seems to have maintained throughout the first half of 1888. The change came when he began to fear that Yohannis would eventually attack him. Now he needed the Italians more than they needed him. He wanted the promised rifles - and more if possible. He undertook to pay for them at Aseb, but was certainly aware that he would be requested to pay in terms of future territorial concessions as well, if he succeeded to hold his own and eventually replace Yohannis as Emperor. It was in this situation that the treaty of Wichale was conceived in Rome in August-September 1888" (Rubenson 1976: 384)

Apparently, it was in the Rome agreement between Menelik and Italy, before the death of Yohannes, that the act of "territorial concession" was initiated. Menelik was negotiating behind Yohannes's back with Italy in order to secure firearms and the throne of Abyssinia. Therefore, it was with a clear conscience, and by conscious preference, that Menelik shaped his foreign policy. He was quite aware that its subsequent outcome was to be the cession of territories, though territories which were not currently under his domain.

The predominant view in this line of argumentation seems to be that Eritrea, an Ethiopian territory, was lost because of the power intrigues and rivalry between the Abyssinian leaders. On the other hand, these conspiracies and treaties signed with the Western powers and regional actors demonstrated not only that the Abyssinian state was yet in its formative stage, but also that there were no demarcating lines that clearly defined the Abyssinian state. Abyssinia was actively engaged in activities of expansion and conquest, on the one hand, and centralisation on the other. In that sense, the Abyssinian state actively participated in the scheme of partition for Africa, first, by conquering and adding alien people to its own territory, and second by centralising its domains. On the other hand, by entering into treaties and conventions with various Western powers in general, and with Italy in particular, the Abyssinian State was a vital actor in bringing Eritrea into existence.

This highlights the question of why Abyssinia signed the various treaties and conventions with Italy concerning Eritrea in the first place, and continued to sign accords which affirmed and reaffirmed Italy's sovereignty over Eritrea. In conjunction with the events of the Battle of Adwa, the related question of why Abyssinia did not attempt to dislodge Italy from Eritrea when it had an ample opportunity to do so remains a point of controversy. "One major question surrounding the Battle of Adwa is why Menelik did not pursue his advantage in chasing the Italians from the highlands or even attempted to liberate the coast itself. In fact, Menelik did enter Eritrea and seize the fort at Adi Ugri. However, by March 18, 1896, Menelik was on his way back to Addis Ababa, leaving Mengesha and Alula in command in the north" (Sherman 1980: 12). Scholars, as well as politicians, have tried to answer these questions and have come up with a variety of suggestions, most of the time deriving from their political convictions, and through a biased interpretation of history. The various suggestions can be summed up into four hypotheses:

a) The 'Eritrea had never been part of Abyssinia' hypothesis. According to this view, the reason why Menelik did not pursue the vanquished Italians to drive them out of Eritrea was because Eritrea was not thought of as part of Ethiopia. One observer comments, "Perhaps because Menelik was expanding southward and had never controlled the north, Italy was allowed to keep its Eritrean possession" (Machida 1987: 17). Menelik fought and defeated the Italians inside Ethiopian territory. When they were pushed back to Eritrea he knew that he had reached his jurisdictional limits, so he interrupted the engagement and turned back. It is also argued that Ethiopia itself was not a centralised and unified state. The condition of Ethiopia at that time can rightly be characterised by the prevalence of different tributary feudal kingdoms and landlords, already engaged in bitter rivalries, with raids and counter-raids to expand and control more territories and claim the title of king of kings. By the time Menelik ascended to the throne, Italy had almost completed its conquest of Eritrea. Therefore, he could not claim Eritrea. So the formation of modern Ethiopia and modern Eritrea took place simultaneously (cf. ELF 1971: 17, 1975: 13; EPLF 1977: 6; Sherman 1980: 32; Pedersen 1987: 193). In that respect, the claim that Eritrea had invariably been an integral part of Ethiopia lacks credibility. Furthermore, whatever the intentions and motives underlying Menelik's actions were, it seems that the treaties negotiated between Ethiopia and Italy were signed with free will.

> The importance of the two treaties (Ucciali 1889; and Addis Ababa; 1900) lies in the inconvertible fact that they were freely negotiated by Menelik, the undoubted master of the united Ethiopia, in his hour of triumph. In them were fixed the frontiers between Eritrea and Ethiopia ... It follows, therefore, that on treaty or juridical grounds, the Emperor Menelik's successors can have no claim on Eritrea (E.A. Chapman Andrew, 'Memorandum on Eritrea', Public Record Office, J2807/2807/1, May 29, 1942) (quoted in Amar 1992: 23)

b) The 'Conspiracy' hypothesis. Some have argued that Menelik's action was motivated by the scheme of dividing the two Tigrinya-speakers, i.e.: the Tigrinya-speakers in Tigray and the Tigrinya-speakers in Eritrea. By dividing them, he intended to reaffirm Amhara domination and hegemony in Ethiopia. Several scholars have commented implicitly or explicitly on this conspiracy theory. Dilebo (1974: 222) writes that Menelik signed a treaty with the Italians in 1889 to hand over the whole of Medri Bahri and its people so that he could secure the imperial throne and the title of Emperor from Emperor Yohannes' son and designated successor, Rasi Mengesha Yohannes. Pedersen shares this view, and notes that Menelik, by letting the Italians stay in the highland of Eritrea, intended to weaken the position of Rasi Mengesha. Menelik was not so sure about Mengesha's loyalty. Thus, by dividing Mengesha's base region, Menelik hoped to weaken his potential opponent's power base (Pedersen 1987: 52-3). A clear illustration of this hypothesis is a letter sent to the Italians by Menelik on the death of Emperor Yohannes urging them to occupy Asmara,

> I would beg your Majesty to give orders to all the generals in Massawa not to listen to the words of the rebels who are to be found in some parts of Tigre and forbid the passage of arms... I would like the soldiers of your Majesty to occupy Asmara and make sure that this route is well guarded and defended. I allow myself to say these things to your Majesty, because I see that God, in his justice, gives me the throne that for so many years I had the right to have and which will give rest and peace to all Ethiopia (quoted by Dilebo 1974: 230).

c) The 'Posterity Threat' hypothesis: the threat Italy posed to Abyssinia in the future. According to this hypothesis, Menelik knew that substantial reinforcements and material were on the way from Italy. He chose to maintain Abyssinia's own sovereignty and independence by sacrificing Eritrea (Sherman 1980:12). Sherman adds, "In effect, Menelik "traded" Eritrea and its inhabitants to the Italians to ensure his title and crown" (Sherman 1980: 11). Rubenson contributes his share in the threat hypothesis by saying that there was always the possibility that the Italians would eventually support rival forces and annex territory, etc. if he failed to follow through with the treaty (Rubenson 1976: 386). A slightly different view maintains that Menelik achieved his great victory at a high price (Wolde Giorgis 1989: 75). Therefore, because of the price already paid and because his army was poorly equipped, the continuation of the campaign would have been inexpedient. Hence, he preferred to discontinue it, and instead enter into a peace agreement with them. The credibility of this view is placed in serious doubt for two reasons. First, the Italians incurred a serious defeat, and as a result, they were not in any position to offer much resistance. Second, in terms of morale and weaponry, the Ethiopians were well off after the victory. For instance, they captured 65 cannons and 11, 000 rifles (Dilebo 1974: 234).

d) The 'Preference of south-west over Eritrea' hypothesis. After pointing out that there was no military or diplomatic impediment to liberating Adigrat, Asmara, and Massawa from the Italians, Dilebo (1974: 235-6) argues that the chief reason was that Menelik preferred to secure his holdings and conquer more of the south-west regions and people, Oromo-Sidama and Kaficho. Delibo's explanation of Menelik's reasons for leaving Eritrea in the hands of Italians after his Adwa victory, moving instead to the south-west, is that he had unfinished business in the south-west. Menelik chose to finish the process of occupation that he had begun before the Italian invasion of Tigray. In addition, Dilebo suggests two reasons why the southwest was so important. First, the abundance of land and labour, and second, the availability of rich natural resources.

In conclusion, these hypothesises or propositions point in one direction, supporting the contention that Eritrea was not part of a united and centralised Ethiopia. In addition, they enable us to draw a safe inference that both Eritrea and Ethiopia emerged as centralised modern territorial entities at the same time. This might explain why Menelik, on different occasions, freely signed treaties with Italy that confirmed Italian sovereignty over Eritrea. The discussion that follows seeks to evaluate the impact of the Wechale Treaty on Eritrean nationalism.

The Impact of the Wechale Treaty on Eritrean Nationalism

Whatever motivation and underlying rationale for Menelik's behaviour might be sought, one thing is clear: that Abyssinia bore as great a responsibility as other actors in establishing Eritrea as an Italian colony. The treaties, conventions and improvisations signed by Abyssinia helped establish the basis for the emergence of Eritrea. If those treaties and accords had not been signed and respected, the destiny of Eritrea might have been quite different. How did Eritrean nationalists appraise it? What effect did it have on the evolution of Eritrean nationalism? These are some of the questions that can be posed in relation to the theme of this section. The most relevant issue that needs to be addressed is the implication of the treaties on Eritrean nationalism.

Scholars of nation formation quite often emphasise the ways in which symbols, mythologies, historical fabrications, legends, and imagined genealogical descent contribute to the creation of nations and national sentiments. Sometimes, even a fallacious perception of oneself can serve as the underlying foundation for the genesis of a nation. We find this view cogently summarised in the now classic, monumental work of Ernest Renan (1882). Renan stated, perhaps somewhat ironically, that "forgetting, I would even go so far as to say historical error, is a crucial factor in the creation of a nation" (Renan 1882: 11). If we accept this statement, the axiom will then be that it is not the truth of what you claim that determines the final outcome, but the success you show in convincing yourself and others of your claims and beliefs. Eritrean nationalists believed that the historical treaties and conventions between Abyssinia and Italy constituted a solid foundation for the truth of their legitimate claim for separate nationhood. Particularly during the armed struggle for independence, the issue of treaties between Italy and Abyssinia that led to the colonisation of Eritrea, especially the Wechale Treaty, was used to mobilise and convince people that the Ethiopian claim was groundless and the struggle for independence was right and just (see Sherman 1980: 32). Additionally, the Eritrean nationalist discourse emphasised the view that Italian colonialism created the Eritrean entity, not as the Ethiopian side tried to present it, that Eritrea had always been an integral part of Ethiopia (see Wolde Giorgis 1989: 69f). Many observers also argued that the beginning of the formation of modern Eritrea started with the genesis of the Italian colonial rule and the treaties that facilitated its realisation. David Pool for instance notes:

> It was the start of a process which created Eritrea as a political unit, joining together the nomadic west and the settled peasant highland, forging an Eritrean sense of identity which was to become the root of the ensuing struggle for independence in the 1960s. ...the Italian occupation established the basis of a different historical and political claim for Eritrean independence and set in motion the socio-economic forces which were to underpin an Eritrean national identity (Pool 1979: 17).

It is well documented that on three[2] different occasions Menelik reaffirmed the claim of Italy over Eritrea. According to the Eritreans, Menelik's "treaties and front demarcations with the Italians between 1889 and 1896, effectively establishing the political boundaries of Eritrea, "were not the work of hasty or dictated treaties; they were free and formal acts of the Ethiopian state."[79]" These demarcations were to be the basis of future Eritrean nationalist sentiments (Sherman 1980: 32). In the eyes of the Eritreans, the Ethiopian action represented de facto recognition that the Medri Bahri was a politically separate entity from Ethiopia. The Wechale Treaty, the Eritreans argued, effectively forfeits any Ethiopian claim on Eritrea (Sherman 1980: 32). Based on this conviction, the Eritreans attempted to articulate their nationalism and their view of a separate nationhood. Throughout the national liberation struggle, Eritrean nationalists tried to establish legitimacy for their struggle based on the colonial creation of Eritrea. The Wechale Treaty occupies an important space in the collective memory of the Eritreans. It was the first legal document with international status and formed a foundation for the creation of Eritrea.

From the point of view of nationalism, beliefs such as those described above are important, because any society needs a starting point for the genesis of its history, its nationhood or its identity. The Eritrean nationalists had to trace their arguments to a point in time from which the existence of a united Eritrea had originated. If the struggle for the independence of Eritrea was to be legitimised and justified, and if at the same time, the need for a set of internal beliefs regarding a common history and identity were to be fulfilled, a construction of consistent history and myths was needed. A national ideology must be constructed in order to create the nation. As Ernest Gellner would say, it is nationalism that creates nations, and not vice versa. Therefore, people believed in the reality that Eritrea was a creation of Italian colonial rule. As a result, the treaties and agreements that contributed to the emergence of colonial rule are considered important components of the emergence of Eritrea. In that context, the Wechale Treaty had important political implications for the growth of Eritrean nationalism.

LEGAL AND ADMINISTRATIVE UNIFICATION

The definition of a nation as an 'imagined community' – an 'abstract community' residing under a common political and legal system–fits very well with the civic conception of nation. The cohesiveness of the legal and political system and the centralisation of certain people under this politico-legal order is viewed as a condition for the emergence of nations. This notion got its start in conjunction with the outbreak of the French Revolution. Following the French Revolution, political philosophers and theorists began to derive their philosophical theories and ideals from the thoughts and ideals of the Revolution with the ambition of analysing the project of nation formation. "The political theory of 'nation', as developed by Diderot and Condorcet, and recorded by Abbé Siéyés in 1789 ('a union of individuals governed by *one* law, and represented by the same law giving assembly'), speaks of a collection of individuals united in supporting a perceived interest; the hierarchical or privileging connotations of 'realm', 'country', 'kingdom', 'territory', and 'race' are smelted into the usage of the 'nation'" (Snead 1990: 231). Of course, this purely political conceptualisation of a nation has been criticised as inadequate, particularly from the eclectic school of thought. Critics mean that the notion suggested in the above conceptualisation of the nation excludes important dimensions which complement the understanding of a nation, nevertheless it is recognised as a useful instrumental framework for capturing and analysing the formation of nations. This is particularly true with the case of France and England and those nations that followed their examples (see Schulze 1998)

The issue of social integration has invariably been a point of contention throughout human social history. In this respect, we encounter two central, competing theories that pertain to social integration through coercion and through a common value system. In the former variant, it is assumed that there exists a dominant political power that imposes integration. In the latter variant, a common value system is envisioned by which individual members come into cohere voluntarily because of the common values that bind them. However, under close scrutiny it appears that the gap between the two is not as great as it seems to be. This is because eventually, even the coercion model may foster the adoption of a common value system through the mobilisation and implementation of legitimising and socialising ideologies to ensure its sustainability and durability (Richmond 1994: 289). In our case, therefore, the analogy to be drawn is that the imposition of the territorial unit called Eritrea by the colonial power structure could be paralleled to that of the coercion model–both in terms of territoriality and societal circumvention. The resultant economic division of labour, communications and administrative integration, social differentiation with its concomitant mutual interdependency, leading to the emergence of some sort of common value system, could be likened with the common value system model.

Scholars of colonialism (as was discussed in the theoretical part) have argued that present-day African political units are the products of colonial rule. Colonialism is perceived as having set in motion the processes of nation formation, *inter alia*, through engendering centralised political and legally standardised units. According to proponents of this conceptualisation, the principal legacy of European rule was the effort to implant a European system of bureaucratic politico-legal administrative structures. The political precept reinforcing this notion of colonial legacy is that, as a result of the colonialists' attempt to reproduce the political and legal traditions which were in place in their homelands, they initiated the process of nation formation–either wittingly or unwittingly. The model, 'state-to-nation' process introduced to explain the African situation is an application of the Western historical experience in which the state assumed the responsibility for constructing the nation. Therefore, it is argued that the colonial state and its successor, the post-colonial state, carried the responsibility of building a nation.

Viewed from this angle, the Italian rule in Eritrea laid the basic infrastructural foundations. In terms of political and administrative structures, the Italians organised Eritrea into modern, compact administrative divisions or provinces (Gayim 1993: 59), based on legal-rational principles and political philosophy. This hierarchical structure produced what Rokkan (1973) calls a centre-periphery division. The evolution of the centre-periphery division and the eventual domination of the centre over the periphery in terms of culture, political and economic power, etc. are viewed by Rokkan as a vital precondition for the emergence of a nation. Italian colonialism created an Eritrea legally organised into urban[3] centre and rural periphery divisions through the act of creating different hierarchically organised administrative divisions, as well as by creating a centre equipped with modern technological products embodied in the capital city. This indicates from the political and legal perspective that Italian rule had initiated a centralising political rule unprecedented in the history of Eritrean communities.

From a jurisdictional point of view, a community starts to be seen as a cohesive, centralised society, when it is governed under the jurisdiction of a common, standardised rule of law. The Italians applied both modern and traditional laws in administering the Eritrean communities. Sherman (1980: 14) notes that during Italian colonial rule, the following four types of law were put into place: a) the Italian penal code, which was applicable to all inhabitants of the colony; b) the Italian civil code, which served as the law in civil cases where one part of those involved was Italian; c) Islamic law, when the person(s) involved were of Islamic faith; and d) customary law exercised in civil matters involving the Christian community (see also Trevaskis 1960: 27).

These four components constituted the aggregated body of the legal system in the colony. Colonial rule, by endorsing and incorporating the traditional codes of behaviour in the modern colonial legal system, established, in a general sense, a co-ordinated legal order. The traditional law enforcers were effectively absorbed in the new legal system in the sense that the work they performed was recognised and made part of the new legal order. Here, one can argue justifiably that Italians failed to fully dismantle customary law and replace it with modern formal law. In fact, the Italians ensured that it was kept intact, especially when it served their purpose, or at least did not stand in their way. Further, a critical reading reveals that different laws were applied to different communities. Hence, a uniform and unitary jurisdictional order was not introduced. The veracity of this argument cannot be disputed, but the fact remains that the disparate laws formed a corporate body of law accepted and recognised by the colonial state. In addition, the sociological significance of the arrangement of the corporate system of law lies in the recognition and acceptance of the various elements as being socially binding. In other words, the enactment and binding nature of the various laws was accepted by the colonial power, thereby producing an integrated general law. The overall effect of the establishment of an aggregate body of legal system was to be witnessed primarily, and above all, in the peace and security of the territory. Pacification and control are invariably associated with stable administration and centralised political and legal arrangements. In this respect, many observers have noted that the Italians enjoyed remarkable success in pacifying and controlling Eritrean society (Trevaskis 1960, Longrigg 1945: 132, Negash 1987:151-4)

Trevaskis, an official of the British Military Administration (BMA), wrote, "perhaps Italy's greatest contribution to Eritrea was that she maintained law and order in a country where they had previously been unknown"(Trevaskis 1960: 104). However, the peace and tranquillity which was established under the Italian rule cannot merely be attributed to the common rule of law which was the upshot of the establishment of the corporate body of a pervading legal system. Apparently, it was a combination of multiple factors, which generated the unprecedented peace and security. Certainly, the pacification of the indigenous communities took different forms and obviously various mechanisms were employed. The heavy-handed nature of colonial rule also contributed greatly to this peace and security. Yet, a peaceful and tranquil society was in the process of transformation, which indicated that a new form of society was coming into existence.

Clearly, the legal and administrative changes that were introduced by Italian colonial rule indicate the direction in which the society was advancing. It might have been very slow, but movement that paved the way for the nation formation process had commenced. The politico-legal integration was further enhanced under the British Administration and the Federation period (the subject of chapter five). The overriding socio-economic transformation, which was set into motion by Italian colonialism, will be discussed in the following chapter.

SUMMARY AND CONCLUSION

Boundary delineation and territorial integration are the first basic measures, or requirements, in the process of nation formation. They are the beginnings from which everything moves. When these are achieved, the remaining elements gradually ensue. According to the notion of territoriality, the identification of a people with a specific territory is a precondition for the emergence of a nation. And this identification of the people with the territory is the result of a centralised existence whose primary marker is its name. The personal identities of individuals are, in part, defined by their territorially-delimited country. Thus, they are free from the traditional forms of identity (non-territorial, parochial, primordial, etc.). This perception conforms to the emergence of what Anderson (1991) calls 'imagined community'. The basic theme of the theory of imagined community is that because of the conception of territoriality, those who reside within a specific territory develop the sense that they are bound together and are different from those who reside outside that territory – although they may never meet face to face. Thus, they believe that they constitute a nation. The importance of territoriality in the formation of nations has always been of a substantial significance. Emphasising this importance Armstrong notes,

> Certainly, early contiguous settlement provided resources for a relatively manageable center...The sense of territorial identity that arose from this contiguous settlement fostered concern for fixed language boundaries and political frontiers, which in turn contributed to polity stability (Armstrong 1982: 296).

The discussion in this chapter has focused predominantly on four vital features of the processes of nation formation in Eritrea, notably territorial centralisation, the demarcation of international boundaries, the compartmentalisation or provincialisation of the territory, and politico-legal centralisation. In the theoretical debate regarding nation formation, a lack of any of these elements is viewed as inhibiting the emergence of a nation. Thus for a nation to arise the fulfilment of these aspects is a necessary prerequisite. These aspects were fulfilled in Eritrea as a consequence of Italian colonialism. Their fulfilment represented the rise of one of the important dimensions of nation formation. Italian colonialism, by effecting these aspects of nation formation, established essential prerequisites for the emergence of the Eritrean nation. Once these requirements were put in place the cohesion and integration of the society became increasingly palpable. This is because territorial integration paved the way for other types of integration. Among such types of integration, social integration is the most important. When Italian colonialism delimited the territory of Eritrea, it also delimited the social boundary of Eritreans by giving citizenship to those who happened to live within the territorial boundaries while denying it to those outside that boundary. One cannot simply cross these boundaries. Legal constraints were introduced for moving out or in that boundary accompanied with sanctions.

It was in this way that Eritrea was created. However, Ethiopian nationalists have always claimed that Eritrean had been an integral part of Ethiopia throughout the 3000-year history of existence of that country. This claim runs counter to the view that Eritrea is the creation of Italian colonialism. This conceptualisation of the existence of Ethiopia, and the belief of a unified Eritrea as being an integral part of Ethiopia throughout history, are unsupported by the historical evidence. Without delving further into details, we can establish that both Eritrea and Ethiopia in their modern form are creations of the 19th century. If, for instance, we take the issue of the name Ethiopia, it is argued that the original name Ethiopia[4] had nothing to do with the present Ethiopia. In fact, in a previous historical period the name referred to Meroe, in present Sudan, and in other times, it referred to all black Africa. Modern Abyssinia was renamed as Ethiopia in 1941, when after the British recaptured the country from the Italians, Emperor Haile Selassie issued a decree that the country was officially to be known as Ethiopia (Perham 1969: 15). Contrary to the "Ethiopianist" claim, it is argued that the Axumite Kingdom had only covered the province of Tigray in present-day Ethiopia and the southern and coastal area of present-day Eritrea (cf. Longrigg 1945, Pool 1979: 14; Sherman 1980: 5; Machida 1987:12). Therefore, the mythology of 3000 years of Ethiopian existence seems to be based on shaky ground. Mythology is an important part of the nation formation project. It has served and is still serving as a useful function of legitimisation. But the point to be made as elucidated by Margery Perham is:

> All nations need the support of a private mythology, most of all when they are struggling to be born or reborn, but they should not expect other people to accept their illusion (Perham 1969: XVI).

Perham made this comment in reference to the Ethiopian mythology. This study's point of departure is that both Eritrea and Ethiopia in their present forms are the creation of the 19th century. Further, they assumed their present geo-political shape during almost the same historical period. The treaties and conventions alluded to in this chapter are the evidence for the when and the how of the creation of modern Eritrea. For the purposes of this study, this has been taken as the starting point for the nation formation process in Eritrea.

Notes

1. The treaties and conventions between Italy and Ethiopia concerning Eritrea were amended several times, representing a formal adjustment to the constantly changing circumstances. After the battle of Adwa, various treaties with the intention of consolidating, reaffirming and updating agreements were introduced, for instance January 1, 1897, June 1, 1899, May 10 and July 10, 1900, April 13, 1901, May 15, 1902, May 16, 1908 (see Dilebo 1974, Ghebre-Ab 1993, Gayim 1993)
2. On three separate occasions, in the Wechale Treaty on May 2, 1889; after the Battle of Adwa of March 1, 1896; and in the Addis Ababa Peace Treaty of October 26, 1896, Menelik affirmed Italian sovereignty over Eritrea (Sherman 1980: 32, Dilebo 1974: 236). Both scholars mentioned share the assumption that Menelik had ample opportunity to drive out the Italians from the highland of Eritrea and port of Massawa at the three occasions mentioned, but that instead he preferred to enter into treaties, which affirmed the sovereignty of Italy over the colony of Eritrea.
3. Towards the end of Italian colonial rule, it is assumed that around 20% of the Eritrean population was residing in towns, that is, one-fifth of the entire society had changed its mode of life to an urban mode of life.
4. The term Ethiopia is assumed to emanate from the Greek term "Aethiopes" which means "burned face". But as it was used by ancient writers it referred to dark-skinned peoples stretching from Africa to India, as they were also referred to as "Western" and "Eastern" Ethiopians. From the 7th Century BC, the term came to be used to

express the civilisation of the region between the Blue Nile and the Atbara River in present day Sudan, and Meroe was the capital of that civilisation (cf. Gayim 1993: 265-66). The Abyssinian kingdom of Axum did not refer to itself as Ethiopia, but rather some inscriptions of the Axumite Kingdom indicated that they were bordered by "the land of Ethiopia", in reference to the Kingdom of Meroe (Gayim 1993: 266, also cf. Perham 1969: 13-4). Margery Perham, however notes that it was probably the immigrant Syrian monk who translated the Bible from Greek to Ge'ez who first applied Ethiopia to Axum (Perham 1969: 15).

Chapter 4

SOCIO-ECONOMIC INTEGRATION: CAPITALIST PENETRATION UNDER EUROPEAN RULE

INTRODUCTION

Socio-economic integration is directly connected with socio-economic transformation. Social theorists have argued that the transformation of society in social and economic terms leads to an interdependence of society that necessitates integration and cohesion. Socio-economic transformation fundamentally accomplishes two functions. First, it dismantles – or at least shakes up – the archaic, primordial and parochial traditional social structures. Second, it either partially or wholly replaces those traditional structures with semi-modern and modern structures. This is the basic assumption of the theory of developmentalism. Theories of modernisation, evolution and diffusion teach us how, among other things, the steady and gradual progress in the socio-economic sphere advances human organisation into an increasingly expanding, more complex, sophisticated, flexible, socially mobile, and adaptive societal organisational structure. Classical sociologists such as Spencer, Durkheim, Tönnies, Marx, and Weber founded their monumental works along this line of argumentation (Harrison 1988, Sztompka 1993). Contemporary sociological knowledge has made a substantial revision of these classical theories and approaches, which are more or less based upon biological metaphors and theory. Yet, contemporary developmental sociology still seems to have stuck with the modernisation, evolution, and diffusion theories, albeit with a different tone and a variety of versions, globalisation theory being the currently fashionable one. An analogy can be drawn from these sociological tenets with respect to the project of nation formation. The perception that economic integration has the effect of political assimilation is stressed by many scholars of social science, "purely economically determined market relations have a politically unifying effect" (Weber 1967: 163). Modernist theorists such as Anderson, Gellner, Hobsbawm and Bendix; and communication theorists like Deutsch, emphasise the importance of socio-economic transformation in the form of industrialism or modernism which gave rise to the formation of nation (see Smith 1998). Social mobilisation theorists such as Huntington (1968) are also interested in the conjunction between institutions and the emergent new social groups.

Taking this basic sociological understanding as our point of departure, if we embark on analysing, interpreting and explaining the implications of the European capitalist penetration into Eritrean society, we are undoubtedly confronted with divergent views and contentions. For the purpose of simplicity and analytical manageability, we can classify these divergent views and contentions into two categories, notably proponents and opponents of the view that a social transformation had taken place under Italian rule. According to the proponents, sufficient socio-economic innovation had taken place to enable us to draw the conclusion that colonial rule engendered considerable structural change (cf. Gray & Silberman 1948, Pool 1979; Gebre-Medhin 1979, 1989; Sherman 1980; Houtart 1980, 1982; Leonard 1982; Killion 1985; Pedersen 1987; Bondestam 1989). In contrast, opponents argue that colonial rule did not engender significant structural changes (cf. Haliday 1971; Erlich 1982, 1983; Negash 1987, Wolde Giorgis 1989, Araya 1990). The predisposition that this study takes as its point of departure is that substantial structural change did, in fact, take place, setting into motion the process of formation of an Eritrean nation.

It is often argued within sociology that social, economic, political or technological transformations lead to the emergence of new social structures, classes and groups, accompanied by differentiation and specialisation of functions in society. This, in turn, leads to the generation of specific new appropriate structures, which fit the emergent modes of relationships and conditions. Social actors, in their quest for specific purposive goals, trigger both intended and unintended outcomes. Sometimes those unintended outcomes may have far-reaching consequences, altering the societal landscape severely. It is with these phenomena in mind that the effects of capitalist penetration in the Eritrean society are scrutinised. The communities that later constituted the Eritrean society had a very minimum common experience of integrated socio-economic life prior to Italian colonial rule. The task of the welding together of the disparate ethno-linguistic groups from what was, at best, a tenuous co-existence, into a homogenous political society was a complex process. However, such a complex process would seem to presuppose a substantial socio-economic base, which would serve to incorporate the different ethnic groups into an integrated network of economic activities (see Leonard 1982: 59). According to Leonard, this material basis corresponds to the subjective formation of a common consciousness, which at least mitigates hostility between, and promotes understanding among, the various ethnic groups. In elucidating the effect of the European colonial rule on the various ethno-linguistic groups in terms of a material basis of integration, Leonard notes,

> The intervention of considerable sums of Italian and British capital during a period of 63 years effected profound economic, social and political changes (Leonard 1982: 60).

Pedersen (1987) supports this proposition when he argues that at the end of colonial rule Eritrea emerged as a qualitatively different socio-economic entity. The cornerstone of such propositions is the belief that a profound socio-economic transformation took place as a result of European colonial capitalist penetration. This, in turn, is believed to have shaped a common Eritrean national identity. The understanding here is that there is a direct connection or correspondence between material transformation and subjective consciousness. In other words, the belief is that socio-economic transformation will lead to the changes in the state of mind or consciousness.

This chapter attempts to elucidate the socio-economic transformation that took place under European colonial rule in Eritrea. In addition to the introduction and summary sections, the chapter is comprised of four sections. Section two scrutinises the changes in communication infrastructure. Section three examines economic innovation focusing on the industrial and agricultural sectors. The fourth section discusses the development of urbanisation. The last section examines the impact of capitalist penetration on social structure. While assessing these structural implications, the focus is centred on the emergence of modern social groups such as the working class, the urban middle classes, the bourgeoisie, and the intelligentsia.

COMMUNICATIONS INFRASTRUCTURE

This section will briefly discuss the expansion of the communications infrastructure under Italian colonial rule. Subsequently, its implications for the integration of the Eritrean society is assessed. Social communication theorists have argued in support of the connection between the increasing expansion of communication and nation formation. The research on nation formation, thus, emphasises the importance of the growth of communication infrastructures to the rise of nations (e.g. Hodgkin 1956, Lipset 1963, Deutch 1966, Smith 1983a). The underlying belief is that the presence of a pervasive communication network interconnects not only the various topographical regions, but it also facilitates the intermingling of the different classes and cultural, linguistic and religious groups. In other words, in terms of cartography, different geographical regions are interconnected and made functionally interdependent. And in terms of culture, politics, and economics, the various social groups are integrated in a process whereby a transcending and binding common identity is created. This is based on some commonly understood and accepted values-system, symbols, and myths. This development should not be viewed as a result of merely the infrastructural communication network, but also as a result of social communication. The expansiveness and pervasiveness of the communication infrastructure generates the conditions in which disparate groups and individuals with different socio-cultural backgrounds are able to interact, through its facilitating mechanisms in the social and geographic mobilisation. This, in turn, creates social networks, social relations and social communications that give rise to common social norms and value systems. One of the leading social scientists advocating the idea that the expansion of communication infrastructures strengthens the cohesion and integration of society is Karl W. Deutsch. Deutsch (1966) gives an elaborate exposition of the role played by communication technology in the formation of nations.

Thomas Hodgkin (1956) also discusses the significant role played by the expansion of the communication infrastructure in the emergence of nationalism in Africa. Another author, who discusses the prominence of the connection between communications technology and nationhood, particularly the dimension of the modern means of transportation, is Thomas Hylland Eriksen. Eriksen (1993:106) suggests that communications technology furnishes the basis for the integration of people into a nation-state by facilitating the integration of people into more complex and larger social systems. This is one upshot of the easy movement of people and goods from one corner of a territory to another. This also may have an unforeseen effect at the level of consciousness that induces the feeling of belonging to a nation. A further elaboration of this point can also be found in Durkheim's sociology, in particular in the notion of the division of labour. Durkheim (1984) depicts how the expansion of modern communications technology helps enable the concentration of population accompanied by the functional differentiation and specialisation that constitute the foundations of modern society. In short, the expansion of the communications technology is an indispensable condition for the rise of nations.

We will now discuss the development of communication technology in Eritrea. The major innovation that occurred in Eritrea as the consequence of the Italian colonial rule is conspicuously demonstrated in the field of communication, mainly the construction of roads, railways, telegraph, postal and telephone systems (cf. Pool 1979: 17, Killion 1985). Indeed, by the 1920s a remarkable achievement was registered. This achievement included 120 km of railway, 570 km of roads and 1,728 km of telegraph lines (Leonard 1982: 66). This expansionary trend continued unabated in the 1930s, and was reaching its peak when it was abruptly interrupted by the outbreak of Second World War. A further example of this rapid expansion and development could be seen in the construction of 1,176 km asphalt roads connecting the most important nascent urban centres. In all, by 1933, a total of 3,596 km of road system construction had been successfully completed (Mesghenna 1988: 186). This was an enormous project by Eritrean standards, and was a remarkably courageous venture, taking into consideration the investment of time, money, and energy necessary and the additional difficulty posed by the harsh topography.

The Italians were quite determined to modernise the communication infrastructure, and never hesitated to employ the best equipment that technology had to offer. Consequently, by 1939, the process of construction was sufficiently advanced that 25 postal offices and 67 telegraph lines were in operation, and 17 localities were equipped with telephone services. In the field of transportation the capacity of the port of Massawa was raised to 1,500 tons and that of the cableway transport to Asmara was raised to 500 tons per day (Leonard 1982:

68). According to the report of the Four Power Commission, at the outbreak of hostilities between the Allied Forces and Italy, there existed "846 transport enterprises and 383 construction enterprises" (FO 371-69370 Ch. 2, p.34). Furthermore, even with the termination of Italian rule and the establishment of British Administration, particularly in the early phase, industrial activity continued to flourish. A scheme by the Allied Powers to make Eritrea a support base in their military campaign against the Italo-German aggression during the remainder of the war reinforced the increased industrial activities. These activities included projects such as the "reconstruction and expansion of the airport of Gura and the Naval Base at Massawa" (FO 371-69370, Ch. 5, p.59). These projects were quite successful due to the adequate availability of heavy machinery and the presence of a skilled Italian work force. Under the British Administration, particularly during the war, the expansion of some sectors of the communication network even increased.

The table below presents the railway construction undertaken by the Italians between 1900-1930.

Table 4.1: Railway Construction

Date	Line	Length in km.
1904	Massawa - Ghenda	75
1910	Ghenda - Nefasit	26
1911	Nefasit - Arborobu	10
1911	Arborobu - Asmara	13
1922	Asmara - Keren	100
1928	Keren - Agordat	86
1929	Agordat - Tessenei	103

Source: constructed from ITALIAN COLONIALISM: A Case Study of Eritrea, 1869-1934 Motive, Praxis and Result (Mesghenna 1988: 181f)

The most conspicuous and important undertaking in the context of communication was the construction and expansion of a railway and road system, which stretched across almost the whole geographical and ethnic perimeters. As can be seen from the table, within a relatively short stretch of time, an extensive railway and road construction project was undertaken, revolutionising the communications landscape. The following facts can be cited as an illustration of the social implications of the communications infrastructure boom: daily, 420 tones of goods (153,000 tons annually) and 1720 persons (627, 800 annually) (EPLF, Italian Colonialism in Eritrea 1882-1941) were transported through the newly established railway system. The communications between the different regions and communities, coupled with the emergence of urban centres and agricultural and industrial project sites, resulted in much-increased interaction among the various ethno-linguistic groups. The urban centres became focal points for the rural population, and the extensive communication network facilitated this. The expansion of the communications infrastructure, therefore, accelerated the economic exploitation by the colonial powers, but it also created opportunities for the local population to move around with less constraint. Further, it geared the velocity of social and geographical mobility.

The foregoing discussion indicates how the development of the communications infrastructure was arguably the most outstanding, palpable success of the Italian colonial rule. It was a revolutionising innovation. This was true, in part, because it represented an unprecedented level of development in the history of the society. Its importance, of course, stretches beyond the facts of mere technological innovation. It was much more significant in its integrative role in the area of economy, social integration and administration. In elucidating the connection between communication technology and nationhood, Eriksen (1993: 105-6) identifies two kinds of communications technology, notably mass media and transportation. In reference to the latter, he notes,

> Modern transportation technology greatly facilitates the integration of people into larger social systems, increasing the flow of people and goods indefinitely. It creates conditions for the integration of people into nation-states, and in this way it may have important indirect effects at the level of consciousness in making people *feel* that they are members of the nation (Eriksen 1993: 106).

In conclusion, there can be no doubt that the communications infrastructure, which was an enormously significant contribution of Italian colonialism, played a great role in integrating and centralising the Eritrean society.

THE ECONOMIC SPHERE

The economic policy of Italy toward its colony of Eritrea was founded upon classic colonial economic doctrine. Hence, Eritrea was intended to serve as a source of raw materials for the metropolitan Italian industries on the one hand, and as a marketplace for Italian products, on the other. In pursuit of these two aims, the Italian colonial authority undertook an ambitious economic infrastructure that was expected to reinforce the expansionist aim of Italy (Sherman 1980: 15). The economy of Eritrea was completely integrated with the metropolitan economy of Italy. For instance, all goods produced in Eritrea were only allowed to be sold in Italy. On the other hand, the territory's needs of imported goods were only to be procured from Italy (see Mesghenna 1988). The colonial economic order produced an all-encompassing, centralised economic structure. In other words, an integrated economic system was established. A division of centre-periphery, or urban-centred and rural-centred economies that were contingent upon each other was established. This complementarity of the two economic spheres, notably the rural and the urban or the traditional and the modern, constituted a hierarchically-structured national economic system. Concomitantly, the emergence of the hierarchically-structured national economic system also had its effects in the social sphere (to be discussed later). In the long run, in the context of the process of nation formation, the overall significance of this economic integration and centralisation was to furnish one of the necessary prerequisites – a common economic life. This common economic life and resultant economic cohesion is an important contributing factor in the emergence of a nation.

The aim of this section is to investigate the economic changes that occurred under European colonial rule, and subsequently, to explore its implications for the nation formation process of Eritrea. The focus is centred on the industrial and agricultural sectors.

The Industrial Sector

In this sub-section a brief account of industrial development during both Italian and British rule will be presented. Industry was predominantly connected with military projects during the European colonial period. The Italian invasion of Abyssinia in 1936 and the allied war campaign in the Middle East during World War II significantly accelerated the industrial boom (Leonard 1982: 65). However, although the military preparations and the state of war at the mentioned occasions supported a great deal of the industrial development, other independent civilian industrial projects were also successful in establishing themselves. Eritrea was used as a military staging area on several different occasions: in the unsuccessful attempt to invade Abyssinia in 1896, in the invasion of both Somalia and Libya, in the occupation of Abyssinia and during World War II. In connection with these events, above all, the construction of the communications infrastructure and military facilities were visibly important. But in addition to these military-related industries, other sectors of industry – in particular industries related to agriculture and mining – also began to flourish. However, it is appropriate from the outset to indicate that when we talk about industry, we mean light industry. In the Four Power Commission Report for the period of Italian colonial rule, the following industries are enumerated: Flour mill, Pasta Manufacturers, Bread Bakeries, Canned Meat, Salted Meat, and Meat Extract Factories, Tanneries, Vegetable Fibre Industry (Sisal and Sanseviera), Dumnut Blank and Button Factory, Cement Factory, Massawa and Assab Salt Works, Soap Factory, Edible Oils Factory, Pirelli Tyre Re-treading Plant, Compounded Liquor Factory (FO 371-69364, Appendix 70).

Taking a closer look, it is possible to separate the Italian colonial era into two periods. These periods are 1890-1930 and 1931-1941. It seems that most scholars of Eritrean history are in agreement that the industrial development of the first period was limited and modest (see e.g. Pool 1979, 1983; Sherman 1980; Leonard 1982; Houtart 1982; Bondestam 1989, Ghebre-Medhin 1989). The available data show that it was in the second period that industry actually began to expand at a considerable pace. Moreover, the wartime period of the British Administration also witnessed the expansion of industry. Therefore, between 1931 and 1945, considerable industrial development was registered. The two most important underlying factors for this rapid expansion were regarded to be the invasion of Ethiopia by Italy and the campaign of the allied forces against the Italo-Germany aggression, which began in 1941. The Four Power Commission pointed out in its reports on industrial development in Eritrea that at the end of the Italian colonial rule, 2,198 industrial firms were in active operation. These included firms engaged in "motor transport, construction, milling, mechanical engineering and in the manufacture of building materials". The overall value of these firms was estimated to be 2, 198 million lire (FO 371-69370, Ch., p.34, Ch. 5, p.58).

According to Leonard (1982), very limited economic activity was undertaken during the first phase[1] of Italian occupation. This is because the attention of the Italians at this point in time was rather on military matters. Italy set out two tasks to be implemented: to pacify the Eritrean society, on the one hand, and on the other, to expand their colonial occupation into Ethiopian territory. The military activity of that period, coupled with the attempt to transform Eritrea into a settlement colony, produced a limited or "small scale development of roads, railways and ports, as well as some construction of military facilities, administrative offices and dwellings" (Leonard 1982: 66). Yet, even this limited development was unprecedented in Eritrean history. The main industrial activities of this phase involved communication and infrastructure construction (discussed above), agricultural and mining industries. The following are an illustration of Eritrean business activities within the agricultural sector: tanning of hides, canned meat, cigarettes, treatment of vegetable fibers, manufacture of buttons, pasta (Leonard 1982: 66).

Leonard also notes that the expansion of light industry and capitalist agriculture in the 1920s led to further expansion of the economic infrastructure. An example of this development is the construction of East Africa's first hydroelectric power station, with the capacity of 2.5 million kilowatt-hours yearly output. By the 1930s, the colony was in possession of four electrical power stations (Leonard 1982: 67). By 1939, this capacity was increased to 15 million kilowatt-hours. Referring to the achievements of what he calls the 'second phase', Leonard notes:

> All in all activity during the second phase was slow and modest. But it was, relative to a small colonial economy, a sustained and basic effort which served as a solid foundation for the rapid development of the third phase (Leonard 1982: 67).

The preparation by the Italians to invade Ethiopia led to intensive economic activity. All the necessary logistics for the successful completion of the campaign were planned and executed in Eritrea, which led to the expansion of economic, and infrastructure projects. The real economic boom came after 1936. During this period, according to Leonard's description, "from a military staging area Eritrea was transformed into an economic staging area" (Leonard 1982: 67). Comparative accounts of this period show a considerable increase in the number of industrial firms. In 1930, there were only 56 industrial firms in the colony. By 1939, the expansion was so enormous that 2,198 industrial firms with a total capital of 2,198 million lire, and 2,690 commercial firms with an estimated capital of 486 million lire could be accounted for. The then-administrative official in the British Military Administration, G.K.N. Trevaskis, appropriately describes this remarkable economic growth as follows:

> With the Italian conquest of Ethiopia in 1935, Eritrea was converted into a base for the exploitation of the Ethiopian hinterland. During the following five years military installations, public buildings, workshops, depots, warehouses, offices, shops, blocks of flats, villas, and encampments were rapidly thrown up. The port of Massawa was enlarged, and linked with Asmara by one of the longest cable-ways in the world. A magnificent network of roads was constructed to supplement the little mountain railway and the few rough tracks which had formerly linked Asmara with the territory's main centres. Modern airports were built at Asmara and Gura; and a number of satellite landing-grounds were laid out elsewhere. All this was carried out by an army of Italian officials, engineers, mechanics, artisans, professional men, and traders, who arrived in the territory after 1935, it was made possible by large-scale imports of mechanical and constructional material and a lavish investment of Italian capital (Trevaskis 1960: 36).

The demise of Italian colonial rule and its subsequent replacement by British rule converted Eritrea into a military staging area for the Allied Forces during the last years of the War. As a consequence of this development, the economy was set on a military footing. Considering the benefit that a well-established infrastructure can give, the British decided to use Eritrea as a main supply base for the Middle East during the War. Therefore, with the help of the Americans they built various elements of industrial and economic infrastructure, which were predominantly for military purposes. The industrial activities during this period can be briefly elucidated as follows: an aeroplane assembly plant in Gura and a naval base in Massawa were constructed, the commercial harbour was renovated into a modern one, workshops in Asmara were converted into a repair base, and a repair and maintenance centre for BOAC aeroplanes was set-up at Asmara (Leonard 1982: 69, Yohannes 1991: 11). In addition, the development of the economic sector that was not directly related to military purposes was also encouraged, particularly because of the demand for Eritrean products in the Middle East during the War. A telling indication of the strength of the civil economy, according to some observers, was that when the military projects were halted, the 14,000 workers made redundant were easily absorbed by the civil sector of the economy. According to the Italian Chamber of Commerce of Asmara, 1,610 industrial firms with an estimated capital of 11.6 million East African pounds were in operation in 1944 (Leonard 1982: 69).

However, with the end of the War, the British, wittingly or unwittingly, took measures that crippled the economy of Eritrea (Leonard 1982: 69). A number of scholars have commented on how the British Administration systematically weakened the Eritrean economy. In an article titled 'why are we destroying the Ethiopian parts?' E, Sylvia Pankhurst (1952) details how the British Administration obliterated port facilities. The British actions which

Table 4.2: Industrial Firms in 1939

Category	Number	Capital (millions of Lire)
Transport	846	1,518
Construction	624	553
Others	728	127
Total	2,198	2,198

Source: Four Powers Commission Report (cited in Leonard, Case of Eritrea 1982: 109)

resulted in the weakening of the Eritrean economy included the dismantling of port facilities, a cement factory, a potash factory, a salt-processing plant, railway equipment, etc. (cf. Pankhurst 1953, Firebrace 1986). Much of this dismantled infrastructure was transferred to India and Sudan, which were British colonies at that time. This destruction of the economic structure had a devastating effect on the social and political realm. Not surprisingly, it is considered to be one of the factors underlying the political turmoil that followed the demise of Italian colonial rule.

The Agricultural Sector

The modernisation process in agriculture entails the introduction and implementation of scientific technology, mechanisation and agro-commercialisation. These changes can be used to distinguish between modern agriculture and traditional subsistence farming. Further, the concomitant emergence of capitalist agriculture is considered an indication of the shift to modernity. A paradigmatic transformation takes place in which the main objective of production becomes the supply of goods for market exchange, and the people involved in production are predominantly wage earners. In examining the Italian agricultural undertaking in Eritrea, one observes quite remarkable changes. The overall Italian agricultural interest in Eritrea was to produce cash crops for the Italian domestic market (Sherman 1980: 15). In that context, those agricultural activities that were important for the subsistence of the indigenous population were more or less neglected. Great priority was given to agro-commercial products that generated cash profits from exchange in Italian markets, or elsewhere on the international market. For these purposes, a large portion of arable land was expropriated from the local population and allocated for agro-commercial projects that were controlled by the colonisers.

Consequently, with the advent of the Italian colonial rule, new agricultural methods were introduced into the Eritrean farming system. This, of course, had a devastating effect on the indigenous economic structure and, as a consequence, resulted in immense suffering among the peasants. The difficulties that the peasants encountered originated from two sources. First, the expropriation of land for agro-commercial purposes deprived the peasants their basic sources of subsistence, upon which they were totally dependent for their survival. Second, the cash crop production did not directly benefit the peasants because it was chiefly produced with the aim of satisfying the Italian market and the Italian settlers in

Eritrea. The impact that this development brought with it was of an immense magnitude because it distorted the socio-economic structure of society. This trend appears to be a universal feature of colonialism. In describing the effect of the commercialisation of agriculture on the peasant household, Gledhill notes that commercialisation creates problems for the peasant household to maintain their subsistence. Therefore, they had to supplement their subsistence with wage labour, and this, in turn, forcibly transformed the peasants into a 'semi-proletariat' (Gledhill 1994: 77).

The introduction of capitalist agriculture generated an agricultural system in which the dominant traditional indigenous farming system, on the one hand, and the modern agriculture based on the capitalist line, on the other, for a time co-existed side-by-side. This meant the introduction of a capitalist sector for the first time in the history of the region. The first step taken by the Italians toward introducing a modern agricultural system and to implement the use of European seeds and fruits, was to examine the suitability of Eritrea for such undertakings. In the intention of fulfilling that aim, an agro-economist professor by the name of Gino Bartolommei Gioli was assigned to carry out the exploration in 1900 (Mesghenna 1988: 135). The result of the study, which was reported in *L'agricoltura nell'Eritrea,* showed that Eritrea had good potential for the cultivation of cereals and tropical agro-industrial products (Mesghenna 1988: 136). Further, Gioli's study proposed the utilisation of the western and eastern lowlands for the production of tropical agricultural products such as fruit, tobacco, coffee, gum, medicinal plants, dyes, cotton, and even cattle breeding (Mesghenna 1988:138). To evaluate these proposals, the study suggested the establishment of agricultural experiment stations.

Accordingly, various experimental sites were established in Keren, Mai Aini, Kodofelassie, Adi Ugri, Agordat, Ghinda, Sabarguma, Hirgigo, Fil-Fil and Solomona. Tests were carried out between early 1901 and January 1902, particularly on cotton and tobacco plantations, producing varied results. But the actual experimental proposition suggested by Professor Gioli was put into action in the summer of 1902 (Mesghenna 1988: 142). The newly founded agricultural research centre was headed by Professor Isaia Baldrati and established four stations, three in the central and eastern lowlands (Ghinda, Fil-Fil and Keren) and one in the highland (Asmara). In the lowlands coffee, cotton, sesame peanut, rubber, sisal, date palms, bananas, papayas, citrus fruits, etc. were tried. In the highland, a variety of products was tested as well. Among other things the test included potatoes, medicinal plants, fodder plants and different types of legumes such as peas, beans, chickling vetch, chick-peas, and lentils (Mesghenna 1988: 143). From what could be judged from the report made assessing the project the outcomes were rather mixed. According to Mesghenna (1988) the *Societa per la coltivazione del cotone* in Eritrea was the most successful investor.

Table 4.3: The production of cotton in quintal (one quintal = 100 KGs)

Year	Production
1904-1905	0.473
1905-1906	1030
1906-1907	2863
1907-1908	5313
1908-1909	3825
1909-1910	5872
1910-1911	9040
1911-1912	11075
1912-1913	4585

Source: Instituto Agricolo Coloniale Firenze, L'agricoltura nella colonia Eritrea e l'opera dell'Italia (Rome, 1946), p.37. (from Mesghenna 1988: 144, 179)

In addition to the projects run by Italians, the indigenous populations were also encouraged to change their farming habits and were induced to take up working as sharecroppers. However, for a number of reasons, the effort to transform the indigenous population into cash-crop producers did not seem to have been a successful project at that time. Most probably as a matter of expediency, the Italians were more interested in the large agricultural area found in the Tessenei plains watered by the Gash River, and the coastal plains and the Barka river valley. These were large areas of land, very much appropriate for large-scale modern agro-commercial farming, and particularly well suited to mechanised agriculture. However, it was not before 1926 that the agricultural orientation was directed completely along capitalist lines (Leonard 1982: 63). This new capitalist agricultural orientation, according to Leonard, brought with it a wide range of opportunities in the form of credit facilities for agricultural investment and financial encouragement, which entailed customs, franchise and tax credits. In addition, in terms of political decisions, the need for agricultural land prompted the colonial authorities to pass a controversial land's act decree, declaring a large portion of the country to be *Domeniale* (state owned land). This decision, although politico-legal in nature, had far-reaching implications, not only in terms of economy, but also in terms of social, legal and structural dimensions.

In the field of animal husbandry, there were considerable improvements. A veterinary service that was set up in 1905 greatly contributed to fighting animal diseases, thereby increasing dramatically the size of animal population. Between 1905 and 1928, the number of animals more than doubled from 1,109,000 to 2,784,485. In addition, a serious attempt was made to develop a fisheries industry (Leonard 1982: 63). Commenting on the achievement of the 1920s Leonard notes,

> It thus appears that the fundamental work of agricultural "development" was carried out in the 1920s. Production generally reached adequate levels in terms of domestic needs and small scale exportation (Leonard 1982: 64).

The modest achievements in agricultural development described so far refer to the time leading up to the 1920s. This development continued at an ever-quickening pace, so that substantial agricultural development took place during the remainder of the European colonial period. Under British rule overall agricultural output considerably increased, and additional new agricultural products such as pasteurised milk, pigs, beer, fishmeal, etc., began to be produced. The following tables illustrate the growth in agricultural production during the twelve years of the Italian colonial period from 1921 to 1932.

Table 4.4 Colonial agricultural production for the years 1921-1932; in thousand quintals.

Year	Wheat	Barely	Durah	Corn	Taff	bultug	Dagus
1921	59	242	248	72	97	10	60
1922	54	146	312	55	91	28	61
1923	54	151	325	46	73	32	51
1924	73	156	377	29	73	59	52
1925	40	160	200	29	35	49	32
1926	62	150	175	16	49	31	43
1927	5	25	85	40	16	11	13
1928	11	27	100	35	15	7	17
1929	10	30	150	40	15	10	12
1930	12	94	200	90	25	20	22
1931	9	202	146	109	51	27	17
1932	14	113	322	128	-	-	27

Year	Oil seed	Legume	Coffee	Cotton	Tobacco	Semi dum	**Semi dum af**
1921	11	62	-	-	-	6	4
1922	11	72	00.5	2	00.6	12	3
1923	20	72	00.6	3	00.2	23	2
1924	95	88	00.6	20	00.4	23	4
1925	35	41	0.1	15	00.8	44	4
1926	21	59	0.2	16	00.8	44	3
1927	7	40	0.2	10	00.3	45	4
1928	7	35	0.2	7	00.8	28	2
1929	9	38	0.3	8	00.7	54	2
1930	10	42	0.4	11	0.2	40	3
1931	9	30	0.4	7	0.3	61	4
1932	7	-	0.8	5	0.3	-	2

Source: Guidotti, R; "L'avvaloramento agricolo della colonia Eritrea," in La Rassegna Italiana Politica Letteraria e Artistica, volume speciale (XXXV), Settembre-Ottobre 1933 (A. XI), ed. by Sillani, T; P.178; and in L'Affrica Orientale Italiana e il conflitto Italo-Etiopico, ed., by Silliani, T; p. 148; Piccioli, A; op. cit., p. 644; Santagata, F; op. cit.; p.73. (from Mesghenna 1988: 175)

Italians settlers supported by the colonial authorities also cultivated various types of fruits, such as oranges, mandarins, lemons, papaya, grapefruit, figs, bananas, mangoes, and apples. These fruits were cultivated in the eastern and western lowlands (Mesghenna 1988: 177). Fruit production continued to be of great significance in the overall agricultural production long after the Italian colonial system ceased to exist. This continuation can be partially attributed to the eventual adjustment of the indigenous people to the new organisation of agricultural activities, and partly to the prevalence of Italian individuals who continued living in Eritrea as agricultural entrepreneurs. Unfortunately, most of these agricultural plantations were destroyed during the prolonged liberation war and since the middle of the 70s, there have been no traces to be found of several of these agricultural projects.

Table 4.5: Fruit plants distributed by the colonial authorities, 1922-1934

Year	Number
1922	6,495
1923	8,040
1924	5,945
1925	6,000
1926	6,000
1927	5,400
1928	6,700
1929	7,000
1930	3,500
1931	4,630
1932	5,130
1933	7,617

Source: Massi, L; "Le piante di frutto coltivato in Eritrea," in L'Agricoltura Coloniale, Anno XXVII, Maggio 1934-XII, n. 5, p.226. (from Mesghenna 1988: 178)

This account illustrates how under Italian and British colonial rules, considerable modern mechanised capitalist agricultural activities were carried out. Highlighting the agricultural achievement during the Italian and British rule, the Four Power Commission reported that by 1940, there were 163 agricultural concessions. Under British rule, in 1947, this number increased to 819 (FO 371-69363, Appendix 37). Without a doubt, Eritrea experienced far-reaching changes in terms of quantity and quality during the period under examination. This development clearly represented an unprecedented expansion in modern capitalist agriculture. In addition, the great expansion of agricultural concessions had played an indispensable role in producing agricultural workers.

Moreover, in terms of its socio-cultural implications, the emergence of the agricultural centres was of great significance. One revealing outcome was that these centres became the locus of activity for job seekers from different regions and ethno-linguistic groups. In turn, this paved the way for the acceleration of the integration process by the very effect of the opportunities that were created for these groups to interact with each other. And in the final analysis, the overall effect could be seen in the dimension of the process of nation formation. In this respect, the main importance of the agricultural centres would be in the role they played in connecting members of the various ethno-linguistic groups.

URBANISATION

In modernisation theory, the emergence of urbanisation is used as a yard-stick for measuring the process of transformation from an archaic traditional society to modern one endowed with modern values, norms, and belief systems. Urbanisation is a process through which a progressive change takes place in society, and in which the society is split into urban and rural – or centre and periphery. In its common usage, it "refers to an increase in the degree to which the proportion of a nation or region's population is to be found concentrated in towns and cities. It is thus a measure of the relative growth of urban populations within a given territory" (Potter 1985: 22). The emergence of urbanisation has at least the following four features: 1) the development of towns and cities - urban centres; 2) the concentration of industries and business activities in these urban centres; 3) the mixture and concentration of people from diverse back-grounds in the urban centres - leading to anonymity, rootlessness, etc. In this manner, members of the various ethno-linguistic groups are forced to compete for the limited resources of goods and services, affecting in the process the interaction and interdependency of the individuals and group members of the various ethno-linguistic communities. 4) The hierarchisation of the economic system in terms of an urban centred economy destined to play a leading role and a subordinate rural economy. This is the development of rural versus urban division of labour. In short, what develops is an interrelation of complementarity between town and countryside, where towns are in need of a supply of unfinished products, food and labour. The countryside is bound to the relationship by its need for finished goods, by its quest for work and the need for markets (cf. Leonard 1982: 83).

In this hierarchical division, there exists an inevitable functional interdependence and specialisation of production. The result is that in general, the urban centres produce finished products while the rural realm offers essential farming and pastoral products. They are also externally connected in a hierarchically ordered economic relationship with the metropolitan economic system – in the Eritrean case with the Italian system. These conditions generate an economic centralisation in society. In other words, a modern market centre is established where not only goods and services are exchanged, but also ideas, values and belief systems, thereby opening the way for the emergence of a mosaic of ideas, values and belief systems. Arguing along this line Thomas Hodgkin suggests:

> By providing opportunities for a greater degree of specialisation, towns enabled men (and women) to acquire new skills and powers.

> By mixing men from a variety of social backgrounds they make possible the discovery of new points of contact and interest. Around these interest there develops a network of new associations, through which for the first time men come to think of their problems as social rather than personal; as capable of solution by human action rather than part of natural order. Thus African towns have this two fold aspects: seen from one standpoint, they lead to a degradation of African civilisation and ethic; seen from another they contain the germs of a new, more interesting and diversified, civilisation, with possibilities of greater liberty (Hodgkin 1956: 63).

By the 1920s Asmara, the capital city, and Massawa, the main port, were relatively developed. But the real development of urban centres was to come in the 1930s (see Leonard 1982: 67-8). The expansion and modernisation of the towns continued uninterrupted, so that in the 1950s, towns like Asmara, Keren, Massawa, Tessenei, Agordat, Decemare grew into modern ones. They were connected by modern roads and railways and equipped with modern municipal services such as water, electricity, telephone and telegraph, hospitals, schools, police, banks, cinemas, shops, hotels and newspapers. The urban population was composed of workers, merchants, functionaries, artisans, domestic servants and notables (Leonard 1982: 77). The urban centre became a focal point where people from both different geographical regions and from various ethno-linguistic groups were able to converge. The underlying reasons for the flow of people from rural areas to the nascent urban centres might have varied considerably. However, irrespective of the particular configurations and variations of the causes, there are in general two theoretical approaches that attempt to explain the flow of people to urban centres. These theories are known in the sociology of urbanisation as the "pull" and "push" theories. In brief, the pull theory regards the attraction of urban life as the primary factor in spurring people to immigrate to urban centres. Conversely, the push theory attributes this movement to inadequacies and poverty in the rural areas that force people to emigrate in search of a better life. Regardless of the underlying causes for migration, what interests us in this study is the convergence of individuals or groups with divergent socio-cultural background into urban centres, and its social, cultural, and psychological implications. Moreover, the significance of this convergence, viewed from the point of departure of the nation formation process is that it represents a step towards the assimilation into and integration of society.

The emergence of towns or urban centres in Eritrea began with Italian colonialism. As far as I am aware, no study has been made of how modern urban centres emerged and developed in Eritrea. Neither does there exist any systematically recorded data. However, based on their physical location and the time and circumstances of their development, it is possible to construct some general interpretations. At least three significant underlying factors and mechanisms can be suggested, through which the emergence of modern towns was realised. These are; (i) the need for administrative centres (provincial capitals) for the administrative divisions; (ii) the growth of industrial and agricultural locations;

and (iii) the expansion of road and railway lines (along which trade centres appeared). In the first case, when the Italians compartmentalised Eritrea into various administrative regions, they established an administrative headquarters in every administrative region or province. The increasingly complex and expanding field of operations of the administrative machinery brought with it the gradual growth of bureaucracy. The concomitant governmental increase in expenditures, and the expansion of public sphere projects such as building hospitals, governmental offices, post offices, schools, airports, banks, etc., also built up the material infrastructural foundation for the rise of urban centres. These administrative locations, which quite often began with a couple of cottages, were gradually transformed into towns.

The second type of factor accounted for was the location of industrial and agricultural activity. As soon as an industrial or agricultural undertaking at a particular area was started, workers and workers' families began to establish residences there. These new residences had to accommodate the basic biological and social needs of the residents. Thus, there arose the necessity for social interaction with other groups who had other social specialities and functions – perhaps in the form of transactions such as the purchasing, selling and exchanging of goods and services (establishment of marketing and market centres). In such ways, a multiplication of the categories of social groups who were engaged in various functions took place. This eventually culminated in the emergence of complex, functionally specialised and interdependent communities. Subsequently, as a logical outcome of this development, the headquarters area or a nearby village would be transformed into a town in which all the functional activities of a town or urban centre could take place.

In the third type of case, the development of towns or urban centres along transportation routes was likely to have been a more or less unintentional outcome. For the most part, it was either villages that were situated along the line of a railway or road, or stations at which trains and buses paused for a while, which were transformed into towns. Here, people from surrounding area came to sell some of their products such as fruits, animals and animal products, food, or handmade goods for passengers. As time passed, these stations were often transformed into permanent trade centres, and subsequently developed into towns.

Those who came from the area surrounding these stations on a daily basis to benefit from small trades and job opportunities saw the advantage of permanently settling in these spots rather than travelling back and forth. Accordingly, small retail stores, coffee and tea shops, and restaurants began to appear in the centres of activity and residence which were to become towns. In this fashion, several small towns appeared along the road and railway lines.

It is worthwhile to point out that in practice, these three categories usually overlap. For instance, a location can be chosen to be an administrative centre, but the administrative centre can also be situated in an agricultural and industrial location, thus creating the necessity for transportation facilities. Hence, these spots emerged as distinctively different, although perhaps not independently from their surroundings. In other words, the interdependence between these small urban centres and the larger rural areas was dialectically interwoven. The overall outcome was a geographic and cultural division between urban centres and rural villages and a nomadic mode of life. This again set in motion what is sociologically conceptualised as the differentiation of society, predicated upon the separation into urban and rural areas, which in turn led to the differentiation in terms of life style, means of income, status, etc. The following table shows the expansion of Eritrean urban centres. The list comprises the main towns in the 1940s. Beginning from virtually zero before Italian colonialism, the total number of people residing in urban centres was estimated to constitute 20 per cent of the total population at the end of 1950s.

Table 4.6 Population Concentration in Towns as by 1940

Town	Population
Asmara	100,000
Massawa	10,000
Keren	10,000
Decamere	5,000

Source: constructed from Richard Leonard's, 'European Colonization and the Socio-Economic Integration of Eritrea', in The Case of Eritrea 1982: 68.

Taken from educational point of view, urban centres are also focal points for the establishment and perpetuation of a modern educational system. Under Italian colonial rule in Eritrea, the expansion of the school system initiated and run by the colonial authority was extremely limited. In addition to the government-sponsored schools there were Missionary schools, which perhaps played a much more significant role than those run by the government. These schools were located primarily in the urban centres: Vittorio Emanuel III in Asmara; Salvago Raggi in Keren; Ferdinando Martini in Massawa; San Giorgo in Adi Ugri; San Michele in Adi Keih (Teklehaimanot 1996). Scholars of the colonial school of thought frequently comment upon the impact of modern western education on the development of colonial societies and the significance of Missionary schools. One such pioneer scholar who discussed the factors that contributed to the emergence of nationalism in colonial Africa is Thomas Hodgkin (1956). In emphasising the role of Western education and Missionary schools, he stresses that, quite naturally, the geographical locus of nationalism were the emergent urban centres.

The debate on the impact of the emergence of towns on the social fabric is, however, not conclusive. Hodgkin (1956: 63) notes, "The point is often made that the new towns of Africa act as solvents, weakening traditional social ties and loosening the hold of traditional beliefs and values". In general terms, this assumption appears to be quite correct. If we take the Eritrean case, many of the Eritreans who moved to the urban centres kept their rural attachment for a long time to come. This attachment took many different forms: as frequent seasonal retreats, sending money to close relatives, possessing legal rights of ownership of private property in the place of origin, continued close contact with relatives and friends, etc. Nevertheless, the strength of these attachments weakens with the passage of time. Commenting on the social changes that occurred under Italian rule, one veteran Eritrean politician expressed it metaphorically in 1946 in the following way: "I am afraid that we have become 'neither fish nor meat', that is we have departed from our culture and yet we have not adopted the European culture totally, we find our selves in a cross-road" (Woldemariam 1995: 124).

In the tradition of sociology of development, particularly evolutionary development theory, the difference between rural and urban is viewed as representing two historical epochs. Therefore, the rural-urban continuum notion as used by scholars in the discipline is meant to illustrate, in a developmental time-trajectory, that the rural represents the lowest end while the urban is supposed to represent the uppermost end. Expressed differently, it is conceptualised along what Mckinney calls "the societal continuum: polar types" of which Ferdinand Tönnies' classification of *Gemeinschaft* and *Gesellschaft* is perhaps the seminal example. In this classification, Gemeinschaft represents the rural whereas Gesellschaft represents the urban (see Mckinney 1966: 102). Furthermore, from the spatio-temporal point of view, the rural is a relic, a vestige of the primitive old, anachronistic, nevertheless sometimes a nostalgically appreciated lost paradise, whereas the urban is taken to symbolise the most recent human development. In a different interpretation this dichotomisation is conceptualised from a complementarity perspective, and is perceived as two modes of one social order. The complementarity[2] perspective applied to the Durkheimian dichotomy of mechanical and organic solidarity in Cohen's (1985) interpretation may also serve us in our examination of the urban-rural connection. Such an orthodox perception of dichotomisation is no longer a widely appealing scholarly discourse. It is not only generally accepted that the rural and urban coexist simultaneously in a temporal space, but also that they complement each other.

Probably one of the most significant aspects of the development of urban centres is their contribution to the emergence and crystallisation of modern political and intellectual groups. "These centres became the most appropriate environment for socio-cultural and political interactions between 'peoples', the forum for the delimitation of social borders of solidarity. Moreover the centres served as the social bases for the formation of the socio-cultural elite" (Lema 1993: 161). In congruence with this summary of the salient role played by urban centres, what happened in Eritrea after the collapse of Italian rule can be taken as indicative. The emergence of political parties in the urban centres, led by the new elites who were the product of the urbanisation process was a clear example. In conclusion, urbanisation as a social process, and through its centralisation and diversification mechanisms, accelerates the cohesion of a society. It is in this sense that its significance for the nation formation process should be evaluated. After discussing the material development generated by colonial capitalist penetration, let us now scrutinise its implications for the indigenous social structure.

CAPITALIST PENETRATION AND ITS IMPACT ON SOCIAL STRUCTURE

So far, the focus in this chapter has been to illustrate the material innovation that took place as a consequence of colonial capital penetration in Eritrea. The ensuing section briefly examines the effects of these material innovations on the social structure. The fundamental perception being pursued is that changes in material conditions lead to changes in social structure. This, in turn, is a prerequisite for the integration and cohesion of the members of society. This development leads to the emergence of certain basic common attitudes and values, which, in turn, furnish the basis for the evolution of a nation. As was pointed out in the introduction of this chapter, a number of scholars have expressed the view that European colonial rule did not bring substantial social structural change. This assessment simply cannot be supported. It is true that the changes were uneven, and it is also true that the vast majority of the rural population was barely touched. Much of the social change that took place occurred in the emerging urban centres. Yet, the rural population did not escape the practical and structural effects of colonial capital penetration, albeit, in the form of a snowball effect, in that a section of the rural population was eventually transformed into an urban population. Moreover, it has to be recalled that there has been – and still is – a persistent trickling of goods and people from the rural areas to the urban centres. Conversely, there is a flow of materials (money and goods) and services from urban centres to the rural areas. Thus, notwithstanding the cautious Italian policy toward the rural population, it would be naive to conclude that the rural population was completely untouched by the colonial capital penetration.

The experiences of history demonstrate that the immediate effects of the classic capitalist industrialisation in Western Europe were manifested in at least three dimensions. First, land was expropriated from the peasantry, ensuring the availability of large areas of land for large-scale capitalist investment. Second, an idle, landless population of peasantry was created, ready to be absorbed into whatever employment the capitalist economic order could offer. Third, the redundant, landless peasant class was effectively converted into wage labourers. The penetration of colonial capital in Eritrea generated effects similar, although to a limited extent, to those of classic capitalist industrialisation. In Eritrea, three different, but mutually interrelated phenomena emerged as the outcome of capitalist penetration. These include: a) the expropriation of land; b) the emergence of landless peasantry; and c) the availability of work opportunities which demanded wage labour (cf. Leonard 1982: 70). From the capitalist economic point of view, the extensive expropriation of land served two purposes. First, it made land available for different capitalist projects, and second, it forced into redundancy a labour force which was crucially needed in the various emerging capitalist projects, including the occupying colonial army (according to some estimations up to 40 per cent of the active labour force joined the colonial army).

Table 4.7: Number of Soldiers in Proportion of the Total Population (1912-1938)

Year	Number of Soldiers	Population	Active Labour Force	% of Active Labour Force
1912	5,990	330,000	82,000	7.3%
1915	7,350	360,000	90,000	8.1%
1925	9,080	480,000	120,000	7.5%
1928	7,050	500,000	135,000	5.5%
1935	60,200	600,000	150,000	40.3%
1938	70,000	614,353	(1939)	

Source: EPLF, Italian Colonialism in Eritrea 1882-1941

To implement their colonial scheme, the Italians were in great need of manpower, particularly to carry out their scheme of colonial expansion, first in Somalia and Libya and later in the successful occupation of Abyssinia. Therefore, the expropriation of land from peasants, viewed from the expansionist scheme, served quite well to solve the need for manpower. The extensive land expropriation at the early stage was carried out in accordance with the Italian plan to transform Eritrea into a settlement colony. Peasants who lost their basic means of subsistence were forced to move to the developing urban centres in search for jobs. In addition, joining the colonial army became an attractive alternative.

Furthermore, the construction of cities, ports, airfields, railways, roads, telegraph lines, irrigation systems and dams, exploration and mining, and the establishment of both large and small agricultural concessions made the expropriation of land necessary, thereby further driving out the peasants from their land. The successful undertaking of these projects required wage labour, thus bringing into existence a new social class engaged in wage labour (Leonard 1982). In depicting this matter Leonard notes,

> In Eritrea as elsewhere, the intervention of European colonization profoundly affected existing social and political structures: calling into existence new classes, modifying the structures of pre-existing classes (above all the peasantry), and remaking political structures, or at least adapting them to suit colonial needs (Leonard 1982: 70).

Besides the expropriation of land, the Italians systematically undertook measures to weaken the traditional elite, thereby depriving Eritrean society of its established leadership and altering the political structure. Perham (1969), highlighting this condition, contends that the occupation destroyed the upper structure of the provincial administration, with the exception that the colonial authorities permitted favoured chiefs to maintain their position (cf. Pankhurt 1964:144).

The pre-colonial Eritrean communities constituted in the highland, of a predominantly peasant population, and in the lowland, one that was predominantly nomadic. The approximate proportion of peasantry was estimated to run between 95 and 98 per cent of the total population (Leonard 1982: 70). But soon, with the penetration of colonial capital into the society and the emergence of urban centres, the proportion of peasants dropped to 80 per cent (Leonard 1982: 71). There were multiple factors behind the drop in the rural peasant population, and the subsequent transformation of around 20 per cent of the population into modern social groups. The economic benefit that could be gained by engaging in agricultural and industrial labour, joining military service, or moving to the relatively comfortable city life when the chance arose to serve in the bureaucratic administration were among the underlying reasons for the change. In the lowland, the introduction of modern agricultural projects by Italian firms in the 1920s also affected the social structure of the community, in particular in the Tessenei area, (EPLF, Italian Colonialism in Eritrea 1882-1941, pp. 157f). By comparison, this new mode of life was more comfortable than the hardship and uncertainty of peasantry or nomadism. Thus, the powerful appeal of a new and relatively comfortable mode of life can be demonstrated by the increasing swelling in the number of residents in the urban centres. The capitalist penetration affected the highland region and the lowland regions to varying degrees. A considerable number of peasants from the highlands migrated to the capital city, Asmara, and other towns in the highland. People from the lowland moved mainly to emerging towns in the lowland like Massawa, Keren, Agordat, Barentu, Tessenei, etc., and also to the capital city. This development naturally led to the geographical division of labour, between an urban and a rural population. The emergence of urban centres, with all the accompanying modern utilities created a hierarchically structured social stratification.

Another consequence of the expropriation of land was the exacerbation of the tension between the poor peasants and the feudal lords, thereby sharpening the class conflict. Moreover, the Italians took some measures that undermined the positions of the upper classes. Besides the logical practical effects of the capitalist penetration, the Italians passed resolutions that led to the subduing of the feudal social order. For instance, during the 1930s several colonial decrees were passed with the intention of abolishing the *resti* land tenure system (cf. Leonard 1982: 73). Further, changes were undertaken that were intended to reform the serf system. The aristocrats' traditional inheritance of serfs upon the death of the father was limited to only the eldest son. This measure was intended to create a concentration of ownership of serfs among the chiefs and conversely, to create serfless *Nabtabs* and *Shumagelle*. In addition, the Italians abolished the feudal dues and services that the serfs were obliged to pay to their masters (FO 371-73841). The accumulated effects of these intended and unintended undertakings were of two types. On the one hand, a highly centralised aristocratic class evolved while the economic power and social status of the aristocracy was simultaneously being eroded. In fact, the Italians attempted to modernise the institution of the chieftainship (Nadel 1945: 86, Leonard 1982: 75). This modernisation of the institution of chieftainship was intended to occur primarily through the formalisation of the office. These measures progressively weakened the power of the aristocratic classes, thereby paving the way for the emergence of an influential middle class, which started to assume the political leadership.

Leonard seems to be convinced that by taking these measures the Italians intended to transform the serfs to economically free political subjects controlled by a centralised and politically powerful aristocratic class. It seems that instead of a scattered and loosely connected serfs, they wanted to create a serf class bound by feudal obligations attached to a more solid political system with a centralised authority. Moreover, colonialism, by circumventing Eritrea within the boundaries of a centralised colonial state espoused by coercive force, impaired the fundamental pillar of the feudal mode of relation. The colonial state overtook the function of protection which was the responsibility of the aristocratic class, and with that the need of feudal obligation was practically removed (Leonard 1982: 76). Accordingly, the legitimacy of the chieftainship as an institution was gradually eroded, leading to the crumbling of the social and political power of the aristocracy.

As a consequence of the capitalist penetration, the serf-aristocracy relationship gradually weakened. Finally, it was dismantled under the British rule. Many serfs benefited from the capitalist penetration, either by being employed in the agricultural concessions and construction works or by joining the army. The increase in livestock, which was an improvement also enjoyed by the serfs, strengthened their economic power. While the serfs' economic strength was steadily enhanced, the economic and political base of the aristocracy was dwindling day by day (cf. Markakis 1987: 59). The effect of the population growth also demographically shifted the social relation to the advantage of the serfs. The paradox of the colonial rule was that while, on the one hand, it attempted to preserve the feudal class distinction by trying to preserve the superstructure, on the other it undermined the system. The scheme of the colonial authority in introducing changes was no more than shaping the society to be compatible with the colonial rule. Observing this, Frantz (1975) argues: "Grazing societies progressively experienced the intrusion of district, regional, and colonial officials into their local activities, with the result that they became more integrated into colonial administrative systems. Sometimes the pastoralists' structures of authority and power were confirmed, although their judicial and executive duties were redefined". Colonialism tried to reform the system without abolishing serfdom.

> The implicit contractual basis of this relationship was destroyed by the advent of European government which by usurping the position of the Shumagulle as protectors of the Tigre upset the social equilibrium of these tribal communities, leaving the Shumagulle with their privileges and freeing them from their traditional obligations. This together with the generally liberal influence of European adminis-

> tration soon encouraged the Tigre to raise complaint against their rulers and to demand reform (WO 230-255).

Concerning the changes in the lowland, the War Office archive also contains the following comment: "A social revolution had taken place peacefully and society had reorganised itself on a new pattern" (WO 230-255). The account presented in this section enables us to conclude that basic social and political structural changes have taken place. It also seems reasonable to conclude that the underlying material basis of the social change effected by the penetration of Italian colonial capital raised the political consciousness, the expectation and the ambition of different social groups not least the serfs. The defeat of Italy raised the expectations of the serfs. But the BMA take-over of the colony dashed their hopes. This led to open rebellion which began in 1942 and continued until 1949, when the British were forced to pass a decree of emancipation of the serfs (Leonard 1982: 77). Leonard contends that the penetration of Italian colonial capital was the underlying factor for the progressive emancipation movement of the serfs, which later became the driving force behind the independence movement.

The impact of colonial capital penetration on the Eritrean society can be summarised in the following manner. The large-scale expropriation of land in effect triggered an alienation of a considerable number of peasants from their basic means of subsistence. The 'statisation' (state ownership) and commercialisation of land forced many peasants to flock to plantation agricultural centres in rural areas, or to the towns in quest for employment. The introduction of industry and communications infrastructure also played a significant role in this social change. In short, in addition to the material impact, this European colonial penetration brought, "a common consciousness - in children and adults, in men and in women, in Christians and in Muslims, in Tigrinya speakers and those of other languages - of common enemies and of a common cause" (Leonard 1982: 78-9). The changes in material aspect inevitably affected the social structure, which gave rise to the emergence of modern social groups.

THE EMERGENCE OF MODERN SOCIAL GROUPS

After discussing the impact of material innovation on social structure, the remainder of the chapter will deal with the development of modern social groups. One of the legacies of European colonialism in the colonial societies is the emergence of modern social groups. Quite often, it is argued that new social groups, i.e., native bourgeoisie, middle class, urban working class and intellectuals, are produced as a consequence of colonialism (Smith 1983b: 72). Prior to the penetration of colonial capital in the Eritrean economy and community, the main classes were the peasantry and the landlords in the sedentary highland community and the serfs and aristocracy in the pastoral and semi-pastoral communities (*Nabtab, Shumagle,* etc.). However, some ethno-linguistic groups lacked any clear class differentiation. Many observers agree about the absence of a feudal socio-economic system in Eritrea akin to its historical manifestation in European societies (e.g. Leonard 1982, Houtart 1982). It has also been argued that it was in the pastoral nomadic communities that this feudal relationship was commonly expressed (Leonard 1982, Bondestam 1989). The view that the feudal relationship was expressed in the communities of the lowland is based on the socio-economic and politico-cultural relationship that existed between the serfs and the aristocratic class, which was absent in the highland population.

Italian colonialism generated new social groups. Those who were employed in the agricultural projects, railway and road construction, and industrial projects formed one part of these new social groups. These groups also included the intelligentsia (teachers, clerks and interpreters) and the urban middle classes (Houtart 1982, Leonard 1982, Killion 1985, Mesghenna 1988, Bondestam 1989). The bourgeoisie class was strengthened after the implementation of the Federation. Before 1890 there were no towns in Eritrea, in the modern meaning of the word (Leonard 1982: 77), with the single exception of the port of Massawa. But by the end of Italian colonial rule, 20% of the population was dwelling in towns, according to the British statistics. "This urban population was made up of workers, merchants, functionaries, artisans, domestic servants, notables, and most probably a number of hangers-on. Of this urban mixture the proletariat and the petty bourgeoisie are the two classes which we must consider" (Leonard 1982: 77-8).

The urban middle class was the most significant one of the emergent new social groups. This is not only because of its magnitude but also because of its socio-cultural influence. This social group played a leading role in the political activities that unfolded in the wake of the Italian rule. The intelligentsia is a social group, which quite often is categorised along with the urban middle class. In the beginning, this social group was very negligible in size, but it later (under British rule) grew quite considerably. The Eritrean working class grew to become a sizeable body by the end of the Italian colonial rule.

The Working Class

One of the effects of the penetration of colonial capital was the differentiation of society. From this process of differentiation, a working class emerged. There were several interconnected factors that contributed to the rise of the working class. The most important of these factors could be described as (i) the emergence of commercial agriculture; (ii) the rise of manufacturing and construction industries; and (iii) the expropriation of land from the peasants by the colonial authority. While the first two factors constitute the emergence of workplaces in which an opportunity for the development of a wage-labourer group was opened up, the last factor refers to the availability of manpower, which, due to the loss of their land or inaducate production, could be readily absorbed in the new projects. Accordingly, it was the combination of these two categories of factors – new opportunity and displacement – that gave rise to the emergence of working class in Eritrea. The land shortage and insufficient productivity forced many peasants to work in Italian commercial agriculture either as sustitution for or complement to farming incomes. This development was not only the ineluctable outcome of the expropriation of land, but also the result of the availability of work opportunities in the agricultural projects, which served as a pull factor. Many people, even those who were not directly affected by the expropriation of land, trekked to the agricultural centres in search for job. The agricultural workers constituted one category of the work force.

A second category of workers included those engaged in industrial activities. Generally, industry encompassed mining, construction, production and food processing. This category of industry was located largely in urban centres or in the suburbs of urban centres. And it was to this category that the majority of workers were drawn. A third category of workers was composed of those who were involved in the public sector – in the bureaucratic establishment, as white-collar workers; public services, port, railway and road activities, etc. In broad terms, the working class was defined by some scholars as composed "of all the salaried workers employed in the infrastructural and public works, light industries, commercialization and distribution services and in the commercial farms" (Houtart 1979: 5).

The size of the working class under the Italian colonial rule was estimated to be not more than 5% of the total population (Leonard 1982: 78). The report by the Four Power Commission of 1948 indicates that in 1935-36 there were 13,020 Italian and Eritrean workers, however in 1937 this number grew to 127, 130. Categorised according to nationality this number would be divided in the following manner: 63,530 Italians, 43,720 Eritreans and 10,680 Sudanese and Yemenites (EPLF, Italian Colonialism in Eritrea 1882-1941). The last phase of Italian colonialism and the initial period of British occupation witnessed a rapid expansion of the working class. With the defeat of Italy, Italian skilled workers began to leave Eritrea, thereby opening opportunity for skilled Eritrean workers to take their places (cf. Bondestam 1989: 54). This development led to the emergence of additional qualified workers in terms of technical knowledge.

It is believed that agricultural concessions that began to expand under Italian colonial rule – and further were multiplied under British administration – employed a significant proportion of the members of the working class. A report compiled by the FPCI for the Former Italian Colonies Report on Eritrea estimated the number of workers engaged in agricultural projects in 1940 at 25,000[3] Eritrean workers and 2,000 Italians (FO 371-69363, Appendix 37). This account included all types of agricultural enterprises. From a gender perspective, there also emerged a special category of workers – females were employed in the domestic sphere as housemaids in Italian households, commonly known in Tigrinya as "*deki bedama*". Many young girls were absorbed into the labour market as domestic labourers. Although there is no documented data available, the employment of women in the household as domestic servants was a widespread activity, so that many female members of the rural household left their villages and immigrated to the urban centres. These *deki bedama* played an important role in supporting their families back in the villages. A characteristic feature of the majority of the Eritrean working class was that they displayed a dual nature, that is, while adapting to the urban way of life they preserved their rural origin (Killion 1985: 285). Moreover, because the salary income was not sufficient many householders were compelled to supplement their income by having extra income generating activities in their villages of origin. These dual characteristics led to some scholars believe that no Eritrean working class emerged (e.g. Negash 1987: 47).

Table 4.8: Principal Areas of Employment outside Agriculture towards the end of British Occupation

Profession	Eritreans	Europeans
Manufacturing industry (figures for 1947)	23,900	5,000
Mining industry[1] (figures for 1947)	3,200	400
Public services (including railways, ports, and roads, figures for 1950)	8,200	2,400
Total	35,300	7,800

1. Because of insecurity in the countryside at this time these figures are lower that they should be.

Source: Rapport de la commission des Nations Unies (quoted in Leonard, The Case of Eritrea 1982: 110).

Seen from the perspective of the process of nation formation, the significance of the workplaces is that the agricultural, manufacturing and construction sites became the locus of convergence where cross-ethnic, cross-cultural, cross-regional and cross-religious interaction took place. Therefore, for the first time in the history of the society, a working class comprising the various ethnolinguistic groups that were subjected to the common exploitation, oppression, and discrimination of Italian capitalist entrepreneurs was born. Noting this development, Houtart elucidates,

> It was multinational in composition and developed a sharp sense of common identity in the course of its inhuman exploitation by Italian capital. Under the Italian fascism, workers had no rights whatsoever. Fascist colonial legislation forbade the formation of associations and trade unions. Due to the brutal and the racial character of the oppression of the working class, its reaction to fascist policies was sporadic and unsustained (Houtart 1979: 5).

It seems appropriate to surmise that in a political fashion, such circumstances would gradually lead to the creation of a sense of solidarity among the workers themselves, and a national awakening and political activism (cf. Yohannes 1991: 11). This speculation makes sense, in part, because the workers would be likely to develop a common dislike, perhaps even hatred, directed toward the foreign capitalists, generated by the harsh treatment, exploitation and oppression. Perhaps it was these common circumstances, as they were described in detail by Killion (1985, 1997), which prompted the active engagement of workers in the nationalist political movement in general, and in the opposition to the Ethiopian encroachment on the Federation in particular.

One of the accumulated effects of colonialism and the penetration of colonial capital was the establishment of the Eritrean trade union in 1952, *the Eritrean General Union of Labour Syndicates*. It also created a national awareness through which the workers would eventually become an indispensable force in the nationalist struggle. Killion (1985), in his study about workers and workers' nationalism in Eritrea, has found that the dockworkers were the first to resist the Ethiopian encroachment. The first strike of its kind by the dockworkers was triggered by the introduction of an Ethiopian identity card. The strike was put down, particularly in Assab, by the Ethiopian military. The struggle of the dockworkers was followed by other sections of the working class, particularly in the Capital City. It culminated in the strikes and demonstrations of 1958, which were brutally suppressed, and in which 88 workers were believed to have lost their lives (see Killion 1985, 1997). These events triggered a powerful underground political resistance, led by the Eritrean Liberation Movement (ELM). Many members of the ELM were workers.

With the emergence of the National Liberation Movement (NLM), the participation of workers in the struggle continued. In recognition of workers' important role in the liberation struggle, the liberation fronts started to organise workers in trade unions in the early 1970s (see ELF 1971, 1975; EPLF 1977). In the beginning, the work of open organisation was mostly undertaken abroad within the exiled Eritrean communities. Later, as the NLM began to establish liberated zones, the task of organising workers inside Eritrea began. In Ethiopian-controlled Eritrean towns, basic workers' rights - freedom of organisation, demonstration, and expression - were prohibited. As a result, workers were organised in clandestine cells since late 1950s. These clandestine workers' cells played important role in the urban activities of the liberation organisations. Further, their participation included physically joining the liberation army, contributing money, smuggling materials from workplaces to the liberation organisations, disseminating political information and propaganda about the Eritrean revolution, rallying workers in support for the struggle.

The Urban Middle Class

By 1950, the number of people living in towns reached 219, 000, according to British statistics. This comprised 20 per cent of the total population of Eritrea (see Trevaskis 1960: 46, Leonard 1982: 77). If one pays attention to the fact that this growth began from virtually nothing, one can imagine how substantial the transformation was. In the Eritrean context, the task of defining and specifying not only the category of the urban middle class, but class in general is complicated. One thing that is clear, however, is that from the classification given by scholars who have touched upon the subject, the category is so broad that a cluster of social groups are encapsulated in it. This hopelessly complicates any attempt to provide a simple definition. Therefore, no attempt at such definition is made here and only some general constitutive indicators are given. It is perhaps possible to make a distinction that would be helpful in understanding the group along the lines of public and private spheres. In his account of the urban "petty bourgeoisie", Leonard (1982) specifies two significant groups, notably merchants and functionaries. With the penetration of colonial capital in the Eritrean society, a considerable number of people started to engage in commercial activities, thereby creating an integrated network of trade and commerce embracing the various ethno-linguistic groups (see Leonard 1982: 79). This is the area that is commonly identified as the private sphere. The rise of new types of commercial activities, in turn, led to the emergence of a new category of social group in the private sector. According to Leonard, this group progressively assumed an important social and political position, a position that further enabled it to make the maximum use of the limited educational possibilities.

The second group of the urban middle class - the functionaries - he lists as composites of the social group, public health assistants, medical orderlies, telephonists, senior clerks, accountants and agricultural supervisors (Leonard 1982: 82). These are categories of social groups related to the public sphere. The expansion of a network of public sphere activities, both under Italian colonial rule and during British Administration, was behind the emergence of this category of urban middle class. Leonard also argues that the expansion of this group really took place under British occupation. This, in turn, proves the immense growth of the public sphere under British Administration, particularly in the area of education. The defeat of Italy also opened up an opportunity for Eritreans to take over some of the civil service jobs previously occupied by Italians. Another group that should be included in the category of urban middle class is the intelligentsia, and it is treated separately below. It could thus be concluded, with fair certainty, that the urban middle class emerged as a result of the rise of two different categories of social groups involved in two distinct social spheres of activity, the private and the public spheres.

In the discourse of modernisation theory, urban centres are perceived primarily as sites of acculturation in which people come into contact with all aspects of modernisation. In an effort to explain the emergence of nations along the lines of modernisation theory, Gellner (1983) formulates the view as follows: modernisation produces nationalism and nationalists create nations. An extension of this view suggests that it is out of the urban middle class that these nationalists emerge. It was the modern urban middle class with its economic, social and political ambitions that was the spearhead of the political struggle. Urban life gave birth to a new and assertive leadership, and to a variable and easily manipulated mass following (Coleman 1960). This idea is based on the fundamental assumption of modernisation sociology that contends that urbanisation unleashes social forces that invest actors with a great deal of ambition and expectation of achievement. Concomitantly, these actors are presumed to show ingenuity in assuming power and political leadership. It is also argued that this ambition drives them to be champions of innovation, and to evoke the masses into resistance against alien domination.

In the wake of Italian colonialism, the Eritrean urban middle class was too feeble, politically inexperienced and beset with internal contradictions, to be able to take on its expected role of political leadership. The source of this lack of capacity was derived from the variation of its composition, which was characterised by sub-national elements such as ethnicity, religion and language. Moreover, this incapacity can also be attributed to the spontaneity and suddenness of the demise of Italian colonial rule. The Eritrean urban middle class was simply not prepared for what unfolded in 1941. In contrast to many Anglophone and Francophone colonies, and particularly to Anglophone colonies in which the colonial power had prepared them before conceding them their independence, the Eritreans had had no opportunity to exercise any sort of self-governance. The philosophy of indirect rule – the model applied in the Anglophone colonies – delegated limited self-rule to indigenous political forces and institutions. This furnished the colonies, according to Mazrui (1983), with vital experience in the art of statecraft and governance – an important asset at the time of independence.

In addition, colonial powers usually opted for a peaceful hand over of political power at the point at which it became clear that an independence movement was impossible to delay or stop. Such a hand-over had to include a transition period in order for an orderly transfer of power to take place, but it was also necessary for a liberal democratic political order to be put in place. Accordingly, political parties were established and permitted to function actively. Political leaders and candidates were groomed, trained and prepared. In contrast to all these, the demise of Italian rule in Eritrea was not only very sudden, but it also was immediately followed by the take-over of another colonial power – a colonial power which arrived with its own agenda.

So it was for a variety of reasons that Eritrea was in a poor position to take smooth steps from colonial to independent status. The Italian implementation of direct rule deprived the urban middle class of the expertise of governance, and the sudden collapse of Italian rule came without the necessary preparation. Even the limited liberal democratic freedom experienced under British occupation was not intended to prepare the territory for independence. The British were convinced that a unified independent Eritrea had no chance of survival. Thus, it seems that their expectation was that the emergence of the Moslem League and the Unionist Party would lead to the partition of Eritrea. With this view as their guidance, they could not play the role of grooming a unified Eritrean leadership that would lead the territory to sovereignty.

In conclusion, the urban middle class, which could have played the role of leadership, was not only taken by surprise – the new situation was accompanied by the intervention of external actors. Hence, the overall outcome of all these factors was that when the future of Eritrea came under consideration, the middle class was in disarray and chaos. This disarray and chaos gave way to the emergence of a divided nationalism.

The Intelligentsia

Social science in general – and political sociology in particular – pays considerable attention to the prominence of the intelligentsia in the process of nation formation. It would be perhaps unthinkable to talk about the discourse of the process of nation formation in nations like Germany and Italy without mentioning scholars like Heinz Herder in Germany, Giuseppe Mazzini and Garibaldi in Italy, or Frantz Fanon in connection with Algeria and Amilcar Cabral in Guinea-Bissau. The contribution of intellectuals is not limited to formulating nationalist ideas and theories. It stretches beyond that toward a practical dimension, in the creation of nationalist movements bearing the historical responsibility of constructing the nation. We find this well formulated in the famous Italian saying, 'we have made Italy, now we have to make Italians' (Neuberger 1994). It is now widely recognised that the intelligentsia was the force behind the emergence of nationalism in the colonial territories. The intelligentsia's leading role arises from what Anderson has designated as their bilingual literacy (Anderson 1991: 115). Moreover, according to Anderson, bilingualism opened the opportunity for learning "through the European language-of-state to modern Western culture in the broader sense, and, in particular, to the models of nationalism, nation-ness, and nation-state" (Anderson 1991: 116). In stressing the key role played by colonialism in the creation of the intelligentsia and the nationalist political leadership another scholar notes, "colonialism ... created nationalist political leadership by an indigenous bureaucracy educated with the values of Western nationalism but subject to discrimination" (Gledhill 1994: 79). It is the need of the colonial states of 'armies of clerks' (Anderson 1991) which facilitated the creation of the indigenous intelligentsia. In the case of Eritrea, referring to the role played by Italian colonialism in the emergence of Eritrean intelligentsia, Houtart (1979: 5) notes, "a handful of Eritreans were trained to become interpreters, low level clerks, etc. These constituted a small intelligentsia". Leonard (1982: 217) also draws a similar conclusion.

Despite the long struggle for independence in Eritrea, we do not find a Mazzini, a Herder, a Fanon or a Cabral – intellectuals of an international calibre. This has probably been a chief weakness in the Eritrean nationalist movement. The history of the development of Eritrean intellectuals can be traced to the expansion of modern education under the guidance of Mission schools. The Italian colonial policy of education was expressed succinctly by a one-time British Administration official: 'keep the Eritrean's belly filled while keeping his brain empty' (Trevaskis 1960). Education for Eritreans' was so limited that school under the guidance of the colonial authority was only permitted up to fourth grade (cf. Trevaskis 1960). In terms of content, the Eritrean student was supposed merely to read, write and understand the Italian language, and to know the basic mathematical operations. The Mission schools produced the few Eritreans with higher educational qualification. The fascist regime closed missionary schools, including the Swedish Evangelical Mission (SEM). As a result, the number of students graduating from European-managed schools decreased. Between 1934 and 1940, about 800 graduated from four-year elementary school, while only 81 received secondary schooling (Killion 1985: 284). Those who obtained higher education attended missionary schools. Woldeab Woldemariam, a journalist and prominent figure in the Liberal Progressive Party, graduated in 1930 from the SEM teacher's college in Belesa (Killion 1985: 305). Tedla Bairu, the first executive of the Eritrean government, was educated by the SEM, and received his secondary education in the Instituto Magistrale of Florence in Italy in 1933 (Killion 1985: 306). Gebre Meskel Woldu, the first president of the Unionists, was French-educated (Killion 1985: 302). It is estimated that between 1894 and 1948 some 20,000 Eritreans received primary education in local languages (Leonard 1982: 81).

Some observers describe the Italian colonial policy toward the indigenous educational efforts as marked by a civilising mission, which was intended, to Italianize the indigenous population (De Marco 1943: 16). This mission of Italianisation was not, however, founded on the principle of egalitarianism, with intention of granting Italian citizenship to the indigenous population. Rather, it was driven by the classical doctrine of colonialism – changing the mental outlook of the population. They were to be impressed with the greatness of Italian civilisation, learn to show respect for the Italian colonising ability, and to be persuaded of their privileged status as a colony under the domination of modern Rome (De Marco 1943: 7-8). Yet, this civilising mission was marked by highly limited objectives. It was not the intention of the colonial authority to produce an all-dimensional civilised, colonised society. Rather, its vision was driven by the functional, instrumentalist, colonialist doctrine of manufacturing a colonial society that was to become a malleable and loyal servant to the colonial master. Therefore colonial education policy was very attentive in making sure that an enlightened and independent mind that defies servitude is not created. There were few areas in which the indigenous population was expected – or permitted – to earn basic skills and knowledge. "The government native school proposed to create a reserve of artists, craftsmen, agriculturists, interpreters, typists, bookkeepers, radio operators, record keepers, native teachers and junior clerks. However, Italy did not plan to overeducate the natives, for fear of creating misfits" (De Marco 1943: 21). It was well known that the primary objective of the colonial policy of education was to produce future soldiers (De Marco 1943: 22). This restriction of education, not only in size but also in the quality and objectives, inhibited the development of the intelligentsia.

The political actors who surfaced in the political arena following the termination of the Italian colonial rule were a blend of the emerging intelligentsia and the traditional elite. In the highland, the elite at the time of the demise of Italian colonial rule was primarily composed of the urban middle class and the landlords and the higher echelon of the ecclesiastical establishment. In the lowland, it was composed of the ruling aristocracy and religious leaders, as well as a nascent urban middle class. The traditional literate elites were mostly of religious origin. Their status was attributed primarily to their ability read, comprehend and interpret the Bible and the Koran. But with the penetration of colonial capital and its social implications, new elites started to emerge. The modern elite was composed of merchants, men who joined the Italian army, and men recruited into the bureaucratic administration as clerks, teachers, interpreters, etc. These groups found themselves on a collision course with the 'old guard'.

To elucidate the new social changes in the composition of the intelligentsia, let us examine first the situation in the primarily Moslem communities of the lowland. Two important measures taken by Italian colonial rulers had a conspicuous effect on the emergence of the new elite in the Moslem communities. First, was the availability of opportunities for the serf class to engage in novel means of subsistence. These involved the possibility of joining the colonial army, of finding employment in railway and road construction works, in mining and agricultural projects, or serving in the lower levels of the bureaucracy. This transformed the life of many serfs. Second, was the change in the tribute system. The Italians passed a decree[4] to abolish the payment of tribute by serfs to the aristocrats. Instead, it was decided that tribute should be paid directly to the colonial state. This act further weakened the economic, social and political power of the old aristocratic class, while the serfs were slowly moving toward their freedom. A social differentiation leading to the emergence of a new elite was taking place. The overall outcome of the change was to pave the way for the development of a skilled new social group that was to constitute the embryo of the emergent modern intelligentsia. The most prominent figure that was the product of this change was Ibrahim Sultan, leader of the Moslem League and former Italian interpreter. He was of serf origin educated in Italian school in Keren. Under British rule, the movement for the emancipation of the serfs gained momentum, led by the new intelligentsia. An organisation, the Moslem League (to be discussed in the next chapter), played a leading role in the emancipation of the serfs.

The British educational policy represented a radical shift from Italian policy. Under British rule, government schools conducted in indigenous languages were established. The number of schools and grade levels jumped enormously. The enrolment of elementary school students, for instance, grew from 2,405 in 1941 to 9,131 in 1950, while middle schools, with an enrolment capacity of 900 students, were also established (Teklehaimanot 1996: 18). Further, an opportunity was opened to Eritrean Moslems for higher education in the Sudan and Egypt. In Egypt, the famous El Azhari University produced a number of Eritrean Moslem intellectuals. The evident result of the growth of the number of Moslem Eritreans who completed their higher education in the Middle East was demonstrated in the inception of the nationalist movement (see Amar 1997). The formation of the ELM in the Sudan and formation of the ELF in Egypt was the legacy of this change in educational opportunity. In their political vision and practices, these nascent intellectuals were very much influenced by the political culture of this corner of the world. The likelihood of Eritrean Moslems acquiring higher education in the Middle East and Islamic countries increased with the later Ethiopian occupation and the advance of the NLM. As the opportunity for education for the Moslems in Ethiopian-occupied Eritrea successively diminished, many Eritrean Moslems travelled to the Middle East in search of higher education. Consequently, a considerable number of Eritrean Moslems were educated and socialised in the Middle East's culture and politics.

Toward the close of Italian colonial rule, particularly after Italy invaded Ethiopia, many Christian Eritreans emigrated to Ethiopia and continued their education there. At the end of the war, several of them were given higher posts in the Ethiopian State machinery. In the aftermath of the Italian rule, this group of intelligentsia played a crucial role in promoting Ethiopian interests in Eritrea. Organised first in the *Yehager Fikir Mahber,* and later in the Unionist Party (discussed in the next chapter), this group struggled to unite Eritrea with Ethiopia. In much the same way as occurred in the Moslem communities, it was the expansion of modern education under the British Administration that produced more educated, ambitious, young intellectuals in the highland Christian region. The successive growth of the new intelligentsia gradually increased the gap between the old and new intelligentsia, and at the same time established the mechanism for the substitution of the traditional intelligentsia by a modern one. Another important dimension is that while most of the Moslems travelled to Arab countries in search of higher education, most of the Christians travelled to Ethiopia after completing their high school education, with some going to Europe. This was to have considerable politico-cultural implications.

Many have stressed that one of the areas in which the British Administration's contribution was clearly seen is in the relative expansion of education and schools. This meant not only that many school-age children from the different ethno-linguistic groups and religions had the opportunity to attend classes, but also that schools became a meeting point for these youngsters from the various ethno-linguistic groups. These schools were slowly to become a rallying place for the growing student resistance against the Ethiopian occupation (see Amar 1997). This, in turn, meant a strengthening of a new intelligentsia that gradually assumed the political leadership of the liberation movement. Overall, it could be said that the expansion of education produced a new intelligentsia that was to play a key role in the process of nation formation.

In conclusion, education under Italian rule was very limited. Under British administration, however, a considerable expansion was seen. The expansion continued under the Ethiopian occupation. However, the Moslem segment of the society felt more and more excluded, and thus had to look for education in the Middle East. The Christians, on the other hand, turned to Ethiopia, Europe and the USA. It could also be emphasised that generally, the intelligentsia began to rapidly expand under the British Administration.

SUMMARY AND CONCLUSION

It is often argued in the sociology of development that economic changes lead to both predicted and unpredicted changes in social, cultural, and personality spheres. This argument is particularly prevalent among those who are proponents of the various branches of the modernisation theory, such as the evolution theory and the diffusion theory. This Chapter has discussed two aspects, first the economic changes that occurred as the result of the penetration of the Italian colonial capital, and second their consequences mainly in the social sphere. I have also made an effort to demonstrate the social changes that took place following the economic transformation.

The correlation between the material base and the corresponding national consciousness is a subject of controversy. In contrast to Leonard, whose conviction is that material growth led to a corresponding national consciousness, Trevaskis, fails to make the connection between the material base and national consciousness despite his great appreciation of the material innovation that accompanied Italian rule. Without resorting to the strictest sense of the notion of the base/superstructure determinist correlation, I have argued in this Chapter that the changes in the material base, in the final analysis, led to social structural changes.

Although there is an obvious shortage of data on the different classes and social groups, it is possible to draw the conclusion that a substantial social transformation had, in fact, taken place. The evidence for this was, in the first place, the emergence of modern towns, ports, airports, schools, hospitals, banks, industries, agricultural projects, and communications infrastructure such as the postal system, telephone lines, telegraph, roads and railway lines. In the second place, following this material transformation, a change in the social structure also occurred. The manifestation of this structural change was the emergence of modern social groups. Illustrative examples of the latter are 1) the emergence of a working class - employed in the manufacturing and construction industries and in the various agricultural projects; 2) the growth of a modern urban, commercial, middle class, which was the result of the emergence of urban centres; 3) a modern urban middle class employed in the civil service and the emergence of two social groups - the soldiers in the colonial army and the female domestic servants employed in the Italian household; and 4) the rise of the intelligentsia (mostly teachers, clerks and interpreters).

Notes

1. He divides the "development" of Eritrea into four phases. The first phase stretches up to the battle of Adwa 1896, and according to him this phase was characterised by the projects of settling Italian settlers and providing the logistical structure needed for projects of military expansion. The second phase included the period between 1896 up to 1930. Here the settlement and military projects were scrapped. The third phase began in the early 1930s and was marked by the rapid economic development and a large number of Italian settlers flowing to the colony. Finally, the fourth phase encompasses the British rule from 1941 to 1952 (Leonard 1982: 61).

2. The Durkheimian dichotomy of an organic and a mechanical solidarity is frequently interpreted by scholars – and according to Cohen (1985), erroneously – as the two extremes of a continuum of developmentalism, notably traditionalism and modernism. In conformity with the former, conventional interpretation, rural society ('community') is perceived as a small, parochial, stable and of 'face-to-face' contact. People interact with one another as 'total' social persons, informed by a comprehensive personal knowledge of each other. Their relationships are often underpinned by ties of affinity and consanguinity. Conversely urban society is characterised by complexity and anonymity, in a process of continual innovation, etc. Furthermore, the two are assumed to be stationed on two extremes of the continuum of the developmental process. Cohen's assertion of the conventional interpretation of the Durkheimian notion of mechanical and organic solidarity as erroneous maintains that Durkheim's complementarity is compatible with the urban/rural dichotomy. The qualities allegedly attributed to 'community' (rural) can readily be found in the society (urban). The symbolic construction of community in a society co-exists with its individualistic dimension.
3. The figure, according to the report, included family members of the workers. But how many family members there were, or whether they were children, spouse, or father and mother is not revealed in the report.
4. The decree which was passed in the year 1931 to abolish the requirement of paying tribute to the aristocratic class seriously shook the power of the *Nabtab* and *Shumagele*. According to the Italians, this measure was intended to institutionalise the office of the chiefs by making it a salaried office instead of depending on an unpredictable income of serfs. But the practical consequence was that the chieftainship as an institution was weakened because its function was taken by the colonial state both in terms of providing security for the serfs, and controlling and determining the tribute system.

Chapter 5

POLITICO-LEGAL INTEGRATION: THE EMERGENCE OF POLITICAL AND LEGAL INSTITUTIONS

INTRODUCTION

The debate among social science scholars regarding the legacy of colonial rule has focused on the role colonialism played in transforming the legal and political systems of the colonised communities, creating more centralised and integrated societies (see Hodgkin 1956, Emerson 1960, Rokkan 1973, Smith 1983, etc.). Today it is a widely acknowledged fact that the current African political entities are the creation of colonialism. Nevertheless, the particular ramifications of colonial rule remain a subject of controversy. In fact, disputes and divergent views characterise the debate. Various sociological theorists, including dependence theorists, modernisation theorists and underdevelopment theorists (cf. Harrison 1988, Kiely 1995) have suggested opposing and competing views concerning the effect of colonial rule on the colonised societies.

The centralisation of politico-legality refers primarily to the implementation of constitutional governance and political liberalism. In light of the arguments and debates concerning the importance of contributions in this dimension, this chapter examines the legal and political institutions that were established as the result of colonial rule. The emergence of legal and political institutions are, then, to be evaluated in the context of the process of nation formation. The viability of this approach should be considered in light of the preceding theoretical discussions. Particularly in the civic conception of the formation of nations, we have seen that the point of emphasis, as a foundation of the emergence of a nation, is the flourishing of a variety of institutions - political, legal, economic, social and cultural. These institutions, according to the theories we have seen, foster cohesion and interdependence in society. From this perspective, institutions are seen as serving as the brick, sand and cement with which the nation is built. Conversely, the absence of such institutions, it is argued, produces a weakly-integrated society. This leads to weak affinities and loyalties, rendering the society fragile, with high probability of disintegration at any time. The integration model alluded to here pertains primarily to political and legal dimensions.

This chapter examines the political development that took place in Eritrea in conjunction with the demise of the Italian colonial rule. It assesses developments that occurred between 1941 and 1961. In doing so, it makes an attempt to analyse and give account of what happened, why it happened and what effects it had in the process of formation of the Eritrean nation. The focus on this particular period is justified, because it was during this period that political parties emerged as a result of political liberalisation under British Administration and the promulgation of the Eritrean Constitution following the federal agreement. These two developments enhanced the politico-legal integration of the Eritrean society that began under Italian rule. The chapter consists, in addition to the introduction and conclusion, of four sections. The first section discusses the emergence of political parties. Section two deals with the schism concerning political solution to the disposition of Eritrea. In section three we examine the federation with Ethiopia and its implications for Eritrean nationalism. The last section discusses the decline of the autonomous state of Eritrea.

THE EMERGENCE OF POLITICAL PARTIES

The emergence of political parties is typically approached from one of two theoretical perspectives. These include mobilisation theory and participation theory. Mobilisation theory (e.g. Pye 1962, Apter 1963, Huntington 1968) explains the aims and ideas of mobilisation and organization strategies intended to accomplish a particular specific mission of central value to the collectivity. Participation theory describes the participation of citizens in national politics as transcending the local and sub-national levels. It is also thought that mass mobilisation and participation are generated by social forces. Such activity quite often takes the form of establishing organisations/parties. In this context, the task of the mobilising force–elites, intelligentsia, and political leaders–is to gear the society towards national development.

Perceived in terms of mobilisation, participation and organisation, the decade of British rule (1941-1952) is unique in Eritrean history. During no other time has the Eritrean political arena experienced a functioning political plurality. However, this decade, sometimes also known as the 'Era of Parties', is full of contradictions and paradoxes. A close examination of the situation in Eritrea along the lines of mobilisation and participation theories shows that significant mobilisation and participation under the guidance of the nascent political parties took place. Commenting on the level of mobilisation, Markakis (1987: 57-8) notes that Eritrean society was more politically mobilised than the societies surrounding it – Sudan or Somalia. The reason for this mobilisation, Markakis suggests, can be found in the economic implications of colonialism for both the pastoral and the peasant sections of the society. He contends that both segments of the society were dramatically affected by colonial economic policies. Concerning the implications of colonial rule, a distinction is made between Italian and British rules. The general view is that while Italy is believed to have succeeded in establishing the material foundation of the Eritrean nation, Britain's contribution is considered to be in the introduction of new political ideas (Longringg 1945, Trevaskis 1960, Ellingson 1977). Trevaskis, for instance, noting these contributions writes:

> A deliberate and indeed cynical, policy of keeping the Eritrean's belly full and his head empty had earned the Italians political tranquillity. During the (British) Occupation, the process was reversed. Eritrean heads were now filled with new ideas gleaned from lectures and books provided by the English Institute and British Information Office, the weekly Tigrinyan newspaper, contact with Indians and Sudanese serving in the British forces, and the liberalism of the British administration. Influences of this kind, married to the economic distress which followed bred discontent and then political consciousness (Trevaskis 1960: 47).

The most significant contribution of the British Administration was political liberalisation. Three principle underlying factors can be postulated concerning the emergence of political parties in this context. The first is the British Administration's policy of political liberalism (Trevaskis 1960). The British attempt to introduce liberal democratic political thought in all its colonies is frequently interpreted as an attempt to transplant the British political tradition into those societies after they achieve their independence (Mazrui 1983). In this way, the continued influence of its political and cultural legacy was thought to be better safeguarded. As is clearly stated in the citation above British officials, in the aim of impregnating their political ideas carried out extensive political enlightenment. The second factor is the need to find a settlement for the colonial territory, and this in turn necessitated dressing it in popular garments. For this purpose, the administrative authorities encouraged the formation of parties (Ellingson 1977: 265). The third factor is the opportunity extended to the elites to determine the future destiny of the society (cf. Markakis 1988, Tadia 1990). This last factor is directly connected with the indigenous political forces and political power. It was enhanced by the relative political freedom that prevailed under the British rule–and the urgent need to determine the future of Eritrea. The elites were faced, for the first time, with the problem of grappling with state power. But this came at a time when they were in disarray, and when political unity had not crystallised. The following lengthy quotation describes the situation cogently.

> 'The Urban natives', real desires are for a greater share in the administration of their country and opportunity for more lucrative employment in its bureaucracy.'[23] It could be added that the pastoralist serfs were clamouring for emancipation, while their masters, as well as the Christian Church and the remnants of the Abyssinian nobility, were yearning for a restoration of their former pre-eminence.... Not surprisingly, each group was inclined to grasp whatever support was

> offered, domestically or from abroad. The unionists embraced Ethiopia and conceded sovereignty in the belief that they were gaining local dominance, and the Muslims flirted with Italy, the lesser evil, since union with Ethiopia spelled complete subordination. Unionist concessions were not made in the spirit of self-abnegation. On the contrary, they were a means toward political aggrandisement. As Trevaskis discerned, 'fundamentally, the reason why they supported the Unionist Party was that they believed their interests would be better served under Ethiopian than under European colonial rule' (1960: 130) (Markakis 1987: 69).

The first association to emerge representing the entire society, the *Mahber Fikri Hager Ertra*[1] (Association for the Love of the Country of Eritrea), was formed in 1941. Available data indicate that this Association was originally formed for the purpose of co-ordinating the relationships between the British Military Administration (BMA) and the Eritrean society. At its early stage, the aim of the Association was defined as a forum of discussion with the intention to participate in ongoing dialogue with the British concerning the day to day practical issues (Markakis 1987: 62-3). In reference to this development the British archive of the War Office (WO) notes: "An Eritrean Council has been formed, under the control of P.O. Native Affairs, to examine grievances and to endeavour to explain the actions of the Administration in cases where they are not understood" (WO 230-106, 1942). However, it was not long before the Association was drawn to political issues. This was expedited by Emperor Haile Selassie's claim to Eritrea after he was reinstalled in the Ethiopian throne in 1941. The Emperor of Ethiopia, in search of support for his goal of political union among Eritreans, targeted the Association. The instrument for this objective became the Society of the Unification of Eritrea with Ethiopia (SUEE), founded in Addis Ababa by the initiative of the Emperor, and also known as *Yehager Fikir Mahber* (Tekle 1999). Amare Tekle suggests that Ethiopia founded an organisation from among Eritreans residing in Addis Ababa and named it *Yehager Fikir Mahber* (in Amharic). This created confusion because it was mixed with the Eritrean Association formed in Eritrea under its Tigrinya name *Mahber Fikri Hager*. Many observers mistook the two organisations as being one. The Church also became a prominent instrument in the unification effort. As Trevaskis (1960: 60) stated it: "by 1942 every priest had become a propagandist in the Ethiopian cause".

> Eritreans in Ethiopian service were dispatched to Asmara to organise support, bringing money and promises to ease their task, and leading members of the Christian community were persuaded their interests lay with the Ethiopian regime (Markakis 1987: 63).

The first signs of the split in the *Mahber Fikri Hager* became clear in 1944, when unionists dominated the Association (Ellingson 1977: 261, Gebre-Medhin 1989: 72) and the independentists started to abandon it. An attempt to resolve the differences between the unionists and independentists led to the meeting

Figure 5.1: Proliferation of political parties

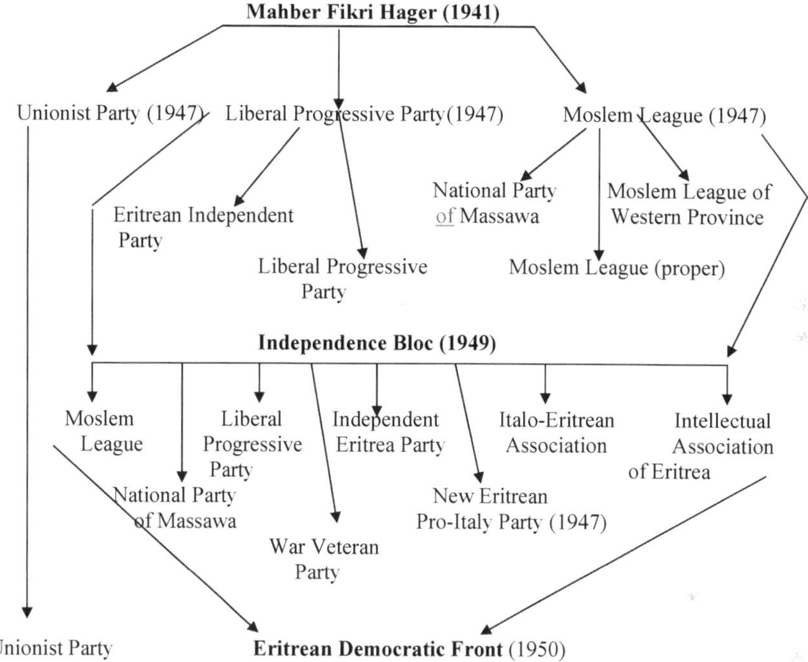

of Bet Giorgis in November 1946. This meeting was convened to discuss the compromise agreement of *Hibret Biwi'el* (conditional union), reached between the unionists and independentists (EPLF 1983: 93-95, Killion 1985: 307). However, the meeting failed to achieve its goals. The failure was attributed chiefly to the Ethiopian Liaison Officer's intervention (Trevaskis 1960: 74), and this effectively sealed the split between the unionists and independentists. In the Bet Giorgis Meeting, it also became quite clear to the Moslems that the only way to counter the intransigence of the unionists was to form their own political party. Consequently, Ibrahim Sultan and Abdulkadir Kebire formed the Islamic Association to challenge the Unionists (Markakis 1987: 64). The year 1947 was a landmark for the proliferation of political parties, and several parties (a total of eight) were formally registered (see FPC 1949). The arrival of the Four Power Commission of Investigation also precipitated the formation of the parties. In 1948, the pro-independence parties formed a common front known as the Independence Bloc (IB). After the UN adopted a resolution of federation in 1950, the Bloc changed its name to the Eritrean Democratic Front (Ellingson 1977: 276-9).

In conclusion, the *Mahber Fikri Hager,* which was originally formed to represent the Eritrean society in its daily interaction with the BMA, was gradually drawn into politics as the issue of the disposition of the territory emerged to the surface. The *Mahber* failed to preserve its original objective of representation of the whole society primarily due to Ethiopian interference. Finally, it was split, with three political parties growing from it: the Unionist Party, the Moslem League and the Liberal Progressive Party. The figure below illustrates the number of parties that originated from the *Mahber*, the split and realignment that took place. In the following sections, the prominent parties will be discussed in some detail.

FORMATION AND COMPOSITION OF THE UNIONIST PARTY

Immediately after Emperor Haile Selassie was reinstated to the Ethiopian throne in 1941, he extended his claim to Eritrea and Italian Somaliland. This claim was made on the basis of historical, cultural, geographical and legal premises. Among the methods through which the cause of unification was intended to be accomplished, was the creation of public support in Eritrea. As a first step towards the fulfilment of this objective, Eritreans living in Addis Ababa were to be organised. This resulted in the formation of an association called *Natsa Hamasien* (Free Eritrea) and 'The Society for the Unification of Ethiopia and Eritrea'[2] (SUEE). These were under the direct control of the Ethiopian government founded in Addis Ababa in 1944 (Trevaskis 1960: 65-6, Ellingson 1977: 269). It was also known in its Amharic name as Yehager Fikir Mahber (Tekle 1999). Its members were high-ranking civil servants of the Ethiopian State. According to Trevaskis (1960: 65-6) the SUEE, based in Addis Ababa and financed and directed by the Ethiopian government, took over the cause of unification from supporters of union in Eritrea. Markakis, too, is of the opinion that members of the SUEE were sent to Eritrea to recruit supporters to the union cause. Accordingly, many leading Christians, including leading members of the *Mahber Fikri Hager* were persuaded that their interest lay with Ethiopia. The latter were also persuaded to rename the *Mahber* to the Association for the Union of Eritrea with Ethiopia, which caused several Moslem–and some of its Christian members–to leave the *Mahber* (Markakis 1987: 63). This account clearly shows how the agents of Haile Selassie targeted the *Mahber*.

Therefore, it was not a coincidence that the same year the SUEE was formed in Addis Ababa, a division in the *Mahber Fikri Hager Ertra* started to emerge. This division is assumed by some scholars to mark the genesis of the Unionist Party[3] (UP) in Eritrea. After it became known that Italy had lost its claim on its former colonies in accordance with the Italian Peace Treaty of 1947 (Becker 1952: 102), and when the British lifted the ban on the formation of political parties, the Association for the Union of Eritrea with Ethiopia changed its name to the Eritrea-Ethiopia Union Party, in short known as the Unionist Party (UP) (Markakis 1987: 64). The UP was officially founded in March 21 1947 (Gebre-Medhin 1989: 97). With respect to the political and social nature of the Unionist Party, scholars of Eritrea differ in their view.

Some researchers have tried to elucidate the nature of the UP by looking into the social and class composition of its leadership. It is broadly accepted that the composite social groups of the Party were a) the higher clergy; b) the aristocracy; and c) the upper section of the urban middle class (Ellingson 1977: 265, Houtart 1982: 223, Leonard 1982: 90, Gebre-Medhin 1989: 97). It is also widely acknowledged that many of the aristocrats from the Moslem communities joined the UP in the union cause due to the serf emancipation movement (Trevaskis 1960: 73, EPLF/British Administration and Eritrean Political Struggle 1941-1950 p. 59). The participation of aristocrats from the Moslem communities in the union cause supports the argument that the popular view–that the Christians supported union while Moslems stood for independence–seems to be not entirely true. Not only were there many Moslems who supported union with Ethiopia, many were also members of the UP. Some studies show that the leadership of the UP, the Central Committee, was comprised of 22 Moslems and 20 Christians (Gebre-Medhin 1989: 197-8).

Unfortunately, data on the UP is very scarce. The secondary material is also permeated with contradictory statements and information, which render it problematic for analysis of the Party. The available studies are inconclusive concerning the Party's aims and time of the formation (the date of its official foundation is given as March 21, 1947–made possible by the lifting of the ban on political activities by the British). According to Negash (1997: 37), the Party was formed in May 5, 1941, the same day that Emperor Haile Selassie returned to Addis Ababa from exile, to seek unification with the motherland. Markakis, referring to *Mahber Fikri Hager* rather than the UP, explains that the formation of the *Mahber* was prompted by the fact that the Italians continued to enjoy their bureaucratic position and their economic welfare under the British rule–something that frustrated some of the future Eritrean political leaders (Markakis 1987: 62). Ellingson argues that the *Mahber* came into existence in connection with Ethiopia's claim for Eritrea and it was changed to the UP in 1944 (Ellingson 1977: 261). Trevaskis (1960: 60) suggests that "*Mahaber Fekri Hager* or the Love of Country Association, dedicated to uniting Eritrea with Ethiopia, came into being during 1942". The account of the Eritrean nationalist discourse also tells that while *Mahber Fekri Hager* was a nationalist organisation representing the whole society, the UP came into existence as the result of the split within the *Mahber Fikri Hager.* This split was triggered by the intervention of Ethiopia (see EPLF 1983).

A point of interest is the base of the UP. While the main base of the UP was in the Hamasen region, the LPP had its base in the Akkele Guzai region. One wonders why the UP sought to unite Eritrea with Shewan-dominated Ethiopia whereas the LPP strove for the united Eritrea-Tigray independence. It might not be possible to provide a straight simple answer. One possible explanation could be that a territorially-based identity was more developed in the Hamasen region than in the Akkele Guzai region. The Hamasen region, perhaps as a periphery of the Tigrean power centre, had gradually drifted away. And already since around the 14th Century, the tension and competition between the power structure centred in the Hamasen and surrounding areas and the power centre in Tigray had grown apart. If this hypothesis is correct, then the motive believed to induce the Unionists to strive for union with the Shewan-dominated Ethiopia cannot be Ethiopian national identity–at least not without accepting the abnegation of their own identity.

This can also be explained theoretically by the notion of centre-periphery. Several scholars (e.g. Rokkan 1981, Rokkan & Urwin 1982) have discussed the connection between periphery and centre in the emergence of nations. The central thesis of the centre-periphery notion is that the superordination of the centre should preside over the complete submission of the periphery. If the periphery possesses the capacity to challenge the centre in terms of economy, culture, military and diplomatic relations, the existence of a cohesive centralised nation is inhibited. Consequently, the periphery develops a separate identity. If we apply this to the case at hand, we find similarity, if not in terms of culture, in terms of economy, military and diplomatic relation. The region had been exposed to outside economic, military and diplomatic intervention since the 15th century. This led to the region retaining its autonomy (see Dilebo 1974, Rubenson 1976, Erlich 1982).

Another explanation is the self-interest hypothesis. Killion (1985) argues that the Hamasen region was the one most affected by Italian colonialism. The aristocrats of the Hamasen lost their land, while the aristocrats in the Akkele Guzai region were able to retain it. The aristocrats in the Hamasen thus expected to regain their land through the union they sought with Ethiopia. The Emperor promised that land that had been confiscated by the Italians would be returned to its owners when Eritrea joined Ethiopia, fostering this expectation. This hypothesis goes on in arguing that those in Akkele Guzai, in contrast, because they could exercise aristocratic power in the rural area, opted for independence. The next section will deal further with this self-interest hypothesis.

Unionism: Ethiopian Nationalism or Aristocratic Self-interest?

The political identity of the Unionist Party (UP) is one of the most contested issues in Eritrean history. The controversy revolves around the question of whether the UP represented Ethiopian nationalism–or was driven by a group of aristocrats who thought that their interests would be better served in the union with Ethiopia. In approaching this controversy, I will make use of the notion of formalist and substantialist. Formalist refers to an interpretation that is based on official statements and structural assumption rooted in imagined culture, religion and history. In the structuralist sense, it is a predeterminist view in that it argues that because of history, religion and culture the unionists manifested Ethiopian nationalism. Identity is here taken for granted, without problematisation. The substantialist perspective, in contrast, refers a mode of explanation that is sensitive to sociological reality. Identity is problematised and made contingent on contemporary sociological conditions. Based on this distinction, we can classify authors like Pankhurst and Pankhurst (1953), Trevaskis (1960), Erlich (1983), Negash (1987, 1997) in the formalist perspective. Those who can be classified in the substantialist group include Ellingson (1977), Leonard (1982), Houtart (1982), Killion (1985), Markakis (1987) and Gebre-Medhin (1989). In search of an explanation, this section will explore the political motives and nature of the UP by drawing upon what is here identified as the substantialist perspective.

The formalist perspective appears to be straightforward. Its arguments are based on the structural premises of the historical, cultural and religious connection of Eritrea with Ethiopia before Italian colonialism began. Thus, the effort by the UP to unite Eritrea with Ethiopia is perceived as originating from Ethiopian nationalism. It provides no space for consideration of the socio-economic transformation generated by European colonialism. Moreover, the basic sources used are the political rhetoric of the party and the archives of the BMA. The social and class origins of the Party are never critically analysed. As a result, this overly simplistic approach fails to appreciate the complex nature of political reality. Conversely, the substantialist perspective makes an effort to interpret and understand the real political cleavages of the period through examining the multiple factors that were involved in determining the political behaviour of the UP, and takes into consideration socio-economic innovation. In short, it is a contextualist approach, which analyses circumstances within the framework of their proper setting, giving a more satisfactory sociological explanation. Proponents of this perspective reject the Ethiopian nationalism thesis and instead employ the self-interest thesis as an explanatory device.

Let us examine the arguments presented by the substantialist perspective. The central thesis espoused by the substantialist perspective is that the UP was motivated by aristocratic self-interest. Several explanations supporting this argument are presented. One of these is that the UP was the creation of Ethiopia and therefore it was not acting of its own free volition. In emphasising this view, Trevaskis (1960: 74) argues that the "party leaders were no longer free agents. They had became servants of the Ethiopian Government". Strong evidence proves Trevaskis' argument – those who attempted to act according to their own volition became casualties. Instances to be cited included: the first president of the *Mahber Fikri Hager,* Gebremeskel Woldu; the first Executive of the Eritrean Government, Tedla Bairu; the speaker of the Eritrean Parliament, Ali Radai and the police commissioner, Tedla Ocbit. These individuals were each sanctioned after actions or statements that antagonised Ethiopian interests. Gebremeskel Woldu was demoted from the presidency of the UP after the compromise agreement reached between the unionists and independentists (Killion 1985: 308) which led to the *Wa'ala Bet Giorgis*. Tedla Bairu was removed from his post when Ethiopia sensed that he was sympathetic toward the federalists (FO371/118738, 1955). Ali Radai and Tedla Ocbit also lost their posts in similar ways. In addition, the use of brute force by the UP was seen as a sign of the lack of confidence in Ethiopian nationalism. Before the demise of Italian rule, there was no sign of Ethiopian nationalism; thus, Ethiopia was forced to enlist the Orthodox Church to agitate for its cause, "by 1942, every priest had become a propagandist in the Ethiopian cause" (Trevaskis 1960: 60). Even within Ethiopia, Ellingson (1977: 261-2) citing the then Chief Administrator of Eritrea, S.H. Longrigg, writes, "the majority of Eritreans in Ethiopia did not, in 1944, favour unconditional union with the Solomonic Crown". Ethiopian nationalism had to be manufactured. The particular means used varied from persuasion to brute force and blackmail (excommunication).

Additional evidence that runs contrary to the Ethiopian nationalism theory is the rejection of the Amharic language as an official language. The UP leadership rejected the idea of the Amharic language as the official language of Eritrea (Trevaskis 1960: 117, Markakis 1987: 69). Markakis (1987: 69) argues that the rejection of the Amharic language, "hinted at the instrumental aspect of unionist attachment to Ethiopia that lay concealed behind the ideological screen woven from religious and historical threads". One can easily find support for this argument in cultural studies. Cultural theories emphasise the importance of language for the development of national identity. Vernacularisation is often presented as a process of the construction of identity. This is because it is believed that it represents the making of unique values, belief systems, symbols and aspirations, which are a vital prerequisite for the development, and perpetuation of a unique identity. The UP's rejection of the Amharic language in favour of the Tigrinya language can be then taken as evidence of maturation of an Eritrean national identity.

Moreover, an illustration presented as evidence of the absence of any substantial Ethiopian nationalism is the reaction of the unionists when Ethiopia began to infringe upon the Federation. Once they realised that Ethiopia was determined to dismantle the federation, the unionists changed their attitude (Greenfield 1965: 305, Markakis 1987: 69). The alliance forged between the leadership of the UP and the aristocrats of the Western Province was also seen as additional testimony to the self-interest nature of the union. It was believed that the two groups joined hands to restore the prerogatives they had lost under Italian rule (Ellingson 1977: 271, Markakis 1987: 69). In the eyes of many aristocrats of the lowland, the Moslem League represented the interest of the serfs. Therefore, the independence it advocated represented an additional, indirect threat to the prerogatives enjoyed by the aristocracy.

Was Ethiopian nationalism even plausible in Eritrea? Both the empirical data and the theoretical debate on the subject of nationalism must be examined to answer this question. With respect to the empirical data, the brief discussion above does not seem to unequivocally support the existence of Ethiopian nationalism. To investigate further on the empirical side, Trevaskis (1960) observed that Eritreans had fought loyally against Ethiopia, and on the side of Italy on two occasions – in the battle of Adwa and in the 1935 invasion of Abyssinia. A contingent of about 50,000 Eritrean soldiers did an impressive job in both conquering and pacifying Abyssinia. In recognition of this service, the Italian government issued a decree in 1937 to treat the Eritreans differently from other subjects of the empire. For instance, they were not to be addressed as natives but as Eritreans, and be given priority for certain jobs and professions (Negash 1997: 17).

The social relationships that existed before Italian colonialism also seem inconsistent with what would be expected according to theories of nationalism. The presence of any significant Ethiopian nationalism presupposes the continuous centralisation and integration of Eritrea under a centralised Ethiopian rule. Comparative historical analysis contends that bureaucratic and territorial centralisation are necessary conditions for the development of nationalism. In the relationship between Eritrea and Ethiopia, these conditions were in short supply. Alternatively, another condition which would need to prevail in order for Ethiopian nationalism to emerge in Eritrea is a congruity of ethnic identity between the ruled subjects and the ruling class that leads to cultural homogeneity – what Smith (1986) refers to as vertical or demotic ethnic identity (religio-ethnic identity). In such circumstances, the evocation of commonality could be brought about without the need for state centralisation and integration on the basis of primordial premises. However, these two fundamental requirements for the emergence of nationalism, state centralisation and ethnic homogeneity were absent in the Eritrean-Ethiopian relationship. This makes it unrealistic to talk about the resurgence of Ethiopian nationalism after close to 60 years of European colonial rule. When the debate on the future of Eritrea began in 'The Eritrean Weekly News' (EWN) in 1944, many of the debaters expressed their opposition to any union with Ethiopia, saying that Eritrea had nothing to do with Shewan Amharas (The EWN 1944). This can be taken as further testimony of the dubiousness of the so-called resurgence of Ethiopian nationalism.

Nationalism is a belief or movement, constructed within a specific socio-cultural context and in a specific spatio-temporal map. It is continuously formulated and constructed by the ongoing socio-cultural and historico-political innovation that guides the quest for political power – a political power that can be seen as the embodiment of a higher collective self-realisation of common identity, and expressed in the form of a sovereign state (cf. Breuilly 1993). All theoretical discussions present a compelling argument that primordial characteristics, unless activated, cannot adequately generate national consciousness, or nationalism. The interplay of factors predicated upon a specific temporal and spatial politico-historical reality, which transforms these primordial characteristics into modern, active political practices, is needed. In our case, the accumulated socio-economic and politico-historical experience of nearly 60 years provides the underlying foundation for the development of nationalism. In other words, nationalism presupposes the purposively-inculcated transcendence of the dormant inherent primordial characteristics to a much more active, conscious political activity. Therefore any attempt to trace the origin of Eritrean nationalism outside the socio-economic and politico-historical experience of colonial rule becomes a metaphysical venture which is characteristic of the "great Ethiopian" thesis. More will be said about Eritrean nationalism in Chapter Eight.

The argument we have followed so far demonstrates that the Ethiopian nationalism hypothesis fails to explain the various discrepancies and paradoxes involved in the history of the UP. The efforts to seek an explanation in primordial features such as ethnicity, language and religion, as has been the tendency in the Ethiopian nationalism hypothesis, does not, therefore, bear fruit. The main premise that the Ethiopian nationalism hypothesis rests upon is religious commonality between the Orthodox, Tigrinya-speaking Eritreans and Orthodox Ethiopia. However, religion is cosmological, thus, by itself is neither necessary nor sufficient for identity construction.

THE INDEPENDENCE BLOC

A coalition of several parties espousing independence for Eritrea, known as the Independence Bloc (IB), was formed in 1949. Elected to its leadership were Rasi Tessema Asberom as president, Ibrahim Sultan as general secretary and Woldeab Woldemariam as deputy general secretary (See Ellingson 1977: 276, EPLF 1983: 95, Markakis 1987: 66-7). The two most important parties in the Bloc were the Moslem League (ML) and the Liberal Progressive Party (LPP). The importance of these two parties rested upon the social fabric they represented. The Moslem League, the largest in the coalition, mobilised and organised the Moslem communities from different regions of Eritrea. The Liberal Progressive Party was chiefly composed of Christians from the highland region of Eritrea. In addition to their complete agreement on the realisation of immediate Eritrean independence with its present boundaries intact, the LPP accepted the demands of the ML for the reinstatement of territory inhabited by the Beni Amer, Beja, and Habab tribes, which it believed to have been annexed by Anglo-Egyptian Sudan (FO 371-63212 Jan 1947 No.13, FO 371-69363). The Moslem League also concurred with the idea of including Tigray in an independent Eritrea, as it was the demand of the LPP (FO 371- 63212 Jan. 1947 No. 13). These compromises showed the readiness of the nationalists to accommodate each other's goals and demands in order to achieve their common objective.

Other parties, smaller in terms of both size and political influence, were also actively operating in the political arena for independence. Many of these smaller political groups were based on more or less specific interests. In contemporary political terminology they could have been identified as interest groups – their main raison d'être probably being primarily the promotion of the particular interests of their members. But these specific interests could not be realised outside of the general national political framework. Moreover, since the achievement of their goals was linked to the general destiny of the society, they assumed a political character and the groups were identified as parties in the generic meaning of the term. To illustrate, the primary purpose of the Veteran Association was to promote the interests of the Eritrean veterans of the Italian army in the form of soliciting unpaid salaries, pensions and other similar benefits (cf. FO 371-63212, 1947: 2). However, the basic common denominator that bound the coalition together was the quest for independence.

The IB, despite its ardent support for independence and numerical majority, failed to realise its announced objective. This failure was the result of a number of underlying factors. First, as a result of the political nature of the coalition, it proved to be quite problematic to maintain unity (FO 1015-600, 1949: 6), thus, vicissitude, disintegration and reintegration characterised the Bloc. The disintegration took place within the ML and the LPP, which weakened both the coalition and the independence movement. Second, the political leadership of the Bloc was unable to provide solid, coherent and effective guidance. The socio-economic origin and composition of the leadership made it essentially impotent. A variety of forces, representing disparate political, economic and cultural groupings were incorporated in the coalition (serfs, aristocrats, religious leaders and urban middle class). As a result, lack of clarity, indecisiveness and opportunism characterised the political behaviour of the leadership. Referring to this state of affairs, and in particular in reference to the two main parties in the coalition (ML and LPP), Houtart (1982: 224) notes that the irresoluteness was attributed to its petty bourgeois class nature. This made it amenable to a variety of political compromises, which, in the final analysis, eroded its basic objectives. It is widely believed that class composition played a key role in the division of the ML. When the serf-dominated ML advocated the independence and emancipation of the serfs many of the members from the aristocratic class abandoned the IB and supported union with Ethiopia. Of course, the list of factors that led to the division within the main partners of the coalition can be expanded, both in terms of internal factors and in terms of external interventions. Moreover, there was a clear indication of the interplay of interventionist forces with vested interest, which created profound obstacles for the achievement of the objectives of the IB. The following political parties comprised the IB.

- The Moslem League
- The Liberal Progressive Party
- The New Eritrean Pro-Italian Party
- The Italo-Eritrean Association
- The National Party of Massawa
- The Veteran Association
- The Independent Eritrea Party
- The Intellectual Association of Eritreans (Ellingson 1977: 276)

Clearly, a profound instability characterised the IB. A recurrent waxing and waning of membership occurred in the ML and LPP, as shown in figure 5.1. The Bloc was to experience its first crisis when the leader of the ML expressed his willingness to co-operate with the New Eritrea Association representing Italians in Eritrea (Ellingson 1977: 277, Markakis 1987: 67). The inclusion of the pro-Italy party in the Bloc isolated those who were disturbed by the thought of Italy's reinstatement as the ruling power of Eritrea. This divisive issue undermined the internal unity of the key parties in the IB. At the same time, the Unionists capitalised on the alleged rapprochement between the Bloc and Italy by exploiting the general fear of an Italian comeback. In addition to this, the naked terrorist actions unleashed against members of the IB by the unionists further undermined the cohesion of the Bloc (Ellingson 1977: 277). Many, in fear for their lives and property, left the independence movement. These developments helped put the independence movement into disarray.

The first party to split off as the result of this disarray was the Independent Moslem League–formed by a breakaway group of former ML members in 1949. This faction, after receiving assurance from Ethiopia that Islamic institutions, norms and values would be respected, accepted the idea of union with Ethiopia. Not long after, three additional factions, notably the Liberal Unionist Party, the Independent Eritrea United to Ethiopia Party, the Moslem League of Western Province followed suit. The Liberal Unionist Party, formed by splintering from the Liberal Progressive Party, was lured to support conditional union by the idea of making compromises with the Unionists rather than ending up in Italian-sponsored independence. This was made more appealing by a pledge from Ethiopia that Eritrea would be allowed to manage its own internal affairs. The Independent Eritrea United with Ethiopia Party (ex-Independent Eritrea Party members) displayed an ambivalent position – that of espousing independence if followed by union. This party held the rather odd position of supporting independence if, after some years, it would lead to union with Ethiopia. The Moslem League of the Western Province took a radically different position. Expressing their opposition to Italian influence in the Moslem League, and rejecting the idea of incorporating the Western Province into Sudan, they advocated continuation of British Administration for the Western Province (Ellingson 1977: 278). In this manner, the Bloc was weakened, thus, unable to accomplish its objective. By the time of the implementation of the United Nations-sponsored federation, the Bloc had changed its name to the Eritrean Democratic Front, comprised of the Moslem League, the Liberal Progressive Party, the New Eritrean Party, the Independence Party, the Italo-Eritrean Association, the War Veterans' Association. At this time, the primary focus of the Bloc was to prevent the Emperor from having a representative endowed with real power in the Executive body of the Eritrean Government, or in Eritrea in general (Ellingson 1977: 279).

It seems that many are generally convinced the Italian factor played an important role in the mistrust and division that developed within the independence movement. It is also clear that this was effectively exploited by the unionists, as well as by Ethiopia. This point is clearly stressed by Ellingson when he says that the difficulties that the parties advocating for sovereignty encountered were attributable to the IB's connection with the Italian community. Ellingson makes this point explicitly, arguing that: "Native Eritreans distrusted the motives of the Italian community in supporting independence but were equally sceptical about joining hands with Ethiopia. The resulting disunity among the anti-unionists helped the Ethiopian Government to convince the U.N. that Eritrea's best hopes for the future lay with the Solomonic Crown" (Ellingson 1977: 280). Yet, although the rapprochement of the IB with the Italians certainly played a great role in weakening the forces of independence, there were also other factors that influenced the general outcome. The most devastating effect of the split within the Bloc was the timing of its occurrence. It happened in the middle of the UN debate on the disposition of Eritrea. The split was used to convince members of the United Nations that support for independence in the Eritrean society was dwindling. In that sense no doubt it was the opinion of Eritreans of this time that formed the basis for the UN decision. In the following sections, I will discuss the two prominent parties in the IB.

The Moslem League

According to some studies, the Bet Giorgis meeting marked a turning point in the formation of the Islamic Association, the predecessor of the Moslem League (see Gebre-Medhin 1989: 96). In the Bet Giorgis Meeting, it became clear to Ibrahim Sultan and his colleagues that it would be impossible to work with the unionists. Acting upon this realisation, Ibrahim Sultan and others walked out of the Meeting. They subsequently summoned a meeting of Moslem dignitaries in Keren in December 1946, to form the Moslem League (Ellingson 1977: 271, Markakis 1987: 65). This timing also coincided with the lifting of the prohibition on political parties by the BMA. A much larger conference was to be convened a month later. Moslems from all over Eritrea were summoned in Keren on January 20–21, 1947, to discuss the political programme and policy to be adopted by the Moslem League[4]. The assembly endorsed a programme similar to that of the Islamic Association and passed a resolution that Arabic and Tigrinya would be its official languages (Markakis 1987: 65). The conference ended with delegates concurring on the demand of immediate independence for Eritrea–or for a ten-year international trusteeship to be followed by independence, if existing circumstances did not allow for immediate independence (cf. FO 371-63212, 1947).

The resolution to adopt Tigrinya as an official language of the League was intended to demonstrate that it was a nationalist party, in spite of its members being exclusively drawn from the Moslem communities. The political leadership that came out from the Keren conference was comprised of the traditional nobility, religious leaders and the new elite whose social origin was based on the serf class. The religious leader of the khatmiya sect, Seyid Abubaker El Mirghani became president, while Ibrahim Sultan was elected secretary-general (Ellingson 1977: 271, Killion 1985: 309). The serfs were the dominant social force in the League, and Ibrahim Sultan (of serf background) became the real leader. It is widely believed that the Moslem League originated in the anti-feudal movement of the serfs, and was led by bourgeois nationalists of serf origin who were influential among their ranks (Houtart 1982: 223-4). The League's two-fold objective regarding the emancipation of the serfs and the mobilisation and organisation of the Moslem communities to partake in the independence movement, put it on a collision course with the old aristocratic elite. This was seen, in the eyes of the aristocrats, as a threat to their prerogatives. Therefore, realising after a while that the League was dominated by the serf emancipation movement, a group of the nobility who had joined the ML began to rally around the unionists (see Trevaskis 1960: 73, Ellingson 1977: 271).

The nobility's urge to desert the ML was reinforced by the League's determination to abolish serfdom. For instance, when they lost influence over the serfs, Kentebai Osman Hidad of Rora and Diglel Gelani of Beni Amer approached the Four Power Commission, pledging their support for a union with Ethiopia (EPLF British Administration and Eritrean Political Struggle 1941-1950, p. 59). Another clear manifestation of this conflict was the split of the Moslem League of the Western Province from the ML proper, led by Ali Musa Radai. To the aristocrats of the Western Province, the ML represented the interest of the serfs. They had a deep suspicion of Ibrahim Sultan, and particularly about his relationship with the pro-Italy Party and the Italians in general. This prompted them to seek alliances with the Unionists in order to safeguard their dwindling socio-economic prerogatives. There also emerged another splinter group under the name of national Party of Massawa representing Moslems of Massawa led by Omar Kadi. This group also supported conditional union with Ethiopia.

In addition to the class cleavages, the League was an umbrella organisation that encompassed the various ethno-linguistic communities of Islamic faith. This composition proved to be detrimental to the level of internal cohesion that was necessary to effectively meet the political challenges they faced. The various ethno-linguistic groups that met in Keren in 1947 to constitute the ML were divided regarding the future of Eritrea. The Tigre and Nara preferred British administration; the Beni Amer chiefs and elders who joined the League opted for immediate independence. The Jeberti of Massawa, the Kunama, the Saho and the Afar were against any connection with the British. Every group had its own grievance and expectation that became a motive to oppose this or that sort of solution. For instance, the Jeberti accused the British of the unemployment caused by the closure of the Royal Naval base; the Kunama had complaints of the way the British treated them. The Saho complained that the British failed to protect them from the Ethiopian aggression. The Afar, on the other hand, were bitter toward the British because of what they believed to be an excessively harsh sentence of their unofficial leader, resulting in his execution (Trevaskis 1960: 74, Ellingson 1977: 271). This ethno-linguistic plurality of the League constituted, for two reasons, its weakness. First, locating the common ground representing the diverse socio-cultural interests became a profound problem. Second, seen in historical terms, these ethno-linguistic groups had a long history of chronic enmity, which still generated suspicion and fear among them.

The irreconcilable interests of the various groups in the ML proved to have a catastrophic effect on the unity of the League. The Moslems of Massawa, formed the National Moslem Party of Massawa in 1947, distancing themselves from the ML. The party was later integrated in the IB (Ellingson 1977: 273, Markakis 1987: 65). However, the inclusion in the coalition of the party composed of Italians whose ultimate intention was the return of Italy again drove a wedge between them and the ML. As mentioned earlier, the involvement of the pro-Italy party in the IB generated an immense amount of suspicion of ML leader Ibrahim Sultan. This suspicion was played upon by his opponents, who accused him of having connections with Italy. The fear that the leader of the ML was leading the movement towards Italian-sponsored independence, thereby bringing back Italy into Eritrea, divided the ML. Some members of the League, lured by Ethiopian promises to preserve their Islamic identity and the use of the Arabic language in schools on the one hand, and to avoid the alleged coming back of Italy, on the other, built a splinter group called Independent Moslem League which favoured union with Ethiopia (Ellingson 1977: 278-9).

The overall effect of these difficulties was the crumbling of the already fragile relationship between the nobles and the serfs. The nobles and the serfs stood, in effect, on different political sides. It seems that the serf's support and desire for independence virtually pushed the nobles to the other side. Therefore, the Moslem nobles allied with the Christian nobles and supported the union cause (Markakis 1987: 60, Pool 1997: 10). These splits so severely weakened the independence movement that it failed to achieve its goal.

In the debate of nationalism and nation formation, the emergence of parties on the basis of primordial identity is often taken as an indication of the absence of or weakness in, collective national identity. This is because such primordial identities are considered as sub-national characteristics. The broadly accepted supposition is that a collective national identity rests on civic identity rather than on primordial identity. The ML was founded on primordial identity. However, they saw the organising of their communities and protecting their interest as compatible with the national interest. In the view of ML members, the Unionists were an externally instigated force. Therefore, the interest of the country was connected with the interest of the ML, because they represented the majority and stood for national sovereignty. Although the rallying point for the ML was Islamic identity, in their convictions they represented national interests. As testimony to this claim, the role played by the prominent figures of the League in the multi-ethnic and multi-religious national association of *Mahber Fikri Hager* can be stressed. Moreover, practical political activity was based on civic premises rather than on sacred premises.

The Eritrean Liberal Progressive Party (LPP)

Another important party in the Bloc was the LPP. Some members of the LPP were important figures in the *Mahber Fikri Hager* before it was purged of those who advocated independence, and before it was eventually reorganised and renamed as the Unionist Party. After efforts to compromise in the *Wa'ala Bet Giorgis* were foiled, the Christian independentist members of the *Mahber Fikri Hager* resolved to form their own party, which they named it

Eritrean Liberal Progressive Party (ELPP). The (E)LPP was the second most important party in the Independence Bloc (IB). Although the exact date of its formation is not known, the "constitutive act" is dated February 18, 1947 (FO 371-69363: 5). This party was primarily composed of Christian highlanders who opposed union with Ethiopia. The prominent leaders in the Party were Tessema Asberom, president of the Party, Seyoum Maascio, secretary-general and Woldeab Woldemariam, a leading member (Ellingson 1977:74, Markakis 1987: 65-6). The Party's objectives were stated as follows: 1) To work for the independence of Eritrea within its current boundaries, and the rejection of any partition of the territory (Eritrea); 2) To bring peace and harmony between the Christian highlanders and the communities of the lowland which had been connected by history, geography, political and economic relationships; 3) To demand the transfer of power to Eritreans from the administering power, in a gradual manner under the guidance and supervision of the U.N.O. within the maximum of ten years; and 4) The incorporation of the Ethiopian province of Tigrai into Eritrea, as the province was connected with Eritrea by language, ethnicity, history and economy. In 1947, the Party demanded the absolute independence of Eritrea. This was to be guided by an Eritrean committee of intellectuals and the present administrative power, under the supervision of the United Nations and through a transition period of not more than ten years (cf. Ellingson 1977: 274).

In the nationalist perception of the LPP, the province of Tigrai was also given a space. It was the position of the LPP that Eritrea and Tigrai were one integrated unit before the division brought about by the Italian colonial rule. They were convinced, as it was stated in the memo the Party submitted to the Four Powers Commission, that "the geographical, ethnic and historical factors concerning the Tigre speaking population, have nothing in common with the Shoan people of Galaz origin" (FO 371-69365, Appendix 101). The Party also requested the reinstatement to Eritrea of the territories annexed by the Sudan, inhabited by the Habab, the Beni Amer and the Beja population (FO 371-69363: 7). The request for the annexation of the presumed territories of Eritrea that were then parts of the Sudan seems a concession to the Moslem League. The Moslem League had, in turn, made concessions to the Liberal Progressive Party in its accepting the annexation of Tigrai–a main demand of the LPP. The demand to incorporate Tigrai with Eritrea can be interpreted as a clear indication that members of the Party had developed a crystallised ethnic identity, which included the province of Tigrai. Undoubtedly, it was in reference to this attitude of the LPP that the BMA in their report of 1944 noted: "In the first place there is the sentimental attachment to the Tigrai - the consciousness of racial and economic unity, and the memory of a long common history. But the Eritreans are strongly conscious of the separate identity of Eritrea, and the ethnic affinity with Ethiopia ends at the border of the Tigrinya block" (FO 371-41531, Oct. 1944). Nevertheless, the party was well aware of the changes brought about by the Italian capitalist economic penetration. Not only Eritrea as a whole, but also the Tigrinya speakers in particular, had developed a distinctive identity, different from that of the Tigrai province. This difference between the two Tigrinya speaking peoples was manifested in the socio-economic development and in terms of life style. In terms of language too, the Eritrean Tigrinya had incorporated a large number of the Italian vocabulary making it distinctly different from that spoken in Tigrai that have incorporated a considerable vocabulary from the Amharic language.

The LPP was believed to elicit its social support, generally, from the urban proletariat and was mainly dominated by the lower petty bourgeoisie and the urban intellectuals from the highland (Houtart 1982: 224). This made the party exclusively representative of the middle class. Perhaps it was because of this social background that the Party was able to adopt a quite progressive political programme. Aware of the economic difficulties Eritrea was likely to encounter, the Party proposed a long-term economic strategy in the form of acquiring a loan from the UN, revitalising the various industrial sectors and other practical policies which could lead to the economic development of the country (cf. Ellingson 1977: 274). In the political realm, the Party advocated that an independent Eritrea should adopt a liberal democratic parliamentary system modelled after that of the British. The latter indicates the influence of the British political system on the LPP. The influence of British political culture was attributed to the British literature that was flowing to Eritrea (cf. Trevaskis 1960) and as the result of personal contact between members of the LPP and officials of the BMA. The endeavour to emulate the British political system exposed the Party to accusations by its opponents alleging that it represented British interests. The unionists campaigned relentlessly to portray the LPP as the creation of the British Administration and thereby isolate it.

Like the other political parties, perhaps much more, the LPP became the victim of terror and manipulation. Unsurprisingly, due to pressures from the Orthodox Church and persistent terrorist actions perpetrated by the Unionists, the LPP began to lose followers, eventually suffering a split within its ranks (cf. Ellingson 1977: 275). This split was reinforced by the alleged involvement of the leader of the Independence Bloc, of which the LPP was a partner, and an opposition to the reinstatement of Italian rule, which opponents of independence accused the Bloc of secretly supporting. A combination of factors, including the fear of renewed Italian domination and Ethiopian threats and promises of non-interference in Eritrean local affairs after the union lured the leadership to split. After meeting Haile Selassie in Addis Ababa, the leaders of the LPP showed a clear division (Markakis 1987: 67). Following this division, in 1950, two factions deserted the IB. A faction named the Liberal Unionist Party, led by Abraha Tessema, was formed. After receiving assurances from Ethiopia that the Eritreans would be left alone to manage their own affairs the Party pledged itself to supporting a conditional union (Trevaskis 1960: 98, Ellingson 1977: 278, Markakis 1987: 67). Woldeab Woldemariam founded the Independent Eritrea United to Ethiopia Party (previous Independent Eritrea Party) which advocated Eritrean independence to be followed by union with Ethiopia (Ellingson 1977: 276, Markakis 1987: 67). At the end, it was the Liberal Progressive Party, led by Tessema Asberom, which stood firm in its position of support for total independence and remained in the Independence Bloc.

The split within the LPP combined with the split in the ML was apparently a contributing factor in the weakening of the independence movement. This split, coupled with the political nature of the various factions of the Independence Bloc (IB), undoubtedly led to the erosion of the firm stand regarding the future of Eritrea.

SCHISM REGARDING THE SOLUTION

In order to understand the nature and origins of the political cleavage that occurred, an examination of the combined social, economic, political and cultural factors that led to it is required. This section concisely examines the possible roots of this schism. Contributing factors can be categorised along the lines of: a) internal structural factors, and b) external factors. To the former belong factors such as economic difficulties and the ensuing social tensions. BMA policies, Ethiopian intrusion, Italian ambition to retrieve its ex-colony and global strategic interests can be linked to the latter. These factors will briefly be discussed in the following paragraphs.

a) Economic Problems. With the cessation of WW II, the economic growth of Eritrea declined. This decline was caused chiefly by two factors. First, Eritrean products were unable to compete with the newly resuscitated economies of Europe, which began to re-supply the markets in the Middle East that had been the domain of Eritrean products during the war (Sherman 1980: 17). The second factor was British economic policy. As a transitional administrative authority, not only were the British unprepared to make new investments – they also started to dismantle the already-dwindling economic infrastructure. We find the widespread dismantling of the infrastructure discussed in detail by E. Sylvia Pankhurst and Richard K. P. Pankhurst (Pankhurst and Pankhurst 1953). The report of the Four Power Commission, shedding light on this British destruction of the economic base, notes that a "number of industrial establishments having stocks and equipment valued at 1, 700 million East African Shillings (£EA 85 million)" (FO 371- 69370 chap. 5, p.59) were closed and dismantled.

Waning economic growth, fueled rampant increases in unemployment and inflation. Many people lost their jobs. Added to this were those returning from the Italian army (cf. Markakis 1987: 42, 58), swelling the number of redundant workers even more. To make matters worse, the price of basic goods was inflated by 600 per cent, while salaries increased by only 60 per cent (Longrigg 1945: 152, Trevaskis 1960: 47). Incomes received through pensions and salaries from the defunct Italian regime ceased to be paid (Markakis 1987: 62). Taken together, these conditions culminated in a general decline of living standards, driving the society to the brink of collapse. However, there were exceptions. In particular, two categories of people seemed to do well in this period of economic hardship. They were the traders in Asmara who were self-employed and the Italian expatriates who benefited from the British employment policies (see Sherman 1980: 17, Teklehaimanot 1996: 10). The accumulated effect of all this, however, led to social tensions.

b) Social Tensions. The economic hardship gave rise to serious social conflicts. The traders in Asmara who were the veins of the city's economy, and who were doing well, were mostly Moslems (Arabs and Jeberti). Many Christians were indebted to them at a high rate of interest, and many encountered difficulties in paying back their debts. This helped exacerbate social relations between the Christian and Moslem communities (Trevaskis 1960: 51). In August 1946, an incident involving the Sudan Defence Force which left 46 Christians dead and more than 60 wounded (Trevaskis 1960: 68, Gebre-Medhin 1989: 78, Negash 1997: 42) further aggravated the tension between Christians and Moslems.

The Italians, although vanquished, turned out to be beneficiaries of the British Military Administration (BMA). Italian office workers were kept in their positions. Priority for business licences was given to Italians on the basis of their expertise and capital. Italian agriculturists were allotted more of the land appropriated from the peasant population in the name of development. Laws promulgated under the Italian era were permitted to continue to operate. The police and the judiciary remained in the hands of Italian officials (Trevaskis 1960: 49, 51-52, 54).

For the emergent Eritrean intelligentsia, whose expectation of Eritreanisation of the bureaucracy was shattered, the disappointment and bewilderment was immense. Their anger was understandably directed toward Italian settlers. The special treatment of the Italians also justifiably raised suspicion among the local population that the British were favouring the Italians (Trevaskis 1960: 51) and this generated more embitterment. Serious resentment against Moslems and Italians grew among members of the Christian community, who saw that their chances of socio-economic improvement were slipping out of their grasp. Overall, the economic hardship and political confusion provoked and escalated social tensions among the various ethno-linguistic groups. Naturally, these conditions furnished fertile ground for any political force that sought to manipulate them to its own advantage. It was in this atmosphere of uncertainty that the Eritrean Orthodox Church and the Ethiopian State attempted to exploit the general confusion of the Christian community.

c) External Involvement. The main actors in the external interference were Ethiopia, Italy and Britain. As we have seen earlier, Ethiopia made claims on both Eritrea and Italian Somaliland in 1941. In its attempt to annex Eritrea, Ethiopia first targeted the *Mahber Fikri Hager.* Later, the UP and the Church became key instruments. Ethiopia employed promises, bribes and coercion to win the support of Eritreans for the 'Union cause' (Trevaskis 1960, Ellingson 1977, Markakis 1987). This Ethiopian involvement in Eritrean affairs, thus, became a significant factor in the division within the Eritrean politics. Italy's interest in Eritrea was initially resuscitated in connection with the emergence of the Eritrean Old Soldiers Association, whose members had claims to salaries (Trevaskis 1960: 79). More concretely, when the issue of the ex-Italian territories was debated in the UN General Assembly, Italy sought actively to persuade the Assembly to let her have some kind of say regarding her ex-colonies (even seeking the return of those colonies). Toward this aim, the Italian settlers and the Italian Embassy in Eritrea were mobilised. They were thought to have spent a considerable amount of money to induce Eritreans to support Italy's continued involvement in Eritrea (Trevaskis 1960: 94-5, Ellingson 1977: 276). After the failure of the Bevin-Sforza proposal (partition of Eritrea worked out by British Foreign Minister Bevin and Italian Foreign Minister Sforza), Italy supported the independence of Eritrea (Trevaskis 1960: 93). This support for independence was viewed by many Eritreans with suspicion. Therefore, the active Italian interest in Eritrea had a negative effect on the relationships between the various political parties, becoming a source of further division.

Britain, as an administrative authority and member of the Big Four Powers, had a double role to play. The British Military Administration (BMA) officials' belief that an independent Eritrea could not survive led to the adoption of the proposal to partition Eritrea (see Longrigg 1945: 174, Trevaskis 1960: 69-70, Morley 1991: 16). Throughout the period, the British Administration was convinced that the only viable solution for Eritrea was its partition between Ethiopia and Sudan. In hopes of achieving this goal, they encouraged the Christian and Moslem communities to develop strong affiliations with their co-religious neighbours. They also showed every effort to promote the Tigrinya and Arabic languages. The Tigrinya Christians were induced to foster close relationships with the Tigreans while the Moslems were induced to bridge their differences with the Sudan. The active promotion of the Arabic language by importing literature from Egypt, opening schools in Arabic, and seeking to open communication between Sudan and the Moslem community of Eritrea, etc., was intended to inculcate a sense of affiliation with Sudan. On the other side, the British entertained the idea of creating an Eritrea-Tigray unity composed solely of the Christian Eritreans and the population of the province of Tigray (Medhanie 1986: 13). For that purpose, they not only actively encouraged a rapprochement between the two groups of Tigrinya speakers, but also devised different ways to realise it–particularly in the early stage of their rule. Any view entertaining the independence of Eritrea was to be discouraged. The following quotation illustrates such inclinations:

> A leading Chief recently mentioned to the S. C. A. O., Adi Caieh, that he hoped that his country would not be handed from one power to another, like a parcel, but would at least be consulted as to its own future. Such suggestions will certainly multiply: and although organised expressions of Eritrean opinion on their own future, may well be more or less embarrassing, it may not be possible to prevent them. Expressions which reach us through either petitions or 'round robins' will probably take the line that they do not want to be handed back to Italy or equally do not want to be handed

> to Ethiopia. ...I take it that *our line is to discourage* (since we cannot gracefully or effectively prohibit) expressions of collective political opinion (WO 230-168, Oct. 1943). (Emphasis added)

The scheme of partition was formally defeated in the May 1949, meeting of the General Assembly when it was presented as the "Bevin-Sforza Agreement" (see Becker 1952: 167-8). However, the British plan of partition and the practical policy that derived from it had a lasting effect on the internal unity of the Eritrean politicians. One of the means used to influence the political process in Eritrea by these external actors, particularly Ethiopia and Italy, was to provide financial support to those parties that supported them. According to Ellingson (1977: 266), the parties that supported independence were largely financed by membership, but the Italian residents in Eritrea also supported them. On the other hand, the Unionists were "handsomely subsidized by the Ethiopian government although, of course this was never publicly admitted". The role of the UN and the USA must also be factored into the above account. The USA, as the new leader of the Western World, assumed a dominant role in the UN. US strategic interests, as they were unequivocally expressed by the then-US Secretary of State and coupled with the Cold War politics, made it necessary that any resolution concerning the future of Eritrea take into consideration US interests (Medhanie 1986: 19). The political theatre performed in the UN General Assembly was seen by many scholars as dictated by global, and in particular, US interests (see Medhanie 1986, Habte Selassie 1989, Bondestam 1989, Pateman 1990, Yohannes 1991, Gayim 1992). Generally, claims as to the viability of an independent Eritrea were received with apprehension by the Western powers. The colonial powers, especially, were not comfortable with the idea of granting independence to Eritrea because of the repercussions it might have on their own colonies (Medhanie 1986: 15). No doubt, such external interference added complexity and difficulty to the already volatile and fragile situation. The involvement of external political actors served, thus, to further expose the vulnerability of the society.

d) Terrorism. In its September 1949, Fourth Session, the UN General Assembly endorsed the idea of confering upon Libya immediate independence, with Somalia to get its independence after ten years of Italian trusteeship. On November 21, 1949, the Assembly decided to send a fact-finding Commission to Eritrea (Trevaskis 1960: 95). The news of the granting of independence to Libya and Somalia was received favourably by the Independence Bloc–but it represented an alarming signal to the Unionists (Trevaskis 1960: 95). The thought of the UN deciding to give Eritrea independence terrified the Unionists. Thus, they resorted to extensive acts of terrorism. Throughout 1948 and 1949, letters and pamphlets were distributed threatening highland Christians and Italians who opposed union (Ellingson 1977: 275). Even the Orthodox Church was actively involved in this issuing of threats. In the column of the newspaper *Ethiopia* the Church warned that religious services such as baptism, communion, marriage, burial and absolution would not be rendered to members of the IB (Ellingson

1977: 275). Between the time of the announcement of the formation of the UN Commission, and its arrival in Eritrea in February 1950, the unionists carried out a comprehensive campaign of terrorism that claimed many lives. It culminated in a five-day battle between Christians and Moslems in February – just at the time of the arrival of the Commission (Becker 1952: 222, Trevaskis 1960: 96). The Andinet, a notorious Unionist Youth organisation, was believed to have carried out many of the urban terrorist acts (Trevaskis 1960: 76, Ellingson 1977: 268). This politics of terror produced the desired results (Erlich 1983: 8). Its dividend was seen in that many members of the IB who feared for their lives and property–and also those who had intended to desert the UP–shifted their allegiance (Trevaskis 1960: 96-7). These blatant terrorist activities struck the independence movement hard that divisions within the Bloc surfaced shortly after the arrival of the UN Commission.

e) Division. Among other things, uncertainty about the future of Eritrea led to a great deal of rumourmongering. Among the stories told, was that after the peace treaty was signed with Italy, the United Nations would give Eritrea back to Italy, and Italians would be given special favours by the BMA. Horrible accounts circulated of deeds supposedly committed – or intended to be committed – by Italian officials who had been left at their posts, or given new post by the BMA. The Sudan Defence Force was described as consistently harassing Churches and priests, with the intention of fostering tension and hatred between the Christian and Moslem communities (see Pankhurst and Pankhurst 1953: 61ff). These stories and rumours, some of them well founded, while many others completely groundless, bewildered the population and produced a confused environment. For Eritrean society–with no experience of political intricacies and complexities, and coupled with the absence of widespread formal education–the complex atmosphere became beyond its comprehension. Under Italian rule, no political activity had been allowed, and this tight control had left the Eritreans without any political experience. When Italian rule collapsed, the desire of the majority of the political elites was described as very simple and modest. This was described by the BMA in its report of June 28, 1941. "Their real desires are more practical: a greater share in the administration of their country and the opportunity for a more lucrative employment in its bureaucracy" (cited in Pankhurst and Pankhurst 1953: 61).

The lack of political experience, coupled with the events and actions described in the brief accounts above (a, b, c and d), formed the underlying basis for the divisions among Eritreans regarding the future of Eritrea. However, it should be stressed that the cleavage that arose at this particular point in time should also be seen as a result of competition between the various factions of elites in their respective efforts to attain political power. Societies that are in their formative processes are invariably characterised by pervasive conflict and competition between categories of elites – either between old and new elites, or between elites of various ethnic origins. In their efforts, therefore, these contesting elites need to rally support from their own social bases, which, in turn, means mobilising grassroots members. Commenting on this matter, Paul R. Brass notes,

> More precisely, it is the study of the process by which elites and counter-elites within ethnic groups select aspects of the group's culture, attach new value and meaning to them, and use them as symbols to mobilize the group, to defend its interests, and to compete with other groups. In this process, those elites have an advantage whose leaders can operate most skilfully in relation both to the deeply-felt primordial attachments of group members and the shifting relationships of politics (Brass 1994: 87).

Undoubtedly, ample examples of such views and perceptions may be found in the modernist conception of nation and nationalism. This is particularly true in the 'invention thesis' whose prominent proponent is Ernest Gellner (cf. Hutchinson 1994). This corroborates the idea that nationalists and elites create national identities either in their quest for power or in their genuine attempt to construct national identity. This top-down approach in mobilisation theory puts the responsibility of mobilisation work squarely on the shoulder of the elites. When the divided Eritrean elites sought to mobilise support from among the people – either with the aim of wielding state power or to create a national identity – they divided the society.

Generally, the Eritrean schism is perceived as resting on two socio-cultural cleavages which generated two kinds of nationalism, one based on Christian identity and another based on Islamic identity (to be discussed later in detail). However, the main cause for the schism seems instead to be the lack of a commonly accepted solution regarding how the future of Eritrea should be determined. The Christian unionists were not convinced about the viability of an independent Eritrea. Many believed that independence would lead to renewed Italian domination. This apprehension persuaded them to seek union with Ethiopia. Arguing along this view Trevaskis (1960: 130) notes, "the reason why they supported the Unionist Party was that they believed their interests would be better served under Ethiopian than under European colonial rule". The Moslems, on the other hand, found association with Ethiopia or with Sudan unacceptable. Therefore, their choice became independence. This division generated two types of nationalism, which could be identified as unionist nationalism and independence nationalism. Yet, in spite of these divisions, it is widely believed that there existed a majority of people in Eritrean society who yearned for independence to guarantee decolonisation[5]. Therefore, many scholars believe Eritrea was denied its independence primarily because of global interests (e.g. Medhanie 1986, Gebre-Medhin 1989, Habte Selassie 1989, Yohannes 1991, Killion 1997, Fessehatzion 1998).

In the literature on nation formation and nationalism, it is argued that the duality of identity and loyalty is the order of the day in polyethnic societies, rather than the exception (more about the duality of identity later). Sociological identity is usually marked by stratification. At various levels, not only are different forms of identity manifested, but one or the other form tends to dominate at a specific point of time and space. One aspect of vital importance in the Eritrean case was that whatever cleavages emerged, and to whatever degree they were sharpened at the political level, one variable remained constant: notably, the acceptance of and commitment to territorial unity. In other words, since its territorial inception, no significant political force ever questioned the legality of that territoriality. Even those who support union thought in terms of a unified Eritrea joining Ethiopia.

In conclusion, insight into the socio-political milieu that unfolded in the aftermath of the Italian rule is essential to properly comprehend the political schism. It must be appraised in the context of its underlying context. It must be recalled that it was an already extremely tumultuous and complex social, economic and political environment in which the formation of parties and the process of determining the destiny of Eritrea commenced. Following the substantialist perspective, it could then be argued that it is only by seriously taking into account these substantial conditions, which both prompted and governed the social and political behaviour of the contemporary Eritrean elites, that we can arrive at a reasonable and meaningful understanding of the cleavage.

FEDERATION AND ITS IMPLICATIONS

The present section will discuss the implications of the institutions and symbols that resulted from the UN-sponsored Federation on the formation of the Eritrean nation. The UN General Assembly Resolution 390A(v) of December 2, 1950, federated Eritrea with Ethiopia (Becker 1952: 229-30). The Federation was put into force on September 11, 1952, and abolished on November 14, 1962 (Fessehatzion 1998, Medhanie 1986). Many scholars have argued that in the transition from feudal socio-economic order to the capitalist socio-economic order, and concomitantly in the building of nations, the role of the state was of crucial importance. The absolute monarchies in Western Europe, accomplished territorial, economic, and political centralisation, through the creation of standardised taxation systems and general mobilisation and recruitment of the masses for the purpose of waging wars. This centralisation was carried out with the intention of consolidating and expanding their territories, but it also had far-reaching consequences for the nation-formation process. In a similar fashion, the colonial states in Africa, through territorial integration, bureaucratic centralisation, economic hierarchisation, the spread of communications, etc. played a vital role in the process of nation building. Thus, the state as a political institution plays an instrumental role in forming, preserving, and perpetuating the nation. Earlier we discussed the two modalities of the process of nation formation notably, state-nation and nation-state. In the state-nation model, the basic responsibility of constructing the nation is bestowed upon the state. Interpreted in the colonial context, this conceptualisation of the role of the state in the formation of the nation is vividly revealed in the formation of territorially-centralised, bureaucratic political administrative units, as many scholars have pointed out (e.g. Hodgkin 1956, Emerson 1960, Seton-Watson 1977, Smith 1983, Anderson 1983).

The establishment of an autonomous Eritrean state with "the widest form of self government" and based on "democratic principles" (Fessehatzion 1998: 23) can be seen as fulfilling two significant objectives in the process of nation formation. First, in terms of symbolic importance – having one's own language, flag, government, parliament etc. – it promoted the development of a sense of common identity. In a more concrete manner, these political and national symbols had an immense importance in the development of imagined collective identity. Although its members could never have direct contact, these symbols helped the collectivity to develop a sense of an 'imagined community' because of their cognisance of these shared common symbols. This occurs through the emotional attachment to those symbols. Evidence of the connection between the national symbols and the emotional attachment to them can be sought in the political behaviour of the Eritrean political parties when the subversion of the federal provisions began. Immediately after the enforcement of the federal system began, the Ethiopian Emperor started to take measures through his representatives that infringed upon the basic pillars of the Federation. This was clearly intended to undermine the autonomy of Eritrea (Fessehatzion 1998). This also drew the attention of Eritrean political forces from across the political spectrum–even several unionists who were believed to have opted for the unconditional union–to defend the federal agreement and the autonomous status of Eritrea.

Opposition to Ethiopian encroachment came even before the endorsement of the Federation by the Eritrean assembly, in the form of resisting the Ethiopian attempt to introduce the Amharic language as the official language of Eritrea (Trevaskis 1960). In addition, the attempt to establish a post of representative with real power in the Eritrean constitution was vehemently opposed. After the enforcement of the Federation, all attempts by the representative of the Emperor to interfere in the internal affairs of Eritrea were resisted. When the activities of the political parties for independence were curbed, new forces like the Workers' Syndicate, the Moslem Youth League and the Young Federalists Association took over the struggle (Killion 1997: 25). Fessehatzion (1998: 34) also adds that an organisation called the Eritrean Youth Peace Council emerged, which was an amalgamation of the Youth wing of the Moslem League and the Unionist Party. The Organisation was formed to ensure the implementation of the Federation, and to oppose its encroachment. The fight outside of the parliament for Eritrean autonomy and the defence of the constitution was spearheaded by the workers and later followed by students (see Killion 1997). The workers (dock and railroads workers) defended democratic rights such as strikes, demonstrations and associations enshrined in the Eritrean constitution.

The second element of importance of the emergence of an autonomous Eritrean state can be seen from the institutional point of view. It can be partially seen as an act of decolonisation in that it replaced colonial political institutions with indigenous national institutions, handing over power to indigenous national political forces. It was perhaps operating from this perception that following the UN resolution of federation, the different political blocs convened a *Wa'ala Selam* (Peace Conference) at Cinema Impero in Asmara on December 31 1950. Both sides agreed to work together to "create a democratic Eritrean state" (Killion 1997: 12), pledging to uphold and protect the autonomous Eritrean State. In that sense, the "UN-mandated autonomous Eritrean institutions" that were put in place, formed a common foundation around which both unionists and independentists could rally, and which formed the basis of Eritrean national identity (Killion 1997: 12). As the IB expressed it in their announcement of acceptance of the federal resolution (see FO 371-90316) the UN-sponsored federal act and the subsequent emergence of an autonomous Eritrean state answered their demands for an immediate hand over of state power to the local population. They perceived the emergence of an autonomous Eritrean state, on the one hand as a fulfilment of their wish of the continuation of Eritrea's territorial unity and identity, and on the other, avoiding total union with Ethiopia.

The process of nation formation is intimately connected with the creation of institutions. Nation as a political community is expressed in terms of civic culture (Smith 1986, 1991). And civic culture presupposes the emergence of multifaceted institutions through which the different sections of society, groups, individuals are co-opted into national political, social, economic and cultural activities. The Montesquieuian division of the state into three organs, the legislative, the executive, and the judiciary, viewed in terms of building political and legal institutions, is a vital step in the direction of constructing a political community or nation. Therefore, in the context of the process of nation formation, the significance of the emergence of the Eritrean autonomous state with its executive, legislative and judiciary organs can be construed as delivering in two dimensions–a symbolic and an institutional one. What can also be added from a symbolic perspective, is the emergence of state institutions and national symbols such as the flag, stamp, parliament, parliamentary building, constitution, schools, languages, national holidays, newspapers, national theatre, national courts, etc. These evoked a sense of national identity and pride, because they were seen as representing a unique Eritrean identity. Political sanctity was conferred on the institutions and symbols. Hence, their desecration sparked opposition from different political forces such as the Eritrean Assembly, workers, students, the Youth Peace Council, the Voice of Eritrea, the Eritrean High Court (see Killion 1997, Fessehatzion 1998). Overall, as Pool (1997:11) notes that the breach of the Federation generated Christian-Moslem co-operation, leading to the emergence of a "modern nationalist organization, the Eritrean Liberation Movement (ELM)".

All this allows us to conclude that the emergence of national symbols and institutions generated a strong feeling of affinity among Eritreans, the evidence of which was expressed in the attempt to defend the constitution and autonomy of Eritrea. In short, the emergence of institutions and national symbols played an indispensable role in furthering the social-psychological formation of a unique Eritrean collective national identity–although they were products of the UN-sponsored federal resolution. The erosion of the Federation and the ultimate collapse of the autonomous Eritrean State will be discussed in the next section.

DECLINE OF THE AUTONOMOUS ERITREAN STATE

This section attempts to briefly explain the downfall of the autonomous Eritrean State of 1952-1962. It will also discuss the opposition to defending the autonomy of Eritrea. The Federation failed for a number of reasons, some of which will be highlighted here. A number of scholars of political constitutionalism have expressed the view that the basic stumbling block of the federal accord rested on its impracticality. Indeed, many even entertained the idea of a conspiracy, based in the argument that the main sponsors of the federal accord were quite aware of the impracticality of the federation. According to this theory, the federation solution was devised because it was deemed possible to award Eritrea to Ethiopia only through a concealed plan. This effectively removed the issue from the UN platform, putting it in Ethiopia's backyard (e.g. Medhanie 1986, Habte Selassie 1989, Gebre-Medhin 1989). Whether or not this conspiracy theory is valid is of only minor significance. Regardless of the sponsors' underlying motives, one result was clear: there existed a profound incompatibility between the political structure the UN was attempting to introduce into Eritrean politics, and the political structure of that entity to which the UN was trying to tie it in a 'matrimonial' bond.

There were several incongruities contained within the federal arrangements. These included, first, demographic factors. The lopsided balance of the population size of the two units to be federated was itself seen as a constraint to the creation of a balanced federal order (Sherman 1980: 27). The second was structural incongruity, with political and constitutional elements forming stumbling blocks that kept the two units apart (see Sherman 1980: 27, Erlich 1983: 7-8, Medhanie 1986: 22). Critics argue that the Eritrean polity and constitutional order promulgated by the UN was founded upon liberal democratic principles–unlike that of Ethiopia. A functioning democracy with political parties, elections recurring at regular, frequent time intervals, freedom of the press, a free labour movement, the right to organise and strike, etc., had been introduced (see e. g. Ellingson 1977, Medhanie 1986, Markakis 1987, Wolde Giorgis 1989, Habte Selassie 1989, Gebre-Medhin 1989). This politico-legal system, based on liberal democratic principles, was broadly seen as incompatible with the archaic feudal political and legal system of the Ethiopian *ancien* regime, which rested on the claim of a divine rule (see Erlich 1983: 8, Araya 1990: 81). This incompatibility was believed to have constituted one of the most important structural constraints inhibiting the emergence of functioning federal system. A third structural incongruity had to do with the legal-constitutional system. The absence of a federal constitution that could regulate and give guidance to the federal arrangement, and with a neutral existence separate from the two autonomous organs of the federation, rendered the arrangement vulnerable to encroachment (Habte Selassie 1989: 38). This important constitutional organ was omitted by the UN Commissioner in the process of the drafting of the Eritrean constitution–a concession to Ethiopian pressure. Instead, the Ethiopian constitution became the federal constitution (ELF 1977: 41ff, Fessehatzion 1998). The absence of a newly structured federal constitution that took into account the federation of two quite different nations enabled Ethiopia to undermine the autonomy of Eritrea.

The encroachment upon Eritrean autonomy had already begun during the constitution drafting process (Fessehatzion 1998). According to Markakis (1987: 93), however, the process began earlier, behind the scenes, before the final arrangement was endorsed in the UN General Assembly. This is believed to have taken place in the discourse between Ethiopia, the United States, Britain and Italy–and without the participation of the Eritrean people. Once the decision on federation had been made by the General Assembly, Ethiopia began to reinterpret federation as a union. Based on this reinterpretation, the Ethiopian Foreign Minister demanded that a number of proposed items be omitted from the Eritrean constitution. The Minister claimed that Ethiopia was entitled to appoint a Governor General for Eritrea as the Emperor's Representative. He also claimed that the Emperor or his representative in Eritrea was entitled to veto power over decisions of the Eritrean Assembly (Medhanie 1986: 21, Fessehatzion 1998: 25) and that this representative should also have the power to nominate, or approve the nomination of Eritrea's Chief Executive, ministers and judges (Fessehatzion 1998: 27). The Minister finally demanded that Eritrea should not have its own flag and official language (Medhanie 1986: 21).

Immediately after the Eritrean constitution had been endorsed by the Eritrean Assembly and by the Ethiopian Emperor, the process of undermining the federation moved into full swing. The constitutional assembly that was established to endorse the Eritrean constitution was, in principle, to be dissolved as soon as it had accomplished its mission. Yet, to the contrary, the assembly was permitted to continue until 1956, at which time a second parliamentary election took place. By this time many opponents of a union with Ethiopia had been silenced or forced to flee for safety.

The representative of the Emperor in Eritrea also proved to be a useful institutional instrument in the Emperor's efforts to undermine Eritrean autonomy. The hostile relationship between the Chief Executive and the Representative of the Emperor was openly known. The Chief Executive attempted to assert his power against the emperor's representative at various occasions (Yohannes 1997). But the most serious problem was the contempt that was conspicuously expressed by the Emperor's Representative toward Eritrean autonomy. To the disappointment of many Eritreans, the Emperor's Representative made it clear from the very outset that regarding the Emperor's, office there were no internal or external affairs. This view was expressed in reference to the division of constitutional discretion between the Eritrean autonomous state and the federal state, or rather, the Ethiopian State.

In his constitutional position as the link between the Eritrean autonomous state and the Crown, the Emperor's Representative played a key role in the progressive weakening of the Federation (Erlich 1983: 8-10, Negash 1997: 90). The office of the Representative of the Emperor was an intentionally constructed constitutional instrument, devised to curb the free activities of the autonomous Eritrean State (cf. Ellingson 1977: 280). Aware of the constraints that such institutionalised constitutional discretion could place on the Eritrean government, the Eritrean parties for independence vehemently opposed the inclusion of any office of the Representative of the Emperor with formal powers in the constitution of Eritrea. However, as part of a compromise, the UN commissioner permitted the insertion of the office of the representative of the Emperor, although without any formal power. In violation of the Eritrean Constitution–and by exceeding his jurisdictional entitlement–the Representative of the Emperor began to interfere in the internal affairs of the Eritrean Government and started issuing orders.

This Ethiopian interference galvanised the determination of many members of the Eritrean Assembly in their opposition. However, as a testimony of the impracticality of the federal setting, the peaceful Eritrean opposition was not heeded. On the contrary, Ethiopia's coercive state machinery began to display its muscle – demonstrating that whenever necessary, Ethiopian objectives in Eritrea would be implemented through the exercise of power. Peaceful demonstrations, strikes and oppositions were violently crushed. There were numerous examples of the use of brute force to thwart any meaningful protest. In 1954, a strike by dockworkers in Massawa and Assab against the introduction of compulsory Federal identity card was suppressed by force (Killion 1997: 22). The 1958 peaceful general strike was also suppressed by force (Killion 1997: 30-33). The case of the *Voice of Eritrea* newspaper, which was closed for publishing articles criticising the violation of democratic rights and infringement of Eritrean autonomy, and the imprisonment of the staff writers (Fessehatzion 1998) provide additional examples.

The Ethiopians viewed the Federation merely as a temporary arrangement, giving them the opportunity to remove the case of Eritrea from the international forum. After they had brought Eritrea into their backyard, they were convinced that they would be able to act in whatever ways that suited them (cf. Erlich 1983: 8, Medhanie 1986: 19, Negash 1997: 145). This Ethiopian attitude toward the Federation virtually guided their policy with respect to its implementation.

The successive, systematic dismantling of the building blocks of the Federation and the effective invalidation of the autonomous status of Eritrea were extremely swift. Within a short period of time, almost all the basic provisions of the autonomy had been dismantled. This dismantling and undermining of autonomy took many forms, and only a few examples are provided here. The political repression that was unleashed as soon as the Federation agreement took effect forced leaders of political parties and trade unions who opposed annexation to flee into exile. Woldeab Woldemariam, Ibrahim Sultan and Idris Mohammed Adem fled the country. This political repression rendered political parties ineffectual–with the exception of the Unionist Party. The trade union movement was forced underground, even though this was a violation of the Constitution. Press freedoms were also curbed–the *Voice of Eritrea* was harassed until it was closed permanently. It became a serious criminal offence to write a dissenting opinion, for example–in spite of the fact that the Constitution allowed harbouring dissenting views. In 1958, the Ethiopian flag replaced the Eritrean flag. In 1959, the Ethiopian Penal Code replaced the Eritrean Penal Law, the name Eritrean Executive was changed to Eritrean Administration and the Chief Executive to Chief Administrator. Finally, on November 14, 1962, the federation was dissolved and Eritrea became a province of Ethiopia (see Erlich 1983: 9, Sherman 1980: 27-29, Medhanie 1986: 26, Markakis 1987: 94, Araya 1990: 81, Pool 1997: 10-11).

Ethiopia claimed that this was done with the consent of the Eritrean Parliament and Government. However, many believe that the decision to abolish the Federation was made solely by the Ethiopian Emperor. To legalise the decision, a written statement was read for the Eritrean Assembly, which had been purged of the opponents of annexation through the years. Even so, strong opposition was shown by the Eritrean Assembly (Medhanie 1986, Gebre-Medhin 1989, Fessehatzion 1998). The decision to abrogate the Federation, as was later described by a then-young officer (and was later to become a senior official of the Marxist regime) who participated in this military show of force, notably Dawit Wolde Giorgis (Wolde Giorgis 1989: 80-1), was made under duress, under threat of a macabre military display of force by the Ethiopian army. This sequence of events fulfilled Ethiopia's ambition to systematically and decisively annex Eritrea.

In his latest book about the Federation, the historian Tekeste Negash absolves Ethiopia from any responsibility, writing that complete responsibility, not only for the rise of the Federation but also for its demise, lies with the Eritrean social forces. (see Negash 1997: 80, 90, 146-7). Arguing that Ethiopia was primarily interested in obtaining an outlet to the sea rather than the total annexation of Eritrea (Negash 1997: 56), he argues that it was the wish of the Unionists which convinced the UN to opt for a federation. "It would, however, be wrong to accuse either the Emperor or his country of 'expansionist ambitions'" (Negash 1997: 54). With respect to the demise of the Federation, he maintains that because the resolution for federation was passed against their wish of an immediate and unconditional union, the Unionists from the very outset put all their energy into making it null and void (at times even against the will of Ethiopia), and within a relatively short period of time succeeded in discarding it.

Neither space nor time permit a detailed discussion of Negash's conclusions, however a few passing remarks seem appropriate. I will limit these comments to the exoneration of Ethiopia, and the characterisation of the consistent effort on the part of the UP for an unconditional union since its inception in 1941. It is true that the Unionist Party did a great service to the Ethiopian cause. However, to claim that Ethiopia had no intention of annexing Eritrea puts one in an awkward position to explain Ethiopia's actions during this period. Already in 1941, the Emperor was claiming that Eritrea was part of Ethiopia, delivering speeches asking the Eritrean people to unite with the motherland (See FO 371/31608, FO 371/ 69353). Ethiopia also founded an organisation by the name of the Society for the Unification of Ethiopia and Eritrea (SUEE) in Addis Ababa and sent its members to influence the *Mahber Fikri Hager*. *The Wa'ala Bet Giorgis* failed because on the eve of the day of the meeting, the unionists were forced to change their mind[6] as a result of Ethiopia's opposition to any form of autonomy for Eritrea (Trevaskis 1960, Killion 1985). Ethiopia also worked hard in the UN to get Eritrea. It is reported that Ethiopia accepted federation only after she was told that there was not enough support for her claim for annexation (Medhanie 1986: 19, Fessehatzion 1998: 22).

We have seen how Ethiopia worked hard to omit clauses that would have strengthened Eritrean autonomy in the process of the drafting of the Eritrean constitution. We have also seen how the Representative of the Emperor interfered in the internal affairs of the Eritrean government–in violation of the Eritrean Constitution. The case of how the first Chief Executive lost his post provides a further illustration of how Ethiopia was determined to breach the Federation. Tedla Okbit, an Eritrean police officer, after being dismissed from his post by the Chief Executive, appealed to the Emperor with the claim that he had been dismissed because of his loyalty to the union (Negash 1997: 118, note 1). This implied that the Chief Executive was less loyal, and the police officer was, in fact, immediately reinstated and even promoted to the rank of police commissioner. It was reported in the British Foreign Office annual review for 1955 that the Chief Executive "has attempted to justify himself with the federalists" (FO 371-118738, 1955). It was not long after these events that the Chief Executive was forced to resign. Commenting on his resignation in an interview with the Swedish newspaper, *Dagens Nyheter,* in 1969, Tedla Bairu said that he resigned in protest against the constant intervention of the Emperor's representative. In fact, it became a custom that any political leader who presumed to deviate from the official Ethiopian line was purged. The first to go was Gebremeskel Woldu followed by Ali Radai, Tedla Bairu, Idris Mohammed Adem and Tedla Okbit.

There are also numerous events that contradict the claim that the UP, since its inception in 1941, had consistently pressed for immediate and unconditional union of Eritrea with Ethiopia. First, the *Eritrean Weekly News* shows that the debate on unity with Ethiopia started in Eritrea in 1944–not before. It was only then that the unity of the *Mahber Fikri Hager* started to crumble. The Moslem members slowly withdrew, followed by the Christians, who later organised themselves into the LPP. This paved the way for the unionists to dominate the Association, signalling the rise of the UP. However, it seemed a slim hope remained, because the groups still sought to bridge their differences until the meeting of Bet Giorgis, after which any such hope was banished to the remote corners. There is no mention in Negash's book about the *Wa'ala* Bet Giorgis. This was the outcome of a compromise agreement reached between the unionists, the Christian independentists and the future Moslem League factions of the *Mahber Fikri Hager*, regarding a conditional union. Concerning an 'unconditional union', the unionists had accepted conditions on different occasions. The *Hibret bewe'el* (conditional union) was one, and accepting the Federation itself and their pledge, in the *Wa'ala Selam*, to uphold it was another. The rejection of Amharic becoming an official Eritrean language can also be mentioned. The conversion from unionist to federalist of people like Omar Kadi (Fessehatzion 1998: 30-40), *Aba* Habtemariam Guru (Fessehatzion 1998: 45-6) and many others, and the young unionists who became ardent federalists (Fessehatzion 1998: 52) belies the 'consistent unconditional union'. Professor Greenfield (1965: 305) also notes that within three years of the implementation of the Federation, a significant shift was seen in the Unionists. All the above accounts show the incorrectness of the argument that Ethiopia bore no responsibility in the rise of the Federation and its demise. It also shows the fallacy of the contention regarding the UP's consistent push for unconditional union, and the view that it was solely the wishes of the UP that gave rise to the Federation and its demise.

The importance of the effect of the arbitrary infringement of the pillars of the Federation, in the context of the process of nation formation, lay in the role it played in polarising the conflict and mobilising Eritreans. Many of the ardent supporters of union with Ethiopia were alienated by the actions of the Ethiopian Empire. The British Police Commissioner of Eritrea, Colonel Cracknell, reported that by 1953 "the more fanatic of the young Unionists, formerly of a 'union or die' attitude, have now changed their cry to 'Federation or die'"(Fessehatzion 1998: 52). Both in its institutional and symbolic sense the Federation inculcated a sense of national identity in Eritrean society. Institutions were established which many Eritreans were able to identify with, cherish and endow with a high symbolic value. The attempt to dismantle them generated strong opposition, which was expressed in different forms. Strikes and demonstrations by students and workers like those of 1954 and 1958 were organised. Petitions were sent to the UN appealing to them to intervene. And finally, an underground political movement led by the ELM began in 1958. Organisations like the Young Federalist Association, the Moslem Youth League and the Eritrean Youth Peace Council were also actively involved in defending the Federation. At a time when the traditional parties for independence were almost silenced or rendered impotent, the emergence of new organisations demonstrated the mobilisation of Eritrean nationalists to defend their autonomy. But most of all, it led to the National Liberation Movement of 1961-1991.

The institutionalisation of basic political and legal organs - political parties, trade unions, parliamentarism, constitutionality, freedom of press, and freedom to demonstrate and organise contributed to the rise of what Killion (1997: 20) has called a "pan-Eritrean nationalist sentiment". So when the process of de-institutionalisation (dismantling of institutions) began, it evoked strong resentment and led to resistance. In this sense, both the institutionalisation and de-institutionalisation contributed to the process of nation formation. In the first case, in terms of the establishment of national institutions with which people were able to identify and feel a sense of pride about, and in the second case, by arousing a sense of defiance and resistance. The prohibition against being educated in one's own languages, the lack of access to newspapers in one's own mother tongue, the deprivation of the possibility of listening to one's own languages and songs on the radio, etc., fostered a deep national resentment. This, in turn, became the midwife of a flourishing Eritrean national consciousness.

SUMMARY AND CONCLUSION

A number of conclusions can be drawn from the discussions in this chapter. An important one with respect to the political parties and the struggle they undertook, is that the Independence Bloc, particularly the Moslem League (ML) and the Liberal Progressive Party (LPP), believed that the people of Eritrea had the right to be independent. This common position was founded on the belief that as a result of Italian colonial rule, the Eritrean society had emerged as an integrated people. As it was stated in their memorandum to the Four Power Commission, they also believed in the historical and economic ties between the highlanders and lowlanders before colonialism. Both parties strongly emphasised in their rejection of union with Ethiopia that Eritrea had never been part of Shewan-dominated Ethiopia. For the Moslem League, the rejection of union was based on existing obvious differences (differences of religion, language, culture, etc.[7]). In the case of the LPP, however, though less obvious in comparison to the ML, the rejection was rationalised by existing differences of ethnic identity and the socio-economic achievement which separated the Tigrinya speakers from the Shewa-dominated Ethiopia. However, the LPP also glorified the last Tigrean domination of Abyssinia and wanted to annex Tigrai.

Another conclusion that can be drawn is that the political debate which unfolded with the demise of Italian colonial rule had radically politicised the Eritrean community. This period brought the various ethno-linguistic groups into direct interaction. The liberal democratic atmosphere introduced by the British rule allowed Eritreans, for the first time, to engage into political debate, dialogue, and negotiation to determine their collective destiny. Serious mistakes were committed because of inexperience, and seen from a nationalist point of view, because of the interference from external forces. Meanwhile the experience of that era shaped the future national politics of Eritrea. This was both in terms of the immediate outcome (the disposition of Eritrea) and in the long term, in the advent of the national liberation struggle.

The understanding of the division of the two political blocs as based merely on the two religions gives a misleading picture of reality. Christians were involved in the independence bloc, while Moslems joined the unionist camp. Neither does the proposition that the unionist movement was based on purely Ethiopian nationalism seem to give an adequate explanation. Common religion that is broadly assumed to be the underlying foundation for the Ethiopian nationalism proposition stands on a shaky ground, because religion, by itself is not sufficient. Besides religion, the Eritrean Tigrinya speakers have nothing in common with the Amhara, which was the dominant ethnic of Ethiopia. The British officials on their arrival had found no sign of Ethiopian feelings in the villages of highland Eritrea. Moreover, the change of heart of many Unionists by the time Ethiopia began to contravene the autonomous status of Eritrea does not corroborate the Ethiopian nationalism proposition.

One would tend to conclude that Eritrean society, like any other colonised society, had its hopes set on taking its own affairs into its own hands. The cleavage reflected the difference in the method chosen to achieve it. The unionists believed they could achieve local domination through union, while for the independentists the choice became total sovereignty. Alluding to the struggles of colonised peoples, Markakis points out that the underlying motive for the struggle of these oppressed peoples has invariably been to capture the twin beneficial effects of colonialism, notably the 'new economy' and the state (Markakis 1987: 70). Access to the state safeguards vested interest, both in terms of capturing the 'new economy' and the ability to influence the decisions made by the state. In the aftermath of the defeat of Italy, the new economy and the state were available for capture. The various ethno-linguistic groups were mobilised with the aim of filling the power vacuum. Capturing the state means assuming the dominant position in terms of economics and politics, thereby exercising one's own will over subordinates. Controlling the state apparatus means gaining everything for the triumphant group–for the loser it can mean losing everything. During the colonial period, the state was in the hands of a power equally alien to all groups. But now the alien power was gone, creating a new opportunity. Therefore, unprecedented mobilisation and organisation of the various ethno-linguistic groups for the purpose of controlling the state was seen.

If this view holds true, then, the reasons that can rationally explain the schism have to be sought beyond what is understood as Ethiopianism (Christianism) vs. Islamism. The line of argument pursued here has followed what has been designated as the substantialist perspective. The theme followed here is rather than a pre-determined structural explanation, a contemporaneous social, economic, political and cultural analysis is needed to understand the cleavage. There is no doubt that the causes emerged from multiple constellations. Available data show that a consistent shifting of strength of support for the political parties and a consistent shift of alignment and realignment of political forces influenced by external and internal factors had taken place. This shows that contemporary factors played a significant role in shaping political positions and attitudes.

Notes

1. Mahber *Fikri Hager Ertra* is invariably translated either as the Society for the Love of the Country of Eritrea or the Party of the Love of the Country of Eritrea (thus SLCE and PLCE respectively). The Association elected a 12-man leadership. Gebre Maskal Woldu, a functionary of high rank in the Italian administration, was elected president, a Moslem merchant Abdulkadir Kebire became vice-president and Harogot Abay general secretary. Other members included Woldeab Woldemariam, Ibrahim Sultan, Hagos Abera, Hagos Ghebre, Demsas Woldencheal, Hassen Ali, Mesghina Gebre-Ezgi, Omar Kadi, Berhanu Ahmedin (EPLF, British Administration and Political Struggle of the Eritrean Society 1941-1950 12-13, Markakis 1987: 63, Gebre-Medhin 1989: 79).
2. The leaders of this association were high officials in the Ethiopian government. Woldegiorgis, one of the founders was the " emperor's minister of the pen"; Dawit Ogbazgi was vice-governor of Addis Ababa; Gabremeskal Habtemariam was director of the Ethiopian Ministry of Posts and Telegraph. The pronounced objective of this association was to help poor unemployed Eritreans living in Addis Ababa, but it was actively involved in the propaganda campaign for the case of union with Ethiopia. According to Trevaskis (1960: 66) the primary aim of this association was to safeguard the union of Eritrea with Ethiopia. In reference to the formation of this association the Pankhursts' note that, " ... the Eritrean Unionist Party was formed in April, 1941, by young Eritreans who had kept in touch with the Ethiopian motherland ..."(Pankhurst and Pankhurst 1953: 61).
3. There is much confusion about the actual formation of the Unionist Party. The confusion is caused partly by the mix between the Unionist Party and the *Mahber Fikri Hager Ertra.* And partly by the name *Yehager Fikir Mahber* (Tekle 1999) given to the Addis Ababa-based Society for the Unification of Ethiopia and Eritrea (SUEE). Lloyd Ellingson (1977: 26) notes that the *Mahber Fikri Hager* changed to the Unionist Party in 1944, this seems to refer to the time when the division in the *Mahber Fikri Hager* took place. G.K.N. Trevaskis (1960: 60) writes that *Mahber Fikri Hager* was formed in 1942 to unite Ethiopia with Eritrea, while Pankhurst & Pankhurst (1953: 61) give April 1941 as the foundation date of the UP. According to Gebre-Medhin (1989) it was formed 1947. Tekeste Negash (1997: 37) maintains that the Unionist Party was formed on 5 May 1941. What Negash refers to perhaps, as the date of formation of the UP is the formation of *Mahber Fikri Hager Ertra*, because he does not make any distinction between the UP and *Mahber Fikri Hager.* There are several indications that *Mahber Fikri Hager* was not the Unionist Party and the Unionist Party was not formed in 1941. Inquiry into the Eritrean Weekly News from 1942 to the end of 1943 shows no indication of unionism. It was in the 1944 issue of the EWN that the debate on the future of Eritrea under the column 'future prospect of Eritrea' began to appear, entailing a debate between the unionist Gebremeskel Woldu (EWN 1944 no. 108, 109) and the independentist Abraha Tessema (EWN 1944 no. 107). Moreover, Woldeab Woldemariam (1995) notes that in 1944, he had formed an organisation with the Moslems that stood for the independence of Eritrea. This shows that it was in 1944 that the UP could possibly have been conceived–after a split between the unionists and independentists took place.
4. At an earlier meeting, December 1946, the spiritual leader of the Moslem community Said Abubaker El Mirghani was elected as the president of the League

while Ibrahim Sultan, an interpreter in the Italian Government and leader of the emancipation movement for the serfs, was elected secretary-general (Ellingson 1977: 270-1, Markakis 1987: 65). Nationalist Christians, anti-union like Woldeab Woldemariam, Tessema Asberom and Abraha Tessema, expressed their solidarity with the basic objective of the League by attending the founding conference (Markakis 1987: 65).

5. According to the public opinion worked out by the UN Commission the representation of the political parties was as follows;

Unionist Party	44. 8%
Moslem League	40. 5%
Pro-Italy Party	9. 2%
Liberal Progressive Party	4. 4%
National Party	1. 1%
Unionist bloc	44. 8%
Independence bloc	55. 2%

This representation shows that there was a clear majority for independence (55.2% against 44.8%). Different diplomatic reports also showed that the majority of the Eritrean population was for independence (Medhanie 1986, Fessehatzion 1998).

6. The *Wa'ala Bet Giorgis* was convened to bridge the schism between the two factions of SLCE and to formulate common principles for the solution of the destiny of Eritrea. Gebre-Medhin (1989) discusses the *Wa'ala* in detail in pages 92-96. Before the actual meeting representatives of the SLCE pro-independence (Hassen Ali, Abraha Tesfu, Woldeab Woldemariam, Abdelkadir Kebire and Berhanu Ahmedin) and SLCE pro-union (Gebremeskel Woldu, Mohammed Omar Kadi, Gorgo Habtit, Taha Adem and Mesghina Gebrezrhi) (EPLF 1983: 93-5) met to discuss a common approach and reached a 12-point agreement. They approached the BMA with their compromise agreement and asked for permission to convene a public meeting which took place in November 1946 in Bet Giorgis (Gebre-Medhin 1989: 94). According to Trevaskis (1960: 74) the "Christian Separatists and the Unionist Party" reached a compromise in October 1946 to the effect that "Eritrea should be an autonomous state within the framework of the Ethiopian Empire". Trevaskis further maintains that this agreement was facilitated due to the absence of the Ethiopian liaison officer Colonel Negga Hail Selassie. On the return of the Colonel from Addis Ababa in November of the same year not only the agreement was discarded but the chief advocate of the agreement and the Secretary General of the Unionist Party Gebremeskel Woldu lost his post. Trevaskis further contends that this showed that if the "Separatists and Unionists" were left alone they could have reached a compromise solution.

7. In the Memorandum presented to the Four Power Commission of Investigation for the Former Italian Colonies Report on Eritrea, the Moslem League expressing their opposition to a partition or annexation of Eritrea, and in demanding the independence of Eritrea forwarded their view in the following way. "The reasons that makes us decide to reject Union or annexation to the Government of SHEWA (Ethiopia) are the differences in race, language, religion and history which all reject any political union of ours with it, especially after Islam had penetrated into its interior. This

moved each of the two countries to do its best to preserve its independence and its characterizing features as a result of the fighting that continued in Ethiopia in the past, particularly in the zones inhabited by the Mohammedans, where there were independent Islamic princedoms until Portugal occupied Massawa in the year 1541 in response to a call of help from the government of Gondar. Then the Turks' occupation followed and their reign continued for nearly 400 years, at times directly and sometimes through governors from the natives themselves; until they surrendered it to the Egyptian Government. Then the Italian occupation came, beginning in the year 1885 and ending in 1940" (FO 371-69365, Appendix 103, Memorandum from the Eritrean Muslem League, November 10th 1947 pp. 3-4).

Chapter 6

THE NATIONAL LIBERATION MOVEMENT AS AN AGENT OF NATION-BUILDING

INTRODUCTION

Scholars of colonialism suggest that the most important factor in the formation of national consciousness in colonised societies is the resistance to foreign domination (Hodgkin 1956, Emerson 1960, Leonard 1982, Smith 1983, Anderson 1991). According to social mobilisation theory, people are generally mobilised to participate in an armed liberation movement by at least three primary reasons. These are (1) national identity; (2) the polarisation of conflict; and (3) the presence of a mobilising organisation (see Pye 1962, Huntington 1968, With 1987). National identity as a factor of mobilisation alludes to a situation in which a people who believe that they constitute a unique identity feel that identity has been violated. The polarisation of conflict, on the other hand, refers to the gap between the contesting sides. Polarisation is said to have occurred when the two sides are unable to reconcile their differences. In this situation, mobilisation is undertaken as a means of rectifying the perceived injustices. The existence of a mobilising organisation involves the rise of a political agent that assumes the role of vanguard in mobilising, guiding and leading the mass of the people with the aim of resolving the conflict. Its mission is encouraging, organising and mobilising the people to participate in the armed liberation struggle.

In addition, the mobilising organisation assumes the task of articulating, interpreting and defining the scope, context, and form of the conflict. The relationship between the mobilising organisation and the people can be described in terms of input and output. Input, pertaining the people's side, takes the form of providing fighters from among their beloved sons and daughters, providing logistics and shelter, gathering information about the enemy and taking care of the wounded and sick etc. in the expectation of the receipt of necessary goods. Output, on the other hand, is attributed to the mobilising organisation. It is expressed in the form of organising and protecting the people, making them participate in the struggle, provide services such as health care and education, and eventually leading them to independence. This interdependency between the mobilising organisation and the population with the aim of realising liberation constitutes the basis of the national liberation movement.

Testing these theoretical premises against the Eritrean reality when the National Liberation Movement (NLM) began, we find a quite high degree of conformity. There was an Eritrean national identity in the background when the liberation struggle was launched in 1961. After the frustrating experience of the attempt at federation, a clear polarisation had developed. A mobilising organisation at last emerged – first in the form of the Eritrean Liberation Movement (ELM) and then the Eritrean Liberation Front (ELF). As it is quite often the case at the beginning of any armed struggle, national mobilisation in the form of participation in the Eritrean armed struggle was limited in the early stages of the NLM. The armed campaign started in one corner of Eritrea and was largely dominated by the Moslem communities. As Smith (1983b: 217-18) observes, it is not rare that liberation movements are started by minority groups and in specific regions, but to be effective, it must eventually embrace the whole nation. The polarisation of the conflict in Eritrea grew in connection with the dismantling of the pillars of the federal agreement. Eritrean nationalists showed strong peaceful opposition to the infringement upon the agreements of the Federation. The opposition was not heeded, and ultimately, the Federation was entirely abolished. This left no option for the Eritrean nationalists but to launch an armed liberation struggle. By the first half of the 1980s, the steady growth of the Eritrean national mobilisation had reached its climax.

An armed liberation struggle, in those societies that have experienced it, is an effective means of mobilisation and a mechanism by which the masses are organised in order to participate in national politics. Participation is accomplished not merely through joining the fighting activities, but also through participating in various civic activities. For instance, people joined the different mass organisations that the liberation fronts established to mobilise and organise the population so that they could participate in the economic, social, cultural and political projects and programmes of the nationalist movement. The Eritrean liberation fronts, starting from the end of the 1960s and deriving from the principle of a people's war, began to organise the society into such mass organisations. Accordingly, at various stages of the NLM, the following mass organisations were established: Union of Eritrean Workers, Union of Eritrean Peasants, Union of Eritrean Women, Union of Eritrean Students and Eritrean Youth Union. It would be reasonable to draw an analogy between the role that conscription played in late Middle Age Europe and the armed liberation struggle of this century's developing societies in terms of national integration and centralisation. In the case of Eritrea, the participation in the Italian colonial army, which had included 40 percent of the active labour force of the population, and which stretched across the different ethno-linguistic groups, already had had important implications for the integration of the society. The sociological relevance of war for the formation of nations is given great significance (see Simmel 1955: 100). In this respect, the commencement of an armed struggle for the independence of Eritrea played a substantial role in the nation formation process.

This Chapter examines the armed liberation struggle, which took place during the period of 1961-1991. It is divided into three central phases, which are, in turn, sub-divided. This periodisation is intended to enable us to examine the historico-sociological evolution of the NLM. These phases are presented sequentially. Phase I encompasses the period between 1961 and 1971. Phase II deals with the period of 1971-1981. And eventually, phase III examines the period between 1981 and 1991. It will be worthwhile to recall from the outset that, in discussing the NLM, the overriding focus is to examine its implications for the process of nation formation.

THE ERITREAN LIBERATION MOVEMENT (*MAHBER SHEWATE/ HARAKA*)

The provisions of the federal accord were either gradually and systematically disregarded, or simply repealed. With that disappeared all democratic rights. Once the avenues for peaceful and democratic political expression were closed, other, less overt, but more effective avenues had to be found for expressing political and national aspirations. This compelled Eritrean nationalists to search for alternative ways to challenge the Ethiopian encroachment. And because all the mechanisms through which political grievances could be channelled were banned, all political activities had to be clandestine. In November 1958, a group of Eritrean refugees in the Sudan took the initiative of organising political activity. Delegates were immediately dispatched to Eritrea to establish clandestine cells, which were formed in groups of seven persons in order to avoid detection by the Ethiopian security forces. As a result of this organisational method, the movement inside Eritrea took the name of *Mahber Shewate* (association of group of seven). In the Sudan, it was known as *Harakat El Tahrir El Eritrya,* Eritrean Liberation Movement (ELM), and better known in its short form, *haraka.*

The activities of the ELM were predominantly urban-based, founded by young Moslem nationalists[1] residing in the Sudan. Its aim was to terminate Ethiopian rule through peaceful means, although later it attempted to launch an armed guerrilla insurrection. They were very much influenced by the nationalist movement in the Sudan, and particularly by the Sudan Communist Party. The strategy of the urban clandestine movement, according to Nawid (1997), was learned from the experience of the Sudanese Communist Party. As soon as they could dispatch their representatives to Eritrea, the work of mobilisation was carried out among the urban population. The mobilisation and recruitment work received an immediately positive response from both the Moslem and Christian communities, and in quite a short time, by April of 1959, clandestine cells had been established in almost all Eritrean towns. The ELM convened its first congress in Asmara in 1960. Employing the slogan "Muslims and Christians are brothers, and their unity makes Eritrea one [nation]", the Movement strove for the unity of Eritrean society. The Movement's three main objectives were unity, independence and building a democratic Eritrea. Its initial method of struggle to achieve independence was to topple the Eritrean marionette government of Asfaha Wodemichael through a revolutionary *coup d'état.* This was to be undertaken by anti-unionist elements of the Eritrean police force and a mass patriotic force, thereby forcing Ethiopia to withdraw from Eritrea (Nawid 1997). This was seen, in contrast to armed guerrilla struggle, as a relatively peaceful means. Therefore, in the early years of the 1960s it concentrated its activities in trying to organise the *coup d'etat.* In fact, a plan of action was drawn up, but prematurely aborted when it was uncovered by Ethiopian security forces. The strategy of achieving independence through a revolutionary *coup d'etat* proved to be unrealistic, at best. In addition to its impracticality, once the scheme was exposed, the Ethiopian security forces inflicted a heavy blow on the ELM. Consequently, the plan was abandoned. Afterwards, toward the mid-1960s, the ELM attempted to undertake armed struggle. However, by the time the movement started to establish military units, the initiative had already been taken by another, rival organisation, the *Eritrean Liberation Front.*

With the entrance of the ELM into the field, the liberation movement encountered its first substantial internal conflict. The discord pivoted around the question of whether there should be two organisations. According to Nawid (1997), the ELM made a proposal to the leadership of the ELF to merge the two organisations. However, the proposal failed because of the ELF's rejection. This led to the first armed confrontation within the liberation movement. The ELM accused the ELF of being responsible for this armed conflict. The ELF, in response, accused the ELM of endangering the liberation movement first, by indulging in the unrealistic strategy of a revolutionary *coup d'etat* to liberate Eritrea, thereby trying to prevent an armed struggle from taking place. Second, when its strategy proved fatal, it attempted to dispatch armed units to the field and in doing so stole arms from the ELF (Ahmed 1997).

The antagonism between the two organisations reached its peak and was eventually resolved through coercive means, ending in the complete demise of the ELM. According to Markakis, the discordance between the two fronts can be explained in structural terms. First, the ELF viewed the ELM as a communist influenced organisation. Second, sectionalism played a significant role. While the leaders of the ELM were from the Keren and Sahel regions, the leaders of the ELF were from the Barka region and this difference of origin contributed to the cleavage. Third, the ELM's attempt to broaden its organisation through recruiting Christians also played not an insignificant role. The leaders of the ELF, and Idris Mohammed Adem in particular, disliked this strategy because in their view, it was the Christians that delivered Eritrea to Ethiopia in the first place (Markakis 1987: 108). According to Mohammed Said Nawid, however, the ELF and ELM disagreed over the ELF leadership's belief that they had the sole mandate of representing the Eritrean people. The leaders of the ELF believed that mandate had been bestowed upon them during the time of political struggle in the 1940s and 1950s. They therefore believed that newly emerging political forces had no legitimacy. Moreover, their view that the Eritrean arena could not accommodate more than one organisation also constituted an irreconcilable point of difference. Ahmed Mohammed Nasir, acquiescing to the latter point admits that the chief reason for the ELF attacking the ELM was its belief that the Field could support only one organisation.

At last, the ELF Supreme Council decided to take military action against the Movement. The obliteration of the ELM unit by the ELF at Ela Tza'ada in 1965 effectively terminated not only the military, but also the political existence of the ELM. Many believe that the legacy of this military action set the precedent for the later civil wars between the Eritrean organisations.

THE FIRST DECADE (1961-1971)

This period, in addition to being the first decade of the armed liberation struggle, also represented a crucial moment in the history of the Eritrean society. First, it marked the beginning of the escalation of the conflict between Ethiopia and the Eritrean people. Second, in spite of all the difficulties that were encountered, this period represented an incremental transformation in the nation formation process. This phase of the history of the liberation struggle of the Eritrean people is characterised by some distinct features. To highlight the identifying features of the period, I will introduce a schematic subdivision. Three sub-periods will be distinguished: a) 1961-1965, b) 1965-1969, and c) 1969-1971. Each of these periods is characterised by certain specific features which distinguish them from one another, and represent a stage of development in the historical trajectory in the NLM in particular, and nation formation in general. The first sub-phase can be identified by several developments, including the commencement of the armed struggle and the establishment of leadership - the Supreme Council (those who gathered in Cairo in 1960 elected the Provisional Executive Committee, which was later changed to the Supreme Council) and the Revolutionary Command. The Eritrean Liberation Army (ELA) was also divided into zones in this sub-phase. The features that highlight the second subdivision included a movement to unite the ELA, resulting in the Tripartite Unity that eventually culminated into the convening of Adobha Conference. The third subdivision is characterised by the take-over of the leadership by the General Command; a split and creation of new organisations; the convening of Awate Conference and First National Congress of the ELF; and the rallying of the other splinter groups toward forming one organisation.

Eritrean political exiles and students met in Cairo, Egypt, in 1960 and decided to form the Eritrean Liberation Front (ELF). A year later a group of poorly armed Eritreans led by Hamid Idris Awate initiated the armed struggle, this marked the beginning of the long National Liberation Movement. Those who played a significant role in the starting of the armed liberation struggle could be separated into three groups: a) political refugees; b) Eritrean students in Cairo; and c) Eritrean soldiers in the Sudanese army. All three groups came from Islamic backgrounds. This background most probably resulted in the fact that the leadership of the ELF, during this period, tended to favour Moslem participation. Therefore the participation on the part of Christians was given either secondary priority or viewed as dispensable (cf. Sabbe 1978: 53-5). The fact that it was Moslems who started the armed struggle and it was in the Moslem area that it first spread has given rise to different interpretations. For example, it has led many scholars to view the Eritrean struggle for liberation as an Arab-inspired sectarian and religious separatist movement instead of a genuine national liberation movement.

The most crucial failure during this phase of the history of the liberation struggle was the absence of an organisation that possessed the capacity to provide potent political control and guidance for the nascent armed struggle. The Movement was characterised by lack of coherent organisation and programme. Osman Saleh Sabbe (1978) attributes the mistakes committed to the leadership's emphasis on the military dimension rather than on its organisational structure. This military focus, indeed, led to the neglect of the relationship between the fighters, the Movement and the populace at large. Its consequence was the development of division within the Movement and the escalation of ethnic and religious conflict. Furthermore, these problems were exacerbated by the personal rivalry among the three prominent figures - Idris Mohammed Adam, Idris Osman Galadewos and Osman Saleh Sabbe.

A factor that had an immense influence on the political thinking of the leaders concerning religious relations was the assumption that the Moslem communities constituted a great majority of the Eritrean society. This view was first expressed by the Moslem League. Expressing this claim in its memorandum to the FPCI, the ML wrote: "The Muslem League of Eritrea, represents the overwhelming majority of the inhabitants of this country, whether *numerically* or from the point of view of *ownership of lands* inhabited by Mohammedans" (FO 371-69365, Appendix 103, 1947, emphasis added). The experience of the pre-Federation and the Federation periods also had a visible influence on the form and content of the armed struggle. The competition and rivalry of the period during which the disposition of Eritrea was being determined (1945-1950), and which accentuated primordial elements, made its imprint on the NLM. The "Moslem majority" view, coupled with the Moslem-Christian division of the 1940s affected Moslem-Christian relations.

The "majority-minority" assumption led the Moslems to believe that the Christians, by virtue of their minority status had to be subordinated. Three factors gave rise to the view that the Moslems constituted the great majority. First was geographical preponderance - the region inhabited by the Moslems constituted four-fifths of the total area of Eritrea. Second, of the nine ethno-linguistic groups that constituted the society, eight either professed Islam or were influenced by it. Third, of a slightly different sort is the argument that, regarding the Eritrean question, the majority of the Christians were believed to have sided with the proposal for union with Ethiopia. This made them suspect in the eyes of many Moslems. In addition to these social structural explanations, of course, there was the political and class nature of the leadership of the liberation movement that had its impact on the course of the struggle.

A theoretical explication of this political behaviour can most probably be found in the theory of sociology of domination. The sociological theory of domination derives most prominently from Max Weber's work. Here social interaction within a specific setting and social relationship is described wherein an individual or group imposes its will on others. This domination presupposes conditions in which the subordinate partners in the social action 'obey' the will of the dominant superordinate (Käsler 1988: 161f). The theory is employed here in a slightly different manner with respect to Weber's tenet of obedience. In this study, in contrast to obedience, resistance to domination is accentuated. The theory of domination as a general overview serves to explain the connection between domination and the conquering power of the state. The state here embodies all the national resources, expressed in terms of economic, social, political, cultural and symbolic resources. The ambivalence demonstrated in the struggle for the independence of Eritrea, on one hand, and (simultaneously) the less accommodative predilection towards particular segments of the society, on the other hand, can be partially understood in terms of the sociology of domination. Social history in general, and the history of nation formation in particular, is marked by violent settlement of disputes between groups seeking to dominate – or to avoid domination. In the formative history of most nations, we learn that certain groups have either succeeded in creating, or attempted to create homogenous nations through suppressing other groups. The variation of the suppression and domination extends from benevolent assimilation to expulsion and genocide or ethnocide. In an historiographic comparative sense then, the experience of Eritrea followed the rule rather than demonstrating the exception in the social history of humanity.

The theory of domination serves to explain and clarify power relationships. Domination, as a relationship framed in a continuum of constellations of power arrangements, stretches between avoiding being dominated, to dominating the contesting partner. Between these two extremities, a variety of compromise configurations can be worked out, the most durable and stable one being, however, a state of equilibrium. As a conceptual instrument, the theory serves to explain the social-psychological behaviour of the actors. While the immediate underpinnings of the idea of domination might be the conquest of state power in a narrow sense, the strategic goal could be the achievement of a permanent social domination in a broader dimension in order to be able to dictate conditions. In terms of the former, the leadership of the ELF was eager to preserve and monopolise power in the organisation. In terms of the latter, the leadership was aiming at the socio-cultural and politico-economic domination by the Moslem communities. In this situation, a suspicion and distrust of the Christian community was fostered. Two factors strengthened this perception. One was the apparent role of the UP in the political drama that led to the federation of Eritrea with

Ethiopia, while the other was the nature of the Ethiopian State and its so-called favouring of Christians. Overall, the strife within the Eritrean nationalist movement could be characterised as moving back and forth along the continuum of the wish to dominate - establish equilibrium - avoid domination.

These prefatory statements are intended to contribute, in a general way, toward analysing and understanding the political behaviour, conflicts and mistakes committed during the period under consideration. In the remainder of this section, the three categories of the periodisation will be discussed in somewhat greater detail.

The Expansion of the Armed Struggle through *'Wilaya'* (1961-1965)

In every armed liberation struggle, the foremost and immediate imperative aim is to expand and consolidate the armed forces (With 1987). Pursuing this axiomatic principle, to expand military capability and to be able to recruit fighters from the people as easily as possible, the ELF established zones or *wilaya*. After the 1965 Khartoum conference, which summoned prominent figures from the field and from abroad for the purpose of reorganisation, a new organisational strategy for the liberation army was agreed upon. Accordingly, the army was first divided into four zones, later into five, representing the nine provinces (Barka, Gash, Sahel, Senhit, Akkele Guzai, Serae, Semhar, Dankalia and Hamasen) as shown in figure 6.1 below. This division of the liberation army into zones was adapted from the Algerian military strategy of establishing territorial zones called *wilaya* (Markakis 1987: 113, Ammar 1992: 57). Actually, it was a Syrian military officer by the name Abdu Al Hak Shata who was operating as military advisor to the ELF who suggested the idea (Ahmed 1997).

According to this strategy, a zone army was to be set up, primarily composed of recruits from the region itself, and with the intention of liberating its own area. The strategy was designed for the purpose of inducing people to participate in the armed struggle. It was believed that if people were asked to liberate their own regions they would be more willing to join the liberation struggle. As a safety valve to avoid the zone army being entirely dominated by fighters from one region, the leadership suggested that the number of fighters from the same region should not exceed 30 per cent of the total size. However, the commander was to be from the region. In addition, the strategy was subject to review after six months (Ahmed 1997). In practice, reality turned out otherwise. Five zone armies were established, each having its own command. The command was accorded broad responsibility. These entailed military, administrative and economic affairs that were performed independently from the Revolutionary Command (RC). One element that had damaging consequence of an immense magnitude for the liberation struggle was the absence of co-operation and co-ordination between these different zones. The Commands carried out their activities as independent organisations that were akin to warlordism. The formation of the RC was intended to serve as a bridge between the Zone Commands (ZC) in the field and the Supreme Council (SC) stationed abroad. But it was rendered impotent because the two organs (the SC and the ZC) established a direct connection by bypassing the bridge in violation of the principle.

Figure 6.1: The structure of the ELF

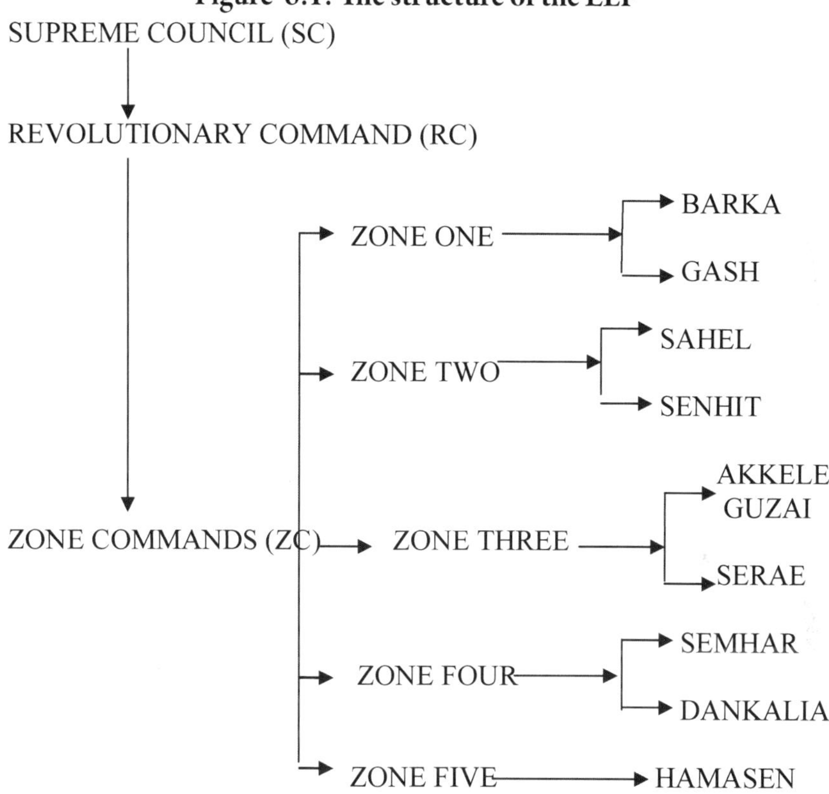

According to the leadership of the ELF, the division of the army into zones was intended to facilitate the recruitment and strengthen the combat capacity of the liberation movement. It was also seen as a device likely to help mitigate competition and rivalry within the liberation movement (Sherman 1980: 74), and, in turn, to foster co-operation and harmony. Unfortunately, the specific socio-cultural embeddeness of the strategy precluded its application in the Eritrean objective reality. Subsequently, it had profoundly negative consequences for the unity of the army. In the beginning, it probably served some of its intended purposes such as recruitment. In the long run, however, it had devastating consequences. It soon became apparent tht the grave mistake that led to the deterioration of the zone armies into rivalry and competition was the division of the ELA into its five divisions on the basis of religion, region and ethnicity (Sherman 1980: 74). Therefore, the practical effect, instead of an amicable coexistence, a spirit of co-ordination between the zones and promotion of their common objective, became a bitter competition to amass larger territories and influence. As a result, persistent boundary squabbles became commonplace. The leaders of the zones indulged in accumulating property by collecting taxes, imposing fines, demanding donations and looting animals from people (Sherman 1980: 74). They were also accused of oppressing the population and committing serious atrocities. In short, they were accused of engaging in all types of arbitrary measures that generated disharmony between them and the people under their control. Contributing to this behaviour was the absence of effective control from the leadership above. In practice, the zone division became a base for sub-national configurations, that is, they became the base for ethno-linguistic gathering. As a result, clan and tribal conflicts beset the liberation army, which, in turn, diluted the nationalist character of the NLM (Toteel 1997).

Observers point out that multiple problems beset the Movement. These include the absence, on the one hand, of an effective and capable political leadership, and on the other, an organisation equipped with a clearly defined and an elaborate political programme. In addition, the stationing of the SC abroad was also seen as part of the problem. The sectarian division in the SC was also considered as constituting a source of inefficiency and disunity. The organisational connection between the SC as a collective leadership, on the one hand, and the zone leaders, on the other, was very loose. The three members of the SC established a direct supervising relationship on an individual basis with the zone leaders on grounds of kinship affiliation, a move quite contrary to the principles of formal bureaucratic administration. Consequently, a patron-client[2] relationship was fostered, thereby undermining the overall organisational structure. The patron-client relationship operated in such a way that members of the SC would provide the necessary logistics and weaponry to their client ZC (Ammar 1992: 58), while the ZC would safeguard the sphere of influence of their patrons (Markakis 1987: 116).

The RC stationed in Kassala, Sudan, which was thought to serve as a bridge between the SC and the field, thereby providing effective political leadership by exerting strong discipline fostering solid unity, failed miserably. The failure of this intermediary organ seems to have been caused by the undermining efforts and intentions of both the SC and the ZC (particularly within three client Commands - Zones One, Two and Four) (Markakis 1987). Indeed, in practice, the leaders of the zone armies operated as independent units with respect to the RC. An element that ensured the autonomy of the zone leaders was perhaps the absence of frequent or effective direct communication between the upper hierarchy and the lower strata of the organisation. This was further strengthened by the fact that the zones were practically dominated by a single ethnic group. This apparent lack of an integrated and well-structured organisation at this formative stage of the struggle was one of the underlying reasons for the problems of the NLM throughout the decade.

The Rectification Movement (1965-1969)

The negative effects of the competition and rivalry between the zone armies were strongly felt by the fighters. Therefore, those who realised the seriousness of the schism began to engage in earnest internal debate. Consequently, a movement emerged from within the liberation movement, commonly known in Arabic as *Eslah,* rectification. This movement to rectify the mistakes of the independence struggle was reinforced by contemporaneous developments. The particular development in this instance pertained to the return of young radical fighters who had been sent for military training and political education in progressive Arab countries, and in China and Cuba. Many of these young fighters, upon their return, were assigned as commissioners in the five zones. In their efforts to rectify the mistakes of the Movement, the first thing they did was organise meetings. The first meeting of this type took place at Aredaibe in 1968. It was attended by the commanders of the three zones (Zones Three, Four and Five) under mottoes such as; 'Unity of the Army', 'Leadership in the Field', 'Human Rights for the People' and 'Correct Relations between the People and the Army' (Markakis 1987: 124).

Other sources attribute the rectification movement to three factors: (a) The *Eslah* movement based in Kassala; (b) the intelligentsia of the "marginalised" zones, in particular, zones four and five; and (c) the "oppressed tribes" in Zone One, the seven tribes known as the *Keser* tribes (Kunama, Nara, Elit, Bisha, Algeden, Betama, Sebderat) who resisted the domination of the Beni Amer in the Barka-Gash region. And in Zone Four, the Marya and Tigre of Sahel resisted the domination of Belain (Toteel 1997). According to Toteel, these "oppressed" groups could not tolerate the domination of the zones by specific ethno-linguistic groups. They demanded that they should have either equitable representation, or their own zone army that exclusively represented them. The second factor was the intelligentsia of the marginalised zones based in Kassala. Many educated fighters were redundantly stationed in Kassala. The RC kept them in Kassala out of fear for their own lives. This was due to the fact that the ZCs harboured some hostility toward the intellectuals. Many of them, having no formal education themselves, perceived the presence of intellectuals as a threat to their power. These educated fighters began an informal, clandestine movement within the Movement, with the aim of correcting the mistakes and weaknesses of the liberation struggle. By reaching a common understanding through discussions and exchange of views with those fighters with a higher educational level who had been sent to the field, the leaders of *Eslah* attempted to reform the organisation. In addition, when the cadres who had been sent to China returned, they were able to reach an understanding regarding the task of tackling the problems of the NLM. The main objective of the *Eslah* was expressed as being to convene a national congress. According to Toteel, members of both the RC and the ZCs were involved in the Rectification Movement. However, there exists a confusion about where, when and by whom the *Eslah* was formed. There is no doubt in Toteel's mind that the *Eslah* was formed in Kassala and received support from the intellectuals of the marginalised zones and the "oppressed tribes" who played a leading role in the rectification effort (Toteel 1997).

The Rectification Movement had as its intention placing the liberation movement on the right course by correcting mistakes committed by zone leaders, thereby unifying the different zone armies. Seen from the perspective of its overall results, however, it failed in realising its mission. Not unexpectedly, it faced strong opposition from the SC and their clients in the ZC. According to observers of the NLM, politically speaking, this movement triggered a struggle between two political forces and trends. These were the old/new, conservative/radical, traditional/modern sets of political trends. The old generation embodied in the SC represented the first element of this dichotomy, while the young generation espousing the ideals and strategies of the new political movement represented the second element of the dichotomy. In this political contest, the old generation employed traditional sectarian methods to preserve its interests. "Their young, radical challengers strove to transcend this debilitating inheritance and to shift the internal political contest to an ideological and political level with which the older generation was quite unfamiliar" (Markakis 1987: 124). The cleavage was to assume a clearer form at a later stage of the struggle in conjunction with the emergence of new organisations.

The effort to unify the army continued in spite of the political cleavages between the leaders abroad and the young generation whose influence was increasingly growing in the field. The first phase of this endeavour culminated in the creation of the Tripartite Unity–the unity of the Zones Three, Four and Five. Two Zones (One and Two), because of the opposition from both the patrons in the SC and the clients in the ZC, stayed out of the Tripartite Unity. Encouraged by the Tripartite Unity, the revolutionary fighters took the struggle one step further to achieve the complete unity of all zones. The bases of Zones One and Two also struggled for unity, and finally it was reached in the Adobha Conference[3] in 1969. This Conference succeeded in uniting the five zones, but at the same time laid the groundwork for the next, much more serious split. The modest, reformist outcome of the Conference appeared to satisfy no one. The conservative old guard thought that the young revolutionaries had gone too far, while the young radicals were annoyed that the conference produced no fundamental change. This dissatisfaction was not limited to the resolution of the Conference, but also concerned its practical implementation. To the dismay of the young radicals, even the modest outcome encountered serious obstacles to implementation. Although the urgency for unity was apparent, the forces that opposed unity were insurmountable. Realising the issues at stake, that is, their personal power, the conservatives were prepared to prevent the process of unity at any cost. As Markakis (1987: 124) expresses it: "The older generation of nationalist politicians used the traditional methods to defend their prerogatives, despite the resulting damage to 'national' unity".

Therefore, the achievements of the Adobha Conference did not last long; it did not have even the time to raise its feet from the ground before a split of a serious nature erupted. However, it is important to point out that the split did not take place along the continuum radical-conservative political thought.

The Emergence of New Organisations (1969-1971)

So far the discord, at least formally, was within the ranks of one organisation. However, developments were soon to take different forms and directions. The struggles of the Rectification Movement and the subsequent outcome of the Adobha Conference struck at the heart of the conflict, notably the power structure. Those who expected to lose much in the power shift made it one of their priorities to assure that these efforts would not erode their power prerogatives completely. Not surprisingly, as a result, all attempts to unify the various units of the organisation achieved only limited and temporal success. Consequently, instead of different military units under the umbrella of one political organisation, there emerged different, independent politico-military organisations. The Eritrean political arena witnessed the simultaneous birth of three new groups, the PLF I, the PLF II, and the Obele group. The motives, objectives and political colour of these groups, of course, varied immensely. This setback in the effort to unify the ranks of the liberation movement was perceived by some observers as epitomising the fragility and feebleness of Eritrean nationalism, particularly from the viewpoint of the need to achieve a cohesive and united nationalist movement. Those who shared this perception tried to qualify their argumentation by referring to the fact that the splinter groups' social bases more or less constituted specific ethno-linguistic groups (see Erlich 1982).

In the aforementioned split and subsequent formation of different organisations, the role of the SC, and particularly of the three prominent figures of the Council, was decisive. When it became clear that the reformists' intention was to curb the power of the SC, the three prominent figures of the Council moved to create their own power base, which assumed sectarian, regional and religious social forms. In the aftermath of the Adobha Conference, several fighters gathered in Kassala, Sudan, fleeing pursuit by the new leadership of the General Command. From there they were flown to Yemen by Osman Salih Sabbe (who formed the *Amana Ama* - General Secretariat) and arrived at South Dankalia (Mohammed Nur 1997). Subsequently, after convening their first meeting on April 4, 1970, at Sodho-eila, they founded the PLF I (also known as the Sedho-eila group). It was predominantly composed of fighters from the Semhar (Red Sea) province. A further split occurred within this group, a larger group remained in South Dankalia while a smaller group moved to Northern Sahel. However in November 1971, the two factions of the PLF I met again at Embahera and were reunited. Simultaneously, the birth of another group was crystallising.

Another group of fighters left the ELF and assembled in Akkele Guzai. In March 1970, this group founded the PLF II or *Selfi Natzinet*, during a meeting at Ala. In contrast to the PLF I, which was primarily composed of Moslems, the PLF II (Selfi Natzinet), was primarily composed of Christian highlanders. After the Awate Conference in 1970, a third group, the Obele, comprising fighters from the Barka region also emerged. Now, these three groups and the *Amana Ama* stationed in Beirut – which, as we have seen above was behind the creation of the PLF I – started to co-ordinate their activities. With the aim of negotiating to strengthen their co-operation, the three groups (the PLF I, the PLF II and the Obele) sent delegations to Beirut to meet the *Amana Ama* (which later changed its name to the *Foreign Mission*) and agreed to work together through a united national front. The three groups created a provisional transitional united administration in October 1972 at Gehteb, whereby they were put under a centralised leadership structure while at the same time, preserving their organisational independence. To strengthen and deepen their unity, the PLF I and the PLF II agreed in 1973 to build one organisation. However, the final act of unification took place on June 13, 1974, when the two were joined by the Obele group. Thus, the Eritrean People's Liberation Forces was formally formed (see Mohammed Said 1994).

The above account illustrates the sequence of events through which the three groups that originally elicited their social base from specific social sections of the society were transformed into the EPLF. Before they joined hands, each group primarily represented a specific ethno-linguistic group. Yet, it must be pointed out that, in spite of the composition of their respective social bases, they strongly disavowed any claim that they were sectarians in their pamphlets, political manifestos, declarations, etc. For instance the PLF II, in their famous pamphlet "We and our Objectives" (1971) explaining why they left the ELF, acknowledged their Christian background, while they denied strongly that they were particularly pro-Christian. Nevertheless, their political rhetoric and propaganda seemed, and apparently was interpreted as emphasising, or displaying, a tone of parochial and primordial sentiments and tendencies. In addition, their appeal at the very outset was more or less directed toward highland Christians. However, once the PLF I and the PLF II were integrated, their composition was totally altered. Moreover, the increasing flow of young Eritreans to the struggle from all ethno-linguistic groups further enhanced the organisations nationalist characteristics. The inclusion of the Obele group in the EPLF seems to have been a tactical and temporary arrangement of convenience, because some months later it and the Foreign Mission left the EPLF. The Obele group, throughout its history constantly represented a very narrow social group and interest.

To summarise, the first decade (1961-1971) of the national liberation struggle was beset with serious problems because of lack of a clear political programme, a capable, disciplined and efficient political leadership and a clearly defined organisational structure. Yet, it opened the way for the mobilisation and participation of the larger population in the armed struggle. Despite numerous problems, Eritrean youth kept joining the armed struggle. The split that took place at the end of the decade brought with it temporary setbacks in the mobilisation and participation of the population, but the tide soon changed. The second decade witnessed so far an unprecedented mobilisation and participation, which also enhanced the nation-building process.

THE SECOND DECADE (1971-1981)

This section discusses the basic characterising features of this second period. First, the introductory part of the overall section (periodisation 1971-1981) introduces, in a quite brief fashion, the outstanding developments that occurred during the period, followed by a more detailed discussion divided into respective sub-periods. This second decade can, for the purpose of analytical investigation, be categorised into three sub-periods: a) 1971-1975, b) 1975-1978, and c) 1978-1981. In brief, the developments that characterised this period can be accounted for as follows: During the first sub-period (1971-75), the ELF convened its First National Congress. It was believed by many to have endorsed a resolution that triggered civil war – a civil war that raged for two years. It was also during this period that the various factions of the EPLF joined hands to form one organisation. In the second sub-period (1975-78) a number of events took place. The 1975 Khartoum unity agreement was one of these events. The ELF convened its Second National Congress during this period, and a split within the EPLF occurred. The period was also marked by a massive flow of Eritreans joining the armed struggle, and in addition, many towns were liberated. The EPLF convened its First Organisational Congress, and finally, on October 20, 1977, a unity agreement was signed between the ELF and EPLF. The developments which marked the third sub-period (1978-81) included the recapture of towns; the recurrence of civil war; the defeat of the ELF, a split within the ELF and its final disintegration.

More concretely, the outstanding developments of this period included the two fronts holding their respective congresses, in which they clearly and elaborately stated their objectives, plans of action and political programmes. The ELF held its First National Congress in 1971 and its Second in 1975. The EPLF held its First Organisational Congress in 1977. The massive flow of Eritreans to the liberation fronts that began by 1973/74 was also another important development. This development marked a major turning point in the mass mobilisation and participation in the liberation struggle. This resulted in that more than 90 per cent of Eritrea being liberated by the end of 1977.

The congresses mentioned above also passed resolutions to establish mass organisations (workers' union, peasants' union, women's union, students' union, and youth union) (ELF 1971: 38, 1975: 41) which enhanced the popular base of the struggle. Above all, the congresses distinctly proclaimed that the Eritrean Revolution was a national democratic revolution and stated its objectives (ELF 1971). The EPLF, at its First Organisational Congress in 1977, also articulated its programme, emphasising the desire to enhance the liberation movement, the task of nation-building and securing the independence of Eritrea. The Congress of the EPLF adopted a comprehensive political, social, economic and cultural programme, believed by many to be more radical. This in some sense reflected the more advanced stage of development which the NLM had reached. This Congress passed several resolutions that are worth some attention. One described a vision of the content and form the Eritrean State should take. Another highlighted the economic policies to be pursued. And in addition, cultural and educational innovations, the social dimensions - workers' rights, women's' rights etc. were clearly emphasised. The equality and unity of the various nationalities were also given top priority (EPLF 1977). As is the case with any national liberation movement with a vision of building a modern, progressive, prosperous and democratic society, we find a number of clauses and propositions in these political programmes which rested on the perceptions and principles of the modernisation theory. In this modernisation enterprise, the authors of the programmes constituted the modernising political actors. With these and many other developments, this second decade marked entry to a stage in which not only the struggle for independence, but also the process of nation formation was markedly propelled forward.

The second decade of the history of the NLM represents a qualitative transformation in many aspects. The NLM, as an agent of nation-building, by endorsing concrete programmes and guiding the prospective direction of the movement and the society in terms of political, economic, social and cultural projects, advanced step-by-step the development of the process of nation formation and the achievement of sovereign nation state. In contrast to the preceding decade, which was characterised by spontaneity and preoccupation with military priorities, this second period was distinguished by the embarking on a comprehensive, clearly thought out plan-of-action. The elements of the plan were then formalised through congresses and concretised by policy implementation with the active participation of the Eritrean masses. The most interesting details emerge with the examination of the three sub-periods of the second decade.

The Consolidation of Rival Organisations (1971-1975)

A couple of events can be highlighted to illustrate this period. As it was pointed out earlier, it was during this period that the ELF convened its First National Congress. This Congress is remembered not only as a turning point, at which the groundwork for the transfer of the ELF was set in place, but also as the Congress that enacted a resolution setting the stage for civil war. It should also be recalled, however, that the Congress avoided any explicit declaration of war. Nevertheless, it effectively closed all avenues of negotiation by demanding that the breakaway groups simply accept the decisions of the Congress and rejoin the "mother" organisation (ELF). It was decided that if the PLF I and the Obele group refused to comply, force would be used (ELF 1971, Toteel 1997). The PLF I immediately denounced the Congress, and at its meeting at Embahera in November of 1971, declared that it would not recognise the Congress. This denouncement became the prelude to the Revolutionary Council's (RC) declaration of war on the group, a war that consumeted the energies of the NLM for the coming two years (1972-74). The Congress's decision pertaining to the PLF II was slightly different from that regarding the PLF I and the Obele group. The Congress stated that due to the social constituency of the PLF II and the sensitivity which accompanied it, the leadership should be extra cautious in its handling of the matter and should try to resolve it as peacefully as possible. Pool (1997: 11) notes that, "sensitive to the legacy of the killing of Christian fighters, the Ala group was not initially a target". In addition, when the RC declared war against the PLF I, it tried to convince the PLF II that they should stay away as the military operation was not directed against them. However, the PLF II was not convinced, rather, it interpreted the appeal as the ELF's tactic to liquidate the different factions one by one. There were clear indications in the language of the Resolution that reinforced their suspicion. The Resolution was not, for example, amenable to any kind of negotiation. Moreover, the fundamental position of the ELF was that the Field couldn't tolerate more than one organisation. This was why the resolution of the Congress stated that the factions should abide by the decision of the Congress and rejoin the ELF.

The three factions of the EPLF, after passing through different transitional stages, consolidated themselves into an organisation that was to gradually grow into a formidable force. Here, two processes were simultaneously proceeding, one entailing organisation building and the other pertaining to securing survival. However, the rapprochement between all three groups that constituted the Eritrean Popular Liberation Forces (EPLF) appears not to have been based on matters of principle, in particular, concerning the Foreign Mission and the Obele group. Evidence supporting this interpretation can be found in the fact that after a while a split took place reflecting a line of division in which the Foreign Mission and the Obele group formed the ELF-PLF. This left the PLF I and PLF II as the constituent groups of the EPLF.

Finally, the civil war came to a halt. Various factors are suggested as contributing to the end of the war. Prominent among these was the ELF's realisation that it could not conclude the civil war to its benefit. A second factor is believed to have been the fall of Haile Selassie, which created a conducive milieu in the highland of Eritrea (see Pool 1997: 11-12) and which also led to an increase in the competition over recruiting followers. A third factor was the pressure put on the organisations by the people to stop the fighting. People's committees were formed and dispatched to appeal to and put pressure on the organisations to initiate negotiations and halt the civil war. Finally, a fourth factor was the dissatisfaction that arose within the rank-and-file of the ELF regarding the continuation of the war (Mahta 1981, Toteel 1997).

In connection with the cessation of hostilities between the organisations, perhaps one additional point that could be highlighted is the increasingly close balance of power between the two organisations. The flow of young Eritreans in great numbers into both organisations had the effect of enhancing the strength of both organisations. Of much more importance, was the fact that the balance of this flow meant that both organisations were growing at an equal pace, resulting in a roughly equal balance of strength. This equilibrium brought the realisation that it would not be possible to defeat the rival militarily. Thus, the only realistic alternative was to stop the civil war and begin dialogue. For this moment, the civil war was halted and unity negotiations began.

Meanwhile, the policy of the new Ethiopian regime toward the Eritrean question was no different from that of the old regime. The unwillingness to find a peaceful and just solution by the military junta for the Eritrean problem, and the subsequent suppression and reign of terror increased Eritrean participation in the armed struggle. In spite of the bloody internecine war, the flow of Eritreans from all walks of life to the liberation movement grew steadily. The flow to the field of younger and more educated Eritreans thus radically altered, both quantitatively and qualitatively, the nature of the NLM as well as the organisations that represented it. Overall, it can be said that this period witnessed a mass mobilisation and participation in the armed struggle that cemented Eritrean nationhood.

The Liberation of Towns (1975-1978)

The two most outstanding developments that distinguish this sub-period are: a) the liberation of most of Eritrea including all but four towns and the subsequent total mobilisation and participation of the society, and b) the complex unity effort undertaken to unify the various factions of the Eritrean revolution. The struggles to mobilise the population and to simultaneously achieve unity and integration have always been two faces of a single political struggle. At this point, the liberation of most of Eritrea by the nationalist fronts highlighted the urgency of mobilising the population and ensuring their participation in the liberation struggle. The process of mobilisation encompassed two interconnected elements. These included encouraging the population to actively participate in the armed struggle for independence and organising them in mass organisations. This, in turn, was supposed to lay the foundation for the future civil society, which would enable the mass organisations to work for their class and social group interest. The mobilisation process also sought to educate the masses both politically and culturally in order to develop national consciousness. In short, a conscious concerted struggle was undertaken to strengthen political and cultural processes. This was done by incorporating the building of civil institutions that safeguard societal interest and the durability of the gains of the liberation movement with the intention of ensuring the goal of nation-building. The convening of congresses, both of the mother organisations and of the mass organisations affiliated to them, was intended to institutionalise legitimacy and enhance national infrastructures as a guarantor of sovereignty and nation-building.

Starting from the second half of 1976, the liberation of villages and towns proceeded in an unprecedented pace. By the end of 1977, more than 90 per cent of Eritrea had come under the control of the NLM. This development brought with it a new phenomenon and a new challenge to the NLM, that of administering towns, which resulted in close interaction between the urban civilian population and the fighters. This, in turn, highlighted the urgent new responsibility of enforcing law and order with a system whose personnel was composed of Eritrean sons and daughters, and replacing the coercive Ethiopian state machinery. In other words, civilian administration was established. Moreover, it became commonplace to see the cherished flag flying over every corner of a street, where, not long ago, it had been only a dream. For many Eritreans, it was the first time seeing their flag. In addition, the fears and insecurities, night curfews, the threat of languishing in prison or the possibility of being executed for minor offences such as singing the Eritrean nationalist song, possessing a pamphlet or because one looked suspicious in the eyes of an Ethiopian soldier, were gone for the majority of Eritreans. It was a revolutionary change, and its sustainability required revolutionary ways. One of the methods used to nurture national identity was to glorify and commemorate the victories through music, poems and songs. Many popular songs rehearsed in those days reflected the changes that were taking place, in particular the liberation of towns, and went like "Eritrea, Eritrea towns became our camps". Here one is prompted to highlight the importance of the construction of myths, symbols and rituals in nation-building (see Hosking and Schöpflin 1997). Myth entailes the act of telling and retelling of stories of combat actions, while rituals involve the commemorating, celebrating and festivities of those combat actions and victories. Symbols stand for the objectification of those stories and narratives through, for instance, designating martyrs' squares and martyrs' tombs.

Therefore, in the effort to construct and foster national identity and reinforce nationhood, symbolic measures were undertaken by the fronts. Such symbolic measures also involved the creation of public spaces through giving names to public places such as streets, public buildings (hospitals, municipalities, schools, squares, banks) from among the names of martyrs, historical battles and places of battles which were to be respected and remembered by the people. Of a high sacred symbolic value in the collective identity of the imagined community – equivalent to the role played by the tomb of the 'Unknown Soldier' – was the *Meda Siwu'at* (Martyrs Square), placed in the centre of every liberated town. These measures incorporate acts of both deconstruction and construction. They were acts of deconstruction, in the sense that old meanings and symbols connected with the occupying power were emptied. They were acts of construction in the endowment of new meaning, value, symbolism and sanctifying national memory. It should not be difficult, therefore, to imagine the immense emotional exhilaration that this development induced in the Eritrean society. National sentiment and feeling reached a boiling point. Its palpable manifestation could be demonstrated in the glorious and enthusiastic participation – without any pecuniary interest – in almost every project that the liberation movement initiated.

The liberation of the towns confronted the fronts with new challenges. These challenges included, among other things, the establishment of a civil administration and other national institutions. Creating new national institutions and designing and initiating economic, social, cultural and political projects became an urgent responsibility. In the towns they liberated the respective organisations established mass organisations (workers, peasants, women, students and youth). For those who were under age, pioneer associations like the *Tzebah* (dawn) and *Merih* (vanguard) were set up. Schools were opened under the guidance of the NLM, with Tigrinya and Arabic being used as languages of instruction. Health and other public services were provided. Political and military education were provided to the civil population. In general, the overriding aim was, extending from short term practical objectives, helping the people to participate in the daily administration, construction, development, security, etc., of their town, with the long term objectives of creating a new society. Emphasising the importance of such programmes initiated by nationalist leaders, Benedict Anderson notes:

> Nationalist leaders are thus in a position consciously to deploy civil and military educational systems modelled on official nationalism's; elections, party organisation, and cultural celebrations modelled on the popular nationalisms of nineteenth-century Europe, and the citizen-republic idea brought into the world by the Americas (Anderson 1991: 135).

The first attempt towards the achievement of national unity between the two fronts after the bloody internecine war resulted in the September 1975 Khartoum Unity Agreement. The basic elements of the Agreement were to establish "One Revolutionary Organisation, with one Political Leadership and One Liberation Army and a Programme of Action" (ELF-PLF 1975). However the unity agreement was immediately rejected by the EPLF's Field Leadership for two reasons: a) the power struggle which was going on between the Foreign Mission (EPLF leadership abroad) and the Field Leadership, b) the strategy of unity agreed upon contradicted its own formula of unification (Sherman 1980: 48). Concomitantly, a split occurred within the EPLF in which the Foreign Mission and some elements of the PLF I and the Obele group on the one hand, and the PLF II and the bulk of the PLF I on the other, formed two separate organisations. The former became the Eritrean Liberation Front-Popular Liberation Forces (ELF-PLF) and the latter the Eritrean People's Liberation Front (EPLF). The split within the EPLF strained the unity effort.

The quest for the unity of the NLM was, however, kept alive, culminating in the October 20, 1977, Unity Agreement. Numerous committees were set up following this agreement. A leadership body was established which was to assume the task of supervising the transition period until a unity congress could be convened. This body came to be known as the Joint Supreme Political Leadership. Other sub-committees were also created, with specific tasks that were subordinated to this joint political leadership (EPLF 1987: 42). This revival of unity was received by the Eritrean people and friends of the revolution as good news. Many thought that the differences between the two main organisations were not only insignificant but also that the organisations should be united in order to achieve their primary goal. In addition, although at the time the liberation movement was enjoying victory, most of the towns under its control, it was expected by all indications that the Ethiopian regime would try to recapture the towns with massive support from the Soviet Union and its allies. Given such expectations, unity within the revolution was seen as crucial in order for the organisations to be able to defend themselves and the liberated areas. However, before unity could be accomplished the expected Ethiopian attack occurred. Within a few months, the Dergue army had reoccupied all the towns.

The failure to achieve unity in the NLM no doubt contributed to the military defeat, although it might not have been the decisive factor. It was not certain that even a united liberation movement would have managed to withstand the formidable Ethiopian forces of aggression backed by massive Soviet Bloc support. The recapture of most of the towns was clearly a serious setback for the liberation struggle. However the national sentiment, the enormous emotional impression and the memory which was inculcated in those towns during the administration of the NLM and the air of liberation experienced albeit brief, were to have a lasting effect. A testimony to this was the fact that many of the inhabitants of these towns followed the retreating fronts, seeking a) to join them as fighters; b) to live as internally displaced refugees under the fronts in camps like *Medeber Tehadso* and *Medeber Solomuna*; or c) to live a refugee life outside Eritrea, particularly in the Sudan.

The Setbacks of the NLM (1978-1981)

The basic features that characterised this period can be simply stated in terms of three interconnected developments. In combination, these constituted a major setback for the NLM. First, with the help of Soviet Bloc intervention, the Ethiopian military regime succeeded in recapturing all the towns that had come under the control of the NLM (cf. Pool 1997: 12). Second was the failure of the unity efforts in the ranks of the NLM. Third, subsequently an internecine war erupted between the two biggest organisations that eventually led to the demise of the ELF. The first development needs no exposition, while the second development will be treated in a later section. Therefore, I will briefly discuss the third one. The question which group was responsible for starting the civil war still generates controversy. Members of the ELF typically claim that it was the EPLF that started it (ELF-RC 1989: 22), while EPLF members answer in kind (see EPLF 1984: 62). In fact, there appears to be some basis for both claims. On June 6, 1980, units of the ELF attacked a unit of the EPLF at Inger, in North Dankalia, forcing the EPLF to retreat from the region (Toteel 1997). If this is taken as the starting point of the war, it was the ELF who bore the primary responsibility for initiating it. On August 28, 1980, the EPLF attacked the ELF in Sahel on the pretext that the ELF had deserted the front lines in Sahel without informing the EPLF. The withdrawal was interpreted by the EPLF as an act of conspiracy or betrayal, undertaken deliberately to weaken it, as this would certainly increase the EPLF's vulnerability to attacks by the Ethiopian army (EPLF 1981: 14). If this is taken as the starting point for the civil war (as is widely accepted), then the EPLF was primarily responsible. These events took place after a promising start that year, and after an accord had been reached in January of 1980, to merge units from both armies, which gradually would have cemented the integration of the fronts.

The underlying factors for the outbreak of the civil war were many. Some of the prominent factors included unilateral negotiations with the Dergue regime and the existence of internal elements that were against unity. In violation of the agreed-upon principle of not unilaterally negotiating with Ethiopia to seek to a peaceful solution for the Eritrean problem, it seems that both fronts were engaged in secret, unilateral negotiations. When the civil war broke out, both organisations began accusing each other of having secret, unilateral contact with Ethiopia. These negotiations increased the already existing mutual suspicions and led to a campaign of bitter recrimination. A second factor was the fact that there had always been forces in both organisations that opposed unity, and they were prepared to use everything at their disposal to sabotage such possibilities. The attack on the EPLA units in North Dankalia was considered to have been of this nature. First, the attack came just days before a planned meeting between representatives of the two fronts intended to implement the integration of military units from both organisations. Additionally, it seems that it was a decision made by the military office alone, that is, without the knowledge of all members of the Executive Committee. The action was undoubtedly taken with the aim of undermining the agreement reached earlier in the year, because that agreement could only be thwarted by military action (Toteel 1997). Within the EPLF, there was also the belief that the ELF had not changed from its behaviour of the 1960s (Tesfai 1997), a belief that was not conducive to unity. Under these circumstances the second civil war between the two organisations broke out in August 1980, lasting almost one year. By July 1981, the ELF had been pushed to the Sudan, which put an end to its military existence inside Eritrea. This marked the end of the civil war and paved the way for the domination of Eritrean politico-military space by the EPLF. The virtual total defeat of the ELF opened a new era in that it gave rise to the hegemony of the EPLF in the final decade of the armed struggle (1981-1991).

THE THIRD DECADE (1981-1991)

Two prominent features distinguish this decade. They are: a) the domination of the Eritrean politico-military arena by a single organisation, after ten years of competition between the liberation organisations; and b) the culmination of the NLM in the independence of Eritrea. A further division into three sub-periods is possible: a) 1981-1984; b) 1984-1989; and c) 1989-1991. One of the main characterising features of this period is the emergence of a single dominant politico-military organisation, and there arose two contending views concerning the implications of this domination. For the sake of simplicity, I have designated the two views as the optimistic and the pessimistic, and they can be also assessed in terms of introvert and extrovert perspectives. The introvert, or internal perspective pertains to the internal unity of the NLM, while the extrovert, or external perspective pertains to its ability to effectively and successfully confront the enemy in combat.

Beginning with the optimistic view, proponents of a single united front contended from the introvert perspective that the emergence of a single dominant organisation in both the political and military realms provide the necessary foundations for success in the liberation struggle by bridging the gap between the ranks of the Eritrean fighters. In addition, it was thus presumed that it would strengthen the cohesion and integration of the society (cf. Iyob 1995: 121-22, EPLF 1984). A liberation movement under the leadership of a unified vanguard was believed to possess greater chances and capacities for building an integrated society. In this context, the emergence of a single dominant organisation was seen as a blessing. From the extrovert perspective, the blessing was construed from the point of view that rather than consuming its energy and resources with internal competition, the Eritrean Liberation Movement would be able to channel all its resources into achieving its basic objective. In fact, according to this view, the emergence of a single front was deemed to be a necessary prerequisite for the successful conclusion of the liberation struggle (cf. EPLF 1984).

The opposite, pessimist view, contended that the domination of the Eritrean politico-military arena by a single front would be detrimental to the society's unity (cf. ELF-RC 1989). Therefore, it was argued that the disappearance of one organisation would inevitably lead to a sense of deprivation and loss on the part of the members of that organisation. This view based its contention on the premise that because the different organisations represent different segments of society, the sudden disappearance of an organisation would exacerbate the divisions of the Eritrean society (cf. Ammar 1992: 106). Proponents of this idea built their interpretation on the belief that the organisations derived the core of their social base from particular segments of the social fabric of Eritrean society. Accordingly, it was believed that the disappearance of one organisation would disturb the socio-religious balance.

Seen in retrospect, it would seem that of the two contrasting views, the optimistic view prevailed. The predicted disintegration and religious conflict did not take place. On the other hand, the NLM was able to direct all its resources to fight against the occupation army, which as a result the liberation of Eritrea was ensured. Perhaps this could have been achieved in a positive way, through ensuring unity of the organisations instead of through military settlement.

The second major phenomenon that occurred in this period, which this section takes up, is the achievement of independence. After a number of decisive military match-ups between the EPLF and the Ethiopian army, Eritrean sovereignty was secured. In the following pages, the key events and developments that took place in the period under consideration will be discussed.

Sub-Period 1981-1984: Post ELF, Fragmentation of the ELF

This section discusses the circumstances leading to the demise of the ELF. These were demonstrated successively, first in the military defeat and eventually, in its fragmentation and dissolution. As we have seen earlier, around the middle of the second decade of the national liberation struggle, the flow of Eritreans joining the fronts grew geometrically. The proportion of this increase coming from the Christian highland part of Eritrea was particularly large. Thereby, the socio-political composition of the organisations, in particular of the ELF, began to dramatically shift. When the ELF held its Second National Congress in 1975, the organisation had a large number of new fighters who were not allowed to participate in the congress. As a result, the Congress failed to adequately reflect the real socio-political changes that were taking place within the ELF. In addition, with the steady increase in the flow of the new recruits into the organisation, the gap between the political power structure and its base kept growing wider. The evidence of this widening gap was clearly expressed in the makeup of the leadership. Representation among the leadership, embodied in the Revolutionary Council (RC) and the Executive Committee (EC), failed to reflect the socio-political forces which constituted the rest of the organs of the ELF. In other words, the issue of power sharing was not adequately resolved in the Congress. Yet the influx of new social force triggered a process of transformation within the ELF which, if fully realised, could have radically altered the organisation. In other words, the condition in which the ELF found itself at this time could have been expressed as a point of transition from the old to the new; the metamorphosis of which was never fully realised. Unfortunately for the ELF, this new reality became its main element of instability.

The emergence of such structural incongruities inevitably evokes tensions and contradictions between the old and the new, necessitating break-points of reconciliation. Such break-points often appear in the form of congresses where one of the central elements of incongruity and conflict, in this case a power struggle, is raised and resolved. Congresses either ameliorate or eliminate contradictions by patching together compromises, or conversely, they exacerbate them by postponing resolution or by their utter failure to find solutions. A proper reading of the sources of current antagonisms is said to amount to finding half the solution to the problem. The second national congress of the ELF was held at a moment when a new internal political force was just beginning to assert itself. Perhaps, in this respect, the Congress came a bit prematurely, in the sense that the new force had not had the time needed to establish itself, get experience, and subsequently strive for the necessary changes in a more effective and constructive fashion. The old political force, conversely, was well established, had experience, and it used its strength to dictate its wishes. Usually the ultimate goal of the political game is to capture the instruments of power. In the Congress, what can be categorised as a reformist clique ensured its grip on power. This outcome diminished the influence of conservative elements in the organisation. However, it failed to produce a radical structural innovation that would generate continuity and harmony between the old political power and the new socio-political base that was emerging as the predominant composite force in the organisation.

Yet, a more serious development to emerge, partly as a result of the new force joining the organisation, was that the base of the old power (the rank and file from the Moslem communities) was slowly abandoning the organisation. Realising that the new arrivals were more radical, educated, and of urban origin the veteran fighters felt threatened that these new forces came to take their place, thus, began to leave the organisation. This, in turn, created an imbalance of power relationships in which the power structure was left with no supporting base. This development was perilous because it took place in an ethno-linguistic and ethno-religious context. That is, both departing and joining forces could be identified with specific ethno-linguistic groups. The result was, thus, the uneasy coexistence of an old political power structure with a new base. This meant a combination of not only apparently irreconcilable forces but also a synthesis of instability and volatility. A manifestation of this precarious political détente was revealed immediately after the congress, when an atmosphere of suspicion and accusation dominated. This tension and mutual suspicion was, however, to simmer for some time before any actual open confrontation took place. A clear indication of the gap was the dominance of the new political force at different levels of the organisation below the leadership, which was indeed demonstrated by the innumerable initiatives, and activities which not only did not involve the leadership, but which also revealed the impotence of the leadership. In fact, one development that quite puzzled observers was that at some point, the ELF reached a stage at which it seemed to be led by the cadres, even earning a reputation as an organisation led by its cadres. This reality created a great confusion in the understanding and interpreting of the political nature of the organisation, not least to the foreign observer, which was led to believe that the ELF was a sectarian, Moslem-dominated and Arab-oriented organisation.

The leadership slowly lost moral authority over its members. The first sign was the 1976-7 uprising, which was crushed violently (cf. ELF-RC 1989: 21). Yet, instead of reading the barometer properly, learning from this episode and subsequently trying to rectify the mistakes, the leadership seemed to prefer to continue as if everything was in order. Another serious problem the ELF experienced during this time was disunity among the leadership. Indeed, it was divided at least in three factions that paralysed the organisation (ELF-RC 1989: 24). A section of the leadership was consistently marginalised and alienated and grew restless. An indication of its alienation was the systematic opposition to the convening of the third national congress of the ELF (cf. Ammar 1992). To maintain its position in the organisation, this faction was not hesitant to use extra-constitutional measures (like the one of 1982). While the internal problems were simmering, the rivalry between the ELF and the EPLF was re-emerging. It was during this time, when the internal situation of the ELF was extremely precarious, that the war between the ELF and the EPLF broke out.

Because it was already in internal disarray, the ELF was not in a position to stand the combined challenge from the EPLF and the TPLF. Almost a year after the second civil war began, the ELF was forced out of Eritrea, ending up in the Sudan.

Following its retreat to the Sudan, the ELF was unable to withstand the tensions and pressures, resulting in its split into various groups. Now, the contradictions that had to date been concealed beneath the surface found the occasion to float freely. This buoyancy, indeed, lost constraint and developed into a hazardous state that seriously affected the already precarious health of the organisation. Inside the Sudan, hence, three factions of the ELF emerged. The fundamental point dividing the groups was how the problems of the organisation should be resolved. The solution that they prescribed was, indeed, dictated by their political ideologies. The political nature of the three groups can be described in the following terms. On the one hand was a rightist, conservative sectarian faction whose ambition was to preserve the status quo or rather, return to *status quo ant.* On the other hand, there was a leftist-oriented radical faction that believed that the ELF could only be saved through undertaking fundamental changes. A third was a reformist group that believed that the ELF could be innovated through mere adjustment and some kind of reform. The first group's proposition failed because simply the *status quo ante* was outmoded. The reformist formula also failed, being too little, too late. The leftist proposition also failed because it deviated too much from the traditional way of doing things in the ELF, and thus, failed to elicit support from the two other components of the organisation. Neither was it able to bring the needed change on its own. In social theory, it is argued that to solve a problem it is a necessary presupposition to be able to define and diagnose it correctly. The first and the third factions failed miserably to assess the situation properly, and were subsequently in no position to come up with a remedy. The second faction was relatively able to define and diagnose the illness but lacked the means to remedy it.

Following the division in the ELF and the subsequent crystallisation of the factions, each faction was involved in unity negotiation with other organisations. The ELF-RC attempted to enter into a unity agreement with the ELF-PLF, but this flirtation did not last long. Therefore, the marriage of convenience had to be terminated, apparently by the initiative of the ELF-RC who came to realise that it could not preserve its autonomy. However, the divorce came at a price. Consequently, the ELF-RC had to pay indemnity for the inconvenience it had created, and this meant further decimation. But perhaps the price was not as high as the one that the ELF-Sagem was to pay. The ELF-Sagem received an ultimatum from the Sudanese Government: it should either go back to Eritrea or join the rank of refugees in the refugee camps in the Sudan. They chose to return to Eritrea. Many, perhaps naively, believed that the EPLF would not bother them, while many others could not imagine any other alternative. Reality proved wrong those who believed that the EPLF would not bother them. With its newly won hegemony, the EPLF was not prepared to accommodate any force that had aspirations of autonomy. Therefore, the ELF-Sagem was for the second time given an ultimatum, this time from the EPLF. The ultimatum split the group. Those who disliked the ultimatum understood their situation too late, and were forced to flee in order to form a breakaway group. The rest had to be content with the generous offer of membership in the EPLF. The ELF-Abdella faction was also to be engaged in a unity agreement commonly known as the Tripartite Unity or Jeddah Agreement orchestrated in Saudi Arabia. Even that attempt failed, and changing loyalties resulted in the group losing members to the other partners in the tripartite unity. The picture was getting more and more messy.

There is no doubt the ELF, in its heyday, captured the hearts and minds of the majority of the Eritrean people. But the turmoil and chaos that followed the defeat and fragmentation of the ELF harmed all three factions, although to different degrees. Generally speaking, the ELF-RC seemed, at the end of the day, in much better condition in comparison with the other two factions. The inability of the three factions of the ELF to patch their differences, and the further fragmentation within each faction undeniably concluded the demise of the ELF. All groups that afterwards continued to operate under the name of ELF were utterly different, both in form and content, from the old ELF.

The EPLF Hegemony

After the defeat of the ELF, the politico-military space of the Eritrean arena fell under the effective dominance of the EPLF. The victory of the EPLF is widely attributed to its organisational strength, centralisation and unity of the leadership (Sherman 1980, Chaliand 1980, With 1986, Pool 1997). Moreover the unity and discipline which characterised the EPLF was believed to originate from two experiences, "the loose controls and internal struggles of the ELF, and an internal crisis. The latter involves a challenge to the leadership by the *manqa* movement" (Pool 1997: 12). Having overcome the challenges to its internal unity and cohesion on two occasions – in 1973 by a radical group and the 1976 departure of the Foreign Mission (ELF-PLF) – the EPLF was widely believed to have succeeded in building a strong, modern organisation. The organisation developed a political culture based on strong discipline and stringent principles of democratic centralisation that were seen by its opponents as being enforced at the cost of democratic rights. Many scholars and observers of the Eritrean revolution had commented that the EPLF was able to build a highly motivated and well-disciplined national liberation army. On top of this quality, the prolific splits that beset the ELF cemented the hegemonic position of the EPLF. Hegemony here is used to mean, without any normative judgement made, the prevalence of a single organisation ensuring unrivalled domination in the military, political, economic and cultural spheres.

Now the EPLF, as the hegemonic organisation, had to make sure that it was capable of 'delivering the goods', achieving independence and nation-building. Its legitimacy hinged on the achievement of independence and ensuring stronger integration and cohesion in Eritrean society. The hegemony of the EPLF can be further analysed by focusing on two dimensions: first, the way in which the issue of unity was treated under the "new order", and second, its performance concerning the independence struggle. The first profound challenge in the military confrontation with the enemy was officially launched by the Dergue on February 15, 1982 (EPLF, *fitzametat,* Special Issue, April 1982). This came immediately after the ELF was driven out from the field in the 'Sixth Campaign'. The Dergue's highly advertised and meticulously designed military campaign was intended to crush the NLM once and for all. The EPLF foiled the Dergue plan, thereby, asserting its determination and capacity to survive. This military confrontation with Ethiopia is discussed in the next two sections.

Since the EPLF had now secured its hegemony, it adopted a formula that was interpreted by opponents as well as observers as a change of a long-held policy of unity. It abandoned the united front formula of unity and began to advocate a national assembly composed of a single organisation (cf. EPLF 1987: 44). For the last ten years, the EPLF had advocated a loose co-operation between the liberation fronts, while its main rival, the ELF, held to the formula of a single integrated organisation. However, the EPLF maintained that it has always been consistent in its view concerning the issue of unity (Mohammed Said 1997, Tesfai 1997). The switch of strategy was directly connected with its military strength. In a statement of clarification of its new policy of unity of 1982, it put it in an unequivocally clear language stating 'when we announce this position we depart from the position of strength'. Moreover, it also declared that the unity of the liberation movement was to be sought, unlike the strategy hitherto pursued (top-down), from the bottom-up. That is, it was to come through uniting the masses. Therefore, under the new hegemonic order, the EPLF made it clear to its opponents that they could in no way aspire to an autonomous existence in the Eritrean political and military arena. The case of the ELF-Sagem is a clear example of this "new order". Even the aborted unity negotiations between ELF-RC and EPLF were governed by the spirit of the political ideology of the new hegemonic order. Tesfai (1997), after rejecting the view that the EPLF had switched its strategy of unity, argues that the EPLF was not prepared to give a renewed life to the ELF, which it believed bore all responsibility for the internal problems of the liberation struggle. He also adds that the EPLF was never convinced that the ELF had changed from its political nature of the 1960's. The shift of position on the issue of unity, not only from the EPLF side but also from the different factions of the ELF, can be explained by the sociological theory of domination, which characterised the relation between the organisations (to be discussed below). The next two sections will deal briefly with the decisive encounter between the EPLF and the Dergue regime.

Military and Diplomatic Shift (1984-1989)

The outstanding elements which mark this sub-period can be identified in terms of the victory of the battle of North Eastern Sahel, the famine of 1984-

85, the unity agreement between the EPLF and the ELF-CL (Sagem), and the battle of Afabet. While the first and the last were of military significance, the other two were of diplomatic and political import. In the early months of 1984, the EPLF scored a major military success over the Ethiopian army. This victory was achieved in North Eastern Sahel, where an entire division of the Ethiopian army was wiped out. It was most probably the biggest defeat of the Dergue army, after the fiasco of the "Red Star", or Sixth Offensive (cf. Adulis vol. I, no. 1, 1984). Its primary significance was that it marked the turning point in the military confrontation, when the military initiative shifted into the hands of the EPLF (Adulis vol. I, no. 1, 1984). The importance of this victory goes beyond mere military success. It was also a significant victory in the social-psychological dimension, the diplomatic dimension and the logistical dimension. This military offensive on the national level was matched by a diplomatic offensive on the international level. It was also supported by intensive economic, administrative and social service undertakings in order to strengthen and accelerate the process of independence and nation building.

After its return to Eritrea from the Sudan, the ELF-CL (Sagem) convened its organisational conference in early 1984 and subsequently attempted to define its relationship with the EPLF. Apparently, subsequent developments led to this group joining the EPLF, which was realised through the unity conference in 1987. Of course, it was not the whole group that joined the EPLF. The EPLF, perhaps aware of the nature of division in the liberation movement, showed sensitivity in its handling of its relationship with the group of the ELF-CL (Sagem) which opted to join it. The representation of the group in the legislative body of the EPLF (Central Committee), for example, was quite generous in relation to its size. Maximum efforts were displayed, not least for diplomatic expediency, to show that an accord had been reached between the ELF and the EPLF. The name of its second congress, "The Second and Unity Congress of the Eritrean People's Liberation Front and the ELF-CL" (Adulis vol., IV no. 2), is a good indication of the emphasis and importance given to unity. Unity attempts with various groups operating outside Eritrea, ELF-RC, ELF-PLF (Sabbe), ELF-PLF (Revolutionary Committee) were also undertaken, but without any tangible result.

The famine of 1984-85, in spite of the dimension of human tragedy it entailed, also played an important role. It became a litmus test for the various actors involved, notably the EPLF, the Dergue and the international community. The Dergue was properly accused of using food for political purposes because of the regime's refusal to allow free access to aid for the needy population under the control of the EPLF, and the TPLF in Tigray. The EPLF staged a concerted diplomatic campaign not only to expose the policy of the Dergue regarding the issue of famine, but also to convince the international community that the root cause of the Eritrean ordeal was the war. It campaigned diligently to convince the international community that a just political solution to the conflict was the only way to resolve the human tragedy. The Dergue, on the other hand, deployed its best skills and tools to squarely place all responsibility for jeopardising the live of the people on the liberation fronts, conversely, attempting to take all credit for itself for any efforts to alleviate the suffering of the people. The willingness of the international community, particularly the main actors, to find a solution not only to the immediate human tragedy but also to the fundamental problem – political conflict – was also put to test.

The diplomatic contest assumed a two-pronged purpose. The first was the saving of human lives menaced by famine and the second finding a solution to the conflict, the cause that had been presented to the international community by the EPLF as the main source of the tragedy. The famine, therefore, assumed a political, diplomatic and juridical dimension directly connected with the people's right for self-determination, and as guaranteeing the sustenance of human life and social survival. The fundamental issue of principle, of who had the right to represent the Eritrean people, was brought into focus. Further, the politics of famine was entangled in contradictory claims, in which the Dergue wished to appear as the sole representative, while the liberation fronts justifiably claimed that the right of representation rested with them. Finally, the politics of famine led to the realisation by the Western community that the government in Addis Ababa had only limited territorial control. The result was that relief aid from western NGOs was routed through the Eritrean Relief Association (ERA), the relief agency of the EPLF. This, in turn, conferred certain legitimacy upon EPLF (Pool 1993). Consequently, a shift was registered in the diplomatic field, so that the EPLF and the Eritrean cause began to win sympathy, in many circles, and calls for a just political solution began to resonate.

Yet, a decisive military victory – to date, the first of its type – was scored by the EPLF against the Dergue army, in the battle of Afabet in March 1988. It lasted only two days, but the Dergue's entire Nadew ('Destroy') command was annihilated (Africa Confidential 1988 vol. 29, no. 9). Undoubtedly, this battle determined the subsequent course and outcome of the war. The distinguished Africanist British historian Basil Davidson compared it with the battle against the French at Dien Ben Phu, in Vietnam, which determined the destiny of that war, ending with the defeat of France. He wrote, "this victory, ... is one of the biggest ever scored by any liberation movement anywhere since Dien Ben Phu in 1954" (quoted in Adulis vol. V, no. 3, April 1988). This historical comparison and prophecy was accurate in that it was not long after the battle, the war was over. As a result of this defeat the Dergue withdrew from several towns, Agordat, Barentu, Tessenei. In preparation for the final assault, the mobilisation and participation of the populace was accelerated. In the following years an unprecedented popular mobilisation was witnessed inside and outside Eritrea and as a result the size of the EPLA grew immensely, by some estimates up to 100,000.

Early in the 1970s, the NLM expressed its earnest desire of co-operation with democratic opposition forces in Ethiopia to bring about social change in the country, and effect the recognition of the right to self-determination of the Eritrean people. Since then, the co-operation attempt traversed varying terrain, reaching its culmination toward the end of the 1980s. Apparently, it was after the battle of Afabet, the EPLF and the TPLF reached an understanding to co-ordinate their military activities, which was frozen for some time, in order to defeat the Dergue. This accelerated the erosion of entrenched power and effected the final demise of the regime. The co-ordination between the EPLF and the TPLF (later EPRDF) was of strategic importance both for the liberation of Eritrea and for democratic changes in Ethiopia. It is this co-ordination that became the underlying basis for the mechanised infantry of the EPLF to take part in the final mopping up operations against the Dergue inside Ethiopia. This effort culminated in the entrance to Addis Ababa and the ascendancy of the EPRDF to power.

With respect to the peace negotiations, the EPLF, now well aware of the weak position of the Dergue, reiterated its readiness to enter into negotiation with the Ethiopian regime. It stated its readiness to finding a political solution to the Eritrean question based on a referendum, the details of which were elaborated in 1980. The main premises of the referendum, commonly known as the seven point referendum proposition were, that the Eritrean people would be given the choice to vote on a union with Ethiopia, a federation, or independence. The Dergue did not outright reject the idea of negotiation and long-drawn discussions began. However, as later developments will prove, the Dergue's acceptance was for tactical purposes. It became increasingly clear that the Dergue was never willing to compromise the territorial unity of Ethiopia. This position was also supported by the superpowers, which had now begun to show interest in resolving the conflict through peaceful means. The Dergue, as well as the superpowers, sought to find a peaceful solution without compromising the territorial integrity of Ethiopia. A referendum as a viable political instrument in finding a peaceful and democratic solution to the conflict had been advocated by the EPLF throughout the decade. Conversely, the Ethiopian regime, apparently aware of the obvious result, persistently rebuffed any calls for referendum.

The Final Journey (1989-1991)

A dramatic unfolding of events marked the last three years prior to the achievement of liberation of Eritrea. Intensive activity took place, both on the battlefield and in the arena of negotiation. Both sides were involved in skilfully staged diplomatic manoeuvring. Since the Dergue rigidly stuck in its view of the indivisibility of Ethiopia, the negotiations failed to produce result. This led to, finally, resolving the conflict through military means. A configuration of disparate circumstances–local, regional and international–produced a climate favourable for the independence of Eritrea. At the international level, the fall of the Berlin Wall in 1989 definitely sealed the end of the Cold War. The fall of the Soviet Union also had worldwide implications. Conflicts which had been raging for decades with the direct or indirect involvement of the superpowers started to ebb. With the onset of the time of *glasnost* (openness) and *perestroika* (restructuring), the blind support based on ideological doctrine that had characterised the Cold War period came to be seen as profane. So the Dergue was told by its allies to find a peaceful solution to the Eritrean problem while its request for increased military hardware was rebuffed. The Dergue regime's hold on power began to slip when the support which it was getting from the Soviet Union and its satellites dropped off markedly. In addition, as a result of the decline of Cold War confrontations, the superpowers pursued a path of co-operation in solving regional conflicts (see Keller 1990/91). Consequently many conflict-ridden regions came to benefit from this New World order; Namibia, Angola, Mozambique, Cambodia, and Nicaragua were some examples. Ostensibly the demise of the Soviet Union and the ending of the Cold War created an environment conducive to the independence of Eritrea (Pool 1993).

At the regional level, the Dergue was weakened by the military success of the EPLF in Eritrea and the opposition in Ethiopia. This weakness was reinforced by its diplomatic isolation, its loss of popular legitimacy at home and the May 1989 coup attempt by the army. As a result of this, the regime became increasingly susceptible to the mounting pressure for peace negotiations. A number of meetings aimed at finding a peaceful solution to the conflict succeeded one another, moving from Atlanta, Georgia to Nairobi, Kenya, then to London. These were first undertaken under the semi-official mediation of former US President Jimmy Carter. This was followed with the co-chairmanship of Jimmy Carter and the former President of Tanzania, Julius Nyerere. Finally, it concluded in the official mediation of the US Assistant Secretary of State for African Affairs, Herman Cohen. Negotiations foundered on the issue of the indivisibility of Ethiopian territory. Even the mediators seemed to harbour a sympathetic view on the issue. Insofar as the Dergue insisted on territorial unity, there could be no peaceful resolution of the conflict. This intransigence required that activities on the military front proceed unabated. Indeed, in the typically logical fashion of 'might is right', all sides seemed to be anxious not to lose the military initiative and maintain the upper hand in it. Historical experience appears to prove the strategy of a potent combination of success on the battlefield with tactical negotiating skill at the bargaining table to assure victory. Driven by that logic, the TPLF first succeeded in destroying the Dergue's state machinery in the whole of Tigray province, followed by the operations of the EPRDF, which dislodged the army of the Dergue from many Amhara regions. All in all, in the military realm, the Dergue was loosing ground at an unprecedented speed. It became increasingly clear to everyone that its ship was sinking deeper and deeper, with no chance of rescue.

At the local level, during these past ten years, the EPLF had been building itself into a formidable liberation organisation. It first secured its hegemony in politico-military terms by defeating its Eritrean rivals. Second, the consistent military victories that it achieved augmented remarkably its skill at conventional warfare. Moreover, its stock of military hardware was elevated quantitatively and qualitatively to a highly competitive level, thanks to the losses of the

Ethiopian army. In short, by the end of the 1980s the EPLF was transformed into a state organisation possessing all the necessary capabilities for taking on state power. While peace negotiation were taking place with the Dergue, there seemed to be a lull in military activities, until a decisive blow left the Dergue army battered. This led to the capture of Massawa on February 10, 1990. When the battle started, Mengistu was quoted as saying that the capture of Massawa would mean the loss of the 2nd Army, and that this, in turn, would mean the loss of Eritrea (Africa Confidential 23 March 1990, vol. 31, no. 6). That assessment was correct. Realising that the continuous possession of the port town by the EPLF was not only a mark of its own incompetence, but was also ringing the bell of its final demise, the Dergue bombed the town with all its might. The aim of bombing the town was to compensate for the military defeat on the ground, thereby hoping to dislodge the EPLF. The massive bombardment, however, did not bring the intended result, except that the port was converted to rubble, and it became the symbol of determination for the Eritrean fighters.

The peace negotiation, in its final phase, was moved to London under the official mediation of the USA. However, during the peace conference in London in 1991 under the chairmanship of Herman Cohen, the negotiation collapsed due to the crumbling of the second largest army in Africa, and the concomitant capture of Asmara and Addis Ababa. As the political dialogue in London aimed at finding a peaceful solution was showing no signs of a breakthrough, the machinery of force was performing its own miracle. Events in the military realm started to unfold at such a great speed that it left behind the theatre being played out at the negotiating table. The state structure of the Dergue literally crumbled in front of the various highly motivated liberation forces. The EPLF triumphantly entered Asmara in May 1991. The war was over and Eritrea was liberated.

THE OVERALL UNITY EFFORTS

In this section, I briefly discuss the reasons for the lack of success of the unity efforts. According to some observers, one of the main weaknesses of the NLM was its failure to unite its own ranks. This was viewed as a sign of the feebleness of Eritrean nationhood and nationalism. The chief factor that supported such perception was the emergence of competing liberation fronts. A basic question that can be posed against such a perception is, of course, whether the existence of various fronts justifies the argument of absence or weakness of nationhood and nationalism. The various Eritrean fronts differed in their view of how to achieve their political goals, but never wavered in their conviction of creating a united sovereign nation, which should be viewed as the foundation of their nationalism. In any case, it is not my intention to argue about whether the existence of a variety of organisations is a yardstick for nationhood and nationalism. The aim is to try to find explanation for the failure of efforts at unity.

The life of the effort made to achieve unification was as old as the disunity itself. To capture the temporal genesis of the pursuit of national unity, thus, will not be easy. It could be located in the era of political parties (1940s), while another possible time frame could be the period of the armed struggle. My own preference is to focus on the quest for unity undertaken through the duration of the armed struggle, with particular emphasis on the period where there existed actively operating rival organisations in the Field (1970-1980). The aim of this section is, to make some contribution toward understanding why the NLM failed to achieve unity in spite of the obvious urgency of need. To do this, I look at several factors, employing politico-sociological concepts such as ideology, ethno-religiosity, asymmetry/symmetry, domination, and the personality of political leaders, which serve to help explain the persistence of the cleavage.

In general there can be discerned two main sets of explanations dealing with the question of unification. These are the ideological and the asymmetry/symmetry explanations. One explanation says that the underlying reason was the ideological difference between the two main fronts (see e.g. Sherman 1980, Chaliand 1980, Erlich 1983). However, scholars are divided when it comes to who was more Marxist oriented. Chaliand seems to be convinced that the EPLF was more Marxist than the ELF, whereas Hamilton says the ELF developed more radical political stance (Sherman 1980: 51). Erlich (1983) argues that while the EPLF's strategy was 'first revolution then independence', the ELF's strategy was 'first independence then revolution'. The logic of Erlich's argumentation is that the strategy of 'first revolution and later independence' tended to postpone the question of unity. On the other hand, the strategy of 'first independence and later revolution' advocated immediate unity. If we can believe this argument, thus the hindrance for unity was ideological difference along the lines of prioritising revolution vs. national independence. The correctness of this assumption is debatable. First, the question of unity has invariably been a matter of high priority. Second, the actual historical course of events refutes such assumptions. Every organisation gave high priority to the achievement of unity, if its accomplishment could be secured on the terms of the respective organisation. The ELF considered national unity as, "a central objective of the Eritrean struggle and a basic precondition for the realisation of victory" (ELF 1975: 45). The EPLF also stressed its commitment for the achievement of broad national democratic front (EPLF 1987b: 40).

The ideological explanation has also been approached from another angle, notably that of either pro-Soviet (the ELF's national democratic revolution), or pro-China (the EPLF's new democratic revolution) (Sherman 1980: 66). This is of course not an ideological difference in the proper sense of the term but rather a difference of orientation within the same ideology. Probably noting this, Melaku Tegegn (1989) argues that no ideological difference existed between the ELF and the EPLF. Toteel (1997) also agrees that in the proper theoretical sense of Marxism-Leninism, it could not be claimed that an ideological difference existed between the two fronts, but that perhaps in their mode of practical operation certain differences could be observed.

The second set of explanations is based on the asymmetry/symmetry theory. The prescription of the asymmetry theory is that in the presence of a significant imbalance of strength between contending forces, incentives for co-operation and reconciliation are removed. It is argued that when such a discrepancy emerges the forces tend to drift apart from each other. The contestants fail to show a genuine interest in reconciliation. The weaker side loses interest because of fear of being dominated, displaying intransigence, while the stronger one entertains the thought of being able to dictate the rules of the game according to its own terms. In the history of the Eritrean internal conflict, there is evidence that upholds this theoretical assumption. Taking a few historical facts that can throw some light on the soundness of this line of argumentation, we can point out the official unity positions of the fronts. The ELF, since its First National Congress (1971) adopted the line of total integration, while the EPLF preferred loose co-ordination. These views of unity are expressed in the formulas of the *National Democratic Front* and the *National United Front* (Markakis 1987: 138). While the former embraces complete unification, the latter prescribes loose co-operation between the organisations (Sherman 1980:62).

The basic elements incorporated in the unity formula expressed by the *National Democratic Front* are, (i) a single front, (ii) one political programme, (iii) one army, and (iv) a single body of political leadership (ELF 1975: 36, 45). This unity formula was advocated by the ELF, and was primarily founded upon its belief that it was stronger, hence, it would be able to dictate the terms of unity. Conversely, the fundamental precepts of the *National United Front* were demonstrated by its preference of a coalition of fronts, with the possibility of retaining their idiosyncratic characteristics in the form of separate structures and autonomous organisations with their own leadership. In the latter formula, it is co-operation between the fronts without loosing individual independence that is envisaged. This position was supported by the EPLF until it became the dominant politico-military force. The EPLF's adherence to this unity formula was attributed to its apprehension of being dominated by its stronger rival (Sherman 1980: 62, Markakis 1987: 138-9). This apprehension was expressed by the EPLF in this way: "Indeed the conspiracy was designed to strangulate, disrupt or dominate the EPLF" (EPLF 1977: 16). Markakis also adds that the EPLF entertained the formula of the National United Front because it, "was confident that its own superior organisation and political capacity would, in the long run, prevail and dominate such a coalition" (Markakis 1987: 139). The credibility of the proposition that the unity formula was dictated by relative power can be more vividly ascertained by the change of heart of both organisations after the defeat of the ELF. In the case of the ELF (the different factions), the old formula was abandoned and they began to advocate for the rights of organisations to an autonomous existence. Conversely, the EPLF also shifted from its original position, adopting a unity formula that favoured total unification (EPLF 1987: 44), because now it became the sole dominant force in the Eritrean arena. The main component of the new unity formula of the EPLF, called *lifnti,* was the formation of a national council in which the political leaders of the various organisations would be represented. In the military dimension, it was suggested that there would be one army and a single strategy. The armies of the various organisations were also expected to join the army of the EPLF. This proposition was rejected by the other organisations because they thought that the EPLF, due to its size would dominate the others. They preferred a much looser coalition that would guarantee their independence.

The theory of symmetry, on the other hand, rests on the assumption of a relative balance of strength. Practically speaking, the close balance is considered to make it virtually impossible for any group to win the conflict in its favour. This also eliminates the fear of being subjected to the mercy of the stronger. This state of stalemate forces the contesting groups to compromise. The period of Eritrean history between 1975-1980 roughly illustrates this situation. With the onset of the second half of the 1970s, the strength of the two fronts was gradually nearing a state of equilibrium. As a result of this near symmetry, the two fronts showed a genuine will and effort to unite their organisations. The first step taken toward this goal was the halting of the first civil war. It was followed by negotiations intended to achieve unity. This led to the October 1977 Unity Agreement, which was based on the precepts of a *National Democratic Front* (Markakis 1987: 144). It was seen as a shift of position of both organisations in that the ELF accepted a transition period while the EPLF became open to the idea of the formation of single organisation. A necessary condition for the symmetry theory to succeed is that external interference should be kept at arm's length. Apart from disturbing the balance of strength, the involvement of foreign elements in the conflict also generates social-psychological and emotional cleavages that can have a lasting effect. This was evidently manifested in the Eritrean conflict that led to the second civil war between the ELF and the EPLF in 1980. The intervention of two external factors of disturbance can be mentioned here: (i) the secret negotiations with Ethiopia and (ii) the involvement of the TPLF in the internal affairs of Eritrea. Following the series of negotiation efforts with Ethiopia, secretly undertaken through the mediation by the Soviets, the East Germans, and the Italian Communist Party, the trust between the organisations suffered immensely (cf. EPLF 1987b: 43). In addition, the involvement of the TPLF in the internal Eritrean conflict by siding with the EPLF (which was seen by the ELF as a significant contributing factor in its ultimate defeat) created bitter resentment among the members of the ELF. This external intervention served as a disturbing factor in the emerging symmetry of power, particularly in the social-psychological dimension, blocking the unity process.

Some scholars have also emphasised the geo-religious and geo-linguistic origins of the conflict (e.g. With 1987, Negash 1987, Amar 1992). This explanation focuses on the Christian-Moslem, Tigrinay-Arabic and highlanders-lowlanders dichotomies. It is here argued that the primary point of difference is basically embedded in the socio-cultural context of the society's demographic makeup. According to this view, each of the two organisations represented their respective component parts of the society, in this case, the Christian Tigrinya speakers and the remaining Moslem communities. It is supposed that while the EPLF represented the Christian highlanders, the ELF represented the Moslem lowlanders.

Yet another factor used to explain the conflict was the personality of political leaders. The concept of the personality of political leaders is used to help explain and understand political conflicts of a personal nature such as particular experiences, rivalry, etc., and their implications for the overall national polity. There are those who emphasise that the personality differences between the leading political figures in the NLM were one of the important elements which hindered the achievement of unity (see Sherman 1980). Yet, there are still others who attempt to find an eclectic explanation. For instance, Pool (1997: 11) notes that, "The complexities of the split cannot be characterized as Christian against Mulsim. Ideology, foreign policy orientation, regional, clan and personal loyalties all played their part". I believe it is the combination of all these elements that can give us clearer picture.

In conclusion, it has to be pointed out that at the bottom of the failure of unity was a competition among elites. Political rivalry for domination played significant role in hindering the unification of the organisations. In this respect, therefore, the theory of domination has much to contribute in explaining and analysing the division within the ranks of the liberation struggle, and the failure to secure unity.

Fig. 6.2 The proliferation of organisations

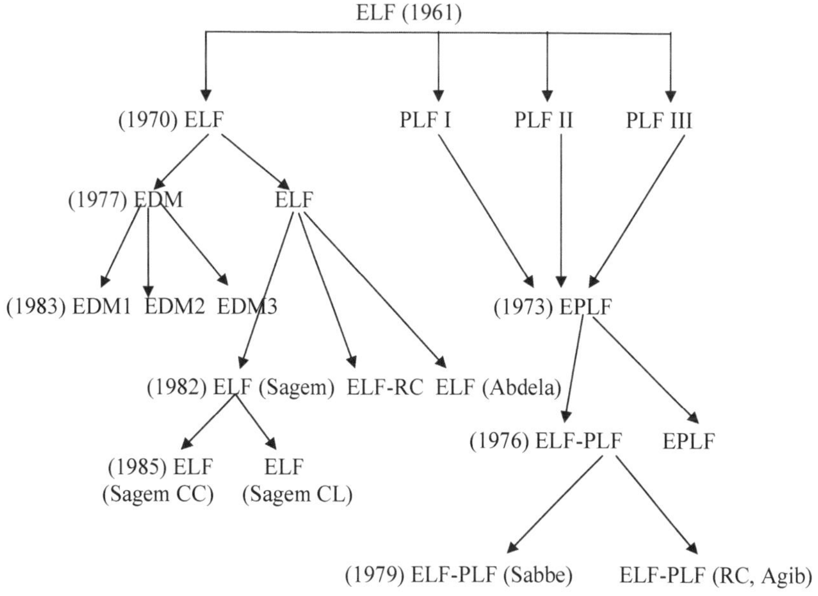

ELF (1961)

(1970) ELF PLF I PLF II PLF III

(1977) EDM ELF

(1983) EDM1 EDM2 EDM3 (1973) EPLF

(1982) ELF (Sagem) ELF-RC ELF (Abdela)

(1976) ELF-PLF EPLF

(1985) ELF (Sagem CC) ELF (Sagem CL)

(1979) ELF-PLF (Sabbe) ELF-PLF (RC, Agib)

Figure 6.2 shows the proliferation of the Eritrean organisations since the 1970s. In 1961, the ELF was founded. In 1970, a split took place, from which there emerged four factions (ELF, PLF I, PLF II and PLF III). This was again reduced to two organisations (ELF and EPLF). Again a split occurred within both the ELF and the EPLF and the proliferation continued as shown in the figure.

SUMMARY AND CONCLUSION

The central focus of this chapter has been to describe the evolution of the liberation movement and its primary internal cleavage. In studying these two elements, it became necessary to examine the political actors and the environment in which the liberation movement began. Therefore, the first decade of the armed struggle was examined by looking into the two dimensions of introvert and extrovert. Observed from the introvert perspective, the Supreme Council (SC) divided the liberation army into zones to ensure maximum mobilisation and participation. From the extrovert perspective, the SC adopted a political and diplomatic policy that presented the armed struggle as a revolutionary liberation movement that was part of the larger Islamic and Arab liberation movement. Both dimensions had a negative effect in the internal development of the liberation struggle. The division of the army into zones hampered the unity of the movement. The three prominent figures of the SC created their own power base through Zones One, Two and Four, thereby establishing a patron-client relation. This situation not only weakened the overall fighting capacity of the army, but it also fettered the development of the National Liberation Movement (NLM) into a genuine revolutionary people's struggle.

In 1970, a split took place in the ELF from which four factions emerged. By 1972, two rival organisations (the Eritrean Liberation Front and Eritrean People's Liberation Forces) began to consolidate. With the emergence of the two new organisations, a generation of young political leadership began to ascend. A National Democratic Programme (NDP) was endorsed, and in the NDP, the social, economic, political and cultural goals of the NLM were clearly articulated. As a result, the NLM began its second decade with a new political course. These changes were called forth by two main factors, first, the unabated flow into the ranks of the liberation movement of Eritrean Christian fighters, and second, the take-over of the political leadership by a younger, more radical generation. By 1973-74, the flow of Eritrean youth into the armed struggle reached a turning point. From only a couple thousand in the first decade, the size of the liberation army increased to tens of thousands in the second decade. The veritable explosion in the numbers of the liberation army resulted in the liberation of villages and towns, and by the end of 1977, more than 90 percent of Eritrea was liberated. The expansive mass mobilisation and participation gave rise to the formation of mass organisations, representing the different social groups. The decade also witnessed two civil wars, the second of which resulted in the defeat of the ELF.

The decade that began with the outbreak of civil war (1972-1974) ended with another (1980-1981). The result of this second civil war ensured the hegemony of EPLF in the last decade of the liberation struggle. The first decade of the armed struggle was characterised by the hegemony of the ELF, which led to split and civil war. The emergence of two organisations and the consequent civil war intensified calls for unity. Numerous attempts were made to unite the organisations, and these, during certain periods, offered hopeful signs. This hope was created when, instead of hegemony, a relative balance of power prevailed between the organisations. Guided by their military strength, the organisations adopted different unity formulas, which, to a great extent, were the source of the failure of unity. The hegemony that followed the defeat of the ELF was accompanied by the liberation of Eritrea.

Overall, the events of this period of Eritrean history played a salient role in the general process of nation formation. The NLM at last forged unity among disparate ethno-linguistic groups around a common sacred objective, struggling for the achievement of national sovereignty. That common struggle, characterised by bitter experience, enriched the repertoire of common national memories, a necessary presupposition for living together. In that respect, the armed struggle for the liberation of Eritrea represents the most outstanding and vital process in a chain of historical events which began in 1890 and culminated in the formation of the State of Eritrea in 1991. Underscoring the immense importance of the period of the armed struggle, several foreign observers as well as Eritreans maintain that in actuality, Eritrean nationalism and nationhood was ultimately formed through the national liberation struggle.

Table 6.1: Summary of the History of the NLM

PHASES	SUB-PHASES	IMPORTANT EVENTS
PHASE I (1961-71): ELF HEGEMONY	1961-65	Formation of ELF ELM destroyed Zonal Division
	1965-69	Rectification Movement Anseba Conference Tripartite Unity
	1969-71	Adobha Conference Disintegration *ELF, PLF I, PLF II, PLF III (Obele) Awate military Conference
PHASE II (1971-81): PARITY BETWEEN ELF AND EPLF	1971-75	First National Congress of ELF First Civil War 1972-74 Unity: PLF I, PLF II; PLF III = EPLF Popular mobilisation and participation Haile Selassie replaced by Dergue Civil War ends Second National Congress of ELF
	1975-78	1975 Khartoum Unity Agreement Split within EPLF Liberation of towns First Organisation Congress of EPLF 20 October 1977 Unity Agreement
	1978-81	Recapture of towns by Dergue, retreat of the liberation movement Second Civil War Defeat of ELF
PHASE III (1981-91): EPLF HEGEMONY	1981-84	Disintegration of ELF *ELF-CL returns to Eritrea *ELF-RC unity with Sabbe *ELF-Abdella Idris unity of the Tripartite (Jeddah Unity)
	1984-89	Military defeats of the Dergue *North Eastern Sahel *Afabet Famine and diplomacy
	1989-91	Second and Unity Congress of EPLF Capture of Massawa by EPLF Peace negotiation Independence of Eritrea

Notes

1. The founding members of the ELM were Mohammed Said Nawid (Beit Asghede) Idris Mohammed Hassen (Beit Asghede), Salih Ahmed Iyay (Belain), Osman Mohammed Osman (Bellow/Massawa), Hassen El Haj Idris (Tigre/Massawa), Habib Ga'as (Afar), Mohammed El Hassen Osman (Afar). The first cell in Asmara to found Mahber Shewate was constituted of Yasin El Gade, Tiku'e Hidogo, Kahsai Bahlbi. The first conference of the ELM was held in Asmara in 1960. Salih Iyay, who was stationed in Keren, represented Senihit, Sahel, Barka and Gash, before the conference, whereas Yasin El Gade, stationed in Asmara, represented *Kebesa*. After the conference Asmara became the centre and Yasin El Gade, Tiku'e Hidogo, Mohammed Birhan led the movement (Nawid 1997).
2. The patron-client relationship pertained to three zones and three members of the Supreme Council. The three zones in question were Zones One, Two, and Four. The patrons were Idris Mohammed Adam who assumed a patronage relationship with Zone One and its commander Mahmud Dinai from the Barka region, Idris Osman Galadewos who became patron to Zone Two and its commander Omar Azaz from the Keren-Sahel regions, and the third patron, Osman Saleh Sabbe who forged a patronage relation with Zone Four and its commander Mohammed Ali Omaro (Markakis 1987: 114f, 284 note 28).
3. The decisions of the Adobha Conference include the formation of a Provisional General Command that was to assume the responsibility of leadership for one year until a national conference was being convened. Accordingly, a Preparatory Committee was set up to organise the conference. Concerning the defunct organisational structure and the respective power bodies the following decision was passed; the SC would stay until the conference was convened, however it should hand over all property to the Provisional General Command. The RC, which was stationed in Kassala was immediately to cease to exist. Furthermore, a committee of inquiry was set up at the request of the radicals and charged with the task of examining the mistakes committed . Perhaps the most important decision of the conference on the grounds of its urgency was the blending of the army that had been divided into five zones.

Chapter 7

COMMON HISTORY AND CULTURE: THE GROWTH OF NATIONHOOD

INTRODUCTION

The importance of common history and culture[1] for the rise of nations was considered in the chapter presenting the theoretical framework. On the basis of those theoretical principles, this chapter will explore the development of common history and culture in Eritrea in a more abstract and theoretically-oriented manner. The aim is to demonstrate how the emergence of common history and culture led to the development of an Eritrean nation. It is not my intention to give an account of Eritrean history in this chapter, because the discussion in the preceding chapters (2-6) deals with Eritrean history. Neither is it my intention to give an account of Eritrean culture. For the purpose of illustration, however, certain events in the social history of Eritrea will be highlighted. These events are discussed under the headings: European rule and resistance against it; Ethiopian rule and resistance against it; the attempts of the NLM to create a cohesive society from the Field; and, the development of literal vernacular languages and its impact in the process of nation formation. These events constitute key elements of Eritrean history. Their presentation in this chapter serves the purpose of demonstrating the connection between historical events and the concomitant development of common culture. The intention is to investigate the implications of common history in the growth of common culture, then show how the two together influenced the formation of the Eritrean nation. Common history and common culture are necessary conditions for the rise of a nation.

Culture, in this study is to be understood as a complex of elements that have resulted from common historical experience (Sewell 1999: 40). The idea of combining common history and common culture in this chapter is based on the view that culture is a product of a previous historical experience. History should here be understood as an accumulation of past events. The century-long history of Eritrea is one of foreign oppression characterised by the experience of domination and exploitation on one hand, and the political struggle of the Eritrean people in opposition to such oppression and exploitation on the other. Eritrean culture is perceived here as the outcome of that history. Referring to the continued intrusion and the accompanying resistance, the ELF wrote in its political programme: "Resistance against invaders and the tradition of remembering our great heroes constitute an important component of Eritrean culture" (ELF 1971: 35). The assumption of this study is that the Eritrean collective identity is generated as a result of this historical experience and its resultant cultural formation.

Common elements of culture are overarching common beliefs, values, symbols, myths, etc. These are, in turn, the outcomes of actual or imagined historical experiences which members of the society have experienced–or believe themselves to have experienced. In this sense culture may be perceived as the accumulated repository of social activities in an historical trajectory. Noting the repository nature of culture, Anthony D. Smith writes, "Culture is both intergenerational repository and heritage, or set of traditions, and an active shaping repertoire of meanings and images, embodied in values, myths and symbols that serve to unite a group of people with shared experiences and memories, and differentiate them from outsiders" (Smith 1998: 187). In this definition, two points of significance for the formation of nations can be extracted. These are the views that culture, while uniting a group simultaneously differentiates them from outsiders. As the result of historical accumulation, culture becomes, in effect, a resource. Understanding culture as a resource leads to the interpretation that, "culture provides" a tool kit of symbols, stories, rituals and worldviews, which people may use in varying configurations to solve different kinds of problems" (Pedriana and Stryker 1997:639). It further constitutes a symbolic resource that enables us to interpret social action. Highlighting this condition Geertz (1993: 145) notes, "culture is the fabric of meaning in terms of which human beings interpret their experience and guide their action".

Following the foregoing conceptualisation of culture, this chapter attempts to trace certain significant epochs and events that contributed to the emergence of an overarching Eritrean culture by way of their power to stick in the collective memory. The temporal point of departure will be the moment of the initiation of Italian colonial rule, since it was in this period the differentiating process began. The central argument is that common culture began to be formed as a result of colonial rule. Arguing in favour of the proposition that colonial history engendered common Eritrean culture, Lobban (1976: 339) notes: "It is my argument that this common tradition of colonial oppression has brought a variety of Eritrean language groups into a common national culture". I too argue along the lines of this proposition. Culture is employed here in a broad context. It is to be construed, paraphrasing Geertz's interpretation, in the sense that Eritrean society from its overall colonial historical experience has developed a set of meanings through which it can interpret its experience and devise guidelines for its prospective actions. Insofar as the driving force behind the development of common Eritrea culture is seen to be foreign domination and the struggle against it, we are by necessity referring to political culture. Political culture is generated by the loyalty to constitutional or political processes and institutions that bind people together despite their ethnic differences (Calhoun 1997: 48).

Since the legal formation of Eritrean territoriality a century ago, the imagined community that has been conjured up in the minds of most Eritreans has an overriding historical reality. The common value on which a common interpretation is based includes elements such as territorial affiliation, the common historical experience of colonial oppression and exploitation, the memory of resistance and struggle against intruding forces, and the appreciation of a common material interest rendered plausible as the upshot of economic interdependence. These are the basic fundamentals upon which Eritrean collective identity rests and which the study focuses on in order to explore the process of formation of the Eritrean nation. The common values serve the society as a yardstick to both refer to its history and simultaneously to commit itself to live together in the future on the basis of an understanding that a common destiny binds it.

The Italian colonisation of Eritrea was preceded by heightened military activities in the region. These military activities involved such powers as Abyssinia, Anglo-Egyptian Sudan, France, Italy and the Mahdists. Of particular interest for our purposes are Abyssinia and the Mahdists. The Abyssinian rulers and the Mahdists endeavoured to subject the various communities inhabiting the soon-to-be territory of Eritrea under their own total control. The Mahdists' effort was directed at the lowland Moslem communities, while Abyssinia mainly aimed at the Christian highlanders. These aggressions met with resistance from the communities, who were eager to preserve their autonomy. In the highland of Eritrea, Rasi Woldenkeal led resistance against Emperor Yohannes' attempt to subordinate the Hamasen region of the highland of Eritrea, while leaders such as Kentebai Hamid Hassen led the resistance against Yohannes and the Mahdists in the lowland. The leaders were, at times, compelled to co-operate against the aggressors (cf. Erlich 1982). Rasi Woldenkeal's retreat to the Halhal or Bahta Hagos' to the Habab people are some of the examples. It appears that these leaders tried to co-ordinate their forces, most probably forced by sheer necessity of survival, but perhaps also by the economic relationships that existed between the various regions. The significance of these acts of resistance and co-operation in the development of Eritrean national identity is that they constituted the precursor or the first building blocks in the formation of Eritrean national memory. The resistances and co-operations were to constitute part of the historical memory and myth of Eritrean nationalists. As with any society, Eritrean society has its own mythology of historical events, epochs, legends and historical heroes and figures. Over the course of history, the Eritrean society has built images and myths of its heroes that enrich its common history and consolidate its common culture. Among those historical legends and heroes are Rasi Woldenkeal, Degeyat Bahta Hagos, Kentebai Hamid Hassen, Fitewrari Kafle Gofar, Rasi Tessema Asberom, Abdelkadir Kebire, Woldeab Woldemariam,

Ibrahim Sultan, Idris Hamid Awate (EPLF 1983, 1987a, Italian Colonialism in Eritrea; Yohannes 1991). The first four figures were resistance leaders at the start of Italian colonialism, the next four figures led political struggles in the 1940s and 1950s, while the last one is celebrated as the father of the armed struggle.

History teaches us that historical figures and legends are quite often judged differently in retrospect. The names of those who are fortunate are placed in the golden memory books, whereas those who are unfortunate swell the list of defamed personalities. Whatever judgement is passed on them, whether they are declared holy or evil, it is clear that legends are built on them that constitute a significant part of the national historiographic repertoire. It is a repertoire which, whether in times of crisis or in times of commemorating treasured memories, serves as a wardrobe from which the individual or group may choose its precious attire, to refresh their minds and feel good. In addition, some of these legendary figures may be appreciated by certain groups or individuals while being hated and despised by others. Such legendary historical figures constitute part of the historical mythology that is a prominent feature in the construction of national sentiment and identity, which in turn provides important ingredients for the process of nation formation.

UNDER EUROPEAN RULE

A common history presupposes territorial integration and political centralisation, enabling a people to share things. In other words, the creation of a common space and the interaction within that space furnishes the conditions for the consolidation of common history. Without a common history, a common culture cannot emerge. As we have seen in earlier chapters, the centralisation and integration of the various ethno-linguistic groups in Eritrea began with Italian colonisation. Therefore, the development of common history and culture is connected with the appearance of colonialism. That is why, in our investigation of the development of common history and common culture, colonialism must be examined. Our examination of European colonialism involves the two colonial regimes, the Italian and the British. The two regimes, despite many similarities, differed in significant aspects such as durability, legality, and content as well as their particular contribution.

Colonial oppression and exploitation clearly mark the history of Eritrea. The importance of this oppression and exploitation for our aim is that all ethno-linguistic groups experienced it. Accordingly, colonial rule contributed to the formation of the Eritrean nation by confining all the Eritrean communities and subjecting them to common oppression and exploitation. The literature on colonialism emphasises the fact that oppression and exploitation evokes resistance (see e.g. Hodgkin 1956, Emerson 1960, Rokkan 1973, Smith 1983). Resistance, in turn, generates nationalism, an anti-colonial nationalism or 'resistance nationalism' (cf. Bruilly 1993: 161f). However, it is not inevitable that oppression and exploitation lead to resistance. The Eritrean situation during Italian colonial rule perhaps provides an example. The commonplace view concerning the Eritrean reaction to Italian rule is that there appeared no noticeable organised resistance. An extreme proponent of this idea is Trevaskis (1960) who says that the harsh Italian treatment of the indigenous population, coupled with material betterment effectively pre-empted any tangible resistance. Trevaskis explains Italian policy toward the indigenous population, putting it sarcastically, depicting it as a policy of filling the stomach while emptying the mind. This policy, according to its proponents, prevented any open opposition from developing. Thus, peace and stability prevailed in Eritrea. Although to date, there is no extensive, systematic, scholarly study of resistance under Italian colonial rule, the limited works available show that in the first five years of Italian rule, resistance was, in fact seen (Negash 1986, Mesghenna 1988, Yohannes 1991). However, for the remainder of the colonial period it seems that the Italians succeeded in pacifying the Eritreans. Roy Pateman (1989), one of the few scholars who attempted to study Eritrean resistance to Italian domination, on the other hand, maintains that a considerable resistance to the Italian colonial rule had occurred, consequently stirring up a distinct Eritrean nationalism.

Though it appears untenable to maintain that no resistance was seen, neither does it seem convincing to claim that any extensive organised resistance existed. Therefore, the account given by Roy Pateman seems to be overstated. Moreover, the evidence presented by Pateman represents what others consider as no more than sporadic and isolated rebellions. By all indications, except for the resistance of the first few years and the isolated, sporadic individual campaigns, peace generally characterised the Italian colonial period. The first significant uprising against the Italians was led by Degeyat Bahta Hagos in 1894, and was prompted by the extensive land expropriation from the peasants. Immediately before the Italian colonial rule there was resistance – both against the Abyssinian Emperor, and against the Mahdists (cf. Erlich 1982). However, these resistances were transformed into collaboration with the emerging Italian power. Many of the resistance figures, to escape Abyssinian and Mahdist domination, sought sanctuary in Italian-occupied Massawa and actively participated in the Italian conquest of Eritrea (see Yohannes 1991). Opposition to aggression from the Mahdists and Emperor Yohannes drove them into collaboration with the Italians, since initially, Italian presence was preferred over either Abyssinia or Mahdist Sudan. Later, when the threat from the Mahdists and Abyssinia abated, those same collaborators turned against the Italians. The resistance to Italian colonisation began when Eritrea fell under complete Italian occupation that continued for the first few years. It seems that the collaborators had not been fully aware of the magnitude and possible consequence of Italian occupation, and when they realised the problems of Italian rule, they rose against it. Effective, organised resistance to Italian rule was rendered difficult by the harsh measures taken against the Eritrean chiefs by the Italians (Negash 1987, Yohannes 1991) who could have led resistance. Informed sources claim that twelve chiefs and eight hundred of their followers were killed (Yohannes 1991: 20, also see Negash 1987: 121) depriving the communities of their traditional leaders. Yet, many individual and isolated acts of resistance did take place. Many of those individuals who resisted Italian rule were forcibly exiled to the notorious prison Island of Nakura in the Red Sea. Many were reported to have died in the prison (Negash 1987: 122). Several attempts were also made to escape from the entirely isolated island prison. A number of these escaping attempts were successful and famous which earned them memorial poems and songs. Nakura, thus, became a symbol of oppression and defiance of Italian colonialism. Many of the poems and songs are well remembered today and constitute part of the historical memory. More significantly, the Eritrean nationalists during the liberation struggle effectively employed them in the nationalist education in the aim of raising national consciousness and building a common culture.

The real collective Eritrean resistance which spanned ethno-linguistic boundaries and which was to become part of the collective experience came with the collapse of Italian colonisation. In multi-ethnic societies, resistance in which the different ethno-linguistic groups collectively participate nurtures common history and culture, and cements national identity. Such a situation was created in Eritrea, in the aftermath of Italian colonialism, particularly with the emergence of political parties under British rule. The British Administration was regulated by the principles of the Hague Convention on occupied enemy territories. In accordance with the Hague Convention, an administrating power assumes a temporary responsibility and mandate. Therefore, in theory, measures that can be taken by that power are restricted by the temporary nature of its tenure. This temporary character had, above all, two visible consequences–one economic and the other political. In terms of economic policy, British rule brought economic hardship that brought about socio-political division. In political terms, in contrast, the liberalisation of politics opened the opportunity for popular mobilisation and participation in which popular political demands were openly discussed. These two elements of instability–political openness on the one hand and economic deterioration on the other–generated socio-political turmoil. This situation fostered resistance that took various forms. The forms of the resistance varied, from that of political parties' legal struggles to that of *shifta* (bandits/outlaws, political or economic ones).

Under the British Administration, conflicts between various rival groups across the border flared up again. Cross-border raids that had been suppressed and contained by the Italian colonial rule resurfaced. Such instances were those between the Hadendowa and the Beni Amer tribes (see Trevaskis 1960: 70-71, Markakis 1987: 59). These conflicts were, however, not limited only to cross-border raids between contesting tribes. Because they also clashed with the British policies, they were also usually directed against colonial rule. The confrontation with the British forces, since it was seen as occurring between the occupier and the occupied, had the effect of raising national consciousness. Moreover, those who were leading the tribal conflict quite often directed their resistance against the British, whom they considered enemies. Individuals like Hamid Idris Awate (widely considered to be the father of the Eritrean armed struggle) and Ali Mohammed Idris were engaged against the British and described their resistance as anti-colonial. On the other hand, followers of the Unionist Party, in their campaign of terror against the Italians and the supporters of independence also clashed with the British authorities. Moreover, they were adamantly against British rule because they saw it as standing in the way of their objective (the union with Ethiopia) which they considered to represent liberation from colonial rule.

Compared to the political struggle undertaken by the emergent political parties, these individual acts of opposition are of meagre importance in the creation of national common history and culture. More significant for the formation of a common history and a common culture was the political activity of the parties during the 1940s. The parties mobilised Eritrean society under the banner of Eritreanism–the Eritrea that came into existence as the outcome of colonialism. Even the unionists campaigned for a territorially united Eritrea to join Ethiopia. This intensive mobilisation and participation in politics thus enhanced the awareness of common Eritrean identity (cf. Ellingson 1977, Markakis 1987).

The depiction here of sporadic resistance is intended to illustrate how such events in the gradual historical trajectory could contribute to the process of nation formation. The contribution of the Italian colonial period is much more material in nature in that the objective conditions for the process of formation of the Eritrean nation were established. The common material interest formed the basis for the emerging common Eritrean history and culture. The British Administration, conversely, helped in forging primarily the subjective conditions, in the consolidation of national sentiment and consciousness.

RESISTANCE TO ETHIOPIAN RULE

Three distinct periods of Ethiopian intervention in Eritrea can be identified. These three periods are examined on the basis of their contribution, to the consolidation of Eritrean history and to the formation of the Eritrean culture of resistance. The first period pertains to the time immediately before Italian colonialism (1879-1889). The second period refers to the British Administration and the Federation, 1941-1962. The third covers the period of Ethiopian occupation of Eritrea from 1961 until independence in 1991. Concerning these periods, we are interested in the particular implications each had for the process of formation of the Eritrean nation. The influence of the second and third periods on the formation of a unique Eritrean culture and identity is relatively clear. The effect of the first period is, however, less self-evident. The reason for this is that in the first period, Eritrea, as Ethiopia itself, was not an integrated territory. Therefore, whatever resistance there had been was of an isolated nature against demands for tribute collection or subjugation by various Abyssinian rulers.

This leads to the question of whether Eritrea had been part of Ethiopia during this period (discussed earlier). We find at least two views pertaining to this question. There are those who recognise the existence of a tributary relationship between the Eritrean highland and Abyssinia (e. g. Dilebo 1974, Greenfield 1980, Davidson 1988). However, these scholars are of the view that because Abyssinia itself was not a centralised and integrated state, it is difficult to say that Eritrea was part of Abyssinia. Nevertheless, they recognise that the highland of Eritrea has had a tributary relationship with Abyssinia but was not an integral part of Abyssinia (see chapters two and three in this work). On the other hand, claims are made that Eritrea had been an indivisible part of Abyssinia from time immemorial (e.g. Pankhurst & Pankhurst 1953, Erlich 1983, Spencer 1984, Wolde Giorgis 1989). Here I will argue along the lines of the first view. This is not to suggest a rejection of the ethnic, linguistic and cultural ties between the Tigrinya speakers of Eritrea and Tigrinya speakers of the northern province of Ethiopia (Tigray). Neither should it be understood as a rejection of the fact that this part of Eritrea has been once the core of the Axumite civilisation.

Available poems, folk songs, oral folklore narratives from the first period of Ethiopian intervention indicate that most of the ethno-linguistic groups have a bitter memory of the Abyssinian kings and princes who used to cross to the Medri Bahri, perhaps on a yearly basis, to collect tribute or simply to raid and take whatever wealth they could find. These raids were so barbaric and so cruel that in the course of them many women, men and children were mercilessly massacred. They were cruel, in part, because they were undertaken with the aim of subjecting the communities by fear and submission. One of the many raids still remembered was that of the regent of Begemdir Wibe. One finds, even to these days, many stories told about his cruelty. Songs and poems have passed from generation to generation, carrying the memories of those days, in both the highland and the lowland. Another point of significance in connection with the formation of collective memory and culture is that these raids aroused opposition from local populations. The unintended effect of these raids on Eritrea was certainly in the enrichment of the collective historical memory which, at a later stage, helped in the development of national identity. Not unexpectedly, many local chiefs and their followers, at one or another time, fought against these raids. They also sought protection and signed agreements with the Italians in Massawa as an expression of their opposition to Abyssinian efforts at domination. Kentebai Hammed Hassen of Habab, Beremberas Kafle Gofar of Dembelas, Sheikh Arey Agaba of the Nara, Deglel Ali Hassen of the Beni Amer, Sheikh Hammed of Marya, Sheikh Omar of Asaurta, Degiat Hadgembes Gilwet, Lij Nighuse, Lij Ghobeze and Abera of Tzeazega, Degiat Tesfamariam and Lij Beyene of Adi Quala, Mohammed Sherif of Ad Ekud (opposing Mahdists) all sought the protection of the Italians in Massawa. From among those who were imprisoned with Rasi Woldenkeal Degiat Tessema Imam and Degiat Mesfine Woldenkeal (the son of Rasi Woldenkeal) also escaped from prison in Tigray and joined the Italians (Yohannes 1991: 12-18).

The opposition to Abyssinian domination also drove these leaders to play an important role in the occupation of Eritrea by Italy. For instance, it was Beremberas Kafle Gofar in 1889 who occupied Keren for the Italians. These actions, therefore, can be considered to represent resistance by Eritreans to Abyssinian domination. Prominent personalities which the nationalist literature commemorates as leaders of such opposition include, Woldenkeal Solomon, Abubaker Nasir, Bahta Hagos, Kafle Gofar, Ahmed Il Idris (EPLF 1987a: 31). The importance of such events and experiences is in the bitter memory they imprint in the mind of the communities which produce sagas, like *bizemen Wibe zitsememe Wibe k'bil nebere* (he who lost his hearings in the tenure of Wibe the only word he utters throughout the rest of his life is Wibe). Those events and the memory of those days helped in generating a unique Eritrean identity and culture. After all, it is the accumulated historical experience and memory, and the mythology of those experiences and memories – actual or putative – which in the final analysis, constructs collective identity. The impact of this repository of memory was vividly displayed when in particular, the Moslem communities vigorously fought the idea of an association with Ethiopia in any of its forms, invoking the memory of the many raids committed by Ethiopia. The Liberal Progressive Party (LPP), too, rejected union with Ethiopia, saying that Eritrea had never been part of Shewa-dominated Ethiopia.

What I have designated here as the first period of Ethiopian intervention preceded the Italian colonial period and the subsequent period of British Administration and the Federation. The latter can be construed as a prelude to the third and total Ethiopian occupation of Eritrea (in the second period Ethiopia was not in control of Eritrea). The second period of Ethiopian intervention in Eritrea began with the Ethiopian claim to Eritrea after the defeat of the Italians. Ethiopian intervention during the British Administration was of an indirect nature. Undoubtedly the Ethiopian claim, coupled with the need for settlement of the territory of the ex-Italian colony accelerated political activities in Eritrea. The Ethiopian claim set the stage for the long confrontation between Ethiopia and Eritrean nationalists, which in the course of time grew in intensity. The initial reaction by the forces of independence to the Ethiopian claim was to strongly oppose it. They opposed it, on the one hand, saying that Eritrea had never been part of Shewa dominated Ethiopia. On the other hand, by pointing to the material change that had taken place under the Italian rule that made it impossible to join with a backward country (cf. Memorandum from ML to FPC 1947, Memorandum from LPP to FPC 1947). Ethiopia's important instrument in its campaign to annex Eritrea became the *Yehager Fikr Mahber* or SUEE, which it organised from Eritreans residing in Addis Ababa. The *Yehager Fikr Mahber* targeted the *Mahber Fikri Hager*, which it eventually succeeded in splitting. With the split of the *Mahber Fikri Hager,* the way was paved for the unity between the *Yehager Fikr Mahber* and the unionist section of the *Mahber Fikri Hager*, which culminated in the formation of the Unionist Party (UP).

Now political activity began to crystallise into formal political parties, providing a more firm shape. Ethiopian intervention, political liberalisation under British Administration and the onset of the debate on Eritrea's future by the Big Four Powers and the UN generated extensive mobilisation in the Eritrean society. At the same time, the more the Big Four Powers (and later the UN General Assembly) showed concerted effort to settle the destiny of the territory, the more intervention by Ethiopia grew bold and desperate. The independentists and the unionists tried to reach a compromise solution which led to *Wa'ela Bet Giorgis,* where an accord was struck on a conditional union. However, the agreement was scuttled because of Ethiopian objection (Trevaskis 1960, Killion 1985). When the Eritrean issue was submitted to the UN General Assembly, the Ethiopian campaign was waged from two directions. First, Ethiopia acted within Eritrea through the unionists, who came to act, as Trevaskis (1960) described them–increasingly as servants of the Ethiopian State. Second, it lobbied in the UN General Assembly to influence the decision of the Assembly in its favour. Finally the resolution of federation was passed, federating Eritrea with Ethiopia. Despite the division among Eritrean nationalists regarding the solution to the settlement of the territory, the activities of this time further consolidated Eritrean identity. This was seen in the increasing growth of resistance to Ethiopian intervention. Once the Federation was implemented, Ethiopian intervention and intentions became crystal-clear. Eritreans were told in a clear language that all Eritrean affairs concern the Emperor. The Emperor, thus, made it his intention that all means necessary were to be used to undermine the Federation agreement and Eritrean autonomy. Again, the unionists in the Eritrean Government played an important role in the aims of the Emperor. The pervasive Ethiopian intervention in internal Eritrean affairs and the blatant breach of the Federation agreement made clear for many who previously favoured union with Ethiopia that the fear of those who opposed union had been well-founded (Ellingson 1977: 261, Markakis 1987: 69). The effect, as predicted by Trevaskis (1960: 130), was the strengthening of Eritrean national identity and national resistance, thereby destabilising both Eritrea and Ethiopia itself.

The Federation introduced national institutions and symbols to Eritrea, which the people came to appreciate. These national institutions and symbols were perceived by the Eritreans as products of their own history. They were also seen as the manifestations of the Eritrean culture in the making–common to all. Ethiopian disregard for this history and culture aroused resistance. The replacing of the Eritrean languages and the Eritrean flag by Ethiopian language and flag in schools, for instance, evoked strong protest by students (Ammar 1997). These protests supported by workers strikes and demonstrations were converted into political demands. The students, in their demonstration of 1962, for example, chanted slogans like *Natzinet Delina Haghizuna* (We Want Freedom Help Us) (Ammar 1997: 68). The situation steadily developed into militancy. This was expressed first, in the low-level peaceful resistance followed by a high-level, violent conflict with the aim of restoring the violated identity and culture of Eritrea. Eventually the move from the low-level to the high-level conflict gave rise to the National Liberation Movement (NLM).

The violation of the federal accord and the eventual incorporation of Eritrea as a province of Ethiopia led to the bloody war for independence, ushering Eritrea into the third period of Ethiopian intervention. The emergence of the armed struggle for independence represented a higher form of resistance. Given the scope and degree of sacrifice, hardship and commitment demanded by war, it is reasonable to expect a relatively high degree of cultural integration and a strong consciousness of one's own history. War usually follows a lower level, simmering conflict. The progress from peaceful resistance to an armed conflict requires moral and psychological preparedness. Consequently, it would be unthinkable to initiate and sustain such a highly demanding undertaking unless a strong belief on one's culture and history is developed. It is said that one dies for his passion, not for material interest (McCrone 1998: 5). Certainly, the Eritrean liberation struggle could serve as testimony to this saying. However, this is not to suggest that a full-fledged popular national consciousness and national identity should be viewed as a necessity from the very outset. What is initially required is for a particular group, or people in a particular region take up the struggle. In the process driven by its own endogenous dynamics, but also with the support of exogenous influences, those requirements are constructed and crystallised in a dialectical morphogenetic development of history and culture. However, at a certain stage of the journey, participation should encompass the whole membership of society. Studies of nationalism indicate that this is the common course of development. Gellner's famous aphorism of nationalism creates nations not the vice versa is an obvious suggestion of this development. Miroslav Hroch (1985) also describes nationalist movements as passing through three phases (elaborated in the next chapter).

Although in the first decade of its history the NLM committed serious mistakes, prompting diverging interpretations regarding its nature (see chapter six of this work), it was a response to the flagrant violation of national rights and could be seen as an indicator of the accumulated frustrations of Eritreans. As such, it represented a higher stage of accumulated experience, not only because it happened to come at a later juncture in the historical progression, but also because of the challenges which had to be confronted, the sacrifices made and price paid. Emphasising the hardship of the task, the expression "we are making our history with our blood" was boldly engraved in the political programmes and mottoes of the Eritrean liberation organisations. Students of the Eritrean revolution agree that the NLM, in its struggle against Ethiopian oppression, shaped the destiny of the Eritrean society and formed the Eritrean nation (cf. Markakis 1987, 1988; Bondestam 1989; Gebre-Medhin 1989; Pateman 1991; Soreson 1991). Making this point Calhoun (1997: 101) notes,

> In fact, it is a paradox to say that the Eritrean nation was *made* largely through its very struggle for independence.[13] But the issue is not only one of military success. During its 30 years of struggle, Eritrea became more socially integrated (for example as members of different religions and ethnic groups fought side by side and formed personal relationships), developed a stronger collective identity - and one that was inscribed deeper into individual Eritreans' self-

consciousness - and spread much more widely a clear conception of Eritreanness based on the rhetoric of nationalism.

Of course, it is not peculiar to Eritrea that a revolution creates a nation. Today, it is common knowledge that while the French political Revolution created the French nation, the English industrial revolution created the English nation. Lipset (1963) also discusses how the American Revolution created the American nation.

The thirty years of armed struggle against what I have called the third period of Ethiopian intervention have moulded a culture of resistance which, no doubt, has united Eritrean society to a greater degree than any other period of its history. Although the divide-and-rule policy of the Ethiopian State was at the beginning, a profound hindrance for the realisation of popular national mobilisation, increasing Ethiopian oppression certainly enhanced the mobilisation and participation of the various ethno-linguistic groups in the NLM. The intensification of the war was more and more characterised by indiscriminate massacres, wanton bombings and burnings, incarcerations, and disappearances, etc., on the one hand, and the pervasive discrimination and domination in every sphere of life, on the other. This induced a massive number of people from towns, including from Ethiopia itself, to join the liberation fronts. The new recruits were from all sections of the society affected by common oppression and prepared to achieve a common goal–that of the independence of their country. To achieve this, they were forced to go to the *Meda* (Field) as *tegadelti* (freedom fighters), adopting a new, collective life. Now I will turn to life in the *Meda* where the habitat of the fighters was situated and where revolutionary history and culture was effectively moulded.

LIFE IN THE FIELD AS A CULTURAL MELTING POT

The concept of melting pot as a metaphor is identified with the Chicago School of sociology, where it was employed in connection with the research of interethnic context (Eriksen 1993: 19). The research was conducted to investigate the extent to which the various ethnic groups were assimilated in the 'English-speaking majority's values and ways of life'. Here it was assumed that all the ethnic groups would melt in the acculturation and assimilation process of the mainstream American culture, thereby forging a single common identity. The metaphor, in the present study, is used in different circumstances, and in a different context from that of the USA. In our discussion of the life in the Eritrean Field[2], we can identify four significant concepts denoting the centrality of the symbolic value of political language in the formation of a nation, notably, *Meda*, *Sewra*, *Tegadelti* and *Meswa'eti*.

The concept of *Meda* (Field) refers to the socio-geographical space that formed the base for the Eritrean liberation fighters in the *Sewra* (revolution) in places distant from the control of the enemy, or from likely encounters. It was a geographical space, often the rural liberated areas outside the control of Ethiopian forces. The liberated areas served as centres for activities of a political, cultural, economic, and educational nature. It was also a social space in which the *Tegadelti* assumed the social role of liberating the nation. It was at the same time abstract and concrete. It was abstract because it could be anywhere within Eritrea, timeless and placeless. In this sense it was a symbol representing a space in which those who had devoted their lives to the *Sewra* 'work' and 'live'. It was also a concrete space because it could be located in a specific time and space. *Tegadalai/Tegadalit* was a name given to the liberation fighter who joins the *Sewra*. *Meswa'eti* (martyrdom) was a sacred sacrifice which every *Tegadalai/Tegadalit* was prepared to make for his nation. *Meswa'eti* was so sacred that words like died, killed, murdered, or death did not exist not only in the daily vocabulary of the *Tegadelti*, but also in the society in general, in reference to the death of *Tegadelti*. "In conversation with dozens of Eritrean fighters, I found that no one ever dies - instead he is 'martyred'" (Berger 1987: 30). The concept *sewu'e/sewi'eti* (martyr) was socially constructed, not only to sanctify the martyred but also to bestow anonymity and equity so that those who sacrificed their lives in the name of the nation could be remembered eternally. This emotionally-charged symbolism made *meswa'eti* bearable.

The *Tegadelti* were individuals of a variety of economic, social, educational, gender and age backgrounds who devoted their lives to the *Sewra*. They abandoned their secure lives among their relatives and friends in towns and villages to live in the field, facing all the imaginable difficulties of such a way of life. They had to endure all kinds of difficulties for the purpose of a higher goal. Many different sorts of social groups and classes intermingled on an equal social basis. Regardless of what social positions they had before they joined the *Sewra*, they lived under the same conditions and on an equal footing (cf. Pateman 1990: 468). For some individuals, it meant the first 'face-to-face' encounter with members of other ethno-linguistic groups. This face-to-face contact or interaction, in turn, engendered a far-reaching transformation of relationships. This started from simple familiarity among interacting individuals to the creation of complex codes of behaviour which, in the long run, tended to generate relations of interdependency, leading to the dialectics of integration. These common sociological norms were reinforced by conscious and intentionally enforced legal codes. The organisations adopted rules and legal codes aimed at promoting the integration of members, and of the society as a whole.

To build the envisioned modern nation, agents of the NLM put great effort into the social engineering of institution building. In an attempt to create some measure of uniformity, a variety of integrative institutions were established: a) In the political departments; institutions of school of cadres were established with the chief function of enlightening, organising and mobilising the masses, as well as the production of a devoted and highly motivated contingent of cadres, endowed with the responsibility to teach and lead the masses; b) in the cultural departments; institutions of cultural troupes were organised. The aim was to educate and to raise the political consciousness of the fighters and the populace at large through revolutionary songs, poems, dances etc. (cf. Pool 1997: 12).

In addition, the goal was also to innovate and to integrate the traditions of the various ethno-linguistic groups through undertaking performance tours in the liberated countryside, towns and abroad. In the latter case, the purpose was to include those in Diaspora in the process of nation formation. c) The social departments were equipped with a variety of institutions such as family care institutions where socialisation and internalisation of norms and values took place among the children of fighters and martyrs. In addition, matrimonial institutions were established so that marriage contracts and rituals could be conducted. Clear pedagogical principles were created to build the newly developing sovereign nation. Nationalist ideology predicated on communitarian philosophy became the main guiding principle. Behaviours and acts emanating from libertarian principles were considered enemies of the collective, sacred goal and thus, needed to be strongly resisted. The creation of a new society was the ultimate aim. To achieve this noble objective, thus, both the body and mind were "nationalised". To accomplish this, a new structure of cultural identity must be constructed. According to the nationalist ideology, libertarianism was perceived as hostile to the objective of building a self-sacrificing, altruistic, disciplined collectivity, because it is fundamentally based on antagonistic, individualistic and egoistic principles. In view of the agents of this social engineering, what is being done is done in order to ensure a smooth transition to a developed and sovereign nation.

Membership in a front could take three forms. The most important one was that of the fighters, full-time guerrilla members. This was the primary force in the NLM. The next level was membership in the satellite mass organisations. A third form involved those who simply happened to reside in area under the control of respective organisation. These gradations required the adoption of at least three categories of rules and regulations that defined, regulated and directed the relationship of the component groups of the organisation. This, in turn, produced a set of complex structures and institutions. The first category, full-time members, consisted of two categories, the army whose main task was fighting and semi-civilian full-time members involved in the civilian sector of the organisation, notably, political, economic, cultural, social and educational activities. The semi-civilian staffs undertook military training in order to act as a reservoir in times of acute military urgency. Whatever the assignment was, in whatever section of the organisation an individual was involved, the life was an egalitarian, collective one (cf. Pateman 1990). The revolutionary vision of constructing a microcosm of an ideal society in the Field was also intended in the long run to encompass and pervade the whole society. Once, in elucidating the role played by the armed liberation struggle, Amilcar Cabral wrote,

> As we know, the armed liberation struggle demands the mobilization and organization of a significant majority of the population, the political and moral unity of the various social categories, the efficient use of modern weapons and other means of warfare, the gradual elimination of the remnants of tribal mentality, and the rejection of

> social and religious rules and taboos contrary to development of the struggle (gerontocracy, nepotism, social inferiority of women, rites and practices which are incompatible with the rational and national character of the struggle, etc.). The struggle brings about many other profound changes in the life of the populations. The armed liberation struggle implies, therefore, a veritable forced march along the road of cultural progress (Cabral 1980: 152).

The NLM struggled with two often-contradictory needs: on one hand was the creation of an effective fighting army, and on the other, safeguarding the reproduction of the society. Sociologically, "every society must have a system of kinship, marriage, and family relations, to regulate mating and birth and the care of infants" (Goldthorpe 1974: 24). This 'miniature society', in the Field, must therefore fulfil such social roles, functions and responsibilities. Such social functions, in anomalous social conditions, become very complex, requiring extraordinary mechanisms. Considering the unspecified duration of the armed struggle, the postponement of such social reproduction functions indefinitely became intolerable. Up to a certain stage of the history of the armed liberation struggle, building a family or initiating a sexual relationship was prohibited. The dilemma of maintaining a balance between ensuring social reproduction to safeguard the survival of the society and creating a disciplined revolutionary army became a challenging task for the NLM. The primary aim was to create a revolutionary army guided by revolutionary national democratic moral and code of conduct. The balance between setting up a fighting liberation army and social reproduction, thus, required that the fighters must not be side-tracked by marriage responsibilities. Eventually when marriage was permitted, it was to be performed in utterly novel conditions, following an orderly pattern in which the smooth functioning of the microcosm society was not affected. All the traditional customs and laws which used to govern the initiation and execution of a marriage contract and ceremony had to be suspended.

In a society in which the bond of family ties was very strong, where norms and values were shaped and regulated collectively within the family structure, and where individual autonomy and initiatives were given meagre space, a sudden departure from such norms can definitely lead to a sort of anomaly. Individuals were streaming to the fronts, leaving behind a secure family life, being divorced from the only code of behaviour which, until then, had shaped and regulated their social behaviour. Consequently, the need arose to establish alternative social codes in order to safeguard the continuation of a social order compatible with novel conditions. The first step along those lines was to succeed in promoting a value system in which members share a strong belief and voluntarily submit to it. This invocation of a normative cultural value was to be derived from the centrality given to the nationalist discourse of the absolute right for self-determination. Only the existence of such a structure of value system and a strong belief in it could ensure the high level of commitment and sacrifice that the struggle required. In light of this, all other needs, behaviours and emotions had to be subordinated to the sole overriding cause. It was only then, that voluntary submission to novel social codes of behaviour could be ensured. Therefore, the liberation organisations had to construct new social codes of conduct.

It has frequently been said that under extreme conditions, groups often develop mechanisms which enable them to make their social life as bearable as possible. Moreover, their internal attachment strengthens in proportion to the suffering they experience. Renan expressed it in this manner: "One loves in proportion to the sacrifices which one has approved and for which one has suffered, ... to have suffered, worked, hoped together; that is worth more than common taxes and frontiers conforming to ideas of strategy; that is what one really understands despite differences of races and language. I have said 'having suffered together'; indeed common suffering is greater than happiness" (Renan 1994: 17). The fronts endeavoured to construct national revolutionary code of conduct, which was intended to substitute for the sub-national norms and values, because the goal was the creation of national revolutionary culture and identity (see ELF 1971: 37, EPLF 1977) through which meanings and values could be clearly conveyed and shared among adherents. For instance, the novelty of the new social contract of marriage took many forms. To begin with, it was based on the free consent and love of the two individuals involved. That is, it was not arranged by parents or family members. No dowry, no material or symbolic exchange was involved, since time, energy and money-consuming rituals had to be abandoned. Moreover, it was founded on the organisation's law which prescribed that both partners were equal. Cross-ethnic and cross-religious marriages became commonplace (Pool 1997: 12). In a society where religious and genealogical purity of origin in a matrimonial contract had been highly valued, this change was a revolutionary innovation. In times of child rearing, the values and norms of the organisation became a substitute for the conventional family. In addition, the practical day-to-day care of the child was taken over by the organisations' institutions. Responsibility had to be transferred from the particular nuclear family to a neutral institution. In a nutshell, a new social structure was put in place, and included a value system to regulate, monitor and lead the creation of the new society founded upon a new order.

The significance of this collectivity, "microcosm society", from the sociological point of view, was that it assumed the role of family, kinship or other primary relationships. Living outside a family network, individual members of the collectivity received consolation and emotional security from their comrades–a function that under normal circumstances was fulfilled by the institution of family. In times of hardship, when one was wounded, became sick, or in the moment of martyrdom, the people who gave consolation, showed affective attachment, in short, that played the role of the family were the people around him or her–regardless of their religion, language, ethnic belonging etc. In this way, strong bonds among the members of this collectivity were built. Moreover, members of the collectivity, in their daily life, developed new patterns of norms and values that guided their behaviour. To be sure, this type of social life contributed toward the construction of a common national culture and a common national identity. This was true not only as a consequence of simply living together, and as a consequence of the concomitant gradual emergence of a value system, but also because of a conscious effort on the part of the fronts to attempt to construct a new society.

Two functional mechanisms were in operation here. First, the individual who joined the liberation movement was expected to demonstrate a sort of internalised comprehension of what would be expected of him/her. That is, getting rid of, or at least suppressing, all social behaviour and conduct considered to be non-revolutionary, not national (sectarian, regional, religious tendencies). The individual had to accept this in principle and be prepared to duly play the role allocated to him/her.

Second, the organisation one joined had a responsibility to focus the necessary attention to mould the individual member to fit in the new "family" structure. In particular, viewed from the gender perspective this project had far-reaching consequences. In a society in which patriarchy and gerontocracy wielded considerable power over social institutions, norms and values, the participation of women in the public sphere represented an emancipation of great dimensions. In Eritrean society, a patriarchally and hierarchically structured society, the position of the female in the family in particular, and in the society in general, was accorded low status (Houtart 1980: 107). In most Eritrean families, the head of the household was the father. In the absence of the father, the eldest son assumed leadership. When there was no male offspring, first the mother, and then the female offspring may follow on the ladder according to age sequence. Often, the activities of the female members of the family were circumscribed around the house (Bondestam 1989: 279). Females were only allowed to act in the private sphere–the public sphere remained a male domain. In the rural areas this might take a slightly different form. Generally, the public sphere here was a secluded social space which most of the time did not involve the female gender (see Wilson 1991).

It was by joining the liberation struggle that women broke this tightly controlled and regulated social relationship. There, at least in principle, they were to be treated on an equal basis with their male comrades. In this new collectivity, all were equal partners regardless of gender, ethnicity, class, religion, language, etc. This sudden emancipation of the female gender was seen as a revolutionary innovation for the status of women (see Pateman 1990: 465-6, Wilson 1991).

In conclusion, the Field, viewed as a melting pot, as an engineering of social construction represented by a "microcosm society", was of extraordinary importance in the societal transformation process. An argument may be made regarding the extent of the achievement and durability, seen against the ideal goals set out by the agents of the NLM. But one thing can be asserted for certain: that it was an enterprise of a profound importance, and of a considerable contribution to the evolution of a common history and of an overarching Eritrean culture. It has been imprinted in the memory of those who participated in this microcosm society an experience of life long. It was a practical exposition of what is commonly expressed by students of nation formation, as the will to perform a glorious history.

VERNACULAR LANGUAGES

Theorists of nation formation place great emphasis on the importance of the emergence of literal vernacular languages for the evolution of nations. It is suggested that literal vernacular language help in generating an imagined community (Anderson 1994: 133-4). Language is an important component of culture. It is in that respect that the implication of a literate language in the creation of a common culture had been emphasised by scholars of nation formation (e.g. Rokkan 1973, Gellner 1983, Anderson 1991). Benedict Anderson, for instance, in his book '*Imagined Communities: Reflections on the origin and spread of nationalism*' (1991), depicts how communities which have no direct face-to-face contact develop the imagination of belonging together through the inculcation of a literate language embedded in books, news papers, schools, music, theatre, poems, Radio, TV, etc. The development of attachments among members of a nation, and the feeling and awareness of belonging to a collectivity which recognises itself as a nation is partly attributed to the emergence of a vernacular language. It is considered that the effects of the literate language spill over, streaming across a territorial map within its limited confinement, cementing individuals who are spread along physically unconnected fields of human geography, through spiritual rivers.

The importance of the rise of the literal vernacular language for the formation of nations is that there develops a popular script that is easily accessible to the layperson. This stands in contrast to the Church script, which is confined to the priesthood. Here, it is not the homogeneity of the group's language that is in and of itself given great importance. Of greater significance is the role played by literal language as medium of communication. The appreciation of the role, literal language plays actually comes from the recognition that it serves to disseminate uniform, standardised information and knowledge across space and time. The same knowledge and information is conveyed to different people. In doing this, it unites groups of people occupying different geographical spaces and living in different times. In this way it helps to create an 'imagined community', a nation.

Moreover, we are told that "print-capitalism" – the mass production of books – should also be seen as responsible for the consolidation of nationalism and national identity. This is so because it multiplies the standardisation of communication and dissemination of uniform information and knowledge, thereby enhancing the 'imagined community'. In this manner, individuals would be able to identify their common identity with other individuals with whom they do not have a face-to-face relationship (Gledhill 1994: 78). The expansion of the communication technology that serves to spread the printed word also plays a vital role in the production and reproduction of nationalist sentiment. In particular, in reference to circumstances in Africa, Anderson (1991: 44-45) notes that Western colonialism brought with it print capitalism. And to this print capitalism is attributed the expansion of printed words which open up access to identical information to an unlimited number of colonised people. This engenders a standardisation of the distribution of knowledge which, in turn, leads to the creation of a common understanding, feeling, and sense of identity. Here the language used as medium of communication might be the language of the colonial power.

In the case of Eritrea the development of a literate vernacular language can, more or less, be connected with the onset of colonial occupation. Moreover, the role played by missionaries in expanding a literate vernacular language in particular of the Tigrinya is of extraordinary importance. A brief historical account of the development of "print-capitalism" or literal language in Eritrea offers some clues as to how Eritrean national identity was reinforced through the course of history in connection with the expansion of print capitalism.

The origin or birth of the development of literal language (here we refer particularly to the Tigrinya language to certain extent also to the Tigre language) can be traced back to the historical engagement of missionary activity. From there, it expanded through Italian colonial rule, reaching its adolescence during the British Administration and the Federation. Finally, it arrived at the age of adulthood during the NLM. The first Ge'ez printing press was installed in Massawa in 1863 by a Lazarist by the name of Biancari. The following year, in 1864, Biancari published a religious book. In 1879, the Lazarists established a second printing press in Keren and started to publish religious books. In 1900, this printing press was transferred from Keren to Asmara. In another development, the Swedish Mission established a printing press in 1885 at Minkulu. With the establishment of Italian colonialism, however, an Italian commercial printing press was established at Massawa. Subsequently, in 1891, a weekly newspaper of the administration called 'Le Eritreo' began to be published. In the same year, another printing press began to publish a weekly newspaper called 'Corri'ere Eritreo' in Massawa.

In 1892, an official newspaper, 'Bollettino Ufficiale della Colonia Eritrea', was started. Between 1903-05 'Bollettino Agricolo Commerciale della Colonia Eritrea', an agricultural and commercial bulletin was published. After 1928, there was only one newspaper, called 'Cotediano Eritreo' in Eritrea, with two pages in Italian and one page each in Tigrinya and Arabic. However in 1935, Tigrinya and Arabic were abandoned and its name changed to 'Eritrea Nuova'. The first newspaper ever to appear in Tigrinya in conjunction with ecclesiastic dissemination was published between 1912-15 by the Swedish Mission under the name *Meli'ekti Selam* (The Message of Peace). By 1917, the Catholic Mission, too, began to publish its own newspaper. The Swedish Mission also published and distributed religious books in Tigrinya, Tigre and Kunama. From 1882 to 1914 the 'Bible Association', based in Britain, published religious publications–five thousand in Tigrinya and one thousand in Tigre (EPLF, Italian Colonialism in Eritrea 1882-1941 pp. 205-6).

Unquestionably, written Tigrinya saw its birth with the coming of missionaries and mission schools (see Pollera 1935: 32). According to Negash (1999: 77) "1895 may be seen as the year that marked the birth of written Tigrinya literature". The appearance of the Ge'ez alphabet printing press meant that the Bible and other secular writings could be printed in the Tigrinya language, enabling the layperson to benefit. This development made the growth of written Tigrinya at least theoretically possible. Yet, the widespread use of written Tigrinya in the public sphere was to wait for some time. Most probably until the demise of Italian colonial rule, the use of the local language as a medium of education was limited to religious centres and activities, particularly the Missionary schools. One of the real developments that characterised the post-Italian period was the marked increase in the expansion of literate vernacular languages. Indeed, it was under British rule that the expansion of literate local languages (Arabic and Tigrinya) started to boom through newspapers, school education and radio transmission. The British initiative to recognise Tigrinya and Arabic as official languages of Eritrea, and the measures undertaken to facilitate their promotion dramatically boosted the expansion of the written languages. The decision in the Federation to use Tigrinya and Arabic as official languages not only further strengthened the development of the languages, but it also reinforced the attachment between the languages and popular sentiment. During this period, numerous publications, particularly novels, started to emerge in Tigrinya. However, only a limited numbers of novels have appeared from earlier periods (see Negash 1999). But it is in this period that popular songs and poems in written form began to flourish. The growth of Eritrean languages in their written forms have undoubtedly consolidated national peculiarity and contributed to the growth of a unique national identity. An illustration of this attachment that can be pointed out is the broad rejection, including that of the Unionist Party, of Ethiopia's attempt to introduce Amharic as the official language of Eritrea during the Federation (see Trevaskis 1960: 117). Seen from the enterprise of nation formation, this was a visible indication of the strong connection between a vernacular language and national sentiment.

The *Eritrean Weekly News* (in Tigrinya and Arabic) was perhaps the first secular newspaper to appear. Established by the British Information Service in 1942, this newspaper played a prominent role in incubating Eritrean national sentiment (Markakis 1987: 64, see also Ullendrof quoted in Negash 1999: 115-16), particularly in its famous column of readers' letters. In this column, the public was offered with the opportunity to air their view concerning the destiny of Eritrea. Accordingly, a live political debate took place. It is believed that this column contributed considerably to the promotion of the motto of 'Eritrea for Eritreans'. The significance of the emergence of the *Eritrean Weekly News* is not only to be seen in terms of the contribution it made in the development of literary language. Of no less significance is the role it played in disseminating uniform information across the territory, thereby enhancing the formation of imagined community. At this time, other newspapers besides the *Eritrean Weekly News* were also in circulation. Overall, under the BMA the following newspapers were in operation:

Il Quotidiano Eritrea - a daily newspaper (Italian)
Eritrean Daily Bulletin
Eritrea Weekly News - weekly (Tigrinya)
Eritrea Weekly News - weekly (Arabic)
Gize Yawaladew - Monthly magazine (Amharic)

Gradually, newspapers associated with the political parties also emerged during this period. One such newspaper was the official voice of the Independence Bloc (IB) called *Hanti Ertra* (One Eritrea). After 1950, when the IB changed its name to Eritrean Democratic Bloc (EDB), the paper was published under the name of *Demtsi Ertra* (Voice of Eritrea). The Unionists too had their official newspaper, called *Ethiopia.* With the implementation of the Federation *Demtsi Ertra* was forced out of publication while *Ethiopia* continued to circulate long after. In general terms, it appears that the emergence of these newspapers, in combination with the expansion of the use of vernacular language as the medium of instruction in schools further reinforced the development of the written form of Eritrean language(s), particularly Tigrinya. This, in turn, could be said to have influenced the growth of Eritrean culture and identity. One manifestation of this could be seen in the conspicuous spread of poems, songs and novels.

During the 1950s, numerous poems and songs were written and sung in Eritrean languages. Some of these poems were devoted to the elucidation of the political developments of the time. Severely criticising those politicians who were considered to be following a faulty political course, they pleaded to them to work for Eritrean sovereignty. They were quite popular, not only because they were written and sung in one of the Eritrean vernacular languages, but also because they widely expressed the feeling of the people. Therefore, they were widely believed to have played a profound role in arousing national sentiment. To cite a few of the political poems and songs of those days,

1. Assembleia B'Haki F'redu Kabti Reshan B'dehan K'twerdu	(MP's do the right thing So that you may leave your offices safely)
2. Abotat'Uwano Ab idom' kelo Limano	(Our misguided elders Although they had their power They went begging)

<table>
<tr><td>3. Shigey Habuni
Ay'te tal'luluni
Intay Gher'e Iye?
Shigey Zei'tbuni?</td><td>(Give me my torch
How long can you deceive me
What have I done?
That you deny me my torch?)</td></tr>
<tr><td>4. Aslamai Kistanai
Wedi Kola Dega
N'Mikhri Tsela'ee
Ayt'habo Waga
Ayt'habo Waga
Keyt'khewn Edaga</td><td>(Moslem and Christian
Lowlander and Highlander
To the enemy's counsel
Do not listen
Do not give it value
or you may find yourself
[Being sold] in the market.)
(Iyob 1995: 92, 101, 103)</td></tr>
</table>

Linguistic studies show that the development and expansion of literal vernacular languages is, overall, determined by the spectrum of space in which it is used. The use of the language in mass media, at school, in speeches, publication of books, poems and in theatre, as well as its daily use as a means of communication in the private sphere, contributes to its growth. In developing societies, the access to many of these resources is very limited. Radio is the most commonly available instrument. It has therefore been the most widely employed instrument in the promotion of national projects, agitation, mobilisation, and education, and in efforts to elevate national consciousness. The limited application of a language means it is less developed. What is most interesting in connection with the process of nation formation, is that the wider space of application of the language not only serves as a vital instrument in the development and modernisation of the language, but also in inculcating an emotional and psychological attachment among the group who use it.

Radio transmission was an important device in the resistance struggle of the Eritrean people against Ethiopian occupation. The first of its type was the one broadcast from Cairo in the 1950s, in both Tigrinya and Arabic. Commenting on this, Markakis (1987: 109) notes: "The broadcasts created a sensation in Eritrea, and provoked Ethiopian complaints to Cairo". Later they were transmitted from Syria, and then from Sudan until the fronts started to broadcast radio programmes from the Eritrean Field. Ethiopia outlawed listening to the broadcasts by Eritrean nationalists, arguing that they were a propaganda instrument of the "bandits". Therefore, people in areas under Ethiopian control could only listen to the broadcasts secretly. Of course, the prohibition and secrecy itself created more sensation and myth. One can imagine, therefore, what this could contribute to the consolidation of national identity and the growth of nationalism. In highlighting the significance of broadcasting for national integration, Anderson (1991: 135) writes, "multilingual broadcasting can conjure up the imagined community to literates and populations with different mother-tongues". As a testimony to Anderson's argument, members of the various ethno-linguistic groups received these broadcasts by Eritrean nationalists with great excitement. From very early on, one of the sticking points in the relationship between Eritrea and Ethiopia was the issue of language. Objections to the suppression of Eritrean languages, first from political parties and then from students, constituted a kernel of Eritrean resistance. Widely seen as an indication of what is known as "language nationalism", many students protested against Ethiopian language replacing the Eritrean languages as the medium of instruction in schools. The consequent national fervour of these students was frequently followed by joining the armed struggle for independence. Many of the students who participated in the student protest of the late 1950s and early 1960s were among the fighters of the ELF of the mid 1960s (see Ammar 1997).

The policy of language, pursued by Ethiopia after the Federation was nullified and Eritrea became a province in the Ethiopian Empire, fettered the development of the Eritrean languages, particularly in their written form. Ethiopian Imperial law was extended to Eritrea, prohibiting the usage of Eritrean languages as a medium of instruction in schools. Aware of the connection between language and nationalism, Ethiopia worked relentlessly to prevent the development of Eritrean languages. Conversely, every means was employed to ensure the spread of the Ethiopian language (Amharic) in Eritrea. Under the rule of Haile Selassie, many books in Tigrinya were burned with the aim of curbing the development of the language (Negash 1999: 10). It was perhaps to pre-empt such acts of suppression of the Eritrean languages that the political parties (including the Unionist Party) opposed the introduction of the Ethiopian language as the official language of Eritrea (see Trevaskis 1960). As is shown by Negash (1999) the next stage in the development process of the Eritrean literal languages, particularly Tigrinya, was to emerge under the NLM in the Field.

In contrast to the areas under the Ethiopian control, all political, social and cultural activities of the fronts directed both to their members and to the society as a whole were undertaken in Eritrean languages. Schools organised by the fronts used Eritrean languages. Materials intended for mobilisation and propaganda objectives were published, including periodicals, pamphlets and leaflets, and books for academic purposes (which entailed the translation of foreign literature into Eritrean languages). These publications were intentionally designed to promote cultural heritage and develop new culture. Undoubtedly all this helped in developing the Eritrean languages. Cultural activities such as revolutionary national songs, poems, radio transmissions, video records, etc., were dramatically expanded. For a brief time, an intensive politico-cultural effort was undertaken which blended both written and spoken forms of the languages, thereby, further strengthening national culture. The NLM created a free space for the Eritrean vernacular languages. Moreover, this free space was utilised optimally, where the agents of language mobilised their resources to articulate and produce new meanings and identity maximising emotional commitment for the common cause. For all purposes and intents, the development of literal vernacular languages, through their employment in all spheres of societal life, was viewed by the Eritrean nationalists as an indispensable part of the broader strategy of constructing a common culture.

The agents of the NLM were well aware of the function of vernacular languages in the development of national identity, hence, priority was given to their promotion and development. Language was not only perceived as a medium of communication but also as a means of expression of intimate feelings and emotions, while simultaneously strengthening those emotions and feelings which are collective by nature. The development of the vernacular languages and in their role as a means of expression of shared feelings and emotions proved to be a powerful force in the furtherance of the liberation struggle and process of nation-building.

TOWARD A COMMON CULTURE

One of the propositions that this study takes as its point of departure is that common culture is the result of accumulated common history. The above selective social-historical narrative brings us to the discussion of the development of a common culture in pursuit of this proposition. In the view of many Western scholars of culture, the absence of common culture is the hallmark of multi-ethnic societies in the developing world. This stand is derived from the understanding about and definition of culture as a mere embodiment of primordial characteristics. This orthodox view fails to make distinction between civic or political culture and ethnic culture. The absence of common culture in turn is used, in the study of nation formation, as an indication of the non-existence or the weak existence of a nation. Multi-ethnic societies, thus, are invariably construed as fragile nations. The reason for their fragility is seen as the absence of this cultural cohesion and integration, which are commonly seen in the eyes of these orthodox theorists as prerequisites for the existence of a fully developed nation.

There are also those who recommend the understanding of national culture in plural form–in the sort "more likely to be understood (in post-modern terms) as a heterogeneous patchwork of fragments than as a homogeneous seamless whole" (James 1996: 106). Such an understanding will allow us to eschew falling into the trap of either/or. We are advised that by distancing ourselves from narrow views of the conception of culture, which are often derived from the distinction between relativism and universalism, perhaps we might be able to devise an analytical framework with which we can bridge the gap. It is suggested that a hybridisation in which stratification and diversification of cultures is accepted is the appropriate conceptualisation, in the sense that different levels and dimensions of cultures are understood to coexist. The dilemma that scholars of nation formation encounter with respect to the culture of multiethnic societies could then be addressed through the recognition of the existence of at least two levels of culture within a societal setting. The first would be the overarching civic culture, which encompasses the different ethnic groups, the national culture. The second level would entail the cultures of each specific ethnic group, subnational cultures. This understanding draws us to the distinction between ethnic culture and political culture. Ethnic culture refers to the primordial heritage of an ethnic group, whereas political culture is seen as the result of political institutions, processes and experiences that are not reducible to the culture of single ethnic group. Commenting on the relation of ethnicity and culture, Calhoun (1997: 48) notes: "Neither social solidarity nor common culture is a monopoly of ethnic groups... Collective identity is not precisely equivalent to or guaranteed by common culture". This indicates that collective identity is created as much by political culture as by ethnic culture. When ethnic culture and political culture coexist, loyalty and solidarity of groups are divided between the two, providing two levels of identity. In the two preceding sections I discussed how the Field helped to integrate the different social groups and classes, and further how the emergence and development of literal vernacular languages contributed to the evolution of an overriding common national culture. The objective of this section is to argue that a general overriding common national culture along the lines of the perception of heterogeneity or hybridisation can be demonstrated. Let us now briefly discuss the development of common civic culture in Eritrea.

According to the scheme pursued here, a common culture is produced as a result of accumulated historical activities and experiences. Thus, culture in the Eritrean context is to be understood in its very generic form as an overriding and embracing. As such, our understanding avoids the perception of culture as a homogenous phenomenon expressed in terms of one language, one religion, and tradition, or in the sense of primordial heritage. In other words, for the purpose of this study, culture is conceptualised as a general framework, which does not negate or exclude subcultures of the various ethno-linguistic groups. Simultaneously, it is to be identified as shared elements that the various ethno-linguistic groups recognise and accept, and through which they express and symbolise their collective national identity. These shared elements would be the product of their shared historical experience. This shared experience contains the political processes of foreign domination and the resistance against it on the one hand, and the different political institutions and symbols which developed along the historical course, on the other. Moreover, it also contains the sentiment generated by the political processes, institutions and symbols. Therefore, Eritrean culture as the reflection of these political processes, institutions and symbols is necessarily political. Markers of this political culture would include national holidays, national symbols and anthems, common historical events and commemorations, national theatre, poems, songs, music and films (depicting common experience), as well as legal and political institutions. In the theories of nation formation, it is widely argued that such symbolic markers constitute the culturalist perspective of a nation (cf. Giesen 1998: 9). Many of these symbolic markers were introduced in Eritrea when the UN sponsored Federation made it possible for Eritrea to have its emblem, flag, seal, constitution, government, parliament, judiciary, political parties, etc. Once these symbolic markers were in place, people began to identify themselves with them. Subsequently, their removal evoked strong opposition such as the strikes by students and workers. It must be added also that the economic innovation that took place under Italian colonialism constituted the material base of the Eritrean national culture.

In its role as an agent with responsibility for transforming the society, the National Liberation Movement (NLM), can be compared with the European capitalist penetration in the country–particularly after 1970. While the implications of European colonial capitalist penetration were more in the material culture dimensions, the implications of the armed struggle were primarily in the dimension of the subjective or spiritual culture. It could be said that the NLM played a decisive role in the formation of common Eritrean culture. However, this is not to suggest that the process of formation of Eritrean culture (spiritual) began only with the emergence of the NLM. Since culture is seen in terms of both material and spiritual dimensions, and since the material and the spiritual dimensions are interconnected, it is possible to say that Eritrean culture has been in the process of formation since the beginning of the Italian period. The contribution of the NLM can be viewed as a continuation, though much more in the spiritual realm. Moreover, it should be emphasised that a conscious effort was made to construct a new national culture. This contrasts with the impression that cultural integration had just started at this stage in the history of the society–as some have tried to portray it. Probably the most important point that occurred at this juncture in the history of the society is that social agents emerged with clearly defined agendas for shaping the destiny of the society. Hence, from the 1970s, the two main political fronts established politico-cultural projects integrated with their respective political programmes to mould not only their members, but also the entire society, according to the envisioned cultural formation. These efforts at cultural formation were implemented through education, music, theatre and political education, which the organisations established in the liberated areas. In other words, Eritrean nationalists created their own cultural discourse and practice with the aim of creating a national culture based on the historical and political experience of society.

The substance of the politics of the cultural projects pursued by the nationalists can be divided into two levels. The first was a long-term, incremental, macro-level campaign–a kind of grand ideology. In more concrete terms, this meant the modernisation of society through a mapped out vision, the purpose of which (the product of the ideal vision) was the creation of a progressive, modern, cultured man. Therefore, the fronts set out complex projects intended to produce a new modern society designed along a more or less Marxist orientation. The second was the short term, pragmatic, day-to-day practical programme. Its purpose was to mould the fighters through the adoption of a common collective revolutionary mode of life, guided by the emergent cultural meanings, values and codes. This, according to the programme of the NLM, was presumed to be a vital prerequisite for the success of the immediate objective of the struggle, notably securing the independence of Eritrea. This, in turn, was to constitute the basis for the long-term project, the creation of a new society. With the aim of achieving this cultural change, cultural troupes were used as strategic instruments. They disseminated revolutionary materials: music, songs, poems, theatre, paintings, posters and T-shirts. In addition, they were also used to interpret and reinterpret tradition, using the past to shape the present but also to create the future.

Those who have studied the liberation struggle have argued that the cultural, political and philosophical principles that guided the collective life of the fighters were based on the idea of creating a multi-ethnic, egalitarian community (see e.g. Pateman 1990). The fronts described their intention to be the creation of a national democratic and revolutionary culture (ELF 1971, 1975; EPLF 1977, 1987). To fulfil this aim, the fighters had to be schooled in the new ideology in order to be free from all the undemocratic, non-revolutionary and non-national backward cultural behaviours and tendencies. The mechanisms chosen to achieve this involved providing basic political and cultural orientation, as well as advanced political teachings adapted from revolutionary theories. The latter in particular, were intended to produce a selected corps of cadres who were afterwards to be dispersed among the fighters and the population as a whole in order to teach politics. Their mission was to promote and safeguard national integration and consciousness predicated on common national culture. At the same time, the fighters were being prepared to help lead the fight against reactionary and undemocratic characteristics such as sectarianism, regionalism, religious or linguistic segregation. For example, they were taught how to avoid conflicts that originate from religious and/or ethno-linguistic differences, etc. For this purpose the main organisations established special institutions for political schooling. For instance, the ELF had a school where selected individuals were trained and dispatched to the different organs of the organisation and the population at large. The courses varied from three months to six months, the three-month course focused on Eritrean history and historical materialism while the six-month course included dialectical materialism. The EPLF also had similar programme. Through such political teaching and general cultural campaigns, the fronts sought to strengthen the common national culture.

In short, the cultural and political teachings were intended to promote thinking and actions consistent with a national spirit. All linguistic, religious and ethnic barriers to integration were to be fought. The broader objective, which was the most important mission of the revolution in terms of culture, was the creation of a common overarching cultural identity that transcended the sub-national characteristics. And it was in that context that the NLM sought to construct an integrated collectivity. In polyethnic societies, beneath the common national culture can be found sub-cultures, social positions and roles grounded in family, kinship, regional, religious, and ethnic or linguistic affiliations. Further, these categories of sub-culture inevitably lead to role allocations and conflicts in relationships. The diversity and complexity of roles constitutes the common national culture of polyethnic societies, allowing for the strategically situated to dominate. The relationship of these sub-cultures is therefore characterised by a perpetual, competitive co-existence, not necessarily in an antagonistic environment, at sometimes even in a situation of complementarity. As components of an overall national culture, diversity and complexity will always encompass elements of contradiction, sometimes leading to hostility. In brief, it is in this context of a diversity of culture that the agents of the NLM, grounded in the modernisation project and social engineering, attempted to fight the backward and divisive elements of the culture and in its place create a new common national culture which would recognise and accept complementarity.

It is very difficult to appraise the success of this project of social engineering undertaken by the NLM. In some specific and concrete areas, it is relatively easy to observe the outcome. The issue of language could be taken as one example. After the brief introduction of both the Tigrinya and Arabic as languages of instruction in schools and as languages of bureaucratic administration under the British Administration and in the Federation respectively, the society was deprived of the chance to use its own national languages in the formal public sphere. It was under the NLM that Eritreans got the chance to learn and develop their languages in schools and use them in the public sphere. Within the fronts, the fighters were instructed in the Eritrean languages. National languages also became the chief medium of instruction in schools and learning institutions organised for the civilian population. These developments led, perhaps, to what Ernest Gellner would call the emergence of an educationally mediated standardisation of culture. Or what Benedict Anderson identifies as print-capitalism's role in creating imagined community by disseminating uniform information and knowledge across space and time. The space allowed for Eritrean languages in the NLM undoubtedly contributed to the broad expansion in written and spoken form of at least the Tigrinya language. Many members of the different ethno-linguistic groups developed the ability to write, read, and speak the Tigrinya language. Arabic was already developed as an international language. Perhaps another local language which could have advanced along with Tigrinya but which showed limited progress was the Tigre language. Some of the reasons for this limited progress can be found in the policy differences of the two main fronts. Whereas the EPLF focused mainly on Tigrinya and Tigre, the ELF focused on Arabic and Tigrinya. Informed sources observed that when books were printed in Tigre by the ELF, they were burned because of objections from some sections of the ELF that the expansion of the Tigre language might compromise the position of Arabic (Negash 1999: 56-60). Overall, the development of national languages, through which the majority of the people can communicate, seen in terms of the emergence of a common culture and thereby in the process of nation formation, is an indispensable fulfilment.

In conclusion, relatively speaking, it would not be unwarranted to propose that through the long journey of the liberation struggle–and even before that as the consequence of the colonial capitalist penetration, a general Eritrean civic or political culture developed. In particular, the historical experience of the liberation struggle has, more than anything else, integrated Eritrean society. Hence, an encompassing common culture developed as a result of that bitter historical experience. Paraphrasing Renan, the will to achieve great things collectively developed out of the legacy of past history imprinted in the memory, which remained a driving force for achieving a further common future. The drawing of this inference has to be understood against the orthodoxy of culturalist approach, these days known as cultural fundamentalism, which conceptualises culture as inherently connected with one homogeneous specific social group and in a primordial context.

CONCLUSION AND SUMMARY

In concluding the chapter, it is appropriate to review and accentuate certain central points. As was pointed out at the beginning of this chapter, common history and common culture are treated together. This is not because they are the same, but because the development of the one (common history) leads to the development of the other (common culture). It is said that, "Culture is more often not what people share, but what they choose to fight over" (Eley and Suny 1996: 9). In this sense, common history is about fighting over something, and the consequence of fighting over something constitutes culture. The long history of oppression and exploitation under both European colonial rule and the Ethiopian occupation has obviously produced a historical repertoire of its own sort. This historical experience of a century-long period has undoubtedly generated a common history full of common sacrifices, common commitments and common achievements. Consequently, this common history rendered possible the development of a shared civic culture through which Eritreans could interpret their experience, guide their future and claim a common national identity.

As with any liberation movement, the Eritrean liberation movement claimed the legitimacy of its common history and an all-encompassing common civic culture. It claimed that during those prolonged years of colonial rule, a history was created that bound together the people inhabiting the territory of Eritrea. This might be considered as compensation for what is seen in the eyes of some observers as a short episode in a long experience of struggle. Numerous ups and downs marked the long nationalist struggle. Yet, it is argued that those ups and downs, which have unfolded along the historical trajectory, actually constitute the common history of the Eritrean society. Eritrean nationalist mythology invokes its legitimacy rather more clearly from the war of liberation and colonial experience (cf. Sorenson 1991: 312). During the liberation struggle phase, Eritrean nationalism constructed a suitable historical mythology in order to establish the just and legitimate nature of its struggle. Thus, expressed in concrete terms, Eritrean identity invokes its legitimacy on the basis of two fundamental points: first, the creation of Eritrea as an integrated entity by Italy, with the birth of Eritrean legal territoriality, and second, the tortuous and lengthy history of the liberation struggle.

History, as a segment of time, perceived both synchronically and diachronically, is built of accumulations of episodes, which together constitute the idiographic identity of a society in the form of what is called culture. Culture, in the final analysis, is what the accumulation of these historical episodes produces. The memories, institutions, value-systems, norms and ethos regulating the political and economic behaviours of the social interactions produced and accumulated along the projection of history bestow upon a people its culture. The Eritrean people, through the projection of its history of colonial oppression and exploitation can be said have developed a common culture through which its common identity is reflected and manifested. The persistent conflict between being ruled and occupied by alien powers on the one hand, and the simple aspiration to be master of one's own house on the other, characterises the political culture of Eritrean society. Common Eritrean culture is composed of the activities and manifestations which occurred along the path of history, either as a result of the manifestation of the activities that have emanated from the above, notably from its rulers (Europeans and Ethiopians), or the ones that have emerged from below, that is, as a result of the social activity of the people itself. In short, it can be maintained that a common culture has emerged with which the people can identify, and which, as Eritreans, they cherish and are willing to make sacrifices for. These were sometimes conscious, such as with the fronts' intentional efforts to create a new society, or at other times unconscious, as with simply moving with the flow of their common history. Culture, thus, is comprehended as the accumulated product of the historical events, episodes and experiences of Eritrean social history. Finally, this account of the emergence of a common civic culture is intended to serve as an indication of the fulfilment of one of the presuppositions for the emergence of nationhood.

Notes

1. In the literature of nation formation simple history and culture are typically used. Here I use common history and common culture to emphasise the history and culture we are talking about refers to the history and culture which is shared in common by the various ethno-linguistic groups. Therefore common history refers to all historical occurrences since 1890, at which time the various ethno-linguistic groups were brought together as a result of Italian colonialism and which is shared by all of them. Common culture, also refers to the transcending civic culture encompassing the various ethno-linguistic groups and which is the result of their common historical experience. A common culture was produced by the political process of formation of the Eritrean nation. As such, it is a political culture.
2. The account of the life in the field is given from the personal experience of the author and from some general observations by other writers. In fact, this part of the Eritrean revolution merits a thorough study. To date, no systematic and comprehensive research has been done. Indeed it is an interesting area which can produce useful sociological work. The fighters were not only expected, but were required to reject all so-called primordial reactionary and antidemocratic sentiments and tendencies. Such feelings and sentiments include sectarianism, regionalism, reli-

gious segregation, localism, etc. When a fighter was asked, for instance, from which village, town or part of the country he or she is he or she was to answer that he or she is an Eritrean and comes from Eritrea. It is common that people in Eritrea identify each other by telling from which part of the country they are. This new attitude is intended to eliminate such parochial views and show others that such characteristics hamper unity and should be eliminated. In their place, national identity should be emphasised. Maintaining such habits and customs in any way was construed as backwards, reactionary, antidemocratic and anti-national, thus, all sought to show that they were free of these shameful attitudes, actively participating in the struggle to eradicate them. Political education, propaganda and mass medial campaigns strongly stressed the necessity to counter such feelings and attitudes–not only among the fighters but also in the society. Harbouring such attitudes and feelings was considered almost as a crime. In the political programme from the EPLF's First Organisation Congress we find the intention to: "Destroy the bad aspects of the culture and traditions of Eritrean society and develop its good and progressive content" (EPLF 1977:28). This indicates how the fronts were making efforts to create a new society. It is in this sense that life in the Field was to function as a cultural melting pot, in which members of the different ethno-linguistic groups were to be blended, and metaphorically expressed, to emerge metamorphosed afterward as a 'new man' (or woman). The fronts pursued this philosophy consciously and actively, because, on one hand, the need for the creation of a united, disciplined and well-integrated fighting army was enormous, but also because it would serve as a good model for the whole society. Accordingly young children were organised in pioneer associations, to be the embryo of the new society under construction, under the names *Tzebah* (dawning), *Keyih Embaba* (red flowers), indicating that they were the pillars of tomorrow's generation. These elements, seen from the process of nation formation, can be considered to be what scholars of nation formation identify as an intentional effort by the modernising intelligentsia in the project of nation-building.

Chapter 8

THE WILL TO LIVE TOGETHER: NATIONALISM

INTRODUCTION

This chapter deals with the growth of Eritrean nationalism. It seeks to trace how the Eritreans developed the will to live together. The will to live together is an intriguing dimension. It can be viewed, on one hand, as the culmination in the fulfilment of the necessary requirements for the rise of a nation, or as a prerequisite for the emergence of those requirements. According to its proponents (e.g. Renan [1882]1991,Schulze 1996: 97-99), when the will to live together of members of a group is achieved, it can then be said that a nation exists. Here it is implicitly acknowledged that there are different degrees of the will to live together, which a community may display during various stages of its history. The will to live together, as a subjective feeling represents nationalism, therefore, they are treated here as one. Nationalism, it is argued, invents nations where they do not exist (Gellner 1983). It is argued too that nationalism replaced religion as the primary integrative force of society in modern time (James 1996: 86, McCrone 1998: 10). In the modernist orthodoxy, nationalism is a recent development, originating in the latter half of the eighteenth century (Smith 1998: 1). It is the child of modernism. It became a force that "broke down the various localisms of region, dialect, custom and clan and helped to create large and powerful nation-states, with centralised markets and systems of administration, taxation and education" (Smith 1998: 1). It stood counter to oppressive imperial tyrannies and declared the right of all people to form their own state. However, the popular and democratic version of nationalism was paralleled by an oppressive, imperial and fascist official nationalism (Seton-Watson 1977, Anderson 1991). In general, we find two analytical approaches to development of nationalism. These are nationalism from above and nationalism from below. The former refers to state or elite-generated nationalism while the latter pertains to mass nationalism. Nationalism is typically initiated by a small group of elite, and gradually to be embraced by the whole population.

Miroslav Hroch (1985:23, 1994) identifies three phases in the development of nationalism: (a) Phase A: the period of scholarly interest - intellectuals seek to construct cultural identity through employing various iconographic elements; (b) Phase B: the period of patriotic agitation - political activists seek to win over as many members of the community as possible; and (c) Phase C: the rise of a mass national movement.

When a group develops a sense of belonging and affiliation and the values, myths and symbols which identify it as a group are commonly accepted and reflected by all members, the will to live together–a conscious one–is believed to be solidly crystallised. This, in turn, is an indication of a transcendence from elite to popular nationalism. Socialisation, internalisation and routinisation of those values, myths and symbols influence this popular will. Nationalism functions here as an important ideological instrument in accomplishing this. It makes effective use of print-capitalism in disseminating nationalist ideas. In Gellner's (1983) formulation, the priests of the high culture (cultural nationalism) will make sure that popular nationalism will be inculcated through mass standardised and academy-supervised educational system.

A brief comment regarding the meaning, interpretation and definition of nationalism might facilitate our understanding of the amorphous concept of nationalism. In the ever-expanding literature on nationalism, we encounter a perplexing array of definitions. Therefore, without getting trapped in the plethora of definitions and interpretations–yet to give a hint of what we are dealing with–I will provide a couple of examples. But first, nationalism is defined in one dictionary of political thought as: "1. The sentiment and ideology of attachment of a nation and to its interests. 2. The theory that a state (perhaps every state) should be founded in a nation, and that a nation should be constituted as a state. Hence, the attempt to uphold national identity through political action" (Scruton 1982: 315). Some visible examples are as follows: nationalism is sometimes juxtaposed with national sentiment, while at other times it is equated with nationalist ideology and language. Yet others associate it with nationalist movements. In addition, we have a differentiation on the basis of either the cultural or the political aspects of nationalism. Hutchinson (1994: 122) strongly urges that we should distinguish between cultural and political nationalism, arguing that these are two entirely different types of nationalism, and, therefore, should not be confused. It has become quite possible to differentiate between 'political' or 'civic' nationalism on the one hand, and 'cultural' or 'ethnic' nationalism on the other (Calhoun 1997: 88). Calhoun delineates three dimensions of nationalism. These are (i) nationalism as discourse, (ii) nationalism as a project, and (iii) nationalism as evaluation (Calhoun 1997: 6). The first dimension refers to the production of cultural understanding and rhetoric which enables people to yearn for nation and national identity. The second dimension concerns social movement and state policies intended to promote the interest of the nation, aiming at one or more of the following: greater participation in an existing state, national autonomy, independence and self-determination, or the incorporation of territories. Finally, the third dimension of nationalism refers to political and cultural ideologies that claim superiority for a particular nation. In an approach similar to that of Calhoun's dimensions, Seton-Watson (1977) distinguishes two meanings of nationalism. One meaning refers to 'a doctrine about the character, interests, rights and duties of nations', and the other refers to 'an organised political movement, designed to further the alleged aims and interests of nations'. For Gellner (1983) nationalism is simply a political principle which uphold the congruity of the political and the national unit.

These differing definitions of nationalism can be simplified into three distinct categories: a) sentiment (a feeling of belonging), b) ideology (a belief that a group constitutes a nation) and c) movement (a struggle for the creation of nation-state or to preserve an already existing one represented by political organisations and states). These three aspects of nationalism may manifest themselves simultaneously–or exist separately. When they appear separately, they typically show different stages of development. For instance, while sentiment can often be seen as the lowest stage, ideology represents the middle stage, and finally, movement, the upper stage. When it reaches the movement stage all three are manifested simultaneously. The stage of sentiment represents the existence of a loosely defined feeling. While the stage of ideology can be seen as marking the rise of an elite who formulate a national ideology, the stage of movement arises when a transition from the formulation of idea to organised action takes place. Movement can be peaceful or violent.

In the view of most Western scholars, the rise of nationalism in Africa is the result of opposition to colonial rule, anti-colonial nationalism (cf. Hodgkin 1956, Smith 1983a, Markakis 1987, Anderson 1991, Gledhill 1994). The principal premise accentuated in this view is that because of economic exploitation and political oppression, people are compelled to rise against colonial powers. In this sense nationalism is viewed as a movement against alien powers. Another dimension of colonialism is bureaucratic centralisation. The salient role played by colonial rule is the creation of a centralised bureaucratic political units accompanied by urbanisation, the creation of market centres and the emergence of modern classes and elites. Moreover, colonialism is believed to have spurred nationalism by depriving the indigenous societies, particularly the new intelligentsia, of its twin creations–notably, the new economy and the state (Markakis 1987: 70). The new intelligentsia targets the state as the epicentre of public goods. This conceptualisation of nationalism, therefore, perceives the struggle of the colonised societies as directed not *against* the state, but rather, for all intentions and purposes, its conquest. After all, as Bruilly (1993) notes, nationalism is a form of politics, and politics is the acquisition of state power. Supporters of this argument believe that it is the intelligentsia's alienation from state resources which is the underlying motive for the emergence of nationalism.

To assess the development of Eritrean nationalism along the three stages of nationalism (sentiment, ideology and movement) mentioned above, we can sketch the following picture: While the period of Italian colonialism (1890-

1941) can be represented as the sentiment stage, the short period between the collapse of Italian rule and the rise of political parties (1941-1946) can be represented by the stage of ideology. The period of 1947-1991 can be represented by the last stage. This third stage latter can be divided into two periods: the time of peaceful political activity between 1947-1961, and the armed struggle of the National Liberation Movement (NLM) between 1961-1991. The third stage combined all three categories of nationalism. Furthermore, the development of Eritrean nationalism can be presented as shown in Table 8.1. The table illustrates the opposition by Eritrean groups to external intervention over the indicated historical period, and its impact on the development of Eritrean nationalism.

According to the scheme pursued in this study, we can roughly identify three stages corresponding to the three types in the evolution of Eritrean nationalism. The first stage refers to the beginning of total Eritrean colonisation by Italy during the period 1875-1890. This is designated as "resistance nationalism", and represents the "incubation stage". The second stage, the period from 1890-1952, is identified as "anti-colonial nationalism", and represents the "formation stage". The third, period, from 1952-1991, is identified as "independence nationalism". It represents the "maturation stage". The distinction of the three types and stages of nationalism helps to elaborate the route of development of Eritrean nationalism, demonstrating important differences among the three. While "resistance nationalism" refers to opposition by the various ethno-linguistic groups to the domination attempts of the Abyssinians, Egyptians and the Mahdists, "anti-colonial nationalism" was directed against established European colonial rule. "Independence nationalism", on the other hand, refers to the political and armed struggle against Ethiopia aiming at realising independence.

One important contention of this study is that a diversity of identity is compatible with the formation of a civic nation in a multi-ethnic society. The type of nationalism that characterises multiethnic societies is, thus, by necessity, civic nationalism. In the model of civic nation, a multiplicity of identity is quite possible–as long as a process of disintegration grounded on that diversity of identities is not actively pursued. Based on this view and through introducing the concept of divided nationalism, this chapter will investigate the development of Eritrean nationalism. The focus is on the territorial and civic dimensions of nationalism. Territorial nationalism refers to territorial affiliation, whereas civic nationalism refers to political affiliation (see Smith 1983a, 1983b).

The chapter consists of the following sections: A Prelude to Nationalism, The Development of Nationalism, Nationalism based on Islamic Identity, Nationalism based on Christian Identity, Ethno-linguistic Diversity and Duality of Identity. Under the heading Prelude to Nationalism, the roots of Eritrean nationalism are traced. The section on the Development of Nationalism discusses the growth of Eritrean nationalism. The sections on Nationalism Based on Islamic Identity and Christian Identity discuss the key division in Eritrean nationalism. Finally, Duality of Identity investigates the two levels of identity, the sub-national and the national.

Table 8.1 Development of Eritrean nationalism

PERIOD	EXTERNAL FACTORS	INTERNAL FACTORS	TYPE	STAGE
1875-1890	Abyssinian attempt to subordinate the highland of Eritrea	Resistances by: Rasi Woldenkeal, Bahta Hagos	Resistance	Incubation
	Egyptian move to conquer Eritrea; Mahdists attempt to control the Moslem lowland	Resistance by various groups of the lowland region, e.g., Kentebai Hamid		
1890-1941	Italian exploitation and suppression; land expropriation, deportation, incarceration, killing, etc.	Organised (like the Bahta Hagos uprising) and unorganised opposition to Italian rule.	Anti-colonialism	Formation
1941-1952	British Administration & Political liberalisation	IB – independence UP - union with Ethiopia, Movements		
1952-1962	Federation and its infringement	Workers', students', the Federalist Youth League, anti-union parliamentarians, etc. opposition	Independence	Maturation
1961-1991	Ethiopian occupation	NLM – armed liberation struggle for independence		

A PRELUDE TO NATIONALISM

The aim of the present section is to give a brief account of the various external interventions and the subsequent elements of resistances immediately before the start of Italian colonialism. These, I believe, can be considered to be the forerunners of Eritrean nationalism. This period witnessed active, interrelated movements involving various actors in the region that came to be known as Eritrea. These actors included the Abyssinian State, Egyptian-Sudan and the Missionaries. Their activities were decisive in influencing the destiny of the people. It seems that already then, the consolidation of Eritrean identity had begun to take root. The people of the Bogos, the Mensa and the Catholics in Akkele Guzai sought European protection from both Egyptian-Sudan and Abyssinia. Rubenson (1976) argues that this marked the beginning of the conception of Eritrea. Emperor Yohannes' attempt to subordinate the highland of Eritrea sparked resistance. Haggai (1982) notes that the people of Hamasen could not accept the infringement of their autonomy by Emperor Yohannes. The Mahdist movement alienated several of the Moslem communities from the Sudan, while at the same time the raids by Alula estranged them from Abyssinia. Consequently, many elites from both the highland and the lowland readily embraced the presence of the Italians in Massawa (see Yohannes 1991). This represented a clear distancing from both the Sudan and Abyssinia. The gradual expansion of Italy also led to the intensification of political pressures from three directions by three separate political powers.

The Italians from their coastal base, the Mahdists from Omdurman, and the Menelik from central Ethiopia were moving to squeeze Eritrea (Lobban 1976:337). Lobban argues that this three-power squeeze, and its resultant implication in the sense of political entrapment, set the stage for the later development of Eritrean nationalism. He continues to argue Eritrean nationalism began to develop as a result of resistance to this alien expansionism. However, he concludes that nationalist spirit rarely developed to the level of mass movement. According to Lobban, this was because there were too many consecutive colonial regimes that replaced one another. This, in turn, gave no chance for the development of a mass nationalist movement (Lobban 1976: 340).

To study the resistance of this period more closely, it is helpful to examine two particular movements more closely. Emperor Yohannes' attempt to place the highland of Eritrea under his absolute dominance is one of these. The second is the Mahdist Islamic movement's expansion to the lowland of Eritrea. The respective communities sought to resist this intrusion, and some co-operation against common enemies took place. Once the Italians were stationed in Massawa, many of the leaders of these communities began to collaborate with them. Resistances were sometimes sporadic while at other times it could be quite organised. The significance of this types of resistance, one could suggest, is that they constituted the foundation of Eritrean nationalism, marking a definite point of mental mapping of exclusivity in the perception of the people. They began to set boundaries between themselves and their immediate neighbours. This could reasonably be called the first marker towards Eritrean nationalism. First, it signified the starting point for the 'we' and 'they' distinction, which is a fundamental characteristic of nationalism. Second, it was used effectively by later Eritrean nationalists to invoke legitimacy in the resistance against Abyssinian attempts to conquer Eritrea. Third, it was used by Eritrean nationalists as a justification of their belief that Eritrea was not a part of Ethiopia when it was colonised by Italy. Fourth, it was used in the NLM as a historical reference point of Eritrean resistance to external intervention (see EPLF 1987a).

This can also be seen against the background of the nationalist movement's effort to construct national mythology. Mythology is perceived here as an important element of nation formation. It is common knowledge that nationalist movements create their own mythologies by elevating convenient events – and conversely by suppressing unpleasant episodes – and by constructing real or imagined narratives that evoke deep sentiment. Anderson (1991: 5) argues that in the historian's eye, nations are modern whereas, in the eyes of the nationalist, they belong to antiquity. Eritrean nationalists referred to this period as representing the temporal roots from which Eritrean nationalism could be traced. The theme being followed here is that aggression produces resistance and resistance creates national identity.

Acts of aggression were committed at this time, leading to resistances led by Degiat Bahta Hagos in the Akkele Guzai region, by Kentebai Hamid Hassen from the Habab tribes and Rasi Woldenkeal in the Hamasen region. The most famous was the one led by Rasi Woldenkeal Solomon. This resistance was given a high profile in Eritrean nationalist discourse, describing it as a nationalist resistance against a foreign aggression. In depicting one of the battles (of 1878), the literature of the Eritrean nationalists recalls that the army of Woldenkeal, fighting for their land and their rights, marched courageously onto the field of battle and butchered the invading army of Rasi Baraiu. And when the invading army fled, they chased them and caught them one by one. This chasing and catching led to the naming of the place as Haz-haz (meaning catch-catch) (EPLF p. 15). The relevance of such historical narratives is in the role they play in constructing historical legitimacy for the cause that the people cherish–and for which they fight.

It is believed that the highland region had its autonomy when Rasi Woldenkeal started his resistance. Erlich (1982: 16) notes that: "With their long tradition of self-government, the people of Hamásén could not easily accept the appointment of an outsider... Thus, Alulá's nomination stimulated support for Rás Walda-Miká'él, and many left for his camp in Halhal, Bogos". It was against this infringement of his autonomous political power that he led his resistance. His resistance might be categorised as the political resistance of a privileged group - nationalism from above as Bruilly would call it (cf. Bruilly 1993). The resistance continued for a couple of years (discussed in earlier chapters) and Woldenkeal was able to score important victories on the battlefield that left strong, lasting memories. One such battle, to which the poem below refers, took place in Asmara in 1878 (see Perini 1997: 81-2). According to Perini, an army of ten thousand led by Rasi Bariaiu Gebretzadiq was defeated, and Rasi Bariau was himself killed in the battle on May 20, 1878 near Bet Meca'e (Erlich 1982: 21). Popular songs and poems appeared in commemoration of those victories, which Eritrean nationalists successfully utilised as historical evidence for their interpretation of the Eritrean history. Such poems were:

Wekharya Adi Segdo tzegibki'do	Fox of Adi Segdo are you satisfied
Wekharya Arbate Asmera tzegibki'do	Fox of Arba'ate Asmera are you satisfied
Wekharaya Asmera tzegibki'do	Fox of Asmera are you satisfied
Wekharya Bet Mekha'e tzegibki'do	Fox of Bet Me'kha'e are you satisfied
Tzegibe'we Weldu zeharedo	Yes I am satisfied thanks to what Woldu slaughtered

Hakhele ghedife brindo	Not only of bone meat but also of red meat

The forces of Rasi Woldenkeal were not able to sustain a protracted resistance, and eventually their resistance was defeated. When Rasi Woldenkeal surrendered in the aim of reaching peace with Emperor Yohannes and was taken prisoner, his adherents did not appreciate his action. The poem below expressed the disappointment.

Girazmatch'do iluka aimewiteen	who told you Girazmatch does not die,
Fitewrari'do iluka aimewiteen	who told you Fitewrari does not die,
B'lata'do iluka aimewiteen	who told you Belata does not die,
Degazmatch'do iluka aimewiteen	who told you Degezmati does not die,
Senadirka zebelkaien bteen	to disperse your Schneiders,
Ktrekib Kitsi'en zeiti'fteen	to succeed or fail you should have tried.
Halhal'do ailekan tznu'e meriet	you have Halhal strong fortress,
Senader'do ailekan tzinu'e biret	you have Schneinder strong weapon,
Intai a'iteweka nab senselet	why should you end up in prison?
	(EPLF pp. 15-16, no date, trans. mine)

To adequately understand and interpret these poems in the context of the formation process of the Eritrean nation and nationalism, an analytical theoretical framework is necessary. Therefore, we turn to Benedict Anderson's celebrated thesis of imagined community. By way of deduction it is plausible to extract from the poems at least three points which have relevance to the emergence of imagined community: a) cherishing victory over invaders–or to borrow Renan's expression 'to have performed glorious deeds'; b) resistance and defiance; and c) one's homeland as fortification. The importance of victories is not only emphasised by theories of nation formation. An enquiry into the Eritrean liberation struggle will show how the Eritrean nationalists employed battle victories in the nation-building process. Scholars of colonialism also stress the connection between the resistance to foreign rule and the emergence of nationalism. Homelands, with their terrains, mountains and valleys, are depicted from a historical perspective in the literature of nation formation as important symbols, providing shelter and fortification against enemies. The importance of homeland as fortification in the poem ("you have halhal strong fortress"), for instance, in terms of territoriality carries a symbolic salience which contributes to the crystallisation of the imagined community. In that respect the poem connects symbolically two distinct regions and communities, the highland and the lowland, thus, indicating the beginning of the emergence of the territorially based imagined community. The culture of resistance and defiance epitomises myth making of a 'forefathers' legacy' type.

The geographical perimeters (territorial limits) of the imagined community are flexible, but not limitless. An imagined community, in Anderson's meaning, emerges when a group visualises a number of people who have never met, but who reside in a certain territory which they all share in common and assume to constitute a nation. The poems could, then, be understood in terms of the contribution they make toward the conceptualisation of an imagined community. This could be made clear by pointing out two things: one, that the forces of Woldenkeal retreated to the Halhal region which was outside their natural homeland, and second, the poem refers to Halhal as providing a strong fortress, thereby making connection between two regions. Of course, one has to admit that one can legitimately argue that the territory where the historico-political act which the poems refer to have taken place encompasses only a limited geographical area compared with the territory later to constitute Eritrea. Nevertheless, its significance can be considered to have implications beyond the contemporary geographical limitations of the time. Later nationalists, for example, could invoke historical origin, like the Moslem League's claim that the Eritrean people were connected by history (Memorandum of Moslem League to the FPC 1947).

Its implication can be understood in two other significant ways: first, it embodies the symbolism of defiance and representation of the collectivity which frequently is preserved through conversion into folk tales–although the members of the collectivity might not (often do not) have a direct contact with and knowledge about each other. Second, it sets a precedent, providing the basis for continuation in that this region was eventually to constitute the central administrative capital of Eritrea. Consequently, all Eritrean nationalists have regarded the location of the administration centre as a common national symbol, which, in turn, was an important political symbol in the construction of an Eritrean nation and nationalism. In other words, it constituted a centre that the peripheries could rally around for symbolic and practical leadership.

Symbolically, this space and the accompanying events became an important spatio-temporal and historical reference point for Eritrean nationalism–part of the repertoire of events and memories. Certainly, the poems were used in the liberation struggle to stimulate and construct what Anderson (1991: 20ff) refers as national imagination. The cherishing of homeland, defiance and victory were intended to contribute to the constitution of a common imagination. Anderson cites poems from materials he has gathered from Indonesia and the Philippines that support his thesis of imagined communities. In parallel, it is possible to make use of his method to interpret our Eritrean poems.

In conclusion, what is important with such elements of resistance is their implication for the psychology, emotion and sentiment and the formation of national consciousness and identity of a people, either as an immediate effect or as a part of the repertoire of national memories. Therefore, in that respect, their influence on the later nationalist movement was of no small significance. Important evidence of this is the widespread use of the above-cited poems in the political and historical education of the NLM. We will next discuss the way in which these events, coupled with the impact of the colonial state generated Eritrean nationalism.

THE DEVELOPMENT OF NATIONALISM

Now, after the brief examination of the circumstances immediately prior to the Italian colonial period in the preceding section, we will proceed with our exploration of the development of Eritrean nationalism. An assertion that can safely be made is that the events and resistances discussed in the previous section, coupled with the economic transformation that occurred under Italian colonialism, formed the basis for Eritrean nationalism. Following the elaboration of the three stages of nationalism we made earlier (sentiment, ideology, movement), we could say that Italian rule generated what we have called the sentiment stage. This stage gave way, during the first half of the British Administration (1941-1946), to the ideology stage, in which a group of elites debated Eritrea's destiny before forming political parties. The third stage, the movement stage, according to our scheme encompasses the period of 1947-1991, which includes the peaceful political movement and the armed liberation struggle.

In depicting the causes of nationalism in Africa, Smith (1983a: 50) highlights a number of factors that can be attributed to the colonial state. These include the emergence of a single political community, the establishment of territorial centralisation, the growth of a unified economic system, the promulgation of statewide laws and regulations, and the introduction of taxation and conscription. All this, Smith argues, brings about territorial affiliation and consciousness. While the resistance preceding colonial rule in Eritrea was primarily based in particular ethnic groups, the emergent nationalism – which would be born under colonialism and was to mature during subsequent periods – encompassed the whole society. The awareness of a common identity, brought into existence as a result of colonial rule, was a continuation of the inchoate identity that was present at the start of Italian colonial rule. A result of the factors pointed out by Smith, Eritrean society first came into existence as the outcome of colonial engineering.

Taddia (1990: 164), discussing the formation of Eritrean nationalism notes, "the evolution of Eritrean nationalism has been linked to external domination and internal socio-economic change brought about by colonialism itself". In the theory of colonialism, the deprivation and alienation of the elite from the state, and the overriding conditions of oppression and exploitation are presumed to lead to the emergence of national consciousness and nationalism. The logical extension of this proposition would be the stance that African nationalism is founded on the territorial consciousness sparked by colonialism. Taddia argues that "social differentiation and the emergence of class structure contributed to the rise of nationalism" in Eritrea.

One line of argumentation attributes the emergence of Eritrean nationalism to the resistance against European colonial exploitation and oppression (see e.g. Sherman 1980; Leonard 1982; Davidson 1980; Houtart 1982; Pool 1979,

1983; Killion 1985, Taddia 1990). Another line of argumentation attributes it to the marginalisation and suppression of Eritrean culture and identity by Ethiopian regimes (e.g. Elrich 1983, Wolde Giorgis 1989, Araya 1990). Generally, both arguments rest on the theoretical explanation that maintains that "exploitation/oppression leads to resistance".

Theories of exploitation and oppression are used to explain the material and social changes that are made possible as the outcome of colonial exploitation and oppression. On the other hand, the theory of resistance is associated with political consciousness and the concomitant opposition to domination. According to the first argument (and a guiding theoretical framework in this study), the economic exploitation and social oppression (racial discrimination) under Italian rule is assumed to generate collective national consciousness. The socio-economic transformation that took place under the Italian colonial regime established the material conditions that fostered Eritrean nationalism in the 1940s (Killion 1985: 274). The socio-economic transformation also generated new urban and salary-based social groups. These new social groups played a leading role in the nationalist movement of the post-Italian period of political activity. The small group of intelligentsia that was the outcome of the limited educational opportunity was employed by the state as teachers, clerks and interpreters. When the Italian colonial state collapsed, this group was among the most affected, and thus became a source of political agitators and organisers. They were motivated by the loss of privileges they had enjoyed under Italian rule. They were also disappointed by the fact that they did not gain from the opportunity that surfaced with the demise of Italian rule. That is, when Italy was defeated, they expected to take over the jobs that had been occupied by the Italians. Instead, the British kept the Italians in their posts.

The theory of resistance explains that the resistance also aims at the state. Accordingly, the activity of political mobilisation in colonised societies focuses on conquering the state's power. Eritrean society, like any colonised society, was politically mobilised for the purpose of 'capturing the state' (Markakis 1987: 67-70). This statement is in agreement with Smith's idea that the underlying motive of African nationalism was to conquer the "territorial-bureaucratic state" inherited from colonialism (Smith 1983a: 51). In Eritrea, while the picture concerning the mobilisation of the various ethno-linguistic groups during the post-Italian period is clear, the picture concerning resistance under Italian rule is less conclusive. Many observers contend that Eritrean resistance to Italian rule was absent, an argument used by these observers to support the claim of the non-existence of Eritrean nationalism under Italian rule (cf. Trevaskis 1960). Pateman (1989), however, argues in support of the existence of a considerable resistance to Italian colonial rule. Indeed, the actual manifestation of nationalism as an active and organised political and social activity in Eritrea emerged largely after the collapse of Italian colonial rule. Yet, this outcome was also a result of the accumulated changes and pressures reflecting the transformation process that Eritrean society underwent under Italian colonial political economy. Therefore, overall, it is possible to suggest that Italian colonialism generated Eritrean nationalism through the socio-economic transformation it brought about. Commenting on the broad effects of Italian colonial rule, Erlich (1983: 4) writes:

> The period of Italian rule contributed by its very length to the strengthening of Eritrean awareness, especially among those who underwent urbanization or served in the bureaucracy and army, although the Italians did very little to promote internal social cohesion.

A veritable politicisation of the Eritrean society took place during the British administration. Under the British Administration during the War years (1941-1945), Eritreans experienced industrial development which brought about profound social and political integration within the colonial borders (Taddia 1990). The end of the War, however, brought abrupt economic decline. The need to settling the Eritrean question prompted the BMA to permit political liberalisation, permitting the formation of political parties. Once political parties were formed, the work of mobilising of Eritrean society proceeded with great intensity. Commenting on the political mobilisation of this period, Markakis (1987: 57) writes: "Political mobilisation in Eritrea involved a larger proportion of the population than was the case in the Sudan and Somalia, because it affected the pastoralists and subsistence cultivators to a degree not experienced by their counterparts elsewhere in the Horn at this time". This unprecedented level of political activity, however, assumed a double-edged role, demonstrating a powerful desire for democratic self-determination, while at the same time exposing the fragility of the society. Two phenomena that became important causes of instability emerged simultaneously. These were economic deterioration and political liberalisation. The former meant the reduction of resources and job opportunities whereas the latter meant an increase in demands. The combined result was social upheaval. These circumstances led to a divided nationalism.

A marginalisation hypothesis is also suggested as an underlying premise for the rise of Eritrean nationalism (e.g. Erlich 1983, Wolde Giorgis 1989, Tegegn 1989, Araya 1990). Proponents of the marginalisation hypothesis differ in their assumptions of when marginalisation took place. There are those who focus on Hail Selassie's breach of the Federation (e.g. Wolde Giorgis 1989) while others point to the Dergue's marginalisation of the Eritrean economic elite (e.g. Erlich 1983). The prime argument here is that the marginalisation of the Eritrean culture, identity and economy by Ethiopia was the cause for the emergence of Eritrean nationalism. In that sense it is seen as the realisation of the Trevaskisian 'prophecy', notably: "The temptation to subject Eritrea firmly under her control will always be great. Should she try to do so, she will risk Eritrean discontent and eventual revolt, which, with foreign sympathy and support, might well disrupt both Eritrea and Ethiopia herself" (Trevaskis 1960: 131). Trevaskis made his prediction in reference to what would happen if Ethiopia attempted to violate the federal arrangement. The marginalisation hypothesis was particularly concerned with the Christian section of the society. It must be acknowledged that there is at least a grain of truth in the marginalisation hypothesis. It is true that marginalisation of Eritrean culture, identity, institutions and economy took place under the Ethiopian rule. And it is certainly also true that this evoked resistance. The significant problem with the marginalisation hypothesis is, however, that it suggests that marginalisation was the sole cause of the rise of Eritrean nationalism. It fails to pay attention to the changes that took place as a result of the penetration of Italian colonial political economy and their effect on Eritrean national identity. It also fails to take into consideration the political mobilisation that began during the British Administration and its impact on Eritrean nationalism. Further, it also fails to appreciate the national institutions and symbols that accompanied the Federation and the emotional attachment which was forged as a result.

Responding to the marginalisation of and infringement upon Eritrean culture, identity, political autonomy, national symbols and institutions, Eritrean nationalism was transformed into what I have designated here as the third, or movement stage, in the form of the armed liberation struggle. The armed struggle represents an intensification of national resistance. As such, it represented a higher stage of the resistance to domination. As a higher form of the struggle to achieve political sovereignty, it strengthened nationalism in the process. The agents of the NLM undertook a conscious struggle aiming at the consolidation of the Eritrean nationalism and nationhood. In that sense, there is little doubt that in the NLM, Eritrean nationalism really reached its pinnacle. The following table presents a brief summary of the various types of nationalism, which are deduced from the literature on nation and nationalism. Using the next table, we are able to locate the forms taken by Eritrean nationalism at various historical stages.

We find eleven types of nationalism highlighted in Table 8.2. Seven of these eleven types can be recognised in the development of Eritrean nationalism. Earlier (Table 8.1) we identified three main types of nationalism, notably "resistance nationalism", "anti-colonial nationalism" and "independence nationalism" which also appear in Table 8.2. The remaining four types appearing in the Table are "unionist", "irredentist", "political" and "territorial" nationalism. These four types can be separated into two groups, with "unionist" and "irredentist" on one side, and "political" and territorial" on the other. This grouping rests on (i) temporal factors, and (ii) aim. While "unionist" and "irredentist" were seen for a short time after the demise of Italian colonialism, "political" and "territorial" characterise virtually the entire period (1890-1991). In that sense, they overlap with "anti-colonial" and "independence nationalism". Concerning the second underlying factor of the grouping, the aim of nationalism, we can say that while political and territorial nationalism seek to build a state based on political and territorial identity, respectively, unionist and irredentist nationalism aims at joining another state or annexing part of a state, respectively. An additional point which perhaps requires further clarification is that in Table 8.1, three basic types of nationalism were highlighted. These have been extended to seven as shown in Table 8.2. As previously mentioned, two were ephemeral while two

Table 8.2 Summary of Types of Nationalism

TYPES OF NATIONALISM	AIM	ITS MANIFESTATION IN ERITREA
Resistance	Resist domination, conquest, etc.	Against Mahdist Sudan and Emperor Yohannes of Abyssinia.
Anti-colonial	Abolition of colonialism	Against Italian colonialism and British Administration.
Unionist	Join another state	The Unionist Party and the Moslem League of the Western Province with Ethiopia and the Sudan respectively.
Independence	Achievement of independence	The IB of 1940s, the NLM against Ethiopian Occupation.
Irredentist	Claim on people/region with "similar" ethnic identity	The ML and the LPP claims on territories in the Sudan and in Ethiopia.
Political	Building state based on political identity	The struggle for independence of the NLM and the political struggle of the 40s and 50s.
Territorial	Establishment of territorial state	The aspiration of Eritreans for sovereignty is based on a territorially based identity.
Separatist	Establishment of a separate state	No
Cultural	Establishment of a culturally unique state or recognition of cultural identity	No
Ethnic	Establishment of an ethnic state or recognition of ethnic identity	No
Diaspora	Aspiration for a homeland	No

others overlap with the two basic types of nationalism. This leaves us with our original three basic types of nationalism.

To briefly examine the manifestation of the seven we will try to locate them in their historical trajectory. The first to be identified is resistance nationalism, manifested in conjunction with resistance against the Egyptians, Mahdist Sudan and Emperor Yohannes of Abyssinia. The second is the anti-colonial nationalism which spans Italian and British rules. In the third and fourth places come both independence and unionist nationalism. Unionist nationalism was displayed by the UP's wish to join Ethiopia and by the desire of the Moslem League of the Western Province to join the Sudan. The IB represented the independence nationalism of that period. In addition, independence nationalism incorporates the NLM. Fifth, irredentist nationalism was displayed during the 1940s when the ML and the LPP claimed territories from both Ethiopia and the Sudan. In the sixth place comes political nationalism, which represents the political struggle of the 1940s, 1950s and National Liberation Movement. Finally, Territorial nationalism refers to the overriding process. Eritrean identity and nationalism is based on territoriality. The remaining types of nationalism – separatist nationalism, cultural nationalism, ethnic nationalism and Diaspora nationalism shown in Table 8.2 – have not been observed in Eritrea.

In conclusion, in studying Eritrean nationalism, while recognising the impact of foreign domination, due attention should also be paid to the inherent need for projecting one's own identity. It was the sense of need to have one's own culture, identity, and the ability to determine one's own destiny - simply to constitute one's own state - which was the basis for Eritrean nationalism. Anderson's assertion that every society, regardless of its level of socio-economic development aspires to constitute its own state seems to fit quite well here. Eritrean nationalism has traversed rough terrain. In our view this complex terrain constitutes the Eritrean body of nationalism. We now turn to several dimensions of this terrain.

DIVIDED NATIONALISM

The appearance of two dominant political parties, the Moslem League (ML) and the Unionist Party (UP), which more or less summoned their social bases from the two main religious communities apparently led to different interpretations of Eritrean nationalism. A very simplistic though dominant view is that Christians endorsed Ethiopian nationalism while Moslems supported independence. Moreover, this division was seen as a reflection of Christian identity versus Islamic identity. The dominance of members of the Moslem communities in the early stages of the armed struggle also reinforced this view. In this conceptualisation, the Christian section was presented as first (pre-federation) endorsing Ethiopian nationalism, and later (in the NLM) reluctant to join the nationalist camp because its interest was accommodated within the Ethiopian state.

In this and the following two sections I discuss the divided nature of Eritrean nationalism. I argue that the division should be understood from within the context of a polyethnic nationalism. In describing, above all, the post-Italian colonialism political schism between the various elites, and the attendant cleavage of the NLM, it also seems to be appropriate to discuss it in the fashion of divided nationalism. According to some observers (e.g. Longrigg 1945, Trevaskis 1960, Erlich 1983, Negash 1987), the division into two competing versions of nationalism that surfaced in the aftermath of Italian colonialism was irreconcilable. The division was interpreted as one between Ethiopian nationalism, as embodied in the UP, and separatism, as represented by the ML. This view is not only too simplistic. It is also incorrect. In particular, it is the juxtaposition of the demand of union with Ethiopia as Ethiopian nationalism, and the view that portrays all Christians as proponents of that union, that I believe is erroneous.

A reasonable alternative interpretation is that the cleavage basically represented two variants of Eritrean nationalism. Indeed, the reason behind the division was the different choices made to resolve the question of Eritrea's destiny. In very general terms, it is true that the division that surfaced between the ML and UP appeared to rest on the religious identities. This was because union with Ethiopia was unacceptable to many Moslems and independence to many Christians seemed unfeasible. Having said this, however, we must bear in mind that many Moslems also supported union while many Christians wished for independence. In addition, for example, *Mahber Fikri Hager Ertra* was a multi-religious organisation until 1944 (see The Weekly Eritrean Newsletter 1941-44). Therefore, the gross generalisations (Christians versus Moslems) conceal an important reality.

In explaining the divided nationalism of the post-Italian rule, we can trace the underlying, contributing factors to divisions in structural and historical dimensions. In terms of the structural dimensions, we look to a) socio-economic dimensions, and b) religious dimensions for explanation. Eritrean society's socio-economic dimension was split into two formations - a sedentary agricultural socio-economic formation and a nomadic pastoral socio-economic formation. Within the religious dimension, the society was largely divided into Christian highlanders and Moslem lowlanders. A variety of historical factors are added to these structural differences, among them are: 1) the uneven distribution of the impact of the colonial political economy in the socio-economic transformation of the society; 2) the Italian policy of treating the different religious communities in different ways; and 3) the Italian portrayal of itself as the protector of Islam during its occupation of Ethiopia (see Killion 1985). The socio-economic change that resulted from the Italian colonial political economy was largely concentrated in the Christian highland, whereas the Moslem lowland was only peripherally affected. In Asmara, the Italians established different residential areas for the Christian and Moslem communities and traditional and religious customs and laws were enforced in each religious community. This reinforced primordial differences, thereby deepening religious division. Consequently, the national movement of the post-Italian era was divided based on sectarianism.

British policies contributed little to ameliorate these already precarious relations. Because they found it corresponded with their overall strategy, the British encouraged the formation of political parties based on sectarianism. Moreover, they were actively engaged in promoting Islamic identity and Christian identity because they believed this would lay groundwork for their scheme of dismembering Eritrea. For instance, they paid special attention to the promotion of learning Arabic. By importing books from Egypt, they actively sought the expansion of Arabic, and extra emphasis was placed on the relationship of the Moslem communities with the Sudan. They simultaneously encouraged the promotion of the Tigrinya language and the relation of the Tigrinya speakers with the Tigray province of Ethiopia. In some British circles too, the idea of uniting Tigrinya speakers from both Eritrea and Tigray under some sort of

British protectorate was seriously entertained as late as the end of the 1940s (Erlich 1983: 4f, see also FO 371-35633, 1943).

Theorists of identity formation argue that multi-ethnic societies display multifaceted identities and loyalties (cf. Duara 1996). The constitutive identity and loyalty in such societies fluctuates, at times reflecting subnational identities and loyalties and at other times emphasising the national level, yet, without totally negating the one or the other. These competing identities and loyalties form a complimentary relationship (Eriksen 1993). As far as they are not seeking to deny each other, and allow themselves to operate within the diversity of identity and loyalty, the internal cleavage remains as a struggle for dominance within a common framework and structure. Struggle for dominance, when exercised within a reasonably acceptable unitary framework – that is, where the aim is not to create different states – merely plays the role of reinforcing a competitive nationalism within a single confinable national framework. In this form of nationalism, in spite of the competition and cleavages, there exist some basic values recognised and accepted by all parties. In the case of Eritrea, the basic value rested on the recognition of the territory created by Italian colonialism.

In spite of the cleavages generated by structural and historical factors, however, the colonial political economy succeeded in integrating the socio-economic systems of the various ethno-linguistic groups at the colonial economic and administrative superstructure level (Killion 1985: 287). Manifestations of this development were witnessed in the political positions taken during the debate of the disposition of Eritrea, which confirmed the existence of basic values with which all parties identified. The rejection of partition, a denominator common to all parties, and the unacceptability of annexation for the majority of parties are only two of these manifestations. A further and important illustration was the acceptance of the resolution of the Untied Nations by the political parties–in the name of unity. According to the BA-Eritrea report (FO 371-90316 March 1951), the parties interpreted the outcome of the UN debate as congruent with their position. A vital element in the UN resolution was the preservation of the territorial integrity of Eritrea.

Partition was rejected. The remaining solution was that either a unified Eritrea would join Ethiopia, or become independent. The option of federating it with Ethiopia became a compromise solution. This compromise solution was accepted by all parties, and in the *Wa'ala Selam* (Peace Conference), they pledged to work together to preserve the Federation. The question that arises here is: why was the compromise solution accepted if the division was as claimed by some, between Ethiopianism and Eritreanism or between Islam and Christianity? This shows that at the bottom of the schism rested a lack of consensus on the options that presented themselves at the time concerning the destiny of Eritrea. The emergence of an independent Eritrean state appeared in the eyes of unionists as a solution lacking a safety valve to protect their aspirations, thus independence was seen as impracticable solution. Conversely, in the eyes of the ML, either union with Ethiopia or partition was unacceptable. Indeed, it was this absence of a commonly accepted solution coupled with the intervention of external forces, which was the underlying basis for the divided nationalism. The Federation became the mutually acceptable solution thereby laying the groundwork for a common Eritrean nationalism.

Some authors, referring to the pre-federation nationalist movement claim that virtually all the Christians preferred unity with Ethiopia (e.g. Trevaskis 1960, Erlich 1983, Negash 1987, Araya 1990). Furthermore, this was perceived as solid indication of Ethiopian nationalism. Conversely, the opposition to unity with Ethiopia and to the scheme of partition was portrayed as an opposition only of Moslems (see e.g. Sorenson 1993: 45). Separating himself from the proposition which sees Moslem nationalism versus Ethiopian nationalism as being the underlying reason for the Eritrean cleavage, Markakis (1987) takes a materialist view as the primary cause for the conflict. He argues, focusing on the twin creation of colonialism, the state and the new economy, that the lack of access to the state and subsequent economic and social disadvantages spurred the Moslems to oppose Ethiopian rule. Meanwhile, the Christians, who believed they would be able to dominate the autonomous Eritrea, allied themselves with Ethiopia. He continues to argue, however, when it became clear to them (the Christians) that their idea had been an illusion, they joined the nationalist movement. This view perhaps could be supported by none other than the first Chief Executive, Tedla Bairu, who in a 1969 interview with the Swedish newspaper Dagens Nyheter said that, "we wanted to create bigger state, however, it was not our desire to be subordinated under an authoritarian system". Markakis too, contends that it was struggle for political power that fuelled the continuous conflict between the Eritrean nationalists.

Before moving on to the next two consecutive sections that deal with the two strains of nationalism that emerged in the 1940s, let us devote a few words of precaution to save ourselves from reifying this division. This dichotomization, based on the religio-linguistic category of Islam/Arabic and Christian/Tigrinya identity of Eritrean society, has been criticised as too simplistic, "reducing complicated relationships to a single binary opposition" (Sorenson 1991: 305). It is true this distinction of identity has its flaws. Indeed, it should be qualified by identifying and recognising all the relevant variables that give the dichotomization its full meaning. These variables must include the structural and historical dimensions discussed above because, within the dichotomised groups, there were to be found considerable differences. For instance, within the lowlander/Moslem category there were internal differences such as ethnicity, language, and religion. Similarly within the highland/Christian category there could also be found ethnic, religious and linguistic differences.

Nationalism Based on Islamic Identity

In the debate on the politics of cultural identity, religion is regarded as one of the components of the construction of cultural identity. As we saw earlier, an association (Moslem League) representing the Moslem communities was established in 1946. Since then, the Moslem communities began to be mobilised on the basis of their religious identity. The ML, which emerged to counterbalance the activities of the unionists, strongly rejected the partition of Eritrea as well as the scheme to incorporate it in Ethiopia. Instead, it demanded the immediate independence of Eritrea with its present boundaries intact. To stress the League's representativeness of the whole of Eritrea, it stated its belief in the peaceful and harmonious co-existence of the Moslem and Christian communities. What appeared to have taken the BMA by surprise was the implacable position of the League with regard to incorporation with the Sudan,

> The League's firm opposition to any form of union with Ethiopia has been no secret for some time past, but its refusal to consider the incorporation of any part of this territory within the Sudan has come as a surprise to those who have thought along the easy lines of a partitioned Eritrea. In this, one may see the first signs of an immature Eritrean nationalism; the Moslem leaders have demanded the "return" of the Beja people in the Kassala province, and have hinted that they are ready to support any Christian demands for the inclusion of the Tigrai within greater Eritrea. From this there may develop a virile Eritrean nationalist movement (FO 371-63212, No. 13 Monthly Political Report January 1947).

As was indicated previously, the League entertained the view that Eritrea was a Moslem country. This belief was indeed grounded in an assumption of the geographic and demographic preponderance of the Moslem communities (FO 371-80984). Geographically speaking, the Moslem communities inhabited 4/5 of the total territory. Concerning demographic composition, however, both Italian and British documents showed a rough balance between Moslem and Christian communities. In spite of this fact, the League continued to believe that in terms of both demography and geography, the Moslem communities represented an absolute majority.

> The Eritrean people are divided into two parties. One is Mohammedan and the other Coptic. The former Mohammedans are two thirds of the population and they occupy nearly nine tenths of land (FO 371-69365, FPC: Report on Eritrea, Appendix 103, Memorandum from the Moslem League 1947).

The leaders of the ML, in their quest for national identity and sovereignty, looked to other Islamic and Arab communities and movements for inspiration and support. For instance, in seeking the independence of Eritrea during the debate over the disposition of Eritrea in the UN General Assembly, they sent telegrams *inter alia* " the Arab League in Cairo and the Moslem League in India" (FO 371-63212, No. 13, Monthly Political Report January 1947). In doing this, they were apparently associating themselves with the contemporary movements for independence in the Middle East and India. With the Middle East in particular, they had close contact through the Arab League. The leadership of the ML frequently stopped in Cairo on their way to New York to present their views in the debate on Eritrea in the United Nations, exchanging ideas with the organisation's officials. Ostensibly, the emergence of independent Arab states and the mobilisation of Indian Moslems under the Moslem League (to form Pakistan) have been an important inspiration for the Eritrean Moslems in formulating their nationalist idea.

The need to have a connection with the Moslem world was also strengthened by Ethiopian involvement and the Unionists' and the Church's association with Ethiopia. This was, in fact, encouraged by the British. Noticing the precipitation of the conflict in Eritrea after the collapse of the Italian rule, Markakis (1988: 52) comments that "most Moslems were alarmed by Ethiopia's claim to Eritrea". The connection between Ethiopia and the unionists became clear to them after the *Wa'ala* Beit Giorighis (cf. Wilson 1991: 21). They came to realise that the only way to challenge the cause of union was by building a countervailing Moslem association. In the view of the leaders of the League, the ML was intended to represent the interest of all Eritrean nationalists. This was clearly indicated by the endorsement of both Tigrinya and Arabic as official languages of the League (Markakis 1987: 65). They also emphasised their beliefs regarding the indivisibility of Eritrean society, which they thought was called forth by the economic interdependence and a common colonial history which bound the communities together.

> Eritrea is a unit which can, by no means be subjected to partition; because life had bound the inhabitants of the high lands to those of the low regions by vital economic necessities. So in the past as in the present, for the same reasons, they have always remained solidly together to a degree that makes their separation an impossibility. Another factor that had strengthened the social relations in all respects was the centralized administration of the regions for a period of nearly 60 years (FO 371-69365, Appendix 103, Memorandum from the Moslem League 1947).

The formation of the ML gave the cleavage a religious form. This was first of all because the various ethno-linguistic groups that formed the League were gathered under the banner of Islam. Second, Islamic values and norms were invoked as the basis of identity, though this was seen as compatible with secular national identity. This compatibility of Islamic identity with secular national identity could be explained by three factors: a) since the Moslem communities constituted the "majority" then their identity represented the national identity, b) the congruity of sub-national identity and national identity - probably it was seen that there did not exist contradiction between the two identities, c) the Moslems were compelled to form the League because of the fact that the unionists became more and more "servants" of the Ethiopian state.

More than a decade later, after the formation of the NLM, the leadership of the ELF too advocated a close relationship with the Arab world. In their diplomatic campaign in the Arab world, they tried to present the Eritrean question as an Arab and Islamic question. The strong Arab influence at this period was, most probably, strengthened by several factors. First, because the veteran political leaders were stationed in exile in Egypt and Syria, they came in close proximity to the liberation struggles in the Arab world, particularly that of the Algerians and the Palestinians. Second, many Moslem students were pursuing their studies in the Middle East, particularly, in Egypt who played significant role in initiating the struggle for independence. Third, many of those who joined the armed struggle in the first couple of years came from the Sudanese army. Fourth, many Eritreans were sent to the Middle East for military training, which certainly influenced their outlook. It has also been suggested that the Arab influence on Eritrean Moslem nationalists originated from their knowledge of the Arabic language. It is argued that this enabled them to be aware of what was going on in the Arab world through reading Arabic newspapers and listening to radio programmes in Arabic (Ammar 1992). The independence of Sudan in 1956, the emergence of Gamal Abdul Nasser as a secular nationalist and the symbolic role this played (particularly for Eritreans in the Diaspora, in Cairo) and the Algerian liberation struggle all had an important influence on the Moslem intellectuals and political leaders (Toteel 1997, Nawid 1997).

Beyond the external influence originating from the Arab countries in the form of inspirational, diplomatic, material and cultural dimensions there is an important endogenous factor which serves to explain this ideology of identity. This is an identity embedded in Islam and the Arabic language, a religio-linguistic dimension. Introducing this dimension is also to introduce a cultural approach. A common thread binding the Moslem communities was that they drew their identity from Islamic values, norms and belief-systems. Being composed of various ethno-linguistic groups, a cultural device was needed to bridge the ethnic and linguistic discrepancies that characterised them. One of the appropriate devices in bridging those differences was to be found in the Arabic language, which through the common domain of religion encompassed the various ethno-linguistic groups. This political-cultural construction of identity had two functional objectives. The first was constructing a collective identity that rests on common denominators of religion and a transcending sacred language. The second objective was to use it as an instrument in seeking political power in order to strengthen the imagined collective identity. In the sense of the former, identity was to be constructed based on Islam and the Arabic language since Arabic, as a religious language, binds the various ethno-linguistic groups professing Islam. In the latter sense, it served as a means of competition for power between elites. Therefore, although there were genuine aspirations for having a language that was connected with transcendental cosmological beliefs, instrumentalist political motives also proved to be influential. Some political leaders and intellectuals have conveniently attempted to utilise this in the past, and still do.

The connection with the Arabic language was important for many reasons, particularly for the intelligentsia. As Pierre Bourdieu, in his seminal work, *Language and Symbolic Power (1991)*, has persuasively expressed it, language is not only an instrument of communication, but also a medium of power. The intellectual significance of Arabic for the elites of the Moslem communities was first, that it enabled them to associate themselves with a literate culture of an international standard. This provided both emotional and intellectual satisfaction. Second, it enhanced their competitive capability in the internal socio-cultural and political competition, against the challenges of the dominant Christian Tigrinya-speaking ethnic group. To resist domination by the largest ethno-linguistic group, therefore, it became a rational political strategy to converge on the Islamic-Arabic language identity. During the armed struggle and guided by this conceptualisation, many political leaders from the Moslem communities used the formula applied by the ML, that is, unifying the Moslems around Arabic and Islam. This dichotomization, which found its supporting rationale in the wish to create socio-cultural symmetry, was not theoretically and empirically grounded anchorage. Rather, it was built on the political constructional strategy of a power play.

> during the first two decades of armed struggle in Eritrea, the Moslems held absolute power in the revolution and wanted to keep it. Generally speaking, they were of the opinion that the Eritrean cause was theirs first and that only they could faithfully guarantee its fulfilment and then safeguard it (Ammar 1992:104).

By the early 1970s, the belief regarding the demographic preponderance of Moslems and its attendant Arab-Islamic identity started to wane–if not by design, by necessity. However, marginal groups continued to champion the ideology (Osman Saleh Sabbe, *Legna El Sewria* - the Baathist oriented ELF-PLF Revolutionary Committee). The conditions which brought about the change could be described as: 1) the realisation of the obstacles to reaching the goals of Eritrean nationalism that were created in the diplomatic sphere as a result of the pursuit of that ideology; 2) a sense of the tension it created within the ranks of the NLM; and 3) the social and demographic changes taking place in the composition of the liberation army. Consequently, the sense that the demography of Eritrean society consisted of more or less equal halves began to become the dominant mode of thinking, replacing the 'majority-minority' view of the 1940s and 1960s. This strengthened the sense of a social equilibrium. By embarking on such a new formula of identity, the ideology of domination was then set aside. Instead of striving to dominate, the tendency shifted towards the creation of a socio-cultural and political balance which was to be based on a socio-cultural bifurcation, in other words, a continuation of identity based on the Islam/Arabic and Christian/Tigrinya nexus, but now of two equal and balanced halves. Since power relationships provided part of the basis for such views, the sense of insecurity and suspicion again began to emerge when the actual balance of strength between the two rival organisations (ELF and EPLF) started to shift, starting from the end of the 1970s and through 1980s.

During the 1980s, there emerged groups who specifically emphasised the Arabic/Islamic vs. Tigrinya/Christian identity of Eritrea (e.g. the Abdullah group in ELF since 1982, the Jihad movement since 1989). Perhaps the attempt of some elites to rally the Moslem communities around an Islamic-Arabic bloc can be explained by the theory of the symbolic construction of group identity. According to this theory, whenever a group feels an actual or imagined threat directed against its basic value systems and norms, it acts forcefully to preserve those substantial value systems and norms. To escape domination, the group seeks to reinvigorate its primordial identity and uses it as a bargaining strategy. In an attempt to preserve their norms and value systems and to avoid domination, elites from the various ethno-linguistic groups of the Islamic faith had emphasised their affiliation to Islam and the Arabic language. Accordingly, on several different occasions attempts were made to create a common objective for all Moslems.

From the above account we can safely conclude that collective identity has quite often been connected with power. Power relationships governed all the shifts of emphasis on the ideology of identity. It is clear that in spite of the sectarian subnational identity, there had developed an Eritrean national identity, nationalism grounded upon territoriality. A clear identification with territorial entity created by Italian colonial rule was revealed on several different occasions (see Chapter 5). We have seen the rise of the territorial awareness or perception that arises from the recognition of the existence of a centralised territory and the affiliation with it. What we have here is the conflation of cultural nationalism embedded in religion and language, on the one hand, and territorial nationalism resting on a colonial created territory, on the other.

Nationalism Based on Christian Identity

This sub-section analyses the view of nationalism based on Christian identity. Unlike the Moslem League or the Jihad movement of the late 1980s and 1990s, there never emerged any organisation under the name 'Christian'. Neither were there individual politicians who openly advocated the promotion of Christianity during the liberation struggle. Therefore, the assessment could not be based on specific organisation's or individual's view. As we have seen earlier, it has been suggested that before the advent of Italian colonialism, a highland identity was already in the making, generated by the continuous autonomous status of the region (see e.g. Dilebo 1974, Rubenson 1976, Erlich 1982). Research also reveals that Italian rule, particularly toward the end, had contributed to the growth of "Tigrinya nationalism". Italy, in fact, is believed to have encouraged the development of "Tigrinya nationalism" during the invasion of Ethiopia in order to weaken Ethiopian opposition. This was further reinforced by the annexation of Tigray to the new governate of Eritrea, established in 1938. This, in turn, is assumed to have led to the subsequent emergence of "Tigrinya nationalism" as one of the leading political movements in the 1940s (Killion 1985: 288). However, this Tigrinya nationalism took on a divided form. From 1944, two separate parties claiming to represent the Tigrinya ethnolinguistic group started to evolve in the Eritrean political arena. These were the

UP whose platform was the union of Eritrea with Ethiopia, and the LPP, supporting independence for Eritrea and incorporating Tigray into its agenda.

The effect of the Italian socio-economic transformation was greater in the Tigrinya community than elsewhere. This resulted in the emergence of a small group of Tigrinya-speaking intelligentsia who were employed by the colonial state as interpreters, clerks, and teachers. When the state collapsed this group lost all its prerogatives. The British takeover of Eritrea was also accompanied by the continued domination of the bureaucracy by the Italians, providing no new employment opportunities to the Tigrinya intelligentsia. The appropriation of more land for Italian commercial projects under the British rule also contributed additional strain at a time in which there existed an already acute shortage of land. Those who were hoping for the return of land that was formerly theirs (among them the Church) were disappointed. Meanwhile the Emperor was making promises to return land to its owners if Eritrea would join Ethiopia. The socio-economic situation of these groups deteriorated dramatically after 1943. Overall, the Christian community – and the middle class in particular – was hit hard. To this was added the conflict with Moslem traders (the Jeberti and Arabs) and the Sudan Defence Force. The incident of 1946 between members of the Sudan Defence Force and some elements of the Christian community led to serious riots. This incident, according to some observers, might have led to the aborted compromise proposal of "the creation of autonomous Eritrean state within a federal union with Ethiopia" between the unionists and Christian-Tigrinya independents which culminated in the Bet Giorgis Meeting (Killion 1985:307). The accumulated effect of these events and developments generated political and economic chaos in the territory.

After the failure of the Bet Giorgis Meeting and following the formation of the independence Bloc, the Christian-Tigrinya in the LPP joined the Bloc. The extensive unionist terrorist campaign, combined with the Italian involvement in the Independence Bloc led to the fragmentation of the Bloc. The Christian independents were, thus, disillusioned. Many of the Christian-Tigrinya led by Abraha Tessema deserted the Bloc to form the Liberal Unionist Party, upholding the idea of the conditional union of Eritrea with Ethiopia (Ellingson 1977: 278, Killion 1985: 215). The rapprochement between the Christian-Tigrinya sections demonstrated the prevalence of strong Tigrinya ethno-nationalism, though yet, it vacillated between independence and union with Ethiopia. This vacillation was, however, to change following the creation of the Federation and the attendant encroachment of Eritrean autonomy by Ethiopia (cf. Greenfield 1964, Ellingson 1977, Markakis 1987, Sorenson 1991).

One question that arises here is whether the desire for union with Ethiopia could be considered to be equivalent to Ethiopian nationalism? No consensus exists regarding the answer to the question. Ethiopian nationalists and Ethiopianist scholars argued that it was Ethiopian nationalism. The underlying assumption of this argument was that Eritrea had always been part of Ethiopia. Therefore, it was claimed when the aberrant period of separation came to an end, the Christians wanted to rejoin the motherland. This inference was also partly drawn from the supposition of the existence of cultural, linguistic, ethnic and historical connection between Eritrea and Ethiopia. Consequently, it was argued that it was natural that the Christians should display Ethiopian nationalism. For proponents of this argument there is no difference between Eritrean Christian identity and Ethiopian nationalism (see Rubenson 1976; Erlich 1983; Wolde Giorgis 1989; Negash 1987, 1997). The adoption of such views leads to the conclusion that the Eritrean Tigrinya ethno-linguistic group did not develop an identity of its own. Undoubtedly, religion and language, as central elements in the construction of cultural identity, appear to have had an important significance in the social construction of identity of the Christian community. But this ethno-religious identity was divided at this particular point in time between union with Ethiopia and independence in regard to the future of Eritrea. The vacillation between the two alternatives was driven by complex factors that extended from the need of preservation of one's identity to the attraction of the practical benefits union could presumably bring. It was also either weakened or strengthened by the feelings of insecurity, suspicion and consternation generating internally from the Moslem communities and, externally, from the Italians, the British and other minority foreign groups.

An argument that counters the contentions of "Ethiopian nationalism" is the one based on the interest hypothesis. According to the supporters of the interest hypothesis, the driving force that propelled the unionists to seek union was their belief that by joining the Ethiopian State, they would be able to safeguard their interest. It is argued that in the aftermath of the collapse of Italian colonialism the traditional elite thought that the opportunity had come to restore their pre-colonial power and status (Gebre-Medhin 1989, Iyob 1995: 65). This, according to their calculation could be possible only by joining hands with the aristocratic class in Ethiopia. Among the new intelligentsia also there was a conviction that, since Eritrea was relatively more developed than Ethiopia, they could assume a dominant position in the union (see Killion 1985, Markakis 1988, Gebre-Medhin 1989, Tesfai 1997).

Two points need to be emphasised in discussing the ethno-national identity of the Tigrinya ethno-linguistic group. These are the autonomy of the highland before the advent of Italian colonialism and the material change which occurred during Italian rule. As we have seen earlier, the highland was autonomous, except for the ten year (1879-1889) rule of Alula, the representative of Emperor Yohannes. As Dilebo, Rebunson and Erlich have testified, it was the encroachment upon this autonomy that led to the resistance of Woldenkeal. This suggests that already then there existed some sort of identity. To this must be added the socio-economic change that took place during Italian rule. It is to be recalled that both the LPP and UP were of the view that Eritrea was more developed than Ethiopia. This was expressed by the LPP, for example, in that their rejection of union with Ethiopia was based partly on that country's backwardness. The UP, taking an opposite view of the same circumstances, was convinced that because Eritrea was more developed; they could play a dominant role in the union. From this, it would be clear that the Tigrinya ethno-linguistic group had developed both ethno-national and territorial identities.

In the theoretical discussion of identity formation, the existence of the significant Other is emphasised. It is also indicated that, depending on the situation, the position of the significant Other shifts (Eriksen 1993). When a group is in conflict with another group it defines its own identity vis-à-vis that significant Other group. After the collapse of the Italian colonial rule, the situation that emerged was a state of uncertainty and chaos with respect to the future of Eritrea. It was in this situation that the various groups were faced with the urgency of defining their identity. In the process of asserting their identity, the unionists were engaged in defining their identity in relation to the significant Other. The significant Other(s) against whom their identity was to be defined were the Italian settlers, the occupying power (BMA) and the Moslem communities. Targeting these groups, the unionists, for instance, directed strong attack against the Italians and the Arabs in Eritrea through the weekly newspaper called *The Voice of Eritrea* issued by the 'Ethiopia-Hamasain Society' from Addis Ababa. They further blamed the Administration for incompetence, and of being the cause of the misery of the Christians (Trevaskis 1960: 66). Later, as mentioned earlier, the unionists changed their significant Other. When it became clear to them that their identity could not be respected in the new association, the position of the significant Other was shifted. Highlighting this point, Markakis (1987: 145) notes that the Christians, when the Federation agreement was violated and their right to be masters of their own house was taken away from them, joined the nationalist camp. The significant Other, against whom the assertion of identity was to be directed now became Ethiopia.

The literature on identity formation points that religion per se is by no means adequate for constituting nationalism (see Eriksen 1993). It must be supplemented by other symbolic and material dimensions. The insufficiency of religion as a sole determining factor of nationalism is clearly demonstrated by the fact that many of those Christians who were believed to have advocated unconditional union because of their religious affiliation changed their mind. This change of mind occurred when the Ethiopian State began to infringe upon the rights and institutions that represented unique Eritrean identity (cf. Greenfield 1965: 305, Markakis 1987: 145). This means that nationalism based on Christian identity needs to be accounted for in the context of the internal Eritrean socio-cultural and political settings.

Of course, neither in the 1940s nor during the armed struggle did there arise any group on the banner of Christian/Tigrinya identity. As we saw earlier, the formulation of Christian/Tigrinya vs. Islam/Arabic identity came from the Moslem elites. The unionists have always wanted to unite a unified Eritrea with Ethiopia. To that end, serious attempts were made to win the Moslem communities over to their side. As matter of fact, as Gebre-Medhin's (1989) work shows, about half of the leadership of the UP were Moslems. Ostensibly the union of Eritrea with Ethiopia benefited primarily the unionists. And in general, compared with the Moslem communities, the Christians were more advantaged, since it was relatively easier for the Christians to occupy high posts in the Ethiopian State. This also became a reason why, in the early stage of the armed struggle, they were less welcomed (see Sabbe 1974).

To conclude, it seems that the autonomy of the highland, combined with the socio-economic changes under Italian rule generated "Tigrinya nationalism". In the 1940s, it was divided between the choices of independence and union with Ethiopia. This division was gradually overcome when it became clear that it was not the intention of Ethiopia to respect their identity. This ethno-linguistic identity existed side-by-side with territorially-based national identity. Uncertainty of the future seems to have been the main reason for the idea of union and the initial reluctance to participate in the armed liberation struggle.

ETHNO-LINGUISTIC DIVERSITY

We will talk about ethno-linguistic heterogeneity in the present section instead of ethno-linguistic homogeneity, and assess its compatibility to the formation of nation. The concept ethno-linguistic, indicates the overlap of common ethnicity and linguistic homogeneity, that is, it represents a group who claims both common genealogical descent (imagined or actual) and a common language. In general, it is possible to highlight the basic characterising features of an ethno-linguistic group. These are (a) a shared language which distinguishes the group; (b) ethnic identity which members of the group commonly claim to have originated from, imagined or actual ancestry, an ideology of shared ancestry (see Eriksen 1993: 35); and (c) a compact homeland in which the group claims an exclusive right of historical habitat. The claim to an imaginary or factual homeland reinforces the social construction of group identity by maintaining a continuous renewal of the cognitive attachment to it.

In the study of ethnicity and interethnic relationships there are two interconnected sets of concepts involved: the objective/primordial and the subjective/relational. These distinctions are based on the opposition between essentialism and constructionism. According to those who adhere to the objective/primordial set of concepts as an analytical device, ethnicity is understood simply based on certain objectively-given properties of a social group. Followers of the subjective/relational set of concepts see ethnicity as perpetually constructed and reconstructed in a specific societal environment, as such it is perceived as being relational and situational (see Eriksen 1993). Therefore, it is stressed that ethnicity should be viewed as an aspect of relationship, not as the cultural property of a social group. Moreover, Eriksen (1993: 34) argues that in a solely mono-ethnic setting effectively no ethnicity could prevail, because simply there is no other group with whom an act of communicating cultural difference can take place. In discussing the concepts of dichotomization and complementarisation in the context of ethnic relations, Eriksen makes also the following distinction, "whereas dichotomization essentially expresses an Us-

Them kind of relationship, complementarisation can be described as a We-You kind of process" (Eriksen 1993: 27). He further suggests that in an interethnic interaction the process of communicating cultural differences presupposes the existence of mutual recognition of those differences. It is this mutual understanding and acknowledgement of cultural differences that Eriksen has labelled as complementarisation. Eriksen continues to argue that, "ethnicity entails the establishment of both Us-Them contrasts (dichotomization) *and* a shared field for interethnic discourse and interaction (complementarisation)" (Eriksen 1993: 28). While the former represents exclusivity the latter represents relationship and coexistence.

Relating these conceptual and theoretical reflections to the Eritrean case, we are able to identify nine ethno-linguistic groups (as we have seen in Chapter 2). Each ethno-linguistic group generally shares language, claims a common ancestry and occupies a specific homeland. Eriksen's concept of complementarisation would be the more appropriate in describing the relationship between the different ethno-linguistic groups. This is because, unlike the concept of the dichotomization, which rests on the dimension of exclusion, the concept of complementarisation is founded on the principle of mutual recognition and accommodation. The common struggle undertaken by the ethno-linguistic groups – on the one hand in recognition and acceptance of the internal differences, and on the other believing in a common destiny – represents what Eriksen has described as complementarisation. Earlier we discussed very briefly the configuration of the nine ethno-linguistic groups. In this section, the discussion will focus on the characteristics which constitute the identity and interrelationship of these ethno-linguistic groups.

Misunderstanding and misrepresentation frequently mark the treatment of the ethno-linguistic groups. They are quite often presented as clearly demarcated, exclusive, solitary, ethnic and linguistic embodiments. However, as will be demonstrated below, there is substantial evidence, primarily oral, but also documented, that shows that throughout history, cross-ethnic and cross-linguistic hybrids have been present. This forces any purely ethnic categorisation out of reality and into the realm of ideal type. This hybridisation often takes place when individuals or groups (families) for various reasons cross their geographical and ethnic boundaries to live in an alien environment. With the passage of time, they begin to adopt and absorb the language, culture, values, norms and belief-systems of the group(s) of the geo-ethno-linguistic space where they began their new life. After some generations, the group may shed its original anthropological features, becoming entirely assimilated into the new group. What remains from its past is memory, which was conveyed from parents to offspring in the form of oral narratives and rituals. One example that could be mentioned, for instance, is the Bet Asghede, the aristocracy of the Habab, who were widely believed to have originated from among the highland Christians (see Trevaskis 1960: 14).

Terms commonly used to identify the ethno-linguistic groups include the 'highlanders' and the 'lowlanders' (*Kebessawian* and *Metahitawian*), and 'Christians' and 'Moslems', though these oversimplify and misrepresent reality. This understanding represents a simple dichotomization of society. The bifurcation carries with it an implicit or explicit religious connotation. A closer examination discloses that *Kebessawian,* in the common usage of the term, refers to the Christian Tigrinya speakers, while conversely, *Metahitawian* refers to the multi-ethno-linguistic Moslem communities. The usage of these terms quite often reflects the politicised nature of the categorisation, the roots of which can be traced to the British rule and most probably to the formation of the Moslem League and the Unionist Party. Basically, the division embodies geographical distinctions, but it also coincides with socio-economic modes and religious differences. Since the era of parties in the aftermath of the demise of Italian colonial rule, these terms have, in practise, been charged with political meanings and values. Occasional instrumentalist manipulation by various intellectual and political actors in the liberation movement has served to reinforce this politicised dimension.

We have two approaches, one is dichotomization, which divides the society into two separate sections based upon religious affiliation. The other, as described above, exhibits a strong tendency to treat each ethno-linguistic group as an exclusive, individual entity, believed to have no relationship with the various other ethno-linguistic groups. These approaches can be summarised as (a) a bipolar conceptualisation, which sees the society as divided into two blocs, (b) a multi-polar conceptualisation, which views the nine ethno-linguistic groups as totally exclusive entities. Though the latter is much closer to reality, both conceptualisations fail to reflect reality adequately. In addition to the political implications accompanying them, they conceal significant characterising features. For instance, if we take the category of *Metahitawian* (lowlanders), as we have seen earlier, the various ethno-linguistic groups (eight in number) are put into one bloc on the basis of their faith, with no consideration of the ethnic and linguistic elements which differentiate them. Similarly if we take the *Kebessawian* (highlanders) we will discover that there are other non-Christian and non-Tigrinya speaker communities.

In addition to the roots shared between some of the languages (e.g. Tigrinya-Tigre, Saho-Afar, Kunama-Nara), many people have a working knowledge of the larger languages, Tigre and Tigrinya. Moreover, there are ethno-linguistic groups which also use other languages as their own, i.e., they are bilingual. The Nara speak Tigre, Bilain speak both Tigrinya and Tigre, some of the Mensa group speak Tigre and Tigrinya, etc. Regarding ethnic origin, the picture is not so clear as it is often made to look. In the Beni Amer, for instance we find groups who identify themselves as *Kebilet Hamasen* (meaning the tribe of Hamasen and which means they have originated from Hamasen, Tigrinya speakers). Also Ad Bigel (which means Adi Bidel in Tigrinya), indicating that these groups have originated from the village of Adi Bidel in the Hamasen, there is also a village named Deki shihay (sons of shihay, from the Saho ethno-linguistic group) (Pollera 1935: 44), etc. Further, Michael Hasama Raka in his book *Zanta Ertra* (1986) argues that all the ethno-linguistic groups of Eritrea are interconnected by blood and origin. This book, which makes use of oral tradition, illustrates in detail how the different ethno-linguistic groups, not long ago originated from some common areas and families. The author takes as evidence for this the names of many clans, families, and villages that demonstrate a common origin. In addition to the communities' belief in the existence of a shared common descent among various groups, archaeological remains also convinced Raka to conclude that the Eritrean society, contrary to the commonplace view, is highly mixed.

The delineation of the ethno-linguistic boundaries, thus, is characterised by fluidity and flexibility. Nevertheless, regarding homeland, in broad terms, we find relative consistency. Notwithstanding the immigration of groups in search for jobs, farmland, grazing areas, etc. every ethno-linguistic group inhabits a particular region, thereby preserving a relative territorial ethno-linguistic homogeneity. This reality, of course, excludes urban centres, which since their inception have become a gathering place for members of the various ethno-linguistic groups. Further, during the NLM, the blending of ethno-linguistic groups increased in the rural areas. This is because some regions were relatively safer than others due to the fact that they were under the control of the NLM. In addition, people also followed the movements of the fighters. Further, it seems also that scarcity of land in the highland had the effect of pushing Tigrinya speakers to emigrate to the lowland regions while many Moslems moved to the highlands, particulary to the capital city.

It is clear that colonialism generated a transcendent identity based on common historical experience and common memory. The importance of the memory of the historical experience of colonialism to the development of a consciousness of belonging to a commonly inhabited territory is emphasised by scholars of colonialism. Referring to Indonesia, Anderson (1991) describes the effect of colonialism as follows.

> From all over the vast colony, but from nowhere outside it...from different, perhaps once hostile, villages in primary schools; from different ethnolinguistic groups in middle-schools; and from every part of the realm in the tertiary institutions of the capital.[12] And they know that from wherever they had come they still had read the same books and done the same sums. They also know, even if they never got so far - and most did not - that Rome was Batavia, and that all these journeyings derived their 'sense' from the capital, in effect explaining why 'we' are 'here' 'together.' To put it another way, their common experience, and the amiably competitive comradeship of the classroom, gave the maps of the colony which they studied ... a territory specific imagined reality which was every day confirmed by the accents and physiognomies of their classmates (Anderson 1991:121-22).

It is possible to relate Anderson's description to the situation in Eritrea where the various ethno-linguistic groups were brought together and subsequently were able to develop a transcendent common identity. After the legal emergence of Eritrean territoriality in 1890, the different ethno-linguistic groups were amalgamated to constitute a society by the same process and the same political forces as those described by Anderson in the situation of Indonesia. They intermingled and interacted in one or another way and in the various spheres of social life: at school, in the market place, in the workplace, in the Mosque, in the Church, in the bureaucracy, in the army and the police force; in death and in life, shared happiness and sorrows in the NLM, and so on. This consequently enriched their common history, common memory, identity and destiny.

The NLM played an important role in the integration of the various ethno-linguistic groups. Although there is no statistical data to show the quantitative participation of the various ethno-linguistic groups, a general assessment is possible. The participation of the different ethno-linguistic groups varied in degree over time. The overall participation of some groups was relatively more than others, and some groups started to participate earlier than others. The case of two groups, the Kunama and the Afar, can be mentioned here to highlight the matter. The participation of the former was marginal, whereas the latter were among the early participants–even though there had also been some aspirations for a united Afar nation. The long history has certainly integrated the various ethno-linguistic groups into a transcendent, common civic identity. Yet, there remain differences at a sub-national level, which has necessitated the emergence of duality of identity. In conclusion, the caution to bear in mind is that the bipolar understanding violates reality insofar it conceals the differences within the blocs, the multi-polar (ethnicity in its pure form) also fails to properly represent the ethno-linguistic interrelationships of Eritrea.

DUALITY OF IDENTITY

Nation is often conceptualised as a unitary and integral entity. Based on this understanding, nationalist thought often attempts to de-emphasise notions of multifarious identity and loyalty. As Calhoun (1997: 46) notes: "In the discourse of nationalism, one is simply Chinese, French or Eritrean. The individual does not require the mediations of family, community, region, or class to be a member of the nation." Nationalists often refuse to acknowledge the quasi-autonomy of subnational identity and loyalty. Instead they invest great effort to combat ethnocentric sentiments and in its place to create a single national identity. Regarding the situation in Africa, one scholar notes, "the basic dimension of national consciousness seems a multi-ethnic structure, without any reference to cultural and linguistic affinity" (Taddia 1990:168). The major challenge facing African nationalists is to construct a common identity that transcends the sub-national cultural affiliations. In that aim members are expected and encouraged as individuals to converge at the national identity level. Nationalism strives to construct common national identity. Arguing along this line Calhoun (1997: 11) notes, "nationalism is a way of constructing identity that does not address such variations so much as it simply posits temporal depth and internal integration".

The efforts of nationalists to create culturally homogenous and coherent nations out of the polyethnic societies quite often ends in failure. The forms of identity that exist today in the polyethnic societies of post-colonial Africa are multi-levels. This reality appears to have induced an approach that–in contrast to the early nationalists' attempt to reject subnational identities out of a preference for homogeneity–has learned to recognise and accept the different levels of identities as composite elements of a collective identity. There is today also a tendency to see these different levels of identity as constituting complementary elements. This multiplicity of identity can, for analytical reasons, be reduced to two levels, a national and a subnational level. This represents a duality of identity, the concept of which rests on the principle of differential identity grounded in two categories of culture: subnational and national. According to the constructionist perspective, culture is the product of social construction, thus, relational and situational (Eriksen 1993). As such, it is characterised by vicissitudes. A duality of identity can theoretically be interpreted as indicating identity and difference in the inner process of identity formation. The relationship between identity and difference, in turn, refers to the contradiction between identity and difference. The contradiction revolves around the fact that the subnational groups, while at the national level crave to retain their national identity, at the subnational level they strive to maintain their difference in counterpoint to the national. Individuals experience dual identity as members of the subgroup and as members of the nation. Such scenarios are commonly observed in less developed societies - they are transitional phases - if one accepts the modernist perspective. This contradiction, according to the modernist conception of nation formation will be a gradual transformation to the individual vs. the nation.

The notion of the duality of identity will help us to make sense of the ambivalence contained in the various types of identity. This ambivalence of identity may certainly be found not only in polyethnic societies, but also in the so-called homogenous societies. In the latter the ambivalence, or rather, the complexity of identity can take the form of family, inner circles in work places, or political organisation, on the one hand, and identity at the level of the nation, on the other. In other words, in modern complex societies the dominant mode of identity is based on a polycentric rather than a monocentric foundation. The discussion undertaken here certainly touches multiple types and levels of identities. However, the main concern, for the purpose of this study, is the duality of identity, notably the national and sub-national types and levels. These are the ones that have a direct bearing on the process of nation formation. Therefore, in spite of the discussion and various examples illustrating the multiplicity of identity, the emphasis in this work will rest on the dual levels of identity.

Fig. 8.1 The Development of Identity

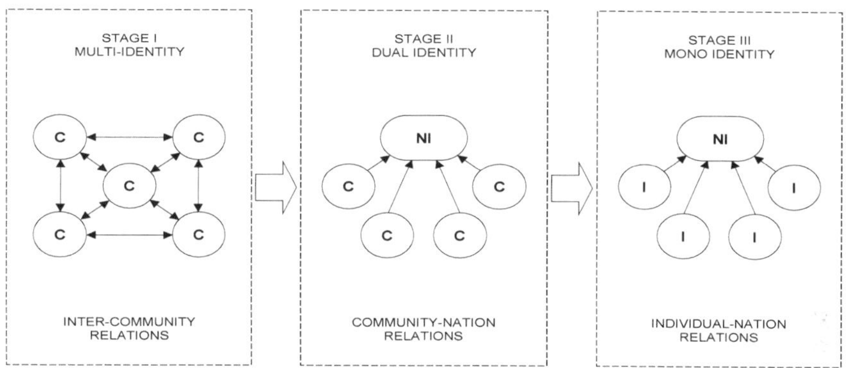

C = Community
I = Individuality
NI = National Identity

Figure 8.1 is intended to present in a very rudimentary manner the evolutionary process of the metamorphosis of identity as is perceived in the classical social theory (see Giesen 1998: 11). As we can comprehend from the above figure the basis of the distinction is the community/collectivity - individuality dichotomy of the politics of identity. For our purpose, in the evolutionary process of the crystallisation of identity in the social history of mankind, three stages are identified. These can be described as multi-identity, dual-identity, and mono-identity. In Gellner's (1983) model these can be represented by the pre-agrarian, agrarian, and industrial stages. In Stage I (multi-identity) the different groups are directly or indirectly interconnected or rather the arrows of relationship are directed in many directions showing an amorphous identity relations in which a collectivity is engaged in a meaningful relationship with various collectivities in a framework of relationships of internality[2]. At this stage the defining factors of identity are primarily the primordial non-political premises. Therefore, the level of an overriding and encompassing structure of identity - nation - has not been reached, thus, the sign NI is absent.

When we reach the second stage the number of arrows indicating relationship are narrowed to a small size, and are patterned only to one direction. Here the various collectivities are patterned in a manner in which their structure of meaningful relationships is arranged primarily toward one central site. A structure of identity emerges in which meaningful relationships of internality give way to meaningful relations of externality, thus building a duality of identity, in the sense individuals pay allegiance both to their own group and to the nation, subnational and national. This type of identity is collective, that is, it is a collective group that has an obligation of allegiance to an internal identity which enters into a relationship with the central entity, the national identity, thus the sign NI . The distinctive development at this stage is that a territorially based consciousness emerges. The collective, by transcending the primordial characteristics which identify it as a group makes a connection to or identification with the territoriality.

A higher body, the state (colonial state) brings about the transcending common identity which through extraction, integration and coercion make possible a transcending convergence of common identity. In the third stage we reach a qualitatively different type of identity. Instead of a collective identification with the nation, we have individuals arranging their own relationships with the nation. We have, in other words, a mono-identity based on the contract entered into between the individual and the nation. All mediations based on group, kinship, region, or religion recede. This view is the fundamental precept of liberal political thought where the individual is thought to affiliate voluntarily with the nation (cf. Greenfeld 1992). This development becomes possible due to the continuous differentiation process in the social structure which gradually sets the individual free from the *collective conscience* (Durkheim 1974) and individuation takes place. The third stage is, according to the scheme implemented here, the highest form which characterises modern nations. What constitutes the identity of the individual is not the set of primordial qualities, but rather civic politics and civic culture, following the civic conception of nation. To locate the stages of development in Durkheim's theme of mechanical and organic solidarity, or in Tönnies' theme of *Gemeinschaft* and *Gesellschaft,* Stage I corresponds to mechanical solidarity and *Gemeinschaft* whereas Stage III corresponds with organic solidarity and *Gesellschaft*. Stage II is transitory. Deriving from this social theoretical perspective we can localise Eritrea roughly as follows. The pre-Italian period can be represented by stage I, in which villages were more or less isolated and there did not exist a binding structure able to rise above the village level. The Italian period and after can be localised in stage II, in which the various villages and ethno-linguistic groups were connected by the structure of territorial integration. Stage III has already begun at this point, and its completion is a goal of the future.

Now we turn to the applicability of the notion of duality of identity to the subject of this study, Eritrea. As discussed earlier, Eritrea is a polyethnic society, composed of nine ethno-linguistic groups. Therefore, the irrelevance of the ethnic or cultural conception of nation to the Eritrean case is indisputable. The alternative, the civic conception of nation, is more appropriate. In spite of internal differences, and since the territorial genesis of present-day Eritrea in 1890, the various ethno-linguistic groups have accepted the present entity of Eritrea. Acceptance of the present entity of Eritrea, however, does not necessarily forfeit the preservation of specific ethno-linguistic characteristics. The cleavages which characterised the society were of a multiple nature. The aspect of cleavage that has relevance to this part of our study, by way of reduction however, is to be limited to the binary division of sub-national versus national identity.

Smith (1994) commenting on the case of Spain, from which an analogy can be drawn to the Eritrean context notes, "yet, most members of these communities share an overarching Spanish political sentiment and culture, over and beyond their often intense commitment to Basque, Catalan or Galician identity and culture". Anderson (1991: 132), in reference to the various ethno-linguistic groups that constitute Indonesia also notes: "Thus, only one of the rebellions of 1950-64 had *separatist* ambitions; all the rest were competitive within a single Indonesian political system". This further supports the notion of the compatibility of the duality of identity notion adopted here. What we have in Eritrea is exactly what Anderson observed in the condition of Indonesia. No part in the Eritrean struggle had a serious ambition for separation; all the cleavages were "competitive"–within a single Eritrea.

From an instrumentalist perspective, the conflict based on sub-national identity could be understood as an internal mechanism of competition either to dominate or avoid being dominated within a shared space. Unlike the idiographic ethnographic feature corresponding to a given ethno-linguistic group, the generic supra-ethno-linguistic features constitute competitive identities. One can belong to the Tigrinya speaking Christian ethno-linguistic group, another to the Beni Amer, while yet another to the Saho, Nara or Belain. Simultaneously, all these individuals can claim a common Eritrean identity. And that claim to common Eritrean identity is based on the overarching commonality of identity which is the outcome of their struggle to determine their common historical destiny. That primordial characteristics are not adequate for the emergence of national identity is now a well known reality. The historical experience of the Eritrean struggle also gives us an ample example of this. There is also empirical evidence to validate the theoretical proposition which prescribes that material interest is one of the basic underlying substances which integrate societies. The rejection of the partition of Eritrea on the basis of ethnic and religious merits, which was intended to lead to the unity of communities of identical ethnicity and religiosity attests to this. The alternative was the acceptance of living together with ethnically and religiously different groups (civic nationalism) on the ground that along the historical excursion a shared socio-economic integration has been achieved. All this supports that a common experience generates the basis for common identity. Shedding light on this aspect of duality of identity, Eriksen notes,

> Being a member of a family does not preclude being a member of an ethnic group; and being a member of an ethnic group does not necessarily preclude being a member of a more encompassing category. However, for that more encompassing group to exist it must be *socially relevant*. It must have some goods to deliver - material, political or symbolic - and those goods must be perceived as valuable by the target group (Eriksen 1993: 76).

Here Renan's famous statement comes to mind: "To have common glories in the past and to have a common will in the present, to have performed great deeds together, to wish to perform still more - these are the essential conditions for being a people" (Renan 1991: 19). The various ethno-linguistic groups of Eritrea have created their common history through their armed struggle which laid a solid foundation for the development of common will which enables them to look to the future (cf. Calhoun 1997: 101). The rejection of the inhabitants of the western lowland of Eritrea to the proposal they join Eastern Sudan (see FO 371-63212, No. 13 Monthly Report January 1947, Raka[3] 1986) is merely one additional indication that colonial rule had created an overriding Eritrean identity. Renan's proposition received a sort of confirmation when that rejection was accompanied by the invocation of a common history. Eritrean nationalists have invariably stressed the plurality of the society. As early as 1971 the ELF in its first national congress declared that all national groups were equal and no single national group would be allowed to dominate others (ELF 1971: 37). It also declared its commitment to respect the culture, language, religion and identity of each ethno-linguistic group along the common Eritrean national identity, thereby recognising the plural nature of Eritrean society and the duality of identity it encompasses.

SUMMARY AND CONCLUSION

Nationalism is often believed to transcend forms of identification in society based on religion, race, language, class, gender, and to encompass them in a larger identity (Duara 1996: 161). In contrast to mono-ethnic society, in polyethnic society, nationalism is considered to be polyethnic or supra-ethnic (Eriksen 1993: 118). And it emphasises shared civil rights rather than shared cultural roots. The discussion on Eritrean nationalism, therefore, refers to an encompassing and transcending supra-ethnic nationalism. In this respect, the divided nationalism of the 1940s reflecting parochial interests can be understood as a manifestation of polyethnic identity. It should be re-emphasised that when we talk about Eritrean nationalism we refer primarily to what is denoted in the discourse of nationalism as territorial and political nationalism or civic nationalism. Smith (1983) commenting on territorial nationalism proposes that its genesis rests on an imposed political entity and is less characterised by the omnipresence of a distinctive cultural identity - in the sense of ethnic cultural identity. Rather, it is, according to Smith, a "politically fashioned and politically oriented identity".

Scholars of Eritrean nationalism attribute the emergence of Eritrean national identity and nationalism to the socio-economic transformation that took place as a result of the colonial capitalist penetration. In addition, by extending the focus to the NLM, they contend that Eritrean nationalism was further strengthened during the armed liberation struggle. It is widely agreed that the origin of Eritrean nationalism is associated with the advent of Italian colonialism. As Sorenson (1991: 312) argues, Eritrean nationalists also, in their invocation of legitimacy in their claim to the right to self-determination accentuated the roots of Eritrean nationalism as being of recent history. Unlike many nationalist discourses that attempt to trace the myth of their nationalist origin to some distant and imaginary antiquity, Eritreans connect it with Italian colonialism.

The notion of the duality of identity is utilised here in the aim of understanding the cleavage as well as to show the compatibility of sub-national identities, on the one hand, and national identity, on the other. This is so, as long as, centrifugal forces do not dominate the national polity. Here it is of utmost importance to make a distinction between the internally containable and uncontainable schisms. Eritrean internal conflict could be seen in the category of an internally containable schism. Research on national identity show that due to the weakness of modern classes and social groups in developing societies, the internal competition to capture the strategic resources takes the form of ethnic or other sub-national forms. Yet, the sociological relationship is characterised by the phenomenon of complementarisation, mutual recognition and acceptance which is imbedded in some means of communication that makes possible the interethnic interaction. Internal conflicts are aggravated when an external enemy tends to associate with one of the contesting forces. In such situation the group that finds itself in a disadvantaged position is compelled to emphasise its primordial identity. From the social-psychological point, this generates defensive mechanisms, which in the absence of normal consensual relation creates a sense of security mediated through excessively asserting your internal primordial identities. It was this sense of fear of being dominated which compelled some Moslem leaders to construct the identity of the Moslem communities and the whole of Eritrea based on primordial characteristics.

On the other hand, the assertion of internal primordial identity can also serve as a tactic of negotiation. In the case of the Moslems, when the felt threat appeared to be coming from two directions, from the Eritrean Christians and the Ethiopian State, the safest way was to negotiate hard. The same was true for the Christians, particularly those in the UP. They felt surrounded by various hostile enemies. Therefore, in their view it was expedient to associate themselves with a friendly power that would strengthen their negotiating position. The presence of these competing identities, however, should not lead us to assume that supraethnic nationalism was precluded. For as Hodgkin (1956: 21) notes in regard to nationalism in Africa, "nationalism operates or tries to operate at a variety of levels: at the level of a particular language-group, or greater tribe, ...; of particular colonial territory".

In the civic conception of nation formation, the primordial characteristics, though important, are not by themselves sufficient to constitute a nation. Therefore, it would not be a convincing argument that Christian Eritreans entertained Ethiopian nationalism because of the primordial characteristics that linked them with Christian Ethiopia. A number of socio-economic and politico-legal dimensions are required which make plausible the transcendence of identity across these primordial anthropological elements. It is in this sense that the legacy of colonial rule fits in the picture. Colonialism has integrated the various ethno-linguistic groups, furnishing the society its commonality. However, as Lobban (1976: 339) notes, "This is not to say that ethnic differences do not exist, but that the abuses from outsiders have synthesized and galvanized Eritrean nationalism more firmly".

Elite competition also constituted one of the underlying causes of the cleavage. In this politics of competition, domination and power relationships played a significant role. Suspicion and the feeling of insecurity are both objective and psychological. As psychological phenomena, they may be generated partly due to the lack of adequate knowledge of the other side, and partly evoked by memory or contemporary experience. As an objective phenomenon, they involve both exogenous and endogenous factors. In terms of the latter, factors such as social, economic, cultural and demographic resources which affect the distribution of power by creating imbalances play a significant role. In terms of the former, real or imagined external threats exacerbate these internal contradictions. One of the component elements of the Eritrean contradiction has been the prevalence of structural imbalance expressed in resource endowment in terms of both material and cultural resources. External factors had also been one of the main dividing elements, the threat coming from the Ethiopian side and from the Islamic-Arab configuration. The psychological impediment to harmony gradually subsided, giving way to the sense of a shared destiny. This was strengthened by life in the Field as a result of the common sacrifices and shared experiences which manifestly grew through the struggle. The structural imbalances, in terms of education, economy and social resources were also narrowed.

In conclusion, we set out to scrutinise the development of Eritrean nationalism starting from the period immediately prior to Italy's colonial reign. We began by examining political resistance of 'privileged groups' ending in the mass nationalism of the NLM. In this process Eritrean nationalism was manifested in different forms and various contexts. From the accounts given, two conclusions can be drawn: a) that the Eritrean cleavage was an internal competitive nationalism; and b) though at the bottom there is a socio-cultural foundation to the conflict, it should not be reduced to simple Christian-Islamic categories.

Notes

1. In the discourse of Eritrean nationalism, two diametrically opposite positions have been observed. These opposite positions can be discerned among the Eritrean nationalists' and the Ethiopianists' promotion of the 'Great Ethiopia' hypothesis. We find these two positions cogently summarised in John Sorenson's book (1993) *Imagining Ethiopia: Struggle for History and Identity in the Horn of Africa*. The argument from the Ethiopianists' side, seeking to refute the nationhood and nationalism of Eritrea, includes, among other things, the charge that Eritrea lacks a historical narrative that goes back into distant history. This is taken to indicate a lack of legitimacy because according to this view, historical glories and symbols in the forms of heroes and sacred places are indispensable in the narrative construction of nationalism. The poly-ethnic composition and short history is also considered,

according to this view, as an indication of the artificiality of Eritrean nationalism. Accordingly this position is unable to perceive Eritrean nationalism outside the Great Ethiopian nationalism with its historical legitimacy grounded on the genealogical descendency of Sheba and Solomon. On the other side of the argument we find the Eritrean nationalist discourse which puts the emphasis of Eritrean nationalism as the outcome of colonialism. Furthermore it acknowledges that it is the result of a gradual process which has to pass through different stages. Instead of looking back to ancient historiographic mythologies the Eritrean nationalist discourse looks forward, a future oriented ideology, which takes the form of building a new modern, democratic, developed and equal society. The imperative need of a powerful myth in the discourse of the construction of nations is emphasised also by Anthony D. Smith (1983). However, in contrast to the former, the historical and cultural myth, by paying attention to the dilemma that the new territorial nations of Africa encounter, he points out that the political myth is what more appropriately pertains to these nations.

2. In depicting the developmental stages I have introduced three terminologies. They are internality, externality, and extra-externality. Internality relationship refers to a meaningful relationship among geographical coterminous groups (villages) - Stage I. Externality pertains to a meaningful relation between geographically coterminous groups and a transcendent supra-organisation - nation - Stage II. Extra-externality relationship is a structure of relations in which a meaningful relation shifts from being one between geographical coterminous groups and nation to one between individuals and nation - Stage III.
3. According to Michael Hasama Raka a meeting was convened in Eastern Sudan in 1949 in which delegates from northern and western Eritrea participated. Among the participants were the author himself and Omar Hasseno. The meeting was initially called to discuss chronic conflicts between the tribes residing on both sides of the border areas. However when the meeting was underway the British administrator of the Sudan, Robert How, proposed that Eastern Sudan should be joined with western Eritrea and a Beja state established. This proposition was received with great enthusiasm from the Sudanese side while the Eritrean side presented its strong protest against the proposition (Raka 1986).

Chapter 9

LOOKING AHEAD: SUMMARY AND IMPLICATIONS

INTRODUCTION

In this work, we set out to examine the process of formation of the Eritrean nation. The century of Eritrean history under consideration (1890-1991) was divided into three periods: a) the Italian colonial; b) the British Administration; and c) the Federation and subsequent occupation of Eritrea by Ethiopia up to Eritrean independence. Overall, the study has made effort to demonstrate 1) the central role played by Italian rule in generating the socio-economic and politico-legal structure of Eritrean society; and 2) the various ways in which the British Administration, the Federation and the NLM primarily contributed to generating national sentiments and consciousness, a feeling of nationhood and a will to live together. A basic proposition of the study was that the fulfilment of these two elements provided the underlying foundations for the rise of the Eritrean nation and eventually, for the State of Eritrea.

This study has advanced the idea that the formation of Eritrea began with the onset of the territorial integration of the colony in 1890. Thus, this date is taken as the point of departure for the study. The fundamental assertion was that two groups of collective actors provided the basis of the making of the Eritrean nation, namely (i) the colonial powers – Italy, Britain and Ethiopia; and (ii) nationalist movements, and more significantly the NLM.

In this concluding chapter, I summarise the main results of the study, focusing on the contributions of the chief collective actors behind the making of Eritrea. I also reflect upon some theoretical issues, discuss post-independence and its challenges, and finally, stress the specificity of Eritrea as a civic nation.

COLONIAL ACTORS

We have identified two fundamental factors in the process of formation of the Eritrean nation that underpinned the process. These were structure and agency. Structure was represented by the socio-economic transformation induced by the penetration of the colonial capitalist economy. The penetration of the colonial capitalist economy generated changes in the social and economic structures of the Eritrean society, leading to the increased interdependence of the various ethno-linguistic groups thereby forging national integration. Agency was comprised of two collective agents. These were the colonial actors and the nationalist movements. It was the interplay of these two agents that contributed to the process of formation of the Eritrean nation. This section deals with the colonial actors – Italy, Britain and Ethiopia.

ITALIAN COLONIALISM

With the advent of Italian colonisation, the various ethno-linguistic communities were centralised under a common bureaucratic administration in which territorially based common identity and integration began to be nourished. This territorial integration and centralisation can be seen as the bedrock of the formation of a nation. Through the organisation of the territory and the communities above the village level, it marked the genesis of the transformation of Eritrea into a nation.

According to the assertions advanced in this study, the primary contribution of Italian rule was in the objective dimension, notably territorial, socio-economic and politico-legal integration. Italy created Eritrea as a coherent geopolitical unit not only through demarcation of its geopolitical boundaries but also through socio-economic transformation. The territorial integration of Eritrea represents the first building block in the process of formation of the Eritrean nation. Following territorial integration and guided by the principle of modern administration, the colonial power undertook a number of measures that further strengthened the process of social transformation. These measures included the introduction of bureaucratic administration, a modern economic system based on capitalist principles, recruitment in the colonial army and a bureaucracy that enhanced societal integration. These social mechanisms – integration, bureaucratic administration, economic integration and recruitment centralised the territory and the society around the Capital City in a hierarchically structured organisation. With these developments, the first step toward the structuration of society was undertaken.

In terms of bureaucratic administration, the territory was divided into provinces and districts. Every province and district was furnished with administrative personnel and the headquarters' hierarchically interconnected. From the point of view of institutional practices, these changes ensured the territorial centralisation and integration of the colony, lending to the overall formation process. The system of recruitment for the army, the bureaucracy and the labour market also brought social integration. Individuals from the various ethno-linguistic groups met and interacted in the colonial army, the bureaucracy and work places. They met in common public spaces with the aim of trading their labour for money. And it was here that they faced common exploitation, oppression and racial discrimination–and humiliation. This exploitation and oppression constituted their newly evolving common historical experience and memory. Common historical experience and memory laid the groundwork for the development of the territorially based imagined community. This became possible as they came to realise that they shared common territory whose occupation constituted the basis of their misfortune.

In the economic realm, the penetration of the Italian capital established a new economic system based on a capitalist principles and modes of production. A monetary economy was introduced in which the peasant and pastoral communities were compelled to carry out their economic transactions according to the rules of a capitalist economic system. They had to trade their farm and pastoral products for money in the market centres, and with that money, they would then buy finished goods to meet their needs back in their villages. These transactions also entailed social dimensions, in that individuals from a variety of different ethnic and linguistic origins met and interacted. In addition, various industries, above all, construction, food processing and mining were expanded, further enhancing the economic integration.

In the agricultural sphere, projects directed along the lines of capitalist principles were undertaken. The establishment of these industries and agricultural projects differentiated the economic structure along the lines between modern economy and traditional economy. The construction of railways and roads, coupled with the expansion of a postal system, telephone lines and telegraphs created a communications network. This network, in turn, enhanced the mobility of people and goods, and both people and products from different corners of the territory could easily be transported. Consequently, the interdependence of urban centres and rural area was strengthened as a result of the expansion of the communications network, particularly the road and railway systems. This interdependence was both economic and social. In economic terms, the interdependence took the form of a new division of labour. The urban centres furnished the rural areas with finished goods, while becoming dependent on the rural for primary products. In the social dimension, individuals who moved from the villages to the urban centres in search of work did not entirely sever their connection with their villages. Indeed, they maintained close contact with their places of origin. At a community level also, the new organisation meant that the villages were dependent on the urban headquarters for social services (schools and health services) and administration. The interdependence was made easy due to the presence of transportation facilities.

The rise of towns was also another outcome of colonialism. The administrative centres and agricultural and industrial sites were gradually transformed to urban centres. The emergence of the towns marked the creation of geographical division between the urban and the rural. Urbanisation brought cultural divisions predicated on the differences between an emergent urban middle class culture and the traditional peasant culture. Economic and technological changes enhanced the possibilities for radical cultural change. A Western-oriented urban middle class culture was entrenched in the urban centres. This Western-influenced urban middle class culture brought new values, beliefs and norms that differed from that of the peasant culture. A division of centre and periphery accompanied the urbanisation process. The emergence of this binary division of centre-periphery, in turn, through the creation of relationships based on interdependence, fostered social and territorial integration.

The economic changes brought by the colonial political economy also led to changes in the social structure. One implication of this structural permutation was evidenced in the stratification and differentiation of society in which one manifestation was the emergence of new social groups such as the urban middle class, workers, and the intelligentsia. This social rupture was the result of the interplay between the temptations and hopes of earning a better life connected with urban life, and the shortage of land caused by Italian confiscation of land (the pull and push). The Italian confiscation of land, particularly in the highland of Eritrea, caused an acute shortage of farmland for the peasants. This forced them to look for an alternative means of subsistence, and at the same time ensured the availability of landless peasants who could easily be incorporated into the capitalist economy as labourers and in the colonial army. These landless peasants thus, filled the agricultural and industrial capitalist projects' need for a labour force, effectively converting them into wage workers. The increasing influx into urban centres in search of work and better life swelled the number of town dwellers. This development, in turn, paved the way for the mushrooming of the urban middle class.

To summarise, the forces of modernisation were set in place with the establishment of Italian colonial rule. The combination of the administrative and legal order, the new economic system, communication technology and the urbanisation process that the Italians set in place generated a new shape of society. This shape, which combined the old and the new, resulted in a transitional social structure. By the end of Italian rule, the colonial political economy had created clear distinctions and stratification in society. New social groups with different ambitions than the old traditional groups were formed (and even the old social groups tasted the new lifestyle). These new social groups played a leading role in the political movement of the 1940s. Generally, Italian colonialism furnished the necessary objective requirements for the formation of the Eritrean nation.

BRITISH ADMINISTRATION

The central proposition developed in the study is that the contribution of the British Administration and the Federation to the process of formation of the Eritrean nation was most significant in the creation of the subjective conditions necessary in raising political consciousness. This section provides a brief account of this contribution. The limited Italian education and the Mission Schools created a group of intelligentsia. This social group is often described, in social theory, as the marginalised or alienated group in that it is found in the crossroads between tradition and westernisation. The group was employed primarily by the Italian colonial state as teachers, interpreters and clerks. When the colonial state collapsed, this group lost most because its primary source of employment had been put out of business. The British Administration, contrary to the expectation of the Eritrean intelligentsia, favoured the Italians in their employment policy in the civil service. Many Italians were allowed to keep their jobs and they were also afforded new job opportunities. The British policy of employment discrimination disillusioned the intelligentsia. They could not return to their traditional occupations, but neither would they be employed by the Administration, leaving them in disarray. Consequently, a stark dislike and suspicion of the British was fostered. It was in such time of confusion that formal organised political activity was permitted.

The first Eritrean organisation representing the various ethno-linguistic groups to emerge was the *Mahber Fikri Hager* (Association of Love of Country), formed in 1941. The initial aim of the organisation was to serve as a bridge between the British Administration and the Eritrean people regarding day-to-day affairs. The activities of the Association shifted to politics as the issue of the disposition of Eritrea began to appear on the agenda of the occupying power and the Big Four Powers, and as the Ethiopian claim to Eritrea grew louder. However, when the probability of Ethiopian intervention became evident, a division within the Association surfaced. The Association fractured into three groups, which eventually formed the Unionist Party, the Moslem League and the Liberal Progressive Party.

The most important effect of the British Military Administration (BMA) on Eritrean society was, above all, in political liberalisation and the expansion of education. Breaking with the restrictive practises of the Italian colonialists, the British introduced democratic liberalism in which the expression of political ideas was tolerated. By 1947, when the ban on the formation of political parties was lifted, several political parties emerged. The new political parties enabled the participation and mobilisation of the communities in national politics. This, in turn, increased political consciousness, leading to the fulfilment of the subjective requirements for the formation of national identity. British rule was also a turning point for the development of the Eritrean educational system. A considerable increase in the number of schools and enrolment was witnessed. In addition, the establishment of middle schools was gradually realised. The expansion of education allowed a greater number of school-aged children to attend schools, not only at the elementary level, but also at the middle school level. This expansion of education in both quantity and quality contributed to the growth of the intelligentsia. In that sense, it can be said that a surge in the development of the intelligentsia came under the British rule.

The end of World War II brought an economic decline in Eritrea. Inflation took hold, and while prices rose geometrically, the rise of salaries was quite meagre. Many industries were closed, causing high unemployment, and this economic hardship led to a decline in living standard. The immediate effect of the economic crisis was visibly reflected in social relations–and evidenced in the spread of social tensions. Most affected by the economic decline was the urban population. Concomitantly, it was in the urban centres that social tensions spread, particularly in the capital, where there was a high level of social conflict. The economic problems, social tensions and alienation of the intelligentsia, combined caused divisions in the middle class. External involvements were also added to the internal social, economic and political factors, exacerbating the divisions. Neither was the British scheme of partition helpful. Therefore, at a crucial juncture of the history of the Eritrean society, the middle class was not able to provide united political leadership. Inevitably, the division in the urban middle class led to a fragmented nationalism.

The divided nationalism broadly reflected the religious cleavage of Eritrean society. The main political parties (the Unionist Party and the Moslem League) were based primarily in the Tigrinya ethno-linguistic group and the Moslem communities, respectively. This is not to say that there were not, for instance, Moslems in the Unionist Party. On the contrary, many aristocrats from the Moslem communities were associated with UP. Conversely, there were many from the Tigrinya ethno-linguistic group who in opposition to the UP, advocated independence. The fundamental basis for the division was actually to be found in the lack of a commonly accepted solution for the disposition of Eritrea. Neither union with Ethiopia nor partition was acceptable solutions to the Moslem League. Conversely, the seeming impracticability of independence of Eritrea, in the eyes of the Unionists, made independence seem an unrealistic solution. Consequently, the Moslem League advocated independence while the Unionists favoured union with Ethiopia. In spite of all this, in 1950, the UN passed a resolution that determined the fate of Eritrea. The resolution on federation was against the announced desires of the parties, however, once it was passed all political parties pledged their support and that they would work together for its success.

A significant legacy of the UN-sponsored Federation was, on top of the rise of national institutions and symbols, the continuation of Eritrean territoriality. The Resolution acknowledged the territorial uniqueness of Eritrea. The decision for federation was made with the explicit understanding that a unified Eritrea, as a unique territory, would be joined with Ethiopia. This acknowledgement was of a great importance in the formation of the Eritrean national identity. It was significant for two reasons. First, it conferred international political and legal legitimacy on the territory created by colonialism, also giving justification to the Eritrean claim of sovereignty. Second, it had an important symbolic function in the development of territorially based particularistic Eritrean national identity. The acknowledgement of the territorial uniqueness constituted the central point of contest between the Eritreans and the Ethiopian State during the Federation. Eritreans strove to preserve the unique identity of Eritrea while Ethiopia's intent was to obliterate that identity. Aware of the implications of the acknowledgement of the territorial unity and the accompanying national institutions and symbols, Ethiopia worked hard to prevent clauses that would confirm and strengthen the unique Eritrean identity from being inserted in the constitution. Already during the debate on Eritrea in the UN, and later in the process of drafting the Eritrean constitution–that is, before the enforcement of the Federation – Ethiopia strove to forestall any clause reflecting the unique identity of Eritrea from being incorporated in the constitution. Furthermore, as soon as the enforcement of the Federation began, the Ethiopian State deployed both covert and overt instruments to undermine it.

The contribution of the Federation was also very important to the rise of national institutions and symbols. The Federation itself was based on the establishment of national institutions and symbols. Accordingly, national institutions that would safeguard and symbolise the unique Eritrean identity were established, such as the Eritrean Government, parliament, judiciary and political parties. The autonomous state was also to be endowed with national symbols such as a flag, national languages, stamps, public buildings, etc. In addition, it was stipulated that the Eritrean Constitution contained a wide range of democratic rights of association, demonstration, press freedom and labour rights. All these institutions and symbols represented Eritrean national identity. As such, they were seen by Eritreans as symbols and embodiments of their unique national character. It was in that respect that they generated strong feelings and inculcated national consciousness. On the other hand, Ethiopia displayed equally absolute aversion to these symbols and institutions because they represented stumbling block to the smooth assimilation of Eritrea into the Imperial State. Subsequently these symbols and institutions became the focal point of intense battles, pitting those who wished to preserve and consolidate them against those who sought their destruction.

According to the UN schedule the preparation of federating Eritrea with Ethiopia was to be completed within two years, 1950-1952. As planned, the drafting of the Eritrean Constitution and the setting up of the Constitutional Assembly was accomplished in 1952. After the Eritrean Assembly and the Emperor of Ethiopia ratified the Constitution, the Administration transferred authority to the Eritrean Government and the federal state (Ethiopian State) on the basis of the constitutional discretion conferred on them, Eritrea was federated with Ethiopia. This brought the end of British Administration and the commencement of Ethiopian domination.

Ethiopian Rule

The relationship of Eritrea to Ethiopia before Italian colonial rule is one of the most disputed aspects of Eritrean history. Ethiopia and its supporters claim that Eritrea has been an integral part of Ethiopia over the three thousand-year history of that country. Eritrean nationalists and their supporters, on the other hand, persistently argue that Eritrea as we know it today is a creation of Italian colonialism. Moreover, they also argue that present-day Ethiopia, like Eritrea, is a creation of the end of the nineteenth century. Therefore, the latter could not constitute an integral part of the former. Whatever claims and counterclaims are made, and whatever relationship had existed, one thing remains clear: Italian colonialism cut the umbilical cord – if it ever existed. This study's temporal point of departure was the colonisation of Eritrea by Italy in 1890. We saw in chapter two that there were three distinctive regions before Italian colonialism. These were roughly the highland, the lowland and the Afar. The first two were connected with regional powers while the last one preserved its independence. We have also seen that when Italy colonised Eritrea, the highland region was under the control of Emperor Yohannes of Abyssinia.

Ethiopian involvement in Eritrea was divided into three phases. The first Ethiopian involvement in Eritrea referred to the rule of Emperor Yohannes' representative Rasi Alula (1879-1889) of the highland. This Abyssinian involvement in Eritrea ended in 1889 when Italy took control of the highland. The second period of Ethiopian involvement (1941-1962) in Eritrea extended over the decade of Federation, beginning when Italian colonialism collapsed in 1941. After his reinstatement to the Ethiopian throne, Emperor Haile Selassie immediately requested that Eritrea be ceded to Ethiopia. He appealed, first to the Big Four Powers, and later to the United Nations General Assembly to transfer Eritrea to Ethiopia. In his claim to Eritrea, he referred to the connection between Eritrea and Ethiopia based on history, culture, identity and economy, which, he asserted, had been forcibly severed by Italy. To make it appear that there was popular Eritrean support for the cause of union, the Emperor formed an organisation consisting of Eritreans living in Ethiopia under the Amharic name of *Yehager Fikr Mahber*. As soon as it was formed, this organisation began to campaign for the union of Eritrea with Ethiopia. Inside Eritrea, it targeted the *Mahber Fikri Hager*, which had originally been formed to serve as a bridge between the local population and the British Military Administration (BMA). The intervention of the Ethiopian state in the internal affairs of Eritrea grew more pervasive, becoming blatant with the appearance of the issue of settlement of the territory on the agenda of the Big Four Powers, and later in the United Nations. As a result of Ethiopian interference, the *Mahber Fikri Hager* was split. Its unionist section, united with the *Yehager Fikr Mahber,* later formed the Unionist Party (UP). The UP was believed to be under complete Ethiopian control. The Ethiopian Liaison Officer, through his control of the UP, worked relentlessly to force Ethiopia's wishes upon the Eritrean people. This led to the division of the Eritrean nationalist movement into two blocs, with one advocating independence and the other advocating union with Ethiopia. This division was an important factor contributing to the UN Resolution of Federation.

The UN Resolution of Federation left Eritrea on the doorstep of the Ethiopian State. It soon became clear that Ethiopia understood the Federation as a union. Thus, it lost no time in its efforts to accomplish the union of Eritrea and Ethiopia. Although the struggle had already begun during the debate regarding Eritrea in the UN General Assembly, the arena was open for Ethiopia after the approval of the Federation. Demonstrating flagrant contempt to the Eritrean constitution and autonomy, the representative of the Emperor declared that so far as the office of the Emperor was concerned, there were no external or internal affairs – everything concerns the Emperor. This statement was made in connection with his interference in the internal affairs of the Eritrean Government, in violation to the constitutionally protected discretion of the Eritrean Government. This statement characterised the policy of the Ethiopian State in Eritrea for the coming decades. Even though the federal accord clearly stated the distinction between the internal discretion of the Eritrean autonomous state and the external discretion conferred on the federal state, the interference of the Ethiopian State in the internal affairs of Eritrea became increasingly aggressive – until Eritrea was finally annexed.

Bent on annexing Eritrea, the Ethiopian State dismantled the pillars of the Federation with the help of its followers in the Eritrean Government. The autonomy of Eritrea was systematically violated and eroded. Political parties that espoused independence were prohibited. Trade union rights were curbed. The Ethiopian official language replaced the Eritrean official languages. The Eritrean flag, stamp, the name of the Eritrean Executive and Eritrean Government, etc. were changed to obliterate the symbols of Eritrean identity and autonomy. On the other hand, new political forces emerged to defend the Federation in response to Ethiopia's increasing infringement of Eritrean autonomy. Many unionists were reported as having shifted position, joining the struggle to preserve the Federation. This demonstrated, as Markakis has described, the instrumentalist nature of their relationship to the union cause. In addition, it also indicated that the institutions and symbols that emerged as a result of the federal accord generated emotional attachment and affiliation whose violation evoked resistance. Eventually, the Federation was rendered null and void by Ethiopia, which, in abolishing it, created a fourteenth province of Ethiopia. The annexation of Eritrea was formally carried out in 1962. Consequently, the political arrangement designed to bind the two units on the principle of equality was gone. These events occurred in clear violation of the Eritrean Constitution that stipulated any change to the constitution and its pillars must come only from the body that promulgated it, the UN General Assembly.

Following annexation, the stage was thus set for another confrontation. Eritrean opposition to the breach of the Federation was swift. This was expressed, first, in the form of peaceful political struggle. When this did not give tangible result the struggle was transformed to violent one. In the same way that Emperor Yohannes' effort to limit the autonomy of the highland led to the resistance led by Rasi Woldenkeal, Haile Selassie's violation of the Federation led to the armed liberation struggle.

This transformed the low-level conflict that characterised the decade of Federation to the high-level conflict, the armed struggle. This ushered in the third phase of Ethiopian involvement in Eritrea, its occupation (1962-1991). Ethiopian occupation reversed many of the changes that had taken place during the previous two decades. The political democracy introduced by the British Administration and guaranteed in the Eritrean Constitution was terminated.

The cultural rights of Eritreans were suppressed. The economy was left to deteriorate, and not only was no new investment encouraged, existing companies were compelled to move to Ethiopia. All indications pointed to a single interpretation – that the measures being taken by the Ethiopian State were aimed at making sure that Eritrea assumed a subordinate position in the Empire. In many aspects, the Ethiopian State actions bore a strong similarity to European colonial policies.

The literature on nationalism shows that political resistance increases in proportion to political oppression. The suffering, misery and humiliation caused by alien domination are assumed to strengthen the determination of the people to strike back. The more the forces of occupation tightened their grip of oppression the stronger grew the resistance (this, of course, should not be taken literary to suggest that any oppression leads to resistance). A close examination of the Eritrean experience will testify to the correctness of this axiom. When the complete occupation of Eritrea by Ethiopia had been realised, almost all recent progress was reversed. The indicators of economic development tipped downward. Fundamental political and cultural rights were suppressed. All this evoked resistance expressed in armed liberation struggle which, in turn, increased oppression. It became apparent that with every success of the NLM, Haile Selassie's regime grew more desperate, resorting to indiscriminate attacks on the civilian population. By the second half of the first decade of the armed struggle, widespread atrocities were being committed by the Ethiopian army. Many villages in the lowland were burned. In 1967, in the wake of these atrocities, the first large exodus of people to the Sudan took place. These acts of terror, however, did not decrease the resolve of the Eritrean nationalists. To the contrary, the struggle grew so steadily that it became more and more clear to Haile Selassie's regime that the harsh military actions were not yielding the expected effects. Consequently, in an act of desperation the regime declared a state of emergency in 1970, to be binding throughout Eritrea. Rural populations in areas where the Eritrean guerrilla were assumed actively operating were ordered to evacuate their villages and be concentrated in the nearest towns or designated area suitable for the army control.

The state of emergency gave the army virtually a free hand. The soldiers were instructed to take all necessary measures to crush the guerrilla army and punish the rural population that was providing them with food and shelter. Under Haile Selassie's regime, practically the whole rural population in the lowland was subjected to unprecedented suppression. However, instead of subduing the NLM these oppressive measures reinforced the determination and will of the Eritrean people. Many young, educated Eritreans, who, on the one hand, were victims of the discriminatory policy of the Imperial State and, on the other, were motivated by nationalist feelings joined the NLM. Consequently, the liberation army grew from a few thousand in the first decade of the history of the armed struggle to several thousand by 1974. Moreover, it also expanded to the highland region. Now Ethiopia faced a serious challenge. Not only was its rule in

Eritrea in question, but even the existence of the *ancien* regime itself was under real threat – a realisation of the 'Trevaskisian prophecy'. The Eritrean struggle for independence contributed a great deal to the downfall of the Haile Selassie regime in 1974. The new military junta (the Dergue) that replaced the *ancien* regime was no different in its policy regarding the Eritrean question – and it was even more oppressive. As soon as it ascended to power, it signalled that it would afford the Eritreans only regional autonomy. The Eritrean nationalists rebuffed this gesture, making it clear in unequivocal terms that they would never accept less than independence.

The Dergue, instead of trying to find a negotiated settlement, resorted to military force. In its campaign to defeat the nationalist struggle, the regime decided to take tough measures against the nationalist organisations and the civilian population. It seemed that the regime was of the resolute conviction that only through brutal measures could it suppress the Eritrean nationalist movement. True to its conviction the regime introduced a policy of terror, which it named 'red terror', to couch it in revolutionary jargon. The red terror which the Dergue unleashed, particularly in the urban centres and especially in the Capital City claimed the life of many innocent people. People alleged to be supporters or sympathisers of the NLM were thrown into prison. Some were shot on the spot, while others became the victims of piano-wire strangulation. Villages in the highland were also wantonly bombarded and burned. The result of this reign of terror was not what the Dergue expected – instead of pacifying the society, it further strengthened its determination. This determination was reflected in the massive flow of new recruits into the NLM. Between 1974 and 1977, the number of the liberation fighters was estimated to grow to tens of thousands. Nevertheless, by the end of 1978, the Dergue regime scored a major victory against the liberation fronts, compelling them to retreat from the urban centres they had recently liberated. This development put the NLM in a defensive position, while the Dergue was back on the offensive. The breakthrough for the NLM in its attempt to shift its position from defensive to offensive came in 1984, when the EPLF destroyed a division of the Dergue army in North Eastern Sahel. Following this victory of the NLM, the EPLF kept the upper hand until the liberation of Eritrea in 1991. On the other hand, the Dergue's indiscriminate attacks on the civilian population escalated to an all-time high – without any sign of success in pacifying the Eritrean society. To the contrary, it seemed that the determination to liberate Eritrea increased in proportion with the intensity of the Dergue's oppression. This was expressed in the expansion of the liberation army, by some estimate it reached around hundred thousand towards the end of the liberation struggle.

This brief account shows the connection between the degree of Ethiopian oppression and Eritrean militancy. The speed of mobilisation and participation in the armed struggle in the early years of the Dergue regime led some observers, like Erlich Haggai, to argue that it was during the Dergue regime that Eritrean nationalism was born. Although the history of the development of Eritrean nationalism testifies to the relation between oppression and political resistance, it is incorrect to attribute the growth of Eritrean nationalism solely to Ethiopian oppression. Nationalism is much more than mere reaction to foreign oppression. As a means of constructing collective identity, it is the result of transformations in social, economic, political, cultural and communicational dimensions. These are by nature indigenous. Ethiopian domination and oppression is, therefore, only one factor among several that induced and fostered the development of Eritrean nationalism and nationhood.

NATIONALIST ACTORS

It was earlier mentioned that the intertwining of colonial actors and nationalist actors played an important role in the formation of the Eritrean nation. While the former were external forces, the latter were internal. This section focuses on those internal forces. In order to trace the development of Eritrean nationalist movement, it is helpful to identify three phases: (i) the sporadic and isolated resistance of 1875-1941; (ii) the phase of organised political movement of 1941-1961; and (iii) the armed liberation struggle or National Liberation Movement (NLM) of 1961-1991. These three phases are distinct from each other with respect to form and content. If we examine the first phase (1875-1941), we can still identify distinctive features between 1875-1890 and 1890-1941. It would not be possible to characterise this period as a nationalist movement in the proper sense of the concept. During the period of Italian rule, the organised nationalist movement was either weak or non-existent, and the real nationalist movement began only after the demise of Italian colonial rule. While the second phase (1941-1961) represents a peaceful nationalist movement, the third represents armed liberation struggle (1961-1991). The overall movement can be studied by reducing it to two phases based on their mode of action: the political movement (nationalist movements) and the armed struggle (National Liberation Movement). The following two sub-sections summarise the development of Eritrean nationalist movements.

Early Nationalist Movements

The eve of Italian colonial rule is considered to be the period in which Eritrean identity was conceived. This is because of the resistance of the elites of the various ethno-linguistic groups to the Abyssinian State and the Mahdists' incursions, and the related attempts of these elites and their followers to seek protection from European Missionaries and diplomats. Sometimes in co-operation with leaders of other ethno-linguistic groups and sometimes alone with their followers, many chiefs from the various ethno-linguistic groups resisted outside domination. The most famous of this was Rasi Woldenkeal Solomon of the Hamasen's resistance against Emperor Yohannes' attempt to put the highland region under his direct rule. Rasi Woldenkeal and his followers fought the forces of Emperor Yohannes from 1876 to 1879. In the Akkele Guzai, Bahta Hagos led resistance against Emperor Yohannes' domination. Bahta Hagos allied with the Saho who were also resisting Abyssinian domination. The common cause of resisting Yohannes' domination became the basis for their co-operation. Bahta Hagos also co-ordinated his opposition against the Abyssinian rulers with the Habab people. When the Italians occupied Massawa, Bahta Hagos found a new ally, started to collaborate with the Italians, and led his resistance from Massawa until Eritrea was colonised by Italy. In the Serae region, a number of local leaders opposed to Emperor Yohannes' authority fled to Massawa, which was then under Italian occupation, and from there led their opposition. They also provided active support to the Italian effort to occupy Eritrea. Kafle Gofar, for example, captured Keren for the Italians.

In the lowland, local leaders resisted intrusions both from the forces of Emperor Yohannes and the Mahdists. Kentebai Hamid of the Habab, for instance, signed an agreement with Italians in Massawa, intended to protect his people. Some of the Beni Amer, the Nara and the Saho chiefs also sought the protection of the Italians. Many of these resistance figures co-operated with the Italians, believing that the Italians would be better than the Abyssinians and the Mahdists. When Italy occupied Eritrea, however, many of these elites rebelled against Italy itself. The resistance against the Mahdists and the Emperor Yohannes of Abyssinia marked the origin of the genesis of Eritrea not only in the sense that they constituted the expression of the emergence of a rudimentary, localised "we and they" distinction in relation to their surroundings. It also represented the active participation of Eritreans in the creation of Eritrea as an Italian colony in opposition to the Abyssinians and Mahdist Sudan. We could conclude this, that although it might not have been possible to speak about Eritrean identity at that time, neither was it possible to speak about Ethiopian identity or Sudanese identity. What did exist was localised identity, which, with the intervention of Italian colonial rule, was to give way to a common Eritrean identity. In this sense, the resistance could be seen as prelude to the growth of Eritrean national identity. Moreover, the significance of this resistance can be evaluated in the context of the construction of myths, symbols and rituals in the nationalist discourse that was later to develop.

With the establishment of the Italian colonial rule, those Eritrean elites who had collaborated with the Italians were punished – not for their collaboration but either for their objection or potential objection to Italian rule. In the first few years of their rule, the Italian authorities, in order to pre-empt any Eritrean resistance, killed, deported to the Island of Nakura or imprisoned many of the Eritrean elites and their followers. These measures deprived the Eritrean people of their leaders, while saving Italy from Eritrean opposition to its rule. The imprisonment, deportation and killing of the elites undermined organised opposition to Italian rule. Although there was scattered individual and isolated opposition to the Italians, the available information indicates that meaningful opposition was seen only at the beginning and toward the end of Italian rule. In the case of the latter, observers refer to the fact that many Eritreans joined the Ethiopian opposition struggle against the Italian fascist regime. The first, and perhaps the last popular organised uprising under Italian rule, was one in 1894 that was prompted by the extensive land confiscation.

The development of the Eritrean nationalist movement took an upward turn after the collapse of Italian colonialism. For the first time, and encouraged by the unfolding situation, an organised nationalist movement began to emerge. The first organisation to appear was the *Mahber Fikri Hager Ertra*, which was first formed to serve as an intermediary between the British Military Administration and the Eritrean people. However, it was slowly transformed into a political organisation. Ethiopia's claim to Eritrea, the emergence of the issue of the settlement of the ex-Italian territories in the agenda of the Big Four Powers, and political liberalisation and the lifting of the ban on political parties by the British Administration all encouraged the appearance of an organised Eritrean nationalist movement. The lifting of the ban on the formation of political organisations in 1947 led to the formal registration of several parties. The birth of political parties paved the way for an extensive and unprecedented mass mobilisation and participation. The demise of Italian colonialism opened the opportunity for the Eritrean elites to finally seek control of the colonial economy and state. The achievement of these aims, however, became a divisive issue. Those who thought that they would benefit more through association with Ethiopia sought union, while those who saw benefit in the sovereignty of Eritrea sought independence. This difference of views divided the nationalist movement into independence nationalism and unionist nationalism.

Although what emerged was a divided nationalism, the effect of the mobilisation on society was of far-reaching magnitude. The entire society was politicised, thereby raising the political consciousness of the people. The weakness of the nationalist movement perhaps contributed to the rise of the Federation. The UN General Assembly (in its official deliberation) presented the solution of federation as a compromise between the 'two wishes' of the Eritrean people. The Federation, as an historical experience, and paradoxically by its failure, contributed to the development of the nationalist movement. As an historical experience, it contributed to the development of the nationalist movement in its introduction of national institutions, values and symbols. And in its failure, which meant the abrogation of the national institutions and symbols, it evoked resistance that promoted the development of nationalist sentiment. On the eve of the implementation of the Federation, the nationalist movement was marked by the struggle for independence on the one hand and union on the other. However, the hallmark of the Federation period was that the nationalist movement strove to preserve the Federation because it was understood as the embodiment of Eritrean identity and autonomy. In other words, the Federation became a rallying point for the nationalist forces which was sealed formally in the *Wa'ela Selam* (Peace Conference) in December 1950, when the Unionists and the independentists pledged to work together to uphold the Federation.

A sign of maturity in the development of the nationalist movement was that when the political parties advocating independence were banned, new nationalist forces, including previous unionists, joined the struggle for independence. The trade union movement became one of the current nationalist forces. The workers movement demonstrated its resistance to Ethiopian violation of Eritrean autonomy through the strikes and demonstrations by dockworkers in Massawa and Assab against Ethiopia's introduction of Ethiopian identity card and in demand of higher wages. This was followed by workers strikes and demonstrations in the Capital City against various Ethiopian violations. Students also contributed their share by striking and demonstrating against the introduction of the Ethiopian language as the medium of instruction in the Eritrean schools. The Eritrean Supreme Court joined the struggle through its efforts to preserve its autonomy. The Eritrean press, particularly the *Voice of Eritrea* became an ardent advocate of the Eritrean Constitution and autonomy. The Young Federalist Association also became a force to be reckoned with.

This resistance was repressed, however, by either the Ethiopian military or the police. When the possibilities for open political resistance grew slimmer, the Eritrean Liberation Movement (ELM) attempted covert resistance. However, neither the covert protest nor the appeals to the UN produced results, leaving the Eritrean nationalists with only one option. That option was the employment of violent means. Therefore, the nationalist movement was transformed to armed liberation struggle, the birth of the National Liberation Movement (NLM).

The National Liberation Movement

By the end of the 1950s, the Federation was as good as dead, prompting Eritrean nationalists to seek an alternative to peaceful struggle. Eritrean political exiles and students met in Cairo in 1960 and resolved themselves to launch an armed struggle for independence. Thus, the long liberation struggle of the Eritrean people began on September 1, 1961. In the first decade of the armed struggle, priority was given to military activity. As such, political and social activities were relegated to the background. The period was characterised by lack of a clearly defined political programme and efficient and committed political leadership. The concentration on military activity and the concomitant inability to articulate functional political and social programmes affected the unity of the liberation army and the process of nation building. Thus, the Movement was beset by internal contradictions, rivalry and leadership impotency. The internal problems led to the reform movement to seek to rectify the weaknesses of the liberation struggle. The reform movement succeeded in achieving temporary unity of the liberation army towards the end of the 1960. Though the achievement of the rectification movement did not last long, it paved the way for a new political course in the coming decade.

The NLM, beginning from the second decade of the armed struggle, undertook a pair of objectives. These two objectives were the liberation of Eritrea with the aim of establishing a sovereign nation state and the building of the nation. In the efforts to realise the first objective, the formation of a well-disciplined and motivated national liberation army was considered to be of decisive importance. Whereas the fulfilment of the second objective presupposed the mobilisation and organisation of the population in order to raise their national consciousness and cohesion. National consciousness and cohesion were thought to be achieved through education where music, cassettes, videos and radio became effective instruments. The traditional means of education, school, was also geared along nationalist lines to enhance national cohesion. Moreover, guided by mobilisation theory, the Eritrean organisations mobilised and organised the population into mass organisations. Accordingly, a workers' union, peasants' union, women's union, students' union and youth union were formed. The objectives of these mass organisations, as defined by the NLM, focused on two elements. First, they were intended to serve as instruments for organising and mobilising the population. They were expected to play an important role in educating, socialising and enlightening the population along the lines of the nationalist ideology, creating a modern, united and conscious society. The second objective of the mass organisations was the realisation of national independence in which the main mechanism was the participation of the population in the armed liberation struggle.

The increasing mobilisation and participation was manifested in the tremendous growth of the size of the national liberation army in the second decade, resulting in the liberation of many towns and villages. This, in turn, opened up the opportunity for further mobilisation, enlightenment and organisation of Eritrean society. Moreover, the establishment of schools, hospitals, local factories, the construction of roads, etc., followed the liberation of towns and villages. The emergence of such institutions further strengthened the integration of society. However, the failure to ensure unity between the Eritrean organisations caused other problems. It inhibited the creation of an environment conducive to achieving a united organisation, capable of safeguarding independence and building a modern, unified society in accordance with the intended aim of the nationalists. The existence of several conflicting organisations was construed as a major weakness of the NLM in its nation building endeavour. This important factor, the establishment of a unified liberation movement was fulfilled in the last decade of the armed struggle. The civil war between the ELF and the EPLF in the Early 1980s concluded with the defeat and eventual disintegration of the ELF. This paved the way for the domination of the NLM by the EPLF, the remaining viable politico-military organisation.

The final decade of the armed struggle passed under the hegemony of the EPLF. This development ensured the establishment of a vanguard organisation, resolving what was generally considered to have been the main weakness of the earlier stage of the Eritrean revolution. The building of a single national liberation army was, thus, realised with the rise of a hegemonic order and the emergence of a single dominant organisation. Yet, in spite of the appearance of a single liberation army, the question of political unity was far from being achieved. This is because the creation of a single liberation army was ensured through the victory of one army over another. The matter of the political existence of the rival organisations was, thus, not decisively resolved. A legitimate concern pertaining to political unity remained to be addressed.

The unity and integration of the liberation struggle that had always been one of the objectives of the NLM assumed a new dimension under the new order. It was seen as a necessary condition for nation formation. Guided by the doctrine of creating a vanguard organisation, the EPLF shifted from its decade-old unity formula of united front to the formula of a single united liberation army. Deriving from the newly adopted doctrine, it invited the forces of the other organisations to join its army. The different factions of the ELF also adopted a new strategy of unity, reflecting its profoundly decreased power and strength, advocating a united front, which they thought would secure their autonomy. This difference of views on how to best achieve unity effectively prevented the unity of the multiple Eritrean organisations from being accomplished. The EPLF continued as the sole dominant politico-military organisation until the independence of Eritrea.

As the sole liberation organisation remaining in the Field, the EPLF bore the responsibility for leading the national liberation struggle and nation-building process to its goal. The new development opened the opportunity to establish the foundations of state structure in the liberated areas. The EPLF built a formidable organisational structure that increasingly assumed the form of state structure. This quasi-state structure, established and operating in the liberated zones, included structures such as security (surveillance and control), social services (education and health care services), economic, agricultural and public administration. There were different departments corresponding to these structures, which resembled government departments. Moreover, in this quasi-state structure, the EPLF assumed the position of a state while the mass organisations and the people's councils represented civil society. In the nation formation process, the EPLF thus assumed the place of the state as the agent of nation-building in disembodied, abstract social relationships.

The NLM was an important instrument in the process of formation of the Eritrean nation. Through the cultivation of historic and symbolic attachments to the territory, it strove to foster a profound nationalist sentiment. The sacrifices being made in the war for liberation for a sacred higher cause – and if necessary that would continue to be made in the future – were also given special emphasis as a mechanism of inculcating national feelings and consciousness. Eritrean history was depicted as endowed with a culture of resistance and heroism, which formed its unique characteristics. Moreover, Eritrean nationalists in the NLM argued that the historical genesis of present day Eritrea began with the appearance of the Italian rule. It was argued that Eritrea developed as a unique territory under colonial rule. As such, the claim of the legitimacy of the history and nationhood of Eritrea was intimately connected with colonialism. In the symbolic dimension, Eritrean nationalists referred as confirmation of the unique Eritrean identity, among other things, to the autonomy, constitution, flag, government, parliament, etc., which were conferred on the Eritrean Federation by the UN Resolution. The NLM accentuated the colonial history and the symbols and institutions which accompanied it with the aim of constructing Eritrean national identity. In short, the Eritrean nationalists' historical narratives and mythology pivoted around the colonial creation of present Eritrea. Consequently, the common colonial experience and the attendant shared culture were strongly stressed. In that way, agents of the NLM were able to connect the emotion, sentiment and affiliation of the Eritrean people to the territory created by Italian colonialism. It has been said that nationalists are the 'high priests' of nationalism, and that nationalism creates nations. The agents of the NLM served as the 'high priests' and Eritrean nationalism undertook the task of creating the Eritrean nation.

THEORETICAL REFLECTIONS

The study of nation formation has gained a reputation as lacking a coherent body of theory. The striking paucity of theoretical integration has infused the study of nation formation with widespread confusion and lack of direction. Efforts to formulate an integrated theory have ended up in conspicuous and total failure. It seems that recently, researchers have come to the realisation that a single theory of nation formation is simply unlikely. It is also not desirable. It is neither possible nor desirable because of the heterogeneous objects of analysis involved in the research of nation formation. The research of nation formation as a general field of study in the social and humane sciences, addresses a wide range of variables which differ to the extreme in terms of culture, history, social structure, polity and economy, rendering it impossible to house them under a single theory. This variability of objects of analysis is crystal-clear, not only when comparison is made between the Western and non-western societies, but also when it comes to the experiences of individual nations within the Western societies. This fact compels one to adopt a very broad theory that has the potential to encompass as many variables as possible. The theory of developmentalism has just such potential. This theory, in a broad sense, describes the transformation processes in social history that leads to the rise of nations. The explanatory value of the theory lies in its encompassing scope and applicability to a variety of cases, irrespective of their radical differences. This is so because developmentalism can be used to study the internal development of each and every case by focusing on their own scope, pace and diversity. Moreover, it helps to identify the general common explanatory factors, at the same time without neglecting the specific differentials.

This study set out as an inquiry of the historical and sociological process by which the formation of the Eritrean nation took place. As a sociological study, it focused on the changes in social structures arising from the interplay between two sets of actors, the colonial powers and the nationalist movements. It is argued that it is the combined effect of the activities of these actors that drove forward the process of formation of the Eritrean nation. This has been explained through analysing the social transformation that took place. The available research reveals that at the root of the theories of nation formation lies the idea of social transformation. A transformation founded on the "great" division of traditionalism and modernism derives from the traditions of classical social theory. In accordance with this theoretical tradition, modernisation entails the secularisation and individuation of society whose potent result is assumed to be the emergence of a social relationship based on rational individual calculation. Based on this expectation, transformation must indicate a transition from community to society and from mechanical solidarity to organic solidarity. The sociological relevance of the process of transformation for the process of nation formation, seen as the change from community to society, is that nations are believed to be the outcome of this change. Conceptualised in this manner, the formation of nations, thus, entails modernisation, secularisation and individuation. In terms of modernisation, relations are to be based on rationality, science and objectivity; in terms of secularisation, nationalism replaces religion; and in terms of individuation, the individual assumes unmediated membership.

The effects of these processes are manifested in both material and spiritual dimensions. In the spiritual dimension, attitudes, behaviours, and ways of thinking and acting change. In the material dimension, economic innovation takes place based on market exchanges, economic integration and interdependence, which lead to social integration and cohesion. According to this project of transformation, social transformation that proceeds from a small face-to-face community to complex abstract society gives way to the formation of nations. Nation formation becomes a reality when social integration based on embodied, concrete face-to-face relationships gives way to social integration governed by disembodied, abstract relationships. This is precisely what happened when Italian colonialism transformed the village and nomadic communities of Eritrea into a larger territorially-integrated society. Mediation in disembodied abstract relationships takes place through extended agency such as that of the state and print-capitalism. These complex, abstract societies are tied together by institutions that are the outcome of the transformation processes. The basic assumption underlying the theory of transformation is that the rise of civic institutions paves the way for the emergence of nations. Such civic institutions include legal (law, courts, judges, jury), political (parties, parliament, enfranchisement, election), economic (market, bank, credit institutions, money and finance institutions), and cultural institutions (values, norms, symbols, music, theatre, cinemas, national holidays). The socio-economic and politico-legal integration of Eritrea generated civic institutions that have had the effect of binding together the society.

Transformation processes, of course, do not take place in a vacuum. Therefore, various groups of actors, among whom the state as a social actor occupies a particularly important position, are involved in the processes of transformation. The absolute state in European social history and the colonial state in the African social history occupied centre stage in the formation of nations. The research of colonialism stresses that the colonial demarcation of territorial units and the concomitant bureaucratic administration established the foundation for the emergence of national units based on imagined communities. More precisely, territorial centralisation and integration is seen as the precondition for the development of nations. Territorial integration, through boundary delimitation – which involves the construction of boundaries between the prospective nations – creates the necessary conditions for the development of the nation. This is so, because boundary-setting constitutes a process of exclusion and of inclusion. Exclusion takes place because those physically separated are to be considered as different, not belonging to "us". At the same time, inclusion takes place, in that those who are demarcated within the delimited space, through abstract imagining, are included in the collectivity or nation. Moreover, in the long run, this territorial belonging induces emotional attachments. An attachment rendered plausible by the shared experience of oppression, exploitation and humiliation as a result of a colonial paternalistic administration which leads to the development of the will to live together expressed in the anti-colonial nationalism.

Theorising about the evolution of the Eritrean nation following the Western theoretical paradigm, if not simply wrong, at least needs qualification. A comparative endeavour sets out to find similarities and differences. In the case at hand, to attempt to find the differences would amount to simply stating the obvious. Therefore the focus would be on pointing out the similarities that warrant theorising about the evolution of the Eritrean nation along the lines of Western theories. The methodological debate, in comparative studies in general, and nation formation in particular, focuses on the generality and contextuality or particularity divisions. The former strives to formulate universal laws or statements while the latter strives to establish the context specific. We have seen earlier that different forces were involved in the historical formation of nations, of which the absolute state and the colonial state assume prominence. It is also commonly accepted that the colonial state was, in many respects, a replica of the European State. As Calhoun notes, European colonisers organised their overseas possessions into colonies modelled partly on European nation-state. Further drawing upon Western experience, the colonial state introduced administrative centralisation, bureaucratisation of governance, popular educational system, taxation, general recruitment in the army (central army) and many other changes which also became part of the societal edifice of the post-colonial social system. Coupled with exploitation and oppression, these changes helped to induce consciousness of a territorially based national identity.

The rise of nations in Europe coincided with the development of capitalism. The premises and mechanisms that facilitated the growth of the capitalist socio-economic system were also responsible for the formation of nations. In examining colonial capitalist penetration in Eritrea, certain observation could be made which enable useful comparison with the European experience. The establishment of the colonial state in Eritrea and the introduction of colonial capitalist political economy could be said, in a relatively similar way, to have been the midwife of the social changes that took place. A change in the social structure, where it was expressed primarily in the formation of new modern social groups, came as the result of the penetration of the colonial capitalist political economy. These forces, the state and the capitalist political economy, all of which were in operation during the formative phase of the nation in Europe, were also active in the process of formation of the Eritrean nation – albeit to different degrees. Above all, the role of the colonial state in the formation of the Eritrean nation was vividly seen in the way it brought about the territorial integration of Eritrea, which was followed by the politico-legal integration. In terms of the latter, a rational-legal system of governance was introduced. Its twin, the capitalist political economy, as its part was involved in changing the economic structure of society. The economic change, on the one hand, led to the formation of new social groups, on the other, it brought about economic integration, which was accompanied by social integration. To the state-capitalist political economy nexus could also be added another factor, the development of communications technology, which was an indispensable factor in the formation of nations.

Communications theorists emphatically argue that the spread of communication technology has brought remarkable changes in social integration, centralisation and interdependence. Roads, railways, postal and telephone systems interconnected different geographical regions as well as making it easy for the movement of goods and people. Moreover, the expansion of what some communications theorists have designated as print-capitalism, in which the dissemination of printed, standardised information became possible, readily served the purpose of integrating the society and the inculcating a feeling of commonality. Colonialism's contribution in the dimension of communications in Eritrea was commendable. The Italian investment in communications in Eritrea is surpassed by none. In testimony to the Italian achievement in the communications infrastructure, thus, many observers have expressed their great admiration. As is also clearly shown in this research the expansion of communications infrastructure, particularly railway and road systems, was very extensive. This enabled vastly-improved connections between different regions and the various ethno-linguistic groups to take place.

The apparent sociological implications of the interconnection of the various regions, as well as the various ethno-linguistic groups resulting from the complex communication network, could be observed in the greater integration of society. The web of communications improvements facilitated the mobility of people and goods. The mobility of people brought in turn, not only an exchange of material products, but also an exchange of traditions, ideas and languages, thereby reinforcing social integration.

POST INDEPENDENCE AND ITS CHALLENGES

Through prevailing in the struggle of liberation, the will to live together has enabled the various Eritrean ethno-linguistic groups to enter into a new phase of their common history. The long formation process that began with the territorial integration of the various ethno-linguistic groups in 1890, ended in the emergence of Eritrea as an independent, polyethnic, civic nation state. With the independence struggle brought successfully to its conclusion, the question that now arises is, is the process of nation formation complete? The answer will, of course, be no. The process of nation formation continues. Two main reasons could be offered regarding the continuation of the process of nation formation. First, as Renan put it, a nation is a daily plebiscite, which must be perpetually constructed and reconstructed. Since membership is voluntary, members' commitment and social solidarity have to be consistently renewed. Hence, this renewal gives rise to the need for the continuation of the formation process. This is particularly true when the social composition comprises various ethno-linguistic groups. Second, Eritrea just emerged as a sovereign nation state composite of poly-ethnicity. This means it is now that the various ethno-linguistic groups must, in earnest, prove their commitment to each other and their abiding by the will to live together – free of the pressures they experienced during the long liberation struggle.

With the formation of the Eritrean nation state the common external enemy that had been so far partly a factor for the unity of the ethno-linguistic groups and their resistance to foreign domination had ceased to exist. But would the unity and integration forged during the course of recent history – and particularly during the liberation struggle, survive? Experience from other national liberation struggles demonstrates that after the common external enemy has been eliminated, the society turns its attention upon its own internal differences. In other words, the secondary contradictions surface, assuming primary position. However, this by no means automatically indicates the derailment of what has been achieved. What it does mean, is that the different ethno-linguistic groups are left to face internal differences that can no longer be deferred or swept under the carpet, as was done during the liberation struggle. Coping with these internal differences, therefore, becomes a litmus test for the strength of the will to live together.

During the National Liberation Movement (NLM), when the civil war between the ELF and the EPLF ended with the defeat of the ELF, it was argued that the unity of the ethno-linguistic groups would suffer. This argument was based mostly on the view that the two main organisations (ELF and EPLF) represented the two religions. However, the predicted disintegration did not take place – apparently the will to live together was stronger than thought by those pessimists. Moreover, this disproved those of the view that the organisations represented the two main religions and that the Eritrean society is divided into two blocs of Christians and Moslems. Furthermore, in spite of ethno-linguistic diversity, the Eritrean society showed remarkable unity when it rallied around the front leading the struggle for independence. What explanations might be found for this unity? The most probable explanation seems to be that the long history of foreign domination had forged a consciousness of common destiny.

In the discourse of nation formation it is quite often argued that common sacrifices, experience of war, a pact entered during struggle form strong basis for a common future and the will to live together. Yet, these can not be an absolute guarantee of the continuation of the will to live together. Studies of nation formation also show that ethnic homogeneity or long common history by itself is not a guarantee for the continuous existence of a nation. Conversely, ethnic heterogeneity or short common history is not by itself an inhibition for the creation of a nation. The particularly bitter experience of the last thirty years and the price paid by the Eritrean ethno-linguistic groups will provide a strong motive for displaying the will to live together. It has been said, after all, that 'one loves in proportion to the sacrifices to which one has consented, and in proportion to the ills that one has suffered'.

If ethnic homogeneity by itself cannot safeguard the formation and/or continuation of a nation, and ethnic heterogeneity is not a recipe for disintegration, what is then required to ensure the formation and survival of a nation? As we have seen, common sacrifices and memory and the values and symbols that result from them tend to create social solidarity. The various ethno-linguistic groups of Eritrea fought together a war of liberation with the understanding and in recognition of the existence of two levels of identity, the ethnic and the civic. This was clearly stated in the programmes of the various liberation fronts. The political education of the fronts emphatically stressed that the various ethno-linguistic groups, on the one hand, in their totality form one nation, and on the other, in their individuality they have separate specific identity. This duality of identity, thus, constituted the body of Eritrean national identity in the past and it will do so in the future. As Calhoun notes, Eritrea became more socially integrated during the thirty years of liberation struggle. The various ethno-linguistic groups have developed a strong collective identity. The common identity and consciousness forged during the long struggle, thus, forms the basis of Eritrean nationhood.

A few paragraphs concerning the future seem to be in order. The future, in this instance, begins from the day of independence. A few years have lapsed since Eritrea achieved its independence. It appears that the will to live together that developed along the course of a century-long history is still intact. The post-independence period will be my next project for research; thus, I will not yet indulge in details. I will try to highlight certain points that have implications for the continued process of nation formation.

Within the last eight years or so a number of institutional formations and arrangements have been taking place which almost certainly have the impact of further enhancing the process of nation formation. To mention only a few, a sovereign Eritrean State was established and has assumed its place in the international community of nation-states. A referendum was held which said yes to independence with a resounding majority. A constitutional assembly set up for the purpose also drafted and approved a national constitution. On the other hand, a number of issues have emerged in the political agenda that seem to create division among the elites. Some of these issues and divisions are residues of the liberation struggle. These include the issue of official languages and the status of the various organisations that were defeated by the EPLF. In the case of official languages, an acrimonious debate is now taking place between the Government and its opponents. In the constitution that was endorsed in 1997, the issue of official languages was resolved through a decision not to have official languages. Instead, the constitution stipulates that all Eritrean languages are equal. This has indeed infuriated those who would like to see Arabic and Tigrinya as official languages. In the matter of the various groups that oppose the EPLF, they were not able to return home. After independence, the EPLF refused to allow them to return as organisations. The EPLF has indicated they are welcome to return as individuals, and those who accepted this condition have done so. Those who declined the offer are still abroad, continuing their opposition.

There is also the issue of democratisation. Although there is no conclusive evidence of the correlation between the process of nation formation and the process of democratisation, the Western historical experience of nation formation suggests a negative correlation. The importance of democratisation for nation formation, particularly in its contribution to institution building cannot be denied. So far, however, the process of democratisation in its liberal version has not been implemented. The ruling party, the People's Front for Democracy and Justice (PFDJ) and the Government are advocating a version of democracy known as participatory democracy, based on the idea of developmental state. The basic principle of participatory democracy is described as being the participation of individuals and groups of various political outlooks and persuasions under a single umbrella organisation. All Eritreans therefore, are invited to participate in the PFDJ. This is strongly criticised by opponents of the government and is by them viewed as a smokescreen to obscure a failure to implement real democracy. The intriguing question, of course, is what the way forward for the continuation of the process of nation formation will look like.

As has repeatedly been pointed out, although the sacrifices, common experience and memory – particularly of the liberation struggle – form strong basis for social solidarity; they are no absolute guarantee that the will to live to together will endure. Therefore, certain basic principles should be carefully observed for this to be possible. There are at least two basic principles that have to be seriously kept in mind:

(1) The recognition of the ethno-linguistic diversity of Eritrea. In the Eritrean Constitution of 1997, we find a statement expressing the value of this diversity. It specifically states that the struggle for a united and developed Eritrea shall be guided by the basic principle of unity in diversity. It is vital that the understanding of this national diversity be thorough and detailed–in theory as well as in practice. It is imperative, for example, that an elaborate, theoretically informed empirical study be undertaken to determine the borders and relationships between the various ethno-linguistic groups. This is important because various groups of elites, without making the effort to really understand the ethno-linguistic composition of society, promote emotionally charged politi-

cal opinions without adequate knowledge of possible consequences. So far, no systematic scientific study of ethnicity is available. Therefore, new research has to be done as a first step–to fill this gap and to depoliticise the discourse, and thereby to base public discourse and debate on more systematic, scientifically-informed knowledge. On the practical aspect, after establishing the necessary knowledge, policies must be designed in such a manner as to correspond with and reflect reality. Political discourse and policies will better serve Eritrea if guided by coherent studies. All actors – the state, individual political actors and elites of the various ethno-linguistic groups – should take great care in paying attention to the polyethnic composition of the Eritrean nation and keep this in mind as they act. Recent debate among politicians has been characterised largely by political rivalry. Generally, two tendencies can be pointed to that characterise the elites. On the one hand, there are groups of elites who emphasise the primordial characteristics, playing down the civic characteristics by exaggerating the religious divisions of the society. On the other hand, there are group of elites who de-emphasise the primordial characteristics and stress on the civic characteristics. What is needed is a practical balance between the primordial and civic characteristics.

It is clear that in the course of the long journey, the development of an overriding common civic culture became possible. Indeed, the civic nationalism of the liberation struggle has led to the emergence of basic values and symbols, through which the Eritrean society is able to interpret its common experience and look forward to its future. Yet, it is also quite clear that there are still differences that distinguish the various ethno-linguistic groups on the basis of their primordial heritages. These differences have existed in the past, and will likely continue to exist in the future. Clear recognition and acceptance of these differences and similarities would foster the continued development of the sense of respect, equality, harmony and self-confidence among the various ethno-linguistic groups which would, in turn, induce national cohesion and integration. Therefore, it is of vital importance to acknowledge and celebrate the unity and diversity that characterise the Eritrean nation.

(2) Avoiding the pernicious division of the society in two religio-linguistic categories. This binary division of society is pernicious because it is based on false assumption that the society is divided in two socio-cultural groups. It glosses over the reality that there are nine ethno-linguistic groups, which can not be reduced to two blocs. For the past fifty years or so, attempts have been made to analyse Eritrean society by using the notion of binary division. The first of such attempts emerged during the British Administration. It is widely believed that in its attempt to partition the territory, the British Administration magnified the Moslem-Christian division of Eritrea. The British were convinced that an independent Eritrea could not surmount the religious division. Later, during the liberation struggle, some observers of the struggle also attempted to explain the conflicts in the ranks of the liberation movement by using this binary divi-

sion. Moreover, some Eritrean groups have used this division in their political competition.

However, as pointed out, this binary division is not anchored in reality. That is, the division of the society into Christian-Tigrinya-highlanders and Moslem-Arabic-lowlanders violates the reality on the ground. This division is based on the assumption that all the ethno-linguistic groups (total of eight) who profess Islam can be parcelled in one bloc, while the Christian Tigrinya speakers constitute another bloc. If we test this assumption against historical facts, we find numerous events and occasions that cast doubt on its validity. That is, reality has proved time and again the artificiality of this binary division. Illustrative examples might be appropriate to expose the inaccuracy of the assumption. For these purposes we can refer to the following historical events: (a) during the 1940s the Moslem League tried to unite the Moslem communities but shortly after its formation a division appeared reflecting the ethno-linguistic diversity of the League. Moreover, it clearly emerged that the various ethno-linguistic groups attending the Keren meeting of 1947 showed different interest and wishes. (b) When the zone armies were established in the armed struggle, opposition arose, in Zone One from the Keser ethno-linguistic groups against the domination of the Beni Amer, in Zone Two by the Maria and Habab against the Belain domination. (c) When the Abdullah Idris group carried out a coupe de'ta in the ELF in 1982 and attempted to form an Islamic and Arab-oriented organisation, it failed because several of the Moslem ethno-linguistic groups (e.g. the Nara, Kunama the Saho) refused to join. It consequently remained small, representing only its own ethno-linguistic group.

All these examples clearly indicate that Eritrea is not a bi-ethnic nation state but a polyethnic nation state comprising nine ethno-linguistic groups. An attempt to reduce them to two blocs will always be a futile endeavour.

ERITREA: A CIVIC NATION

I began this study with the argument that the presence of the five emergent dimensions of nation formation (territorial integration, politico-legal integration, socio-economic integration, common history and common culture) generate the sixth: the will to live together. Moreover, I stated conversely, that the visible availability of all the six dimensions indicates the formation of a nation. It must be observed that all of these analytical dimensions form the basis for the conception of a civic nation. The criteria applied in the ethnic conception of nation are, on the other hand, categorically different. Concepts related to the civic nation are a duality of identity and the will to live together. These three categories of concepts (civic nation, duality of identity and will to live together) are treated together in this section because of the way they interrelate with one another. A brief statement might help to clarify this. The civic conception of nation, as will be shortly illustrated, is based on criteria characteristic of a collectivity that is not of primordial homogeneity. This state of reality necessitates a duality of identity. A collectivity marked by duality of identity needs the development of the will to live together to bind it as a nation. The underlying assumption in the dimension of the will to live together is that common experience, memory and sacrifice generate the will to live together. These subjective aspects, however, need to be supplemented by material conditions. Such material conditions develop as a result of economic integration through which different groups are rendered economically interdependent. This interdependency, in turn, enhances the will to live together, thereby ensuring the cohesion and integration of the nation.

This research started with the territorial integration of the various ethnolinguistic groups in 1890 and ended with the emergence of Eritrea as sovereign nation state in 1991. It investigated the transformation of society over a hundred-year period. The question that follows is what is the result of this transformation or formation process? Has Eritrea emerged as a culturally homogenous (in its primordial sense) nation as nations are sometimes perceived? The response to this question is, of course, unequivocally no. But before grappling with the question of what has become of Eritrea, I would like to briefly recount the debate on the two basic conceptions of nations. The research of nation formation identifies two conceptions of nation, notably ethnic and civic. As we have already seen, the conception of ethnic nation is founded on the premise of primordial characteristics in which the markers of a nation are common language, religion, ethnicity and tradition. Conversely, the civic conception of nation is based on modern characteristics such as citizenship, political identity, binding institutions, and common experience that evoke the will to live together. These two conceptions gave rise to the identification of two types of nations, notably 'cultural' or 'ethnic' nation and 'political' or 'civic' nation. Other fundamental distinguishing characteristics can be found in the notions of voluntarism and determinism. In the civic nation, membership is voluntary, while in the ethnic nation it is pre-determined. In the former, at least in theory, the individual has a choice because he/she is not born into it, whereas in the latter one is simply born in it.

A civic nation typically–though not invariably–displays a duality of identity. Since one characteristic feature of civic nation is multi-ethnicity or multi-linguality, we have at least two levels of identity. The first level will be the primordial one–the sub-national identity. The sub-national identity consists of the specific identity of a particular ethno-linguistic group. The other identity will be the civic one, a national identity that is an overarching, transcendent, common one, a supra ethno-linguistic identity. Consequently, two classes of hierarchically ordered identity coexist, bound by the will to live together. Culture is the primary marker of identity. As far as the culture of polyethnic societies is concerned, even there, we have duality, sub-national culture(s) and national culture. The national culture is primarily a political culture derived from the political experience and identity of the particular society. Conversely, the sub-national culture(s) refers to the culture of specific ethno-linguistic groups, which is based on their specific primordial heritage.

To return to the question posed above–the result of the transformation process–the point of departure of this study has been that the basis of the formation of the Eritrean nation was established by the colonial state through territorial compartmentalisation, administrative and legal centralisation, economic integration and the creation of relevant civic institutions. The process through which these developments took effect also brought with it a history of common experience and memory, which its members could lean on to find legitimacy for their claim of collective identity. An identity formed along the course of the formation of common history and through the construction of selective identity markers resting on civic premises. Since the socio-cultural composition of Eritrean society that emerged as a result of colonialism is pluralistic, it fits in the civic conception of nation. Realising this, Eritrean nationalists in the NLM declared that Eritrean national identity is founded on the basis of both collective and individual membership. The collective membership refers to belonging to a particular ethno-linguistic group (mediated membership), while individual membership denotes the individual becoming a member of the civic nation (unmediated membership). More precisely, this means that the individual–because of his/her own ethno-linguistic identity, and since the ethno-linguistic group is, as a group, a member of the civic nation–assumes membership. On the other hand, the individual has direct membership in the civic nation. As any nationalist movement wishes, however, priority was given to the aim of achieving national identity based on individuality. In the nationalist outlook, members are accepted as individuals regardless of family, kinship, class origin or gender. With the aim of achieving this goal, the agents of the NLM adopted political programmes that were intended to accelerate the construction of a new Eritrean identity. Ideally, this identity would transcend parochial socio-cultural boundaries. Agents of the NLM, thus, in an attempt to build a civic nation, followed the principles of modernisation theory.

It is worthwhile to point out that a cultural group is not the same as an ethnic group. Groups of different ethnic background may well display cultural similarities. A clear example of this phenomenon can be drawn from the Eritrean ethnic and cultural settings. The cultural boundaries between some ethno-linguistic groups are very diffuse. Besides common religion (perhaps because of common religion), which transcends both formal and informal ethnic boundaries, two groups considered to be ethnically different may manifest identical cultural traits, or vice versa. As an illustration, we can mention the closeness of the Belain Moslems to the culture of the Tigre speakers, while the Christian Belain are closer to the Christian Tigrinya culture. A particular ethnic group may display diversity of culture derived from religious differences. Another case is the closeness of the Nara and the Beni Amer–a case of ethnic difference but cultural similarity. Ethnic studies stress the importance of establishing "a field of complementarity", which among other things pertains to a shared language in which interaction takes place. That is, for an interethnic relationship to prevail, a communication mediated through a commonly intelligible language is required. The case of the Eritrean ethno-linguistic groups referred here testifies to the fact that closeness of culture is mainly the result of a shared linguistic knowledge. The examples cited above indicate the prevalence of the "field of complementarity" – a field of shared space in which the ethno-linguistic groups interact and process their relations with respect to linguistic and cultural similarity and interaction between the various ethno-linguistic groups.

Eritreas social composition places it in the category of polyethnic nations. Consequently, when we talk about nation formation, we refer necessarily to the civic conception of nation. The integration and cohesion of society in the civic conception is presumed to emerge as a result of the establishment and development of secular public institutions. These institutions include economic, social, political, legal and cultural ones. Furthermore, these institutions, in general terms, embody symbols, values and norms that the society can identify with in order to develop the will to live together.

While it cannot be denied that a certain level of economic, political, cultural and historical interaction took place among the various ethno-linguistic groups of Eritrea before Italian colonialism, it was indisputably under Italian rule that these relationships were organised and integrated centrally. The political and economic centralisation that occurred under the Italians undoubtedly furthered the evolution of Eritrea as a cohesive civic nation. It may be recalled that in earlier chapters, we examined research on Eritrean nationalism which emphasised the importance of the socio-economic changes that occurred as the outcome of the penetration of colonial capital. Quite often, those who stress the pertinence of the socio-economic change argue that the implications of material changes for overall societal integration were far-reaching. This line of argumentation is based on the assumption that economic innovation necessarily leads to a corresponding political consciousness and identity. An illustration that can be taken as a sign of the emergence of Eritrean national identity rendered possible by Italian colonialism – transcending ethno-linguistic divisions and as the outcome of the socio-economic integration and cohesion – can be shown by: a) the rejection of the Moslem communities of the plan to incorporate them in Sudan; b) the rejection by many highland Christians of the total annexation of Eritrea by Ethiopia; and c) the resistance of all Eritreans to the division of Eritrea.

These examples show the rise of a unique socio-economic entity with which its members can identify, while simultaneously defining the boundary lines between them and their neighbours. This development may be attributed primarily to Italian colonial penetration. As was pointed out earlier, the Moslem League and the Liberal Progressive Party in particular, by rejecting union with Sudan and Ethiopia and by demanding territories which they thought were parts of Eritrea, strove for the independence of the territory of Eritrea – a territory that had been created by Italy. This was a clear manifestation of territorial or civic nationalism. The advancement of civic nationalism earned currency during the second phase (the NLM) of the process of nation formation. At this time, clearly defined projects of mobilisation, participation, institution building and societal transformation were undertaken by the agents of the NLM. These were programmatic undertakings clearly aiming at the construction of a civic nation. Consequently, unlike earlier periods a conscious project of transformation from the *Field* based on the understanding of the diversity of the society assumed primacy in the struggle. Finally, it has to be concluded that as civic nation, Eritrea displays combined characteristics of the primordialist/modernist and the ethnic/civic in its ethno-linguistic diversity. Thus, its nationhood is based on the unity of these diversities.

To conclude, this study has advanced the thesis that the various ethno-linguistic groups of Eritrea have developed a will to live together as a civic nation. This will to live together was generated by (a) colonial oppression and exploitation; (b) the resistance to foreign domination; (c) the war of liberation and the attendant sacrifices and the memory of these events and experiences; and (d) the material interest brought by colonial political economy.

Chronology

1557	Ottoman Empire occupies coastal area
1865	Egypt replaces the Ottomans
1869	Italian Company buys land in Assab
1882	Italy occupies Assab
1885	Italy occupies Massawa
1889	Wechale Agreement
1890	Italy declares the birth of its first colony of Eritrea
1894	The Bahta Hagos upraising
1896	Battle of Adwa
1935	Italy invades Ethiopia
1941	End of Italian colonialism
	Formation of Mahber Fekri Hager
1945	Four Powers discuss Eritrean case
1947	Italy renounces her colonies
	Formation of political parties
	FPC representatives sent to Eritrea
1948	Eritrean case referred to UN General Assembly
	UN Commission arrives in Eritrea
1950	UN Resolution 390A (V)
1952	Federation implemented
1953	General Union of Labour Syndicates established
1955	First Executive forced to leave his post
1956	Second parliamentary election
1957	Eritrean flag lowered, replaced by Ethiopian flag
1958	Formation of ELM
1959	Eritrean Penal Law replaced by Ethiopian Law
1960	Formation of ELF

The name " Eritrean government" changed to "Eritrean administration", "Chief Executive" to "Chief Administrator"

1961	Armed struggle begins
1962	Annexation of Eritrea by Ethiopia
1965	Division of ELA into Zone units - Zemene kiflitat
1968	Anseba Conference
1969	Adobha Conference
1970	Awate Conference
1971	First National Congress of ELF
1972	First civil war begins
1974	End of first civil war
	Fall of Emperor Haile Selassie
1975	Second National Congress of ELF
1977	First Organisation Congress of EPLF
1978	Recapture of Towns by Dergue army
1980	Second civil war
1981	End of second civil war
1984	Battle of Eastern Sahel
1987	Second Organisation Congress of EPLF
1988	Battle of Afa'abet
1990	Liberation of Massawa
1991	Liberation of Eritrea

Glossary

Diglel	Paramouncy of the Beni Amer Federation
Enda	Clan
Eslah	Reform
Haraka	Movement (Arabic)
Kebessa	Highland, Plateau
Mahber Shewate	Association of Seven
Metahit	Lowland
Omda	Feudal rank in the Beni Amer Federation
Sheikh	Feudal rank in the Beni Amer Federation
Wilaya	Military Units
Sagem	return
Resti	Private ownership of land
Diesa	Collective ownership of land
Gulti	A land given to an official for services rendered
Meriet Worki	Land bought
Wa'ala	Meeting
Chiqa	Village chief
Hibret Biwe'el	Conditional unity
Hanti Ertra	United Eritrea
Zemena Kflitat	The period of zones
Meda	Field
Tegadelti	Fighters, (sig.) Tegadalai (male), Tegadalit (female)
Sewra	Revolution

References

ARCHIVES

FO 371-31608, 1942.*Ethiopian Claims to Eritrea*

FO 371-35631, 1943. *Ethiopian Irredentism in Eritrea*

FO 371-35633, 1943. *Anglo-Ethiopian Relations, Committee on Ethiopia Report on Future Policy Towards Ethiopia.*

FO 371-41531, BMA Oct.1944. *Psychological and Political Attitudes of the Population*

FO 371-63175, 1947. *An Enquiry into the Method of Ascertaining the Wishes of the Inhabitants of Eritrea Regarding their Future Government and an Estimate of the Response.*

FO 371-69331 *A Historical Survey*

FO 371-69353 Telegrams, *Ethiopia Claim to Eritrea and Italian Somaliland*

FO 371-69363 *Eritrean Liberal Progressive Party*

FO 371-63212, BMA, 1947. No. 13 *Monthly Political Report* January 1947

FO 371-63212, BMS, 1947. No. 15 *Monthly Political Report Eritrea* - March 1947

FO 371-69363, Appendix 18, Four Powers commission of Investigation for the Former Italian Colonies, Report on Eritrea. *Letter of Tigre Representatives*, date Keren 25th November 1947.

FO 371-69363, Appendix 37. Four Power Commission of Investigation for the Former Italian Colonies Report on Eritrea, *Agricultural Concessions*

FO 371-69364, Appendix 70. Four Power Commission of Investigation for the Former Colonies Report on Eritrea, *Principal Pre-occupation Industries*

FO 371-69365, Appendix 101. Four Power Commission of Investigation for the Former Italian Colonies Report on Eritrea, *Liberal Progressive Party - Memorandum*

FO 371-69365, Appendix 103. Four Power Commission of Investigation for the Former Italian Colonies Report on Eritrea, *Memorandum from the Eritrean Muslim League*, 10th November 1947.

FO 371-80984

FO 371-69370, *The Administrative and Judicial System*, Chap. 6

FO 371- 69370, *General Survey of the Economic Structure as at Present Existing Chap.2*

FO 371-69370, *Trade and Industry*, Industry under the Former Italian Administration, Chap.5

FO 1015-600, *BA Eritrea, Eritrea*: Annual Report for 1949

FO 1015-853, *BA Eritrea, Eritrea*: Annual Report for 1950

FO 371-118738. *Eritrea: Annual Review for 1955 Four Power Commission of Investigation for the Former Italian Colonies*, Report on Eritrea April 1949

WO 230-168, BMA Oct. 1943. *Tel. Ref. No.36/86, D/O SECRET*, by Stephen Longrigg

WO 230-255, *Tribal Organisation in the Western Province*

WO 230-106, *BMA Half-Yearly Report*, For Period 1st January to 30th June, 1942

OFFICIAL PUBLICATIONS

Association of Eritrean Students in North America & Association of Eritrean Women in North America, 1978. In Defence of the Eritrean Revolutions. New York

Association of Eritrean Students in North America, 1977. Selected Articles from Vanguard: Official Monthly Organ of the Eritrean People's Liberation Front

Ethiopia, A Weekly News Letter (in Tigrinya), an official voice of the Association of the Love of the Country of Eritrea with Ethiopia - one Ethiopia 1952 no.295-395, 1954 no. 473-536

Disposition of Italian Colonies, Department Of State, Division of African Affairs, 1949

The Eritrean Weekly News (Tigrinya) 31-8-1942 - 31-12-1946 (a weekly newsletter), Published by Ministry of Information, Public Information Office, BMA

ORGANISATIONAL SOURCES

Adulis, vol. V, no. 3, April 1988 (Published Monthly by the Foreign Relations Bureau of the EPLF - European and North American Desks)

Adulis, vol. IV, no. 2, Special Issue (Published Monthly by the Foreign Relations Bureau of the EPLF - European Desk)

ELF 1971. The Eritrean Revolution: *A Programmatic Declaration*: Approved by the First National Congress Held inside the Liberated area, 14th October-12th November 1971. Damascus, ELF Damascus Office

ELF, 1977. Eritrea and the Federal Act. Presented to the Afro-Arab Summit Conference by the Eritrean Liberation Front Cairo, March 7, 1977.

Eritrean Liberation Front, 1975. *Political Programme Approved by the 2nd National Congress of the ELF*: Liberated Areas, May 22, 1975 (2nd ed.). Beirut ELF Foreign Information centre

ELF, Eritrea: History, Geography and Economy, (no date)

Eritrean Liberation Front, 1978. *The ELF's National Democratic Line*. The ELF Foreign Information Centre, Beirut

ELF-PLF, 1971. *Eritrea: A Victim of UN Decision and of Ethiopian Colonial Aggression*: An appeal of the Eritrean people to the 26th Session of the UN General Assembly, New York.

ELF-PLF, 1975. *Khartoum Unity Agreement, September 1975*, ELF/PLF Information Office

ELF-RC, 1989. *National Democratic Programme of ELF*, The General National Congress, 28 June - 6 July 1989

EPLF/Selfi Natzinet Ertra, 1974. Short History of the Eritrean Struggle and why the Eritrean Popular Liberation Forces was Founded (in Tigrinya).

Eritrean People's Liberation Forces, 1971/1974. *What was Our View about "National Congress"?* (Intai *Neiru Re'utona Bza'aba " Hagerawi Guba'e"* - Tigrinya).

EPLF Eritrea and Its Struggle (No date, *Ertran Kalsan* - Tigrinya)

EPLF 1977. *National Democratic Programme of the Eritrean People's Liberation Front*: Adopted by the First Congress of the EPLF on January 31st, 1977

EPLF, 1977. Importance of Historical First Congress of EPLF in Eritrean Revolution. A paper presented to the 8th Congress of Eritrean for Liberation in North America, 15-22 August 1977 (in Tigrinya).

EPLF. *Eritrean People Liberation Forces* (not date, Tigrinya)

EPLF 1978. Memorandum. Adopted by the First Congress of the EPLF on January 31st, 1977.

EPLF, *Ftzametat*, Special Issue, April 1982 (in Tigrinya).

EPLF, 1981. *Mahta*, There is no Revolutionary Movement without Revolutionary Theory. Vol.7, No. 4. (In Tigrinya)

EPLF, 1983. M'msrat Wetahaderawi M'mhdar Engliz'n Nai Mahber Fikri Hager M'enawn (The Establishment of the BMA and the Demise of the Association of the Love of the Country of Eritrea)

EPLF. Mimhidar Britanian Poletikawi kalsi hizbi Ertran, 1941-1950 (British Administration and Political Struggle of the Eritrean People, 1941-1950)

EPLF, 1984. About Prolonged War (*ztenawhe wgi'e*), by the Information and Propaganda Section of EPLF

EPLF, 1987a. Eritrea and its Struggle: From Ancient to 1941. Information and Propaganda Department of EPLF.

EPLF, *Second Organisation Congress's Documents*, 12-19 May 1987b (in Tigrinya)

EPLF, Italian Colonialism in Eritrea 1882-1941 (in Tigrinya, no date)

EPLF. Beni Amer: From past history, 1928. (In Tigrinya translated from Italian by EPLF, no author or publisher of original work)

NEWSPAPERS AND PERIODICALS

Africa Confidential vol. 29, no. 9, 29 April 1988

Africa Confidential, vol.29, no. 11, 25 May 1988

Africa Confidential, vol. 31, no. 6, 23 March 1990

Allahar, Anton L., 1996. 'Primoridalism and Ethnic Political Mobilisation in Modern Society', in New Community Journals Oxford Ltd. no.22(1)1996, pp.5-21.

Ammar,Wolde-Yesus, 1997. 'The Role of Asmara Students in the Eritrean Nationalist Movement: 1958-1968', in Eritrean Studies Review vol.1, no.1, 1997.

Araya, Mesfin 1990. 'The Eritrean Question: An Alternative Explanation', in The Journal of Modern Africa Studies, 28, 1(1990) pp. 79-100

Connor, Walker, 1993. 'Beyond Reason: The Nature of the Ethnonational Bond', in Nationalism, Routledge, no. 16 (3) 1993 pp. 373-389

Dilebo, Getahun, 1974. 'Historical Origin and Development of the Eritrean Problem 1889-1962', in A Current Bibliography on African Affairs 7:3, 221-44

Ellingson, Lloyd, 1977. 'The Emergence of Political Parties in Eritrea, 1941-1950', in Journal of African History, XVIII, 2, Pp. 261-281

'Ethiopia: The fighting in Eritrea continues', Africa Confidential, vol. No. 24, November 27, 1970

Fessehatzion, Tekie, 1998. 'A Brief Encounter with Democracy: From Acquiescence to Resistance During Eritrea's Early Federation Years', in Eritrean Studies Review vol.2, no. 2, 1998

Haines, C. Grove, 1947. 'The Problem of the Italian Colonies', in The Middle East Journal 1,4

Helliwell, J.F., 1994. 'Empirical Linkages Between Democracy and Economic Growth', in British Journal of Political Science Vol.24. Cambridge University Press. Pp. 225. 248.

Hutchinson, John, 1992. 'Moral Innovators and the Politics of Regeneration. The Distinctive Role of Cultural Nationalism in Nation Building', in International Journal of Comparative Sociology, Brill, no. 33 (1-2) 1992 pp. 101-117

Hroch, Miroslav, 1994. 'The Social Interpretation of Linguistic Demands in European National Movement', in The Social Interpretation of Linguistic Demands in European National Movements. European University Institute 1994 pp. 3-37

Hussey, E. R., C.M.G, 1953. 'Eritrea Self-Governing', in African Affairs

Instituto Coloniale Italiano (M.K.G) 1947, 'Italy in Africa', also, in World Today, 4(2); pp. 62-73, 1947

Johnson, Michael and Trish Johnson, 1981. 'Eritrea: The National Question and the Logic of Protracted Struggle', in Journal of the Royal African Society, vol. 80, no. 319, pp. 181-195.

Joireman, Sandra Fullerton, 1996. 'The Minefield of Land Reform: Comments on the Eritrean Land Proclamation', in Africa Affairs (1996), 95, 269-285

Keller, Edmond J., 1990/91. 'International Perspective on the Eritrea-Ethiopian Conflict', in Horn of Africa vol.13, no 3&4 1990, and vol.14, no. 1&2 1991.

Killion, Tom, 1997. 'Eritrean Workers' Organization and Early Nationalist Mobilization: 1948-1958', in Eritrean Studies Review vol. 2. no. 1, 1997

Lipset, Seymour Martin, 1994. 'The Social Requisites of Democracy Revisited: 1993 Presidential Address', in American Sociological Review Vol. 59 No.1

Lobban, Richard, 1976. 'The Eritrean War: Issues and Implications', in Canadian Journal of African Studies Vol. 10 No.2 1976.

Markakis, John 1988. 'The National Revolution in Eritrea', in The Journal of Modern African Studies, 26, 1(1988), pp. 51-70.

Nadel, S. Freddy, 1945. 'Notes on Beni Amer Society', in Sudan Notes and Records, vol. 26 Pp 51-94

Nadel, S. Freddy, 1946. 'Land Tenure on the Eritrean Plateau', in Africa 16, 1: 1-21. London, Oxford University Press.

'On the Shores of the Red Sea', in Tricontinental 1968, PP. 56-70

Pankhurst, Richard, 1964. 'Italian Settlement Policy in Eritrea and its Repercussions 1889-1896', in Boston University Papers in African History, vol. One, Jeffrey Butler (ed.,). Boston University Press Boston, Mass.

Pankhurst, E. Sylvia, 1952. Why are we Destroying the Ethiopian Ports?, with an Historical Retrospect 1557-1952 and, Asmara: the Heart Disease of a Lovely Modern City. Essex, " New Times and Ethiopia News" Books

Pateman, Roy, 1989. 'Eritrean Resistance During the Italian Occupation', in Journal of Eritrean Studies vol. III, 2(1989)

Pateman, Roy, 1990. 'Liberte, Egalite, Fraternite: Aspects of the Eritrean Revolution', in The Journal of Modern African Studies vol. 28, 3(1990), pp. 457-472

Pateman, Roy, 1991. 'The War in Eritrea: Drawing to an End?', in The Horn Review vol.1, no. 1

Paul, A, 1950. 'Notes on the Beni Amer', in Sudan Notes & Records Proceedings of the Philosophical Society of the Sudan Vol. XXXI - Parts I & II. Alexandria, Whitehead Morris Egypt

Pedriana, Nicholas and Stryker, Robin, 1997. 'Political Culture Wars 1960s Style: Equal Employment Opportunity-Affirmative Action Law and the Philadelphia Plan', in The American Journal of Sociology Vol. 103, No. 3 (November 1997): 633-91

Pool, David, 1981. 'Revolutionary Crisis and Revolutionary Vanguard: The Emergence of the Eritrean People's Liberation Front', in Review of African Political Economy

Pool, David, 1993. 'Eritrean Independence: The Legacy of the Derg and the Politics of Reconstruction', pp. 389-402, in African Affairs vol. 92, no. 368.

Sorenson, John 1991. 'Discourse on Eritrean Nationalism and Identity', in The Journal of Modern African Studies, 29, 2(1991), pp. 301-317.

Taddia, Irma, 1990. 'At the Origin of the State/Nation Dilemma: Ethiopia, Eritrea, Ogaden in 1941', in Northeast African Studies, vol. 12, no. 2-3, 1990

Tekle, Amare, 1991. 'Ethiopia: Myths and Consequences', in The Horn Review vol.1, no.1

Teklehaimanot, Berhane, 1996. 'Education in Eritrea During the European Colonial Period', in Eritrean Studies Review, vol. 1, no. 1, 1996

Van den Berghe, Pierre, 1978. 'Race and Ethnicity: A Socio-biological Perspective', in Ethnic and Race Studied, 1, 4, 401-411

Woldemichael, Berhane, 1987. 'A Comparative Analysis of the Armed Conflict in Eritrea and South Sudan', in Journal of Eritrean Studies Vol. 2, No.1

Yohannes, Okbazghi, 1987. 'The Eritrean Question: A Colonial Case?', in The Journal of Modern African Studies, 25, 4(1987), pp. 643-668

Zernatto, G., 1944. 'Nation: The History of a Word', in Review of Politics 6, 1944, 351-66.

INTERVIEWS

Ahmed, Mohammed Nur, 14 August 1997. Asmara, Eritrea

Iyay, Saleh, 1997. Asmara, Eritrea

Mohammed Nasir, Ahmed, 1996. Stockholm, Sweden

Mohammed Nur, Taha, 1997. Asmara, Eritrea

Mohammed Said, Al Amin, 1997. Asmara, Eritrea

Nawid, Mohammed Said, 7, 10, 13, April 1997. Asmara, Eritrea

Tesfay, Alemseged, 1997. Asmara, Eritrea

Toteel, Ibrahim Idris, 4, 27 July 1997. Asmara and Massawa, Eritrea

Tzeggai, Yohannes, 1997. Asmara Eritrea

BOOKS AND ARTICLES

Abrams, Philip, 1982. Historical Sociology. England, Open Books.

Abu Shanab, Robert Elias, 1971. The Eritrean Revolution. Review Publications (India), and Eritrean Liberation Front Damascus Office.

Adam, Heribert, 1994. 'Ethnic Versus Civic Nationalism: South Africa's Non-Racialism in Comparative Perspective', in South African Sociological Review, 7 no. 1 October 1994

Allardt, Erik, 1970. 'Types of Protests and Alienation', in Mass Politics: Studies in Political Sociology, Erik Allardt and Stein Rokkan (eds.). New York, The Free Press-

Amin, Samir, 1980. Class and Nation, Historically and in the Current Crisis. London Heinemann Ibadan Nairobi.

Ammar, Wolde-Yesus, 1992. Eritrea: Root Causes of War & Refugees. Baghdad, Sindbad Printing Co.

Anderson, Benedict, 1991/1983 (2nd.ed.) Imagined Communities: Reflections on the origin and spread of nationalism. London New York, Verso.

Anderson, Benedict 1994. 'Imagined Communities' pp. 89-96, in Nationalism, John Hutchinson and Anthony D. Smith (eds.), Oxford. New York, Oxford University Press

Aren, Gustav, 1978. Evangelical Pioneers in Ethiopia: Origins of the Evangelical Church Mekane Yesus. EFS Förlaget Stockholm, The Evangelical Church Mekane Yesus Addis Abeba

Anttila, Sten T., 1993. Aspects of Macro-Sociological Methodology. Uppsala, Acta Universitatis Upsaliensis, Ph.D. thesis.

Armstrong, John A., 1982. Nations before Nationalism. The University of North Carolina Press Chapel Hill

Apter, David E., 1963. 'Political Religion in the New Nations', in Old Societies and New States, Clifford Geertz (ed.), 1963. New York, The Free Press.

Balibar, E., 1988. 'The Nation Form: History and ideology', in Race, Nation, Class: Ambiguous identities. Paris, La D_couverte.

Becker, George Henery, 1952. The Disposition of the Italian Colonies 1941-1951. PhD. Thesis University of Geneva Annemasse Imprimerie Granchamp

Bendix, Reinhard, 1964. Nation-Building and Citizenship: Studies of our changing social order. New York London Sydney, John Wiley & Sons, Inc.

Berger, Carol, 1987. ' Eritrea: The Longest War', in Africa Report, March-April 1987.

Beyer, Peter, 1994. Religion and Globalization. London. Thousand Oaks. New Delhi, Sage Publications

Bhabha, H.K. (ed.), 1990. Nation and Narration. London and New York, Routledge

BMA-Eritrea, 1943. Races and Tribes of Eritrea. Asmara

Bondestam, Lars, 1989. Eritrea med rätt till självbestämmande. Uddevalla, Clavis Förlag

Brass, Paul R., 1994. 'Elite Competition and Nation-Formation', in Nationalism, John Hutchinson & Anthony D. Smith (eds.)

Breuilly, John, 1993. Nationalism and the State. Manchester, Manchester University Press.

Bryant, Christopher G.A, 1995. 'Civic Nation, Civil Society, Civic Religion', in Civil Society: Theory, History, Comparison, John A. Hall (ed.). UK, Polity Press.

References

Cabral, Amilcar, 1980. Unity and Struggle: Speeches and writings (trans. by Micheals Wolfers). London, Heinemann

C. G. and Brenda Z. Seligman, 1910. 'Notes on the History and Present Condition of the Beni Amer (Southern Beja)', in Sudan Notes and Records.

Calhoun, Craig, 1995. 'Nationalism and Difference: The Politics of Identity Writ Large', in Critical Social Theory. Blackwell, Oxford UK & Cambridge

Calhoun, Craig, 1997. Nationalism. Buckingham, Open University Press

Chaliand, Gerard, 1980. 'The Guerrilla Struggle' in Behind the War in Eritrea, Basil Davidson, Lionel Cliffe and Bereket Habte Selassie (eds.)

Chatterjee, Partha, 1993. The Nation and Its Fragments: Colonial and Postcolonial Histories. Princeton, New Jersey, Princeton University Press

Clapham, Christopher, 1995. 'The Horn of Africa: A Conflict Zone', in Conflict in Africa, Oliver Furley (ed.). London, New Your, Tauris Academic Studies.

Clapham, Christopher, 1996. Africa and the International system: The politics of State Survival. Cambridge University Press

Cliff, Lionel and Lars Bondestam, 1983. Eritrea: Popular Participation and the Liberation Struggle. Roma, Auletta di Montecitorio.

Cohen, Anthony P., 1985. The Symbolic Construction of Community. London and New York, Routledge

Coleman, James S., 1960. The Politics of the Developing Areas, eds., Gabriel A. Almond, James S. Coleman.N.J., Princeton

Connel, Dan, 1980. 'The Changing Situation in Eritrea', in Behind the War in Eritrea, Basil Davidson, Lionel Cliffe and Bereket Habte Selassie (eds.)

Connell, Dan, 1993. Against all Odds: A Chronicle of the Eritrean Revolution. Trenton NJ., The Red Sea Press

Connor, Walker, 1987. 'Ethnonationalism', in Understanding Political Development, by Myron Weinerand Samuel P. Huntington, 1987. Harper Collins Publishers.

Connor, Walker, 1990/1994. ' When is a Nation', (from 'When is a Nation?', Ethnic and Racial Studies, 13/1 (1990), 92-100), in Nationalism, John Hutchinson and Anthony D. Smith (eds.)

Davidson, B., L. Cliffe and B. Habte Selassie (eds.), 1980. Behind The War in Eritrea. Nottingham, Spokesman

Davidson, B., L. Cliffe (eds.) 1988. The Long Struggle of Eritrea for Independence and Constructive Peace. Nottingham, Spokesman

Davidson, Basil, 1992. The Black Man's Burden: Africa and the Curse of the Nation-State. London, James Currey

De Marco, Roland Reinald, 1943. The Italianization of African Natives: Government Native Education in the Italian Colonies 1890-1937. New York, Bureau of Publications Teachers College, Columbia University.

Deutsch, Karl W., 1963. 'Nation-Building and National Development: Some issues for political research', in Nation-Building, Deutsch & Foltz (eds.) 1963. New York, Atherton Press.

Deutsch, Karl W., 1966. Nationalism and Social Communication: An Inquiry into the Foundations of Nationality. Massachusetts, and London, The M.I.T. Press, Massachusetts Institute of Technology.

Diamond, L., J. J. Linz, S. M. Lipset (eds.), 1988. Democracy in Developing countries: Africa, V.II. Boulder, Colorado; Lynne Rienner Publishers and London, England, Adamantine Press Limited.

Downs, A., 1957. An Economic Theory of Democracy. New York, Harper & Row.

Duara, Pranenjit, 1996. 'Historicising National Identity, or Who Imagines What and When', in Becoming National, Geoff Eley and Ronald Grigor Suny (eds.)

Duchacek, Ivo D., 1987. Comparative Federalism: The Territorial Dimension of Politics. Lanham New York London, University Press of America

Durkheim, Emile, 1977. The Evolution of Educational Thought: Lectures on the Formation and development of Secondary Education in France. London, Routledge and Kegan Paul (1904-5, Published posthumously 1938)

Durkheim, Emile, 1984. Division of Labour in Society. London, The Macmillan Press

Eisenstadt, Samuel N., and Stein. Rokkan, (eds.) 1973. Building States and Nations: Models and Data Resources, vol. I. Beverly Hills London, Sage Publications-

Eley, Geoff and Suny, Ronal Grigor, 1996. 'Introduction: From the Movement of Social History to the Work of Cultural Representation', in Becoming National, Geoff Eley and Ronald Grigor Suny (eds.). Oxford University Press.

Emerson, Ruper, 1960. From Empire to Nation: The Rise of Self-assertion of Asian and African Peoples. Cambridge, Massachusetts, Harvard University Press

Emerson, Rupert, 1963. 'Nation-Building in Africa', in Nation-Building. Deutsch & Foltz (eds.) 1963: New York, Atherton Press.

Emerson, Rupert, 1971. 'The Prospects for Democracy in Africa', in The State of the Nations, Michael F. Lofchie (ed.)

Eriksen, Thomas Hylland, 1993. Ethnicity and Nationalism: Anthropological perspective. London, East Haven, Pluto Press.

Erlich, Haggai, 1982. Ethiopia and Eritrea During the Scramble for Africa: A Political Biography of Ras Alula, 1875-1897. African Studies Center, Michigan State University

Erlich, Haggai, 1983. The Struggle Over Eritrea, 1962-1978: War and Revolution in the Horn or Africa. Stanford, California, Hoover Institution Press

Fanon, Frantz, 1963. The Wretched of the Earth, Preface by Jean-Paul Sartre. New York, Grove Weidenfeld (translated by Constance Farrington)

Fathi, Schirin H., 1994. Jordan - An Invented Nation? Tribal-State Dynamics and the Formation of National Identity. Hamburg, Deutsches Orient- Institute

First,Ruth, 1983. 'Colonialism and the Formation of African States', in States and Societies, ed., David Held.

Frantz, Charles, 1975. Pastoral Societies, Stratification and National Integration in Africa, Research Report No. 30, Scandinavian Institute of African Studies.

Friedman, Jonathan, 1994. Cultural Identity and Global Process. London, Thousand Oaks, New Delhi, Sage Publication

Gayim, Eyasu, 1993. The Eritrean Question: The conflict between the right of self-determination and the interests of states. Uppsala, Iustus Förlag AB

Gebre-Medhin, Jordan, 1979. The Eritrean Case: A Critical Appraisal of Peasants and Modernization Studies in Developmental Anthropology. A Thesis Submitted to the Faculty of Purdue University

Gebre-Medhin, Jordan, 1989. Peasants and Nationalism in Eritrea: A Critique of Ethiopian Studies. Trenton, New Jersey, The Red Sea Press.

Geertz, Clifford, 1963. 'The Integrative Revolution: Primordial Sentiments and Civil Politics in the New States', in Old Societies and New States, Clifford Geertz (ed.). New York, The Free Press

Geertz, Clifford, 1973/1993. The Interpretation of Cultures, Selected Essays. London, Fontana Press

Gellar, S., 1973. 'State-Building and Nation-Building in West Africa', in Eisenstadt and Rokkan (eds.) Vol. II

Gellner, Ernest, 1983. Nations and Nationalism. Oxford UK & Cambridge USA, Blackwell Publishers.

Gellner, Ernest, 1993. 'Nationalism and the Development of European Societies', in The Future Of The Nation-state In Europe, Livonen (ed.)

Gerth, H.H., and C. Wright Mills (eds.). 1967. From Max Weber: Essays in Sociology. London, Routledge and Kegan

Ghaber, Michael, 1993. The Blin of Bogos, (ed. by Wolde Yesus Ammar). Baghdad Iraq

Ghebre-Ab, Habtu, 1993. Ethiopia and Eritrea: A documentary Study. Trenton, NJ, The Red Sea Press

Giddens, Anthony, 1985. The Nation-state and Violence. Cambridge, Polity Press.

Giddens, Anthony 1994. 'The Nation as Power-Container', in Nationalism, John Hutchinson & Anthony D. Smith (eds.)

Giesen, Bernhard, 1998. Intellectuals and Nation: Collective Identity in a German Axial Age. Cambridge University Press

Gledhill, John, 1994. Power and Its Disguises: Anthropological Perspective on Politics. London, Boulder, Colorado, Pluto Press

Goldthorpe, J.E. 1974 (2nd edit.). An Introduction to Sociology. Cambridge University Press

Goody, J., 1973. 'Uniqueness in the Cultural Conditions for Political Development in Black Africa, in Eisenstadt and Rokkan (eds.) Vol. II.

Goor, Luc van de, Rupesinghe, Kumar, Sciarone, Paul, 1996. Between Development and Destruction: An Enquiry into the Causes of Conflict in Post-Colonial States. The Netherlands Ministry of Foreign Affairs (DGIS) The Netherlands Institute of International Relations Clingendael

Goulbourne, H., 1987. 'The State, Development and the Need for Participatory Democracy in Africa', in Popular Struggles for Democracy in Africa, Peter Anyang' Nyong'o (ed.). London and New Jersey, The United Nations University Zed Books Ltd.

Gray, J.C. & L.Silberman, 1948. *The Fate of Italy's Colonies*: A Report to the Fabian Colonial Bureau, with Contributions by an Observer in Eritrea. London, Fabian Publications

Greenfeld, Liah, 1992. Nationalism: Five roads to modernity. Cambridge, Massachusetts London, England, Harvard University Press.

Greenfield, Richard, 1965. Ethiopia: A New Political History, London

Greenfield, Richard, 1980. 'Pre-Colonial and Colonial History', in Behind the War in Eritrea, Basil Davidson, Lionel Cliffe and Bereket Habte Selassie (eds.). Spokesman

Habermas, Jurgen, 1981 (tr. 1987 by Thomas McCarthy). The Theory of Communicative Action. Lifeworld and System: A critique of functionalist reason, vol. 2. Boston, Beacon Press.

Habte Selassie, Bereket 1980. 'From British Rule to Federation and Annexation', in Behind the War in Eritrea, Basil Davidson, Lionel Cliffe and Bereket Habte Selassie (eds.)

Habte Selassie, Bereket, 1989. Eritrea and the United Nations and Other Essays. Trenton New Jersey, The Red Sea Press.

Hague, R., and Harrop, M., 1987. Comparative Government and Politics: An introduction (2nd edit.). Macmillan Education LTD.

Haile, Semere, 1988. 'Historical Background to the Ethiopia-Eritrea Conflict', in The Long Struggle of Eritrea for Independence and Constructive Peace, Lionel Cliffe & Basil Davidson (eds.)

Hall, John, A. (ed.), 1998. The State of the Nation: Ernest Gellner and the Theory of Nationalism. Cambridge University Press

Harrison, David, 1988. The Sociology of Modernization and Development. London and New York, Routledge

Hayes, C.J.H., 1931. The Historical Evolution of Modern Nationalism. New York, Richard R. Smith, Inc.

Held, David et al, eds., 1983. States and Societies. Blackwell, Oxford UK, Cambridge USA

Hobsbawm, Eric J., 1990. Nations and Nationalism Since 1780: Programme, myth, reality. New York Port Chester Melbourne Sydney, Cambridge University Press.

Hodgkin, Thomas, 1956. Nationalism in Colonial Africa. London, Frederick Muller LTD.

Hosking, Geoffrey and Schöpflin, George (eds.), 1997. Myths & Nationhood. London, Hurst & Company.

Houtart, Francois, 1982. 'Social Aspects of the Eritrean Revolution', in The Eritrean Case

Houtart, Francois, 1980. 'The Social Revolution in Eritrea', in Behind the War in Eritrea

Hroch, Miroslav, 1985. Social Preconditions of National Revival in Europe: A Comparative Analysis of the Social Composition of Patriotic Groups Among the Small European Nations (translated by Ben Fowkes). Cambridge University Press

Hughes, A., 1981. 'The Nation-State in Black Africa', in The Nation-State, Leonard Tivey, (ed.). Oxford, Martin Robertson.

Huntington, Samuel P., 1968. Political Order in Changing Societies. New Haven and London, Yale University Press.

Hutchinson, John, 1994. Modern Nationalism. London, Fontana Press

Hutchinson, John & Anthony D. Smith (eds.), 1994. Nationalism. Oxford New York, Oxford University Press.

Hutchinson, John, 1994. 'Cultural Nationalism and Moral Regeneration', in Nationalism, John Hutchinson and Anthony D. Smith (eds.)

Iyob, Ruth, 1995. The Eritrean Struggle for Independence: Domination, Resistance, Nationalism 1941-1993. Britain, Cambridge University Press.

Inggers, Georg G., 1968: The German Conception of History: The National Tradition of Historical Thought from Herder to the Present. Wesleyan University Press

James, Paul, 1996. Nation Formation: Towards a Theory of Abstract Community. London Thousand Oaks New Delhi, Sage

Kaplinski, J., 1993. 'The Future of National Culture in Europe', in The Future of the Nation-state in Europe, Livonen (ed.)

Kemiläinen, Aira, 1964. Nationalism: Problems concerning the word, the concept and classification. Jyväskylä Kunstantajat Publishers.

Kemiläinen, Alipor, 1993. 'Patriotism and Nationalism', in The Future of the Nation-state in Europe, Jyrki Livonen (ed.)

Kiely, Ray 1995. Sociology and Development: The impasse and beyond. London, UCL Press.

Killion, Tom, 1985. Workers, Capital and the State in the Ethiopian Region, 1919-1974, Ph.D. thesis, Stanford University.

Kothari, R., 1973. The Confrontation of Realities: Realities on an International conference, pp. 99-116, in Building States and Nation vol. I. S. N. Eisenstadt and S. Rokkan (eds.)

Krejci, J., and Vitezslav Velimsky, 1981. Ethnic and Political Nations in Europe. London, Croom Helm

Käsler, Dirk, 1988. Max Weber: An Introduction to his Life and Work. Polity Press.

Käufeler, H., 1988. Modernization, Legitimacy and Social Movement: A study of socio-cultural dynamics and revolution in Iran and Ethiopia. Ethnologisches der Universiteit Zurich.

Lema, Antoine 1993. Africa Divided: The Creation of "Ethnic Groups". Lund, Lund University Press

Leonard, R., 1982. 'European Colonization and the Socio-Economic Integration of Eritrea', in The Eritrean Case

Lewis, I. M. (ed.), 1983. Nationalism & Self Determination in the Horn of Africa. London, Ithaca Press.

Liebenow, J.G., 1986. African Politics: Crises and challenges. Bloomington and Indianapolis, Indiana University Press.

Linz, Juan, 1973. 'Early State-Building and Late Peripheral Nationalisms Against the State: The Case of Spain', in Building States and Nations, vol. II, S.N. Eisenstadt and Stein Rokkan (eds.)

Lipset, Seymour Martin 1963. The First New Nation: the United States in Historical and Comparative perspective. London, Heinemann.

Lipset, Seymour Martin, 1970. 'Political Cleavages in "Developed" and "Emerging" Polities', in Mass Politics: Studies in Political Sociology, Erik Allardt and Stein Rokkan (eds.). London Collier-Macmillan Limited, New York The Free Press

Lipset, Seymour Martin, 1983 (2nd. ed.). Political Man: The social bases of politics. London, Heinemann

Livonen, L., (ed.) 1993. The Future of the Nation-state in Europe. England and USA, Edward Elgar.

Locke, L.F., W.W. Spirduso and S.J. Silverman, 1987. Proposals that Work: A guide for planning dissertation and grant proposals. Newbury Park. Beverly Hills. London, Sage Publication. Sel. chapters: Pp.16-82, 170-222. Stencil.

Lofchie, M.F., 1971 (ed.). The State of the Notions: Constraints on development in independent Africa. Berkeley, Los Angeles, London, University of California Press.

Longrigg, S.H., 1945. A Short History of Eritrea. London, Oxford University Press.

Machida, R., 1987. Eritrea: The Struggle for Independence. Trenton, New Jersey, The Red Sea Press

Markakis, John, 1987. National and Class Conflict in the Horn of Africa. Cambridge University Press

Marshall, T.H. and Tom Bottomore, 1992. Citizenship and Social Class. London, Concord, Mass; Pluto Press

Mazrui, A. A. & Tidy, M., 1984. Nationalism and New States in Africa. Nairobi Ibadan London, Heinemann Educational Books Ltd.

Mazrui, A. A., 1983. 'Francophone Nations and English-Speaking States: Imperial ethnicity and African political formation', in State Versus Ethnic Claims: African policy dilemma, Rothchild & Olorunsola (eds.) 1983. Colorado Westview Press.

Mazrui, A. A., 1973. 'Traditional Cleavages and Efforts of Integration in East Africa', in Eisenstadt and Rokkan (eds.), Vol. II

McCrone, David, 1998. The Sociology of Nationalism. London and New York, Routledge

McKinney, John C., 1966. Constructive Typology and Social Theory. Appleton-Century-Crafts

Medhanie, Tesfatzion, 1986. Eritrea: The Dynamic of National Question. Amsterdam, B.R. Gruner

Mesghenna, Y., 1988. Italian Colonialism: A Case Study of Eritrea, 1869-1934, Ph.D. thesis. Lund - Sweden, Studentlitteratur

Merrit, R.L., 1963. 'Nation-Building in America: The colonial years', in Nation-Building, Deutsch & Foltz (eds.). New York, Atherton Press.

Mohammed Said, Al Amin, 1994. The Eritrean Revolution: Advances and Pitfalls (Sewra Ertra: Msguamn Mnqulqaln)

Montserrat, Guibernau, 1996. Nationalism: The Nation-State and Nationalism in the Twentieth Century. UK, Polity Press

Morley, John, 1991. Eritrea Fifty Years Ago: An Eye Witness Account. London RICE

Mukangara, Daudi, 1979. The National Colonial Question in Ethiopia with Particular Reference to Eritrea part one. The University of Dar Es Salam Department of Political Science

Neergaard, Anders, 1997. *Grasping the Peripheral State: A Historical Sociology of Nicaraguan State Formation.* Lund University, Lund Dissertation in Sociology 13

Negash, Ghirmai, 1999. A History of Tigrinya Literature in Eritrea: The Oral and the Written, 1890-1991. Universiteit Leiden, Research School of Asian, African, and Amerindian Studies (CNWS)

Negash, Tekeste, 1986. No Medicine for the Bite of a White Snake: Notes on nationalism and resistance in Eritrea, 1890-1940. Uppsala, Reprocentralen HSC

Negash, Tekeste, 1987. *Italian Colonialism in Eritrea, 1882-1941: Policies, praxis and impact*, Doctoral dissertation, Uppsala

Negash, Tekeste, 1995. 'Competing Imaginations of the Nation: The Eritrean Nationalist Movement, 1953-1981', in Dimensions of Development With Emphasis on Africa, ed. Tekeste Negash and Lars Rudebeck. Uppsala, Reprocentralen HSC

Negash, Tekeste, 1997. Eritrea and Ethiopia: The Federal Experience. Uppsala Nordiska Afrikainstitutet

Neuberger, Benyamin, 1977/1994. 'State and Nation in African Thought', (from 'State and Nation in African Thought', in Journal of African Studies, 4/2 (1977), 199-205), in Nationalism, John Hutchinson and Anthony D. Smith (eds.)

Nisbet, Robert, 1973/1976. The Social Philosophers. Paladin

Nisbet, Robert, 1980. History of the Idea of Progress. London, Heinemann

Nisbet, Robert, 1986. The Making of Modern Society. Britain, Wheatsheaf.

Noam, C., R. Mortimer, J. Ravenhill, D. Rothchild, 1992. Politics and Society in Contemporary Africa. Boulder, Colorado; Lynne Rienner Publishers

Nzongola-Ntalaja, 1987. 'The National Question and the Crisis of Instability in Africa', in Africa: Perspectives on Peace and Development, Emmanuel Hansen (ed.). London and New Jersey, Zed Books

Olukoshi, Adebayo O. and Liisa Laakso, eds., 1996. Challenges to the Nation-State in Africa. Nordiska Afrikainstitutet, Uppsala in cooperation with Institute of Development Studies, University of Helsinki

Oommen, T.K., 1997. 'Introduction: Conceptualizing the Linkage between Citizenship and National Identity', in Citizenship and National Identity: From Colonialism to Globalism, T.K. Oommen (ed.). New Delhi. Thousand Oaks. London, Saga

Oyelaran, Olasope O. and Adediran, Michael Olu, 1997. 'Colonialism, Citizenship and Fractured National Identity: The African Case', in Citizenship and National Identity: From Colonialism to Globalism, T. K. Oommen (ed.)

Pankhurst, E. Sylvia and Richard K. P. Pankhurst, 1953. 'The Dismantling of the Ports' pp.257-266, in Ethiopia and Eritrea: The Last Phase of the Reunion Struggle 1941-1952, E. Sylvia Pankhurst and Richard K. P. Pankhurst (eds.), Lalibela House

Perham, M., 1969. The Government of Ethiopia. Evanston, Illinois, Northwestern University.

Perini, Ruffillo, 1905/1997. Di Qua Dal Mareb (*Mareb-mellase, t*rans. into Tigrinya by Vitorio Roncali.). Roberto Chairamonte

Pollera, Alberto, 1935. *De Kebat Hizbitat Ertra* (Natives of Eritrea, originally written in Italian, translated by Aba Yisac Ghere-Iyesu)

Pool, David, 1979. Eritrea: Africa's Longest War. London, Anti-Slavery Society

Pool, David, 1983. 'Eritrean Nationalism' pp. 175-193, in Nationalism & Self Determination in the Horn of Africa, I. M. Lewis (ed.).

Pool, David, 1997: Eritrea: Towards Unity in Diversity. Minority Rights Group Report

Potholm C. P., 1979. The Theory and Practice of African Politics. Englewood Cliffs, New Jersey 07632, Prentice-Hall.

Potter, Robert B., 1985. Urbanisation and Planning in the 3rd World: Spatial Perceptions and Public Participation. London & Sydney, Croom Helm

Przeworski, A. & Teune, H., 1970. The Logic of Comparative Social Inquiry. New York London Toronto Sydney, Wiley-Interscience.

Pye, Lucian W., 1962. Politics, Personality, and Nation Building. New Haven and London, Yale University Press.

Ragin, C.C., 1987. The Comparative Method: Moving beyond qualitative and quantitative strategies. Berkeley California London, University of California Press.

Raka, Micheal Hasama, 1992. The History of Eritrea (Zanta Ertra in Tigrinya). Asmara, Franchescana Printing Press

Renan, Ernest, [1882]1991. 'What is a Nation', in Nation and Narration, Homi K. Bhabha (ed.). London and New York, Routledge.

Renan, Ernest, [1882]1994. 'Qu'est-ce qu'une nation?', in Nationalism, John Hutchinson & Anthony D. Smith (eds.)

Richmond, Anthony H. 1994. 'Ethnic Nationalism and Post-Industrialism', in Nationalism, John Hutchinson and Anthony D. Smith (eds.), Oxford University Press

Rivkin, A., 1969. Nation-Building In Africa: Problems and prospects, John H. Morrow, (ed.). Rutgers University Press, New Brunswick New Jersey.

Rokkan, S., 1975. 'Dimension of State Formation and Nation-Building: A possible paradigm for research or variation within Europe', in The Formation of National States in Western Europe Charles Tilly (ed.:)

Rokkan, Stein and Urwin, Derek W., 1982. 'Introduction: Centres and Peripheries in Western Europe', in The Politics of Territorial Identity: Studies in European Regionalism, Stein Rokkan and Derek W. Urwin (eds.). London. Beverly Hills. New Delhi, Sage Publications

Rokkan, Stein, 1981. Mobilization Centre-Periphery Structures and Nation-Building: A Volume in Commemoration of Stein Rokkan, Per Torsvik (ed.)

Rothchild, D., Olorunsola, V. A., (eds.) 1983. State Versus Ethnic Claims: African Policy Dilemma. Boulder, Colorado. Westview Press.

Rubenson, Sven, 1976. The Survival of Ethiopian Independence. Heinemann, Addis Ababa University Press

Rustow, D.A., 1967. A World of Nations: Problems of political modernization. Washington, D.C., The Brookings Institution.

Sabbe, Osman Saleh, 1974. The History of Eritrea, (trans. by Muhammad Fawaz Al-Azem, Dar Al-Masirah Beirut).

Sabbe, Osman Saleh, 1978. Origin of the Eritrean Conflicts and its Resolution (mebokel *grichitat ertran afetathuun,* in Tigrinya)

Schoenfeld, Dagobert, 1904/1974. Colonial History of Eritrea 1850-1889: Eritrea and Egyptian-Sudan, Berlin (trans. by into Tigrinya)

Schulze, Hagen, 1996. States, Nations and Nationalism. Blackwell Publishers

Scruton, Roger, 1982. A Dictionary of Political Thought. London, Macmillan Press

Seton-Watson, Hugh, 1977. Nations and States: An enquiry into the origins of nations and the politics of nationalism. London Methuen.

Seton-Watson, Hugh, 1977/1994. 'Old and New Nations', pp. 134-37, (from the Nations and States), in Nationalism, John Hutchinson and Anthony D. Smith (eds.)

Sherman, Richard., 1980. Eritrea: The unfinished revolution. New York, Praeger

Sherman, Richard, 1980. *Eritrea in Revolution*, Ph.D. thesis. Michigan, London; University Microfilms International

Shils, E., 1963. 'On the Comparative Study of the New States', in Old Societies and New States

Sheth, D.L., 1973. 'Comparisons of Developmental Processes Within and Across Nation-States: Analysis of the Indian Case', in Building States and Nations, vol. I, S.N. Eisentstadt and Stein Rokkan (eds.).

Simmel, Georg, 1955. Conflict and the Web of Group-Affiliation (translated by Reinhard Bendix). Glencoe, Illinois, The Free Press

Slowe, Peter M., 1990. Geography and Political Power: The Geography of Nations and States. London and New York, Routledge.

Smith, Anthony, D., 1983a. State and Nation in the Third World. Great Britain, Wheatsheaf Books LTD.

Smith, Anthony, D., 1983b. Theories of Nationalism, 2nd ed. New York, Holmes & Meier publishers.

Smith, Anthony, D., 1986. The Ethnic Origins of Nations. Basil Blackwell

Smith, Anthony D., 1986, 1989/1994. 'The Origin of Nations', (From the Origins of Nations, Ethnic and Racial Studies', 12/3 (1989), 349-56), in Nationalism, John Hutchinson and Anthony D. Smith (eds.), pp. 147-54. Oxford/New York, Oxford University Press.

Smith, Anthony, D., 1991. National Identity. Penguin Books

Smith, Anthony D., 1998: Modernism and Nationalism. London and New York, Routledge

Snead, J., 1990. 'European Pedigree/African contagions: nationality, narrative, and communality in Tutuola, Achebe, and Reed', in Nation and Narration, Komi K. Bhabha (ed.)

Sorenson, John, 1993. Imagining Ethiopia: Struggle for History and Identity in the Horn of Africa. New Brunswick, New Jersey, Rutgers University Press

Spencer, John H., 1984. Ethiopia At Bay: A Personal Account of the Haile Selassie Years. Michigan, Reference Publication

Stalin, Joseph, 1994. 'The Nation', in Nationalism, John Hutchinson & Anthony D. Smith (eds.)

Strayer, J. R., 1963. 'The Historical Experience of Nation-Building in Europe', in Nation-Building, Deutch Foltz (eds.) 1963. New York, Atherton Press.

Sztompka, P., 1993. The Sociology of Social Change. Oxford & Cambridge USA, Blackwell

Tekle, Amare, 1964. The Creation of the Ethio-Eritrean Federation: A case study in Post-war international relations (1945-1950). University of Denver, Ph.D., in political Science, international law and relations

Tekle, Amare, 1999. A Response to Professor Bahru Zewde, http://www.Primenet.com/~ephrem2/eritreanoau/bahru.htm/, accessed 25-01-99

Tilly, C., 1975. 'Western State-Making and Theories of Political Transformation', in The Formation of National States in Western Europe, Charles Tilly (ed.). New Jersey, Princeton University Press.

Tilly, C., 1984. Big Structures Large Processes Huge Comparisons. New York, Russel Sage Foundation.

Trevaskis, G., Kendy N., 1960. Eritrea: A colony in transition 1941-52. London New York Toronto, Oxford University Press

Väyrynen, R., 1993. 'Territory, Nation-state and Nationalism', in The Future of the Nation-state in Europe, Jyrki Livonen (ed.).

Wallerstein, I., 1971. 'The Range of Choice: constraints on the policies of governments of contemporary African independent states', in The State of The Nations: constraints on development in independent Africa Lofchie (ed.). Berkeley, Los Angeles, London University of California Press.

Weber, Eugen, 1976. Peasants into Frenchmen: The Modernization of Rural France, 1870-1914. Stanford, CA, Stanford Univeristy Press

Weber, Max, 1948. From Max Weber: Essays in Sociology, Translated, Edited and with an Introduction by H.H. Gerth and C. Wright Mills. London and Boston, Routledge and Kegan Poul

Weber, Max [1948]1994. 'The Nation', in Nationalism, John Hutchinson & Anthony D. Smith (eds.)

Wiberg, H., 1983. 'Self-Determination as an International Issue', in Nationalism & Self Determination in the Horn of Africa, ed., I. M. Lewis.

Wilson, Amrit, 1991. The Challenge Road: Women and the Eritrean Revolution. London, Earthscan Publications

With, Peter A.K., 1987. Politics and Liberation: The Eritrean Struggle 1961 - 1986. Denmark, International Forum.

Wolde Giorgis, Dawit, 1989. Red Tears: War, Famine and Revolution in Ethiopia. Trenton, New Jersey 08618, Red Sea Press

Woldemariam, Woldeab, 1987. A Short History of Eritrea. Oslo, Norway

Woldemariam, Woldeab, 1995. *Mrutzat Anketzat Ato Woldeab* (Selected Articles of Ato Woldeab), 1941-1991, Tuquabo Aressi (ed.). Asmara, Hedri Publishers

Woolf, Sara, 1990. An Incomplete Decolonization: From Italians in Eritrea to Eritreans in Italy

Yohannes, Okbazghi., 1991. Eritrea, a Pawn in World Politics. University of Florida Press / Gainesville

Yohannes, Zemehret, 1991. Mekete Antzar Etalyawi Megza'eti ab Ertra (Resistance Against Italian Colonialism in Eritrea)

Young, Crawford, 1983. 'Comparative Claims to Political Sovereignty: Biafra, Katanga, Eritrea', in State Versus Ethnic Claims: African Policy Dilemma, Donald Rothchild and Victor A. Olorunsola (eds.).

Young, Crawford, 1994. The African Colonial State in Comparative Perspective. New Haven and London, Yale University Press

SYMPOSIA, REPORTS AND MEMORANDA

Bairu, Z., 1988. The Impact of Modern Industry on Eritrea During European Colonial Rule. R.I.C.E. 1988 Conference on Research and Development. Held in Eritrea, 15th - 21st July 1988.

Department of State, 1949. Memorandum of Conversation: Visit of the Ethiopian Vice Minister of Foreign Affairs.

Ellingson, Lloyd, 1978. 'The Origins and Development of the Eritrean Liberation Movement', in Proceedings of the Fifth International Conference on Ethiopia, Robert L. Hess (ed.), Chicago.

References

Eritrea: The Way Forward, Proceedings of a Conference on Eritrea Organised by the United Nations Association on the 9th November 1985. United Nations Association-United Kingdom

Firebrace, James, 1986. 'The British Responsibility Towards Eritrea and the Moral Responsibility of the International Communities', in Eritrea: The Way Forward

General Assembly, 1948. The Disposition of the Former Italian Colonies

Houtart, Francois, 1979. Social Aspect of the Eritrean Revolution, Eritrean Symposium London: 12/13.1.1979.

Kadi, Mohamed Omar & Woldeab Woldemariam, 1957. *The complaint of the Eritrean People Against The Ethiopian Government*: Being a list of the flagrant violations of the U.N. Resolution 390 A. Submitted to the General Assembly of the United Nations in the name of the Eritrean people, on November 1957

New Eritrea Pro-Italia Party, 1949. *Memorandum*: For the General Assembly of the United Nations Organisation, to the General Assembly of the United Nations Lake Succcess, New York, U.S.A.

Nzongola-Ntalaja, 1988. Nation-Building and State Building in Africa: Paper prepared for presentation at the Fourth Symposium of the special Commission on Africa, Harare, Zimbabwe, June 6-9 1988.

Pool, David, 1980. Ethiopia and Eritrea: The Pre-Colonial Period, Manchester University (paper presented to the International Tribunal of the Rights of peoples)

Research and Information Centre of Eritrea (RICE), Notes on the Italian Colonization in Eritrea (no. date)

Sharawi, Helmi, 1980. The Eritrean Revolution: From National Political Organisation to Armed Struggle (paper presented to International Tribunal for the Rights of Peoples).

Tegegn, Melakku, 1989. Eritrea: Problems of the Nationalist Movement. Paper Presented to the Fourth Annaul Conference on the Horn of Africa/

Index